# COMMUNITY EDUCATION

## PRINCIPLES AND PRACTICES FROM WORLD-WIDE EXPERIENCE

# COMMUNITY EDUCATION

## PRINCIPLES AND PRACTICES FROM
## WORLD-WIDE EXPERIENCE

*The Fifty-eighth Yearbook of the
National Society for the Study of Education*

PART I

*Prepared by the Yearbook Committee:* C. O. ARNDT *(Chairman)*,
WILLARD W. BEATTY, STEPHEN M. COREY, EDGAR DALE,
RICHARD HEINDEL, *and* WILLIAM W. WATTENBERG

*Edited by*

NELSON B. HENRY

1 9 NSSE 5 9

*Distributed by* THE UNIVERSITY OF CHICAGO PRESS • CHICAGO, ILLINOIS

The responsibilities of the Board of Directors of the National Society for the Study of Education in the case of yearbooks prepared by the Society's committees are (1) to select the subjects to be investigated, (2) to appoint committees calculated in their personnel to insure consideration of all significant points of view, (3) to provide appropriate subsidies for necessary expenses, (4) to publish and distribute the committees' reports, and (5) to arrange for their discussion at the annual meeting.

The responsibility of the Yearbook Editor is to prepare the submitted manuscripts for publication in accordance with the principles and regulations approved by the Board of Directors.

Neither the Board of Directors, nor the Yearbook Editor, nor the Society is responsible for the conclusions reached or the opinions expressed by the Society's yearbook committees.

Published *1959* by

. THE NATIONAL SOCIETY FOR THE
STUDY OF EDUCATION
*5835 Kimbark Avenue, Chicago 37, Illinois*

*Printed in the United States of America*

# The Society's Committee on Community Education

T. L. GREEN
*Chief of Mission for UNESCO in Ceylon*
*Colombo, Ceylon*

HORACE HOLMES
*Program Associate, Ford Foundation*
*New York, New York*

LLOYD H. HUGHES
*Program Specialist, Fundamental Education Division, UNESCO*
*Paris, France*
*Formerly Deputy Director, CREFAL, Patzcuaro, Mexico*

A. HURBLI
*Program Specialist, Fundamental Education Division, UNESCO*
*Paris, France*
*Formerly Deputy Director of Arab States Fundamental Education Center*

GLEN LEET
*Program Director, Save the Children Federation*
*Norwalk, Connecticut*
*Formerly Chief of Community Development Unit*
*Division of Social Affairs, United Nations*

WILLFRED O. MAUCK
*President, Bureau of University Travel*
*Newton, Massachusetts*

MARGARET MEAD
*Associate Curator of Ethnology, American Museum of Natural History*
*Adjunct Professor of Anthropology, Columbia University*
*New York, New York*

PEDRO T. ORATA
*Program Specialist, Department of Education, UNESCO*
*Paris, France*

RICHARD W. POSTON
*Director, Department of Community Development, Southern Illinois University*
*Carbondale, Illinois*

CHANDOS REID
*Assistant to the Superintendent, Waterford Township Public Schools*
*Pontiac, Michigan*

THEODORE D. RICE
*Professor of Education, Wayne State University*
*Detroit, Michigan*

RICHARD P. SAUNDERS
*President, Save the Children Federation*
*Norwalk, Connecticut*

DAVID E. SCANLON
*Professor of Education, Newark State Teachers College*
*Newark, New Jersey*

LILY TSIEN
*Librarian, Educational Clearing House, UNESCO*
*Paris, France*

# Editor's Preface

Most of the volumes in the National Society's series of yearbooks have been prepared for publication at the suggestion of members of the Board of Directors or as a result of communications voluntarily presented by individuals or by several persons in collaboration, sometimes serving as spokesmen for a professional association. Occasionally the officers of the National Society circularize the membership of the Society with the request for a suggestion of a desirable topic for consideration by the Board. In 1954, in response to such a request from the Directors, a member of the Society proposed consideration of the subject *international programs of education*.

Some months later, when this topic was being discussed, along with other suggestions, the Board asked Messrs. Melby and Corey to make some inquiries regarding current interest and opinion among teachers and school administrators with respect to types of instructional experimentation in operation or under consideration in different countries. They presented their report at the next meeting, suggesting that the Board invite Professor C. O. Arndt of New York University to prepare an outline for a yearbook representing his point of view with reference to international education. His proposal was approved and the yearbook committee was appointed. It was in this manner that the problem of international education became the object of the yearbook committee's concern and has now been published as Part I of the Society's Fifty-eighth Yearbook.

The objectives of the yearbook committee and the reports of contributors (usually out of their own experiences) explain the conditions under which the United Nations and its agencies, particularly UNESCO (emphasizing fundamental education) and the Bureau of Social Affairs (concerned with community development), have labored with and for the vast populations in underdeveloped areas. These activities and the further benefits visualized give full assurance that the implications of the title of the yearbook, *Community Education: Principles and Practices from World-wide Experience*, will, with certainty, meet the expectations of the founders of UN and UNESCO and of the teams of trained specialists who now minister to the wants and needs of the beneficiaries of the services provided.

NELSON B. HENRY

# Table of Contents

PAGE

OFFICERS OF THE SOCIETY FOR 1958–59 . . . . . . . . . ii

THE SOCIETY'S COMMITTEE ON COMMUNITY EDUCATION . . . . . v

ASSOCIATED CONTRIBUTORS. . . . . . . . . . . . . . v

EDITOR'S PREFACE . . . . . . . . . . . . . . . . vii

INTRODUCTION, *C. O. Arndt* . . . . . . . . . . . . . xiii

## SECTION I

### Basic Principles

CHAPTER

I. THE NATURE AND PURPOSE OF COMMUNITY EDUCATION, *Willard
W. Beatty* . . . . . . . . . . . . . . . . . . . 3

Setting in Which Community Education Developed. What Community Education Is About. What Are the Requisites for Change? Difficulties Which Are Encountered. The Problem of Adequate Staffing. Operating Principles.

II. HISTORICAL ROOTS FOR THE DEVELOPMENT OF COMMUNITY EDUCATION, *David Scanlon* . . . . . . . . . . . . . 38

Early Forms of Cultural Transformation. Education by Missionaries. Impact of Industrial Revolution. Community Education in the United States. Early Mass Education Movements.

III. CULTURAL FACTORS IN COMMUNITY-EDUCATION PROGRAMS, *Margaret Mead* . . . . . . . . . . . . . . . . . 66

The Changing Climate of Opinion. The Situation during World War II. Three Case Studies. Our Present State of Knowledge. Adult Capacities To Learn.

CHAPTER                                                                    PAGE

IV. PSYCHOLOGICAL FACTORS IN COMMUNITY EDUCATION, *Leonard
    W. Doob* . . . . . . . . . . . . . .    97

    Social Setting. The Form of Behavior. General Predispositions.
    Problems in Method.


V. WORLD LITERACY: ITS STATUS AND PROBLEMS, *William S. Gray* .   122

    Recent Literacy Developments. Extent of Illiteracy Today. Role
    of Literacy in Community Education. Levels of Literacy. For
    Whom Should Literacy Training Be Provided? Directing Agen-
    cy and Staff. Relation of Literacy Programs to Public Educa-
    tion. World-wide Similarity in Basic Reading Processes. Basic
    Problems in Teaching Adults To Read. Organization of Literacy
    Instruction. Methods of Teaching Adults To Read. Learning
    through Reading. Supplementary and Follow-up Reading. The
    Teaching of Handwriting. Measurement of Literacy Compe-
    tence.

## SECTION II

### Representative Programs

VI. THE GRASSROOTS APPROACH TO EDUCATION FOR COMMUNITY IM-
    PROVEMENT, *Pedro T. Orata* . . . . . . . . .   149

    Narrowing the Gap between Educational and Social Progress.
    Examples of Community Improvement. Guiding Principles. Im-
    provements Attained through Community-School Approach..


VII. LESSONS LEARNED THROUGH INTERNATIONAL AND BILATERAL PRO-
     GRAMS FOR COMMUNITY EDUCATION . . . . . . . .   170

        I. Teaching and Scientific Development. *Willard W. Beatty*
       II. The American Bilateral Programs in Community Education,
           *Willfred Mauck*
      III. Helping the Asian Villager Help Himself, *Horace Holmes*
       IV. Community Self-help Enterprise and the Private Welfare
           Agency, *Richard P. Saunders*


VIII. COMMUNITY EDUCATION IN THE TRUST TERRITORY OF THE PA-
      CIFIC ISLANDS, *Robert E. Gibson* . . . . . . . .   217

      America's Purposes in Micronesia and Need for Education. Ex-
      amples of Community Education in Trust Territory of the Pacific
      Islands. Community Education in Yap.

CHAPTER                                                                    PAGE

IX. LESSONS IN COMMUNITY EDUCATION LEARNED THROUGH TECHNI-
CAL ASSISTANCE PROGRAMS, *T. L. Green* . . . . . . . 237

Agencies Involved. The Background. Some Examples of Problems
Encountered. Some Lessons Learned. The Nature and Operation
of Limiting Factors. Training. Influencing Attitudes to Community Education. Team Responsibilities. Some New Basic Concepts Needed.


X. COMMUNITY EDUCATION IN SOUTHERN ILLINOIS, *Richard W.
Poston* . . . . . . . . . . . . . . . . 268

Pope County. Brownfield. The Enablers.


XI. INSTRUCTIONAL MATERIALS IN COMMUNITY EDUCATION, *Edgar
Dale* . . . . . . . . . . . . . . . . . 283

Introduction. Developing the Instructional Program. Some General Principles. The Media of Instruction. Instructional Materials
for Adults of Limited Reading Ability. In Conclusion.

SECTION III


*Leadership Training*

XII. UNESCO'S INTERNATIONAL TRAINING CENTERS . . . . . . 307

I. Educational and Cultural Development, *Willard W. Beatty*
II. Training Educational Leaders for the Americas, *Lloyd H.
Hughes*
III. The Arab States Fundamental-Education Center, *A. Hurbli*


XIII. TRAINING IN COMMUNITY EDUCATION AND DEVELOPMENT AT THE
UNIVERSITY OF LONDON, *T. R. Batten* . . . . . . . 334

Basic Problems in Community Education. Organizing the Train-
ing Program at London. Objectives and Methods of the Training
Program. Attacking the Problems of the Training Course. Use of
Group Methods in Training.


XIV. PERSONNEL FOR OVERSEAS SERVICE, *Harlan Cleveland* . . . 344

Training Is Efficiency. Cultural Empathy. The Transferability
of Institutions.

CHAPTER                                                                    PAGE

XV. EDUCATIONAL LEADERSHIP THROUGH WORKSHOP PROCEDURES,
*Theodore D. Rice* and *Chandos Reid* . . . . . . . 358
Demands upon Educational Leaders. Purposes and Limitations
of Workshops in India. Workshops in Pakistan. Lessons Learned
from Workshops in India and Pakistan. Present Role of Workshops in India and Pakistan. Values and Limitations of the Workshop Procedure.

XVI. THE UNITED NATIONS PROGRAM OF COMMUNITY DEVELOPMENT,
*Glen Leet* . . . . . . . . . . . . . . . . 379
Community Development in the Villages of Greece. Community
Development in Greek Cities. The Egyptian Welfare Center
Program. The UN as an Agency of Governments. Community
Development Defined. The UN as an Agency of Governments.
Community Development Endorsed in UN Assembly. Role of
the People in Community Development. The Program Could Be
Improved.

SECTION IV

*Summary and Selected Readings*

XVII. PRINCIPLES AND PERSPECTIVES, *The Yearbook Committee* . . 397
Some Basic Principles. Problems for American Education. Conclusion.

SELECTED READINGS ON COMMUNITY EDUCATION, *Lily Tsien* . . . . 405

INDEX . . . . . . . . . . . . . . . . . 413

INFORMATION CONCERNING THE SOCIETY . . . . . . . . . i

LIST OF PUBLICATIONS OF THE SOCIETY . . . . . . . . iii

# Introduction

C. O. ARNDT

Those who planned and wrote this yearbook recognize an epoch-making opportunity in the present moment of history. Man has now wrested such powers from nature that he is able to satisfy the basic material needs of the human race. He can do more. By the development of a world-wide program of community education, conceived with boldness and executed with decision, he can enable his fellow men to participate effectively in economic and social progress toward a world community. To the furtherance of this prospect the yearbook is addressed.

## Titling the Study

The yearbook committee tentatively adopted the title "Fundamental Education," using the term in the sense in which it was originally fashioned and subsequently developed by UNESCO. Fundamental education was understood to mean a kind of minimum and general education which was designed to help underdeveloped populations understand the problems of their immediate environments and their rights and duties as citizens. The translation of such community understandings into appropriate community improvements was regarded as a further essential element of the concept.

As writing progressed, however, it became apparent that the title "Fundamental Education" is not sufficiently comprehensive. After careful study, it was decided to use as the title for the yearbook *Community Education: Principles and Practices from World-wide Experience*. The committee will not prove sensitive to criticism of the title since we are aware that we are working in an area in which terminology is in flux and in which variants of the several expressions used in the title are operative not only in UNESCO and the United Nations but in the world at large.

Inevitably, since essential elements in the solving of problems include altering the ways of thinking, changing the behavior patterns of people, and helping those people develop new skills, education is seen as the key to the development of attitudes and abilities. This means that educational science is, in such instances, called upon to work out ways of helping people learn how to help themselves.

An early outcome of the UNESCO projects has been the formulation of an important hypothesis. This hypothesis states that the most relevant and functional material which can be found for building an indigenous school curriculum in countries newly free and underdeveloped resides in the problems of daily living which people in these countries face at community level. Among these problems are: village pools and wells, how to build and maintain them; personal hygiene, how to foster it among all villagers; community responsibility, how to move toward it from present family responsibility. There are indications that more and more countries are testing the above hypothesis, and some have reached the point of saying: We have tested and are now ready to act. Community education is becoming a trend in the free and underdeveloped countries of the world.

Some lessons learned in these endeavors are, in their turn, throwing light upon educational issues in all countries. This yearbook, then, has a dual purpose; first, to bring together the working principles and ideas needed by educators who work directly in underdeveloped countries and by those who prepare these workers in educational institutions; secondly, to make clear how the principles thus articulated are significant for education in all countries of the world.

The yearbook, itself, has four sections: (1) basic principles, (2) representative programs, (3) leadership training, and (4) final summary chapter and a short bibliography, prepared through the help of UNESCO.

## Organization of the Yearbook
### BASIC PRINCIPLES

Section I in the yearbook, and particularly the chapter concerning "The Nature and Purpose of Community Education" sets forth the meaning of community education as it is used in this volume. Major effort is placed upon revealing the nature of fundamental human needs as they were observed and studied by competent people in various parts of the world.

The analysis made in the chapter on "Historical Roots for the Development of Community Education" lends perspective to the examples later cited in the yearbook. Examples are drawn from both ancient and modern history. They reveal flashes of insight on the part of man through the ages, which evidence his awareness that there is value in sharing ideas with people in other lands.

A chapter on "Cultural Factors Basic in Community-Education Programs" follows. Anthropological theory and direct field experience give dynamic to the chapter. The analysis should prove challenging in leading readers to thinking realistically about the problems which the underdeveloped countries of the world face today. A key and troublesome question has been how best to bring about changes which are needed in underdeveloped countries. Operative cultural forces must be understood and enlisted if innovations are to be accepted and recognized as permanently desirable.

The examples of social change presented and analyzed in the chapter are sufficiently comprehensive to enable the reader to assess their effect upon entire cultures.

"Psychological Factors in Community-Education Programs" are next considered. They are pragmatically structured to make them suggestive and challenging to fieldworkers. They provide the fieldworker, as well as the reader, with a forward-looking goal, down-to-earth suggestions, and psychological principles upon which to build a modern program of community education.

One of the instrumentalities basic to the building of an effective program of community education is the development of literacy. Considered by many to be an essential first step in community education, literacy programs were given such emphasis as to cause them to sweep throughout the world like a tidal wave. The analysis in the chapter on "World Literacy" provides needed perspective to the efforts of high-speed literacy enthusiasts. Elementary reading demonstrably can be developed rapidly if conditions are favorable. Yet, reading skills can be forgotten quickly if appropriate reading materials are not provided and if cultural urges conducive toward growth in literacy are absent. After giving thought to what has been done in the field, and after considering other relevant factors, a breakthrough is effected with action-level proposals which grow out of the author's long and distinguished study of literacy.

The second section of the yearbook presents descriptions of work being done in community education throughout the world. To give the reader a live understanding of what is implied, this section opens with a chapter telling in down-to-earth, realistic fashion what is a "Grassroots Approach to Education for Community Improvement." Having an appreciation of the types of problems to be tackled, and of what the educator lives with, the reader can then see fuller implications in the necessarily condensed pictures of the over-all programs having regional or world-wide scope.

In the next chapter of Section II, titled "Lessons Learned through International and Bilateral Programs for Community Education," examples of work in progress under the auspices of UNESCO, United Nations, and United States foundations are described and analyzed. Examples are drawn from institutions and agencies whose interests are world-wide and whose commitment to community education is deep-seated. Each organization has modified both its approaches and the content of its programs in the light of experience gained in the field. Each is continuously engaged in evaluation and research upon its work with the view of discovering better ways by which to carry it forward.

The description of purposes and practices developed by United States government agencies since the acquisition of a new territory at the close of the second world war is set forth in the chapter on "Community Education in the Trust Territory of the Pacific Islands." The reader is thus enabled to learn how the United States government proceeds today at the action level. Perception is facilitated not only by the recency of the work but also by its concern with a relatively small population. The quite scattered nature of the islands which make up the Trust Territory necessitates novel approaches in the several localities since they have had little contact with one another in former years. Lessons learned upon one island are later used to good advantage as community education is begun or furthered elsewhere.

The chapter on "Lessons in Community Education Learned through Technical-Assistance Programs" provides many diverse examples to illustrate the impedimenta which retard and obstruct the well-intentioned efforts of technical-assistance experts sent into underdeveloped countries to expedite improvements in standards of living through community education. Observable types of obstruction which are described as particularly significant include: inability on the part of many visiting experts to speak the local language and their lack of intimate knowledge regarding local and national customs, including prestige factors. Stress is placed on the development in a given underdeveloped country of attitudes of the people at community and national levels which are congenial to the efforts of technical-assistance workers. The observation is made that we have been so concerned with the overt factors motivating cultural change, such as demonstration of the greater effectiveness of a steel plow compared with the traditional single-fingered wood plow in turning the soil, that we have neglected to point out the concomitants within the culture which must be watched and utilized if social change is to be furthered effectively. There is urgent need, therefore, to give critical thought to the conceptual bases of our beliefs and actions.

As mentioned earlier, there is need for community education to meet fundamental needs also in countries which are highly developed industrially. Therefore, the chapter on "Community Education in Southern Illinois" was prepared for inclusion in the yearbook. Initiative and leadership for community education in this instance are provided by Southern Illinois University, particularly its Department of Community Development. Resisting the pressures exercised by accrediting agencies to conform to the established pattern for the operation of universities in the nation, this institution is committed to the development of a better prospect in life for the people living in southern Illinois.

In a series of short, narrative descriptions, the author relates how the enterprise came into being, how local citizens were involved in decision-making; in short, how it has functioned thus far. It is apparent that time and hard work by the local population will be required to meet adequately the needs of the people in the community studied. The leadership of the university is well aware of this fact and is proceeding accordingly.

In almost all programs some thought must be given to the preparation and employment of instructional materials. The chapter on "Instructional Materials for Community Education" sets forth general principles determining decisions in this area and includes illustrations from successful endeavors in this field.

## LEADERSHIP TRAINING

To develop a program of community education internationally, a prime requisite is obviously the training of leaders for work in underdeveloped countries situated in the various regions of the world. Aware of this need, UNESCO first established the Centro Regional de Educación Fundamental para la America Latina (CREFAL) in Patzcuaro, Mexico, in order to train leadership teams for North and South America. These teams, in turn, would train other teams in their countries of origin. Later the Arab States Fundamental Education Center (ASFEC) was set up at Sirs-el-Layyan, Menounfia Egypt, for the purpose of training leaders in community education for the Near East. Both centers have now been in operation for a number of years and have gathered experience through their own endeavors. It is fortunate, therefore, that experienced administrators from both centers have prepared definitive statements for the yearbook. These are presented in the chapter "UNESCO's International Training Centers."

Beyond the effort of UNESCO, which was actuated by the need to train leaders for its fundamental-education program, many agencies and institutions have long been at work training leaders for community education. It was possible to make only a sampling of some promising experimental approaches now under way. Three examples have been selected and are here presented in a series of three chapters. In the first of these, "Training in Community Education and Development at the University of London," the author describes the procedures through which personnel, largely experienced, are prepared for engaging in technical-assistance work in underdeveloped countries. Emphasis is placed upon the development of self-reliance and resourcefulness on the part of each member of the group, the staff serving as consultants and assuming direction only as a last resort. After the group has developed sufficient self-reliance to warrant field work, visits are made to villages and small towns to study community agencies at work. The study groups include personnel from underdeveloped countries, and it is significant for these people particularly to note that industrialized England also has problems with co-ordination of the efforts of social agencies in its rural and small-town communities.

Especially in the United States, where many institutions of higher learning prepare technological experts and where there is a general culture receptive to such experts, there is a problem of getting them ready to work in quite different cultures. The chapter on "Personnel for Overseas Service" centers around this problem. So to speak, the expert must learn to enlarge his focus of attention so that he can be as sensitive to human variables in community improvement as he is to the technical factors around which his resourcefulness and trouble-shooting ability tends to center. More harm than good is done if he is scientifically diligent but is a heavy-footed blunderer, culturally speaking.

The next chapter in this section, "Educational Leadership through Workshop Procedures," presents an adaptation of the workshop approach to the needs of Indian teachers and administrators. It is apparent that the workshop approach, so successfully developed in the United States had to be modified considerably to fit into the culture pattern of India. The most important factor in the success of the enterprise seems to have been the apparent skill by which teachers and administration were actuated to examine their own problems and to seek their own solution to these problems.

SUMMARY AND SELECTED READINGS

The final chapter of the yearbook, "Principles and Perspectives," is an effort by the committee to ferret out operational principles derived from the thinking and experience of those who wrote the chapters in Section I. References are subsequently made to ways by which these principles function in other chapters of the yearbook.

## Learning To Plan at World Level

Having given a quick overview of the yearbook, some of the major undertakings in which this nation has become involved as it assumed new responsibilities for planning not only at national but at world level are here briefly high-lighted.

The devastating effects of two world wars during this century were such as to catapult the United States into a position of world leadership. Rich natural resources, together with a highly developed and still developing technology, were dynamic internal forces in the nation's forward surge.

World leadership by its very nature calls for the assumption of responsibilities at regional and world levels. History did not allow the United States to have a period of tutelage before its assumption of leadership responsibility as it had Rome and, more recently, Britain. The United States has had to learn fast and is forced to act while it is yet in the process of learning. In these circumstances, mistakes, often on an extensive scale, have been made and have been discernible at world level. Thus, in the decade of the twenties of this century, private financial institutions in the *United States* made extensive loans to Western Europe in an endeavor to further solvency and to strengthen the economy of those nations. The effort was only temporarily successful, and the people of the United States enjoyed a period described by Charles Beard as the decade of the golden glow. The glow was short-lived, however, since Western European countries, unable to make repayments on their loans, defaulted.

The United States learned something from this experience. After World War II when the payment for surplus war materials to be left abroad was under study in Congress, a wise, statesmanlike decision was taken by that body. It was to have foreign currency payments placed into funds which would be used for the subsidy of scholarships for United States and foreign students. Many students from abroad were thus enabled to study in the United States, and many American students were enabled to study abroad. No moratorium on debts on this occasion but, rather, a constructive, imaginative program designed to foster international understanding.

The economic dislocation of Western Europe which was brought on by large-scale destruction during the second world war caused the government of this country to think realistically about finding ways to help the involved nations re-establish their economies and become viable once again as independent nations. The Marshall Plan came into being, a plan which revealed that the leadership of the United States could plan upon a large, regional scale. It was a mammoth undertaking and proved highly successful not only by serving the national interest but strengthening world peace as well. Such was the pervasive effect of this plan that it served to stimulate creative thinking on the part of the leadership in many nations of Western Europe. The concept of the Atlantic Community emerged. Further evidence of the contagion of this large-scale community planning was the development of the Schumann Plan and, more recently, of both Euratom, which is designed to further co-operation toward the peaceful use of atomic energy, and the European Economic Community.

Having gained useful experience with the relatively successful Marshall Plan, United States leadership next gave thought to the underdeveloped areas of the world, such as South Asia and the Near East. The people of the countries newly free were looking over their ancient walls upon the outside world intent upon finding a feasible plan which gave promise, if followed, of leading them surely out of their underdeveloped status to a more abundant life. They were in quest of food and more food for a rapidly rising population. They desired, moreover, to learn how to harness the machine to the end that it would, in various ways, strengthen their efforts to wrest a better livelihood from nature. The authoritarian elements within Communism were not, to most of them, deterrents, since freedom had long not been their lot. They were either yet living in colonial status or had just emerged from it.

As a highly industrialized nation, United States leadership was relatively conversant with the means and ways by which Western Europe could be helped once again to regain its strength. Many of its people possessed the technical and mechanical skills needed for the functioning of an industrialized society. Western Europe needed essentially to have machinery and material resources to rebuild its industrial plants. If these resources were supplied, they could largely fend for themselves. Our contacts with Europe having been long and close we knew fairly well how to deal with its nations and peoples. South Asia, by contrast, was largely in preindustrial status and was generally unknown to us. Thus, we had to learn by experience, for example, that it was not desirable to send these countries tractors and harvesting machines of the kind used in the United States. Needed, it was learned, was a period of careful, first-hand study of local conditions by the United Nations, the United States, and other nations which desired to help underdeveloped countries. In time, studies were undertaken to determine the nature of the fundamental needs which obtained in these underdeveloped countries and how these needs could be met. We have learned something through experience during the past decade, but we yet have far more to learn.

The leadership of this nation is learning to think and plan in terms of human welfare at world level. In doing so, it is actuated, as are other nations, by an enlightened national self-interest. But is there not something deeper which should inspire the people of this country? Concern for human welfare stems from the very heart of American democracy, this nation having been built upon the proposition that each human being is in himself significant.

As a nation, the United States today is challenged to develop the maturity to think and plan technical-assistance programs with other nations which are actuated by the desire to help meet the needs of people in communities everywhere because human beings are involved.

SECTION I

# BASIC PRINCIPLES

# CHAPTER I

# The Nature and Purpose of Community Education

WILLARD W. BEATTY

## Setting in Which Community Education Developed

Ten countries of the west embracing about 6 per cent of the population of the non-Communist world constitute the economic upper class of the nations in world society.[1] They produce about 65 per cent of the net national product of the non-Soviet area.[2] The per capita national product of this group ranges from Denmark, where the value is $750.00 annually, to the United States where it exceeds $1,870.00.[3] More than two-thirds of the people of the non-Soviet world live in countries where the real income per head is but a tiny fraction of what it is in the highly developed countries; i.e., in the twelve poorest countries the per capita product is less than $50.00 per year. These twelve countries of the Free World contain about one-third of the population and produce less than one twenty-fifth of the total national product.[4]

More distressing than these discrepancies is the fact that all the evidence indicates that the wealthy are becoming wealthier while the poorer areas are becoming relatively poorer. In the richer countries there has been an increasing trend toward equality of opportunity; on the other hand, most of the poorer countries have preserved as great internal inequalities among individuals, classes, and

1. Gunnar Myrdal, *Rich Lands and Poor*, pp. 3-6, 8. New York: Harper & Bros., 1957.

2. "Per Capita National Product, 1952-54," *United Nations Statistical Papers*, Series E, No. 4. New York: United Nations, 1957.

3. *Ibid.*

4. "An International Comparison of National Products and the Purchasing Power of Currencies," *United Nations Statistical Papers*, Series E, No. 1. New York: United Nations Organization of European Economic Cooperation, 1949.

regions as there have ever been. In many, the inequalities are still growing.[5]

A closer examination of all these facts reveals a phenomenon which students of the field have come to refer to as the "vicious circle of poverty." Winslow has described it as it relates to health: "It was clear . . . that poverty and disease formed a vicious circle. Men and women were sick because they were poor; they became poorer because they were sick and sicker because they were poorer."[6]

Myrdal points out that both the "haves" and the "have nots" are aware of this condition and that the adoption of the newer term, "underdeveloped countries," implies a value judgment that it is an accepted goal of public policy that the countries so designated should experience economic development.[7]

As the richest country in the world, the United States has for many years accepted the responsibility to contribute both money and the personal service of many of its citizens in an effort to reverse this process of deterioration. Both in Congress and in the country at large there is little agreement as to whether we have been pouring money down a rathole or winning friends and helping to build a better world for ourselves and for our international associates.

## CHRONIC ILLNESS WIDESPREAD

Millions of people all over the world are chronic sufferers from endemic diseases, such as yaws, bilharziasis, malaria, hookworm, trachoma, sleeping sickness, or amoebic dysentery, which steadily sap their energies and rob them of both the will and the strength to work. Many of these sufferers do not know what afflicts them and are part of a culture complex that neither recognizes the sources of their diseases nor possesses the skilled scientists or medical men to provide relief. Other millions live in a milieu which produces trained specialists who know the answers. The victims are, however,

5. Gunnar Myrdal, *An International Economy*. New York: Harper & Bros., 1956.

6. C. E. A. Winslow, *The Cost of Sickness and the Price of Health*, p. 9. World Health Organization Monograph, Series No. 7. Geneva, Switzerland: World Health Organization, 1951.

7. Gunnar Myrdal, *Rich Lands and Poor, op. cit.*

too poor to command the specialists' services; and strong pressures within the culture resist or restrict free public medical services.[8]

### POVERTY, DISEASE, AND PRIMITIVE METHODS REDUCE PRODUCTION

Other millions are dependent for a livelihood on a degenerative agriculture and are bound to the land, either as peons or tenant farmers.[9] In many cases, their major efforts are directed to the production of export crops like cotton, coffee, rubber, bananas, wool, beef and hides, tea or sisal, with barely enough land reserved for food crops to keep the workers and their families alive. Such exploitation is usually associated with absentee landlords, dishonest overseers, extortionate taxation, and continuous pressure to sell the best of the crop and depend on the runts for breeding stock or seed. Such irresponsible exploitation leads to deforestation to provide crop lands and to furnish material for housing and fuel. This results in sheet and gully erosion of the hillsides and crop lands and the choking of the rivers with silt which, in turn, causes floods. When the trees are gone, dung and agricultural wastes are used for fuel, thus robbing the soil of natural fertilizers, and land fertility rapidly diminishes.

Millions more are skilled handicrafters whose ability to make shoes, weave cloth, fire pottery, carve wood, or whose possession of any one of many needed manual skills equipped them to enter the old-time barter markets and trade for needed food or other objects. They are today facing competition from cheap factory-made products from the cities. Many must either leave home to seek possible employment in cities or adapt their skills to newer demands.

Half of the people of the world can't read or write.[10] Some of them are illiterates in countries of advanced culture to whom the opportunities for schooling have not been extended. The great majority are nonliterates of a culture which has never produced a written language and for whom no printed literature or periodical press exists.

With the increasing demand for speed in the transportation of

8. World Health Organization Reports.

9. Food and Agriculture Organization Reports.

10. *World Illiteracy at Mid-century*, chap. iii. Paris: UNESCO, 1957.

men and materials, hundreds of millions of these people find themselves still dependent on canoes, pack animals, or what they can carry on their own backs for communication with the outside world.

The unifying fact about these disadvantaged billions is that in many cases the same peoples suffer from several different handicaps at the same time. Malnourishment, disease, economic exploitation, serfdom, and illiteracy are concommitants of poverty and isolation.

### PRIMITIVE CONDITIONS TAKEN FOR GRANTED

Until fairly recently, such conditions were accepted by many of the victims as part of their lot in life. "They knew their place," whether they were cockneys on the streets of London, fellahin in the valley of the Nile, peons on a Latin-America finca, or share-croppers in the American south. The accident of birth had determined their status in life, and only a miracle could change that status. Many undoubtedly dreamed of a Cinderella-like transformation; but their religions have persuaded them to be satisfied with what they have without envying their "betters" and to pray for a better life in the hereafter.

The American and French revolutions probably were the best advertised declarations that there was something wrong about these "unalterable relationships" and that poverty and exploitation were not necessarily either sanctified or inevitable. Unable to bring about changes in their homelands, millions of the impoverished fled to the United States during the latter half of the nineteenth century, and France has for generations welcomed political exiles from neighboring countries.

While the great religions preached acceptance of one's lot, they also sought to ameliorate the conditions of the poor through the benevolence of the wealthy. However, there was inherent in much of this benevolence, whether by wealthy Moslems, high-caste Brahmans, or Christian millionaires, the general assumption that the poor were that way because they lacked the desire and the stamina to become anything else. As detailed by Scanlon in the next chapter, there were many instances of efforts to ameliorate conditions among the lower classes of the Western nations in the years following the industrial revolution.

CHALLENGES OF THE EARLY TWENTIETH CENTURY

In our own generation several events have shown that existing conditions need not be permanent. In 1914, Henry Ford and James Couzens, newcomers in the industrial field who were already challenging many traditional practices, reached the conclusion that their dream of a motor car for everyone could not be realized until the employees of their own enterprise could afford to buy the cars they were building.[11] The Ford Company, therefore, inaugurated a $5.00 a day minimum wage for all employees in its industrial empire and opened the door to the economic transformation of the United States.

In 1917, during the First World War, a *coup d'état* by Nicolai Lenin and his associate Bolshevist leaders enabled them to establish a "dictatorship of the proletariat" over the Russian masses. Regardless of how the Western world may interpret the results of the Russian Revolution, it is quite evident to the world at large that a great social change took place in Russia, in the course of which the established order was upset and pre-existing class distinctions were destroyed. However, it has since become evident that this "new order" is setting up new classes.

In 1918 Woodrow Wilson's Fourteen Points gave expression to a new political concept—that of "self-determination." Proposed as an implied solution to the position of the disparate elements of the Austro-Hungarian Empire, it since has been urged as justifying independence for Colonial areas throughout the world.

In 1924, as a result of an entirely normal election in Great Britain, Ramsey McDonald became the first labor Prime Minister of Britain. In 1945, the second labor government with Clement Attlee as Prime Minister made the dramatic decision which recognized the demands of half the British Empire for freedom from alien domination. The apppearance of Burma, India, Ceylon, and Pakistan among the nations of the world was public announcement that another great social change was under way and that it was not limited to people whose skin is white.

11. William Richards, *The Last Billionaire: Henry Ford* (New York: Charles Scribner's Sons, 1948); Harry Barnard, *Independent Man: The Life of Senator James Couzens* (New York: Charles Scribner's Sons, 1958).

To the causes of ferment listed above must be added another historic event of particular significance to the colored races. It was the early success of the Japanese in the second world war, both in challenging the United States at Pearl Harbor and in sweeping the British, the French, and the Dutch from their colonial possessions in the Pacific. The prelude to this drama had been played in 1905 when Japan defeated Russia, with many Western nations applauding her victory. While the ultimate defeat of the Japanese in 1945 may have been partially due to the fact that they treated their fellow Orientals—the Chinese, Indo-Chinese, Filipinos, Burmese, and Indonesians—as badly or worse than the former white administrators whom they supplanted, the long-range effect of their military successes was to destroy the myth of the white man's invincibility. And, since the departure of white administrators, the Asian nations have demonstrated abilities at self-government which generations of dominant whites had assured them that they lacked.

Finally, as we enter the Atomic Age, it is possible to envision sources of power which are not dependent on water, coal, or oil, and which may permit a more rapid and effective industrialization of underdeveloped areas than has previously appeared feasible.

### CONDITIONS CAN BE CHANGED

These are just a few of the events which demonstrated to the common people of the world that conditions could be changed. It was also revealed that many of the "underdeveloped areas" of the world, where poverty, illiteracy, disease, malnutrition, and economic exploitation were particularly in need of attention, were those which had been administered as colonies or protectorates of the Western powers for many years, without being permitted to share the scientific advances of Western culture.

The demand of India (and other colonial areas) for independence had not been a demand of the princely puppets who held their posts at the pleasure of the dominant power; it was a demand from leaders speaking for "the people."[12] And, when independence was granted, the first steps taken by the new government were toward

12. Frank Moraes, *Jawaharlal Nehru: A Biography*. New York: Macmillan Co., 1956.

basic improvements in health, food supply, general living conditions, and economic development.

The extreme contrasts between what the West has and what the underdeveloped areas of the world do not have are in no sense defensible. Neither are they any longer necessary. Western science, with a degree of success which we of the Western world are only now beginning to realize, has at last produced the techniques which make possible a healthier, better nourished, and richer world for all. Through the discovery or development of antibiotics, vaccines and sera, chemotherapy, and pesticides, medical science possesses the tools with which to wipe out many of the age-old diseases. Where local understanding and co-operation can be developed, it has become possible to destroy or control the sources of many infectious or parasitic conditions. Our biologic experimentation has not only continued the age-long process of adapting food plants to new environs but, through cross-fertilization, has produced new and more abundant species and, through chemical fertilization and mechanization of farm equipment, has multiplied many-fold the productivity of an acre of land. Similarly, through the development of new means of transport, many areas of the world have skipped the eras of animal-drawn transport, the railroad, and the truck, and have plunged directly into the age of airplanes.

It is significant that today the news that poverty, malnourishment, sickness, and poor housing are not God-given and inevitable has reached down into the thinking of the submerged masses all over the world. Political leaders around the world are recognizing that improvements are not merely possible but necessary; and that, where intrenched privilege stands in the way, it must be controlled or removed. Either the knowledge and techniques of modern civilization and its respect for human dignity will be voluntarily shared with the rest of the world, or a rising resentment of underdeveloped peoples will ultimately destroy the Western way of life.

### ADVANCED COUNTRIES NEED HELP, TOO

Only by implication has it been suggested that many of the steps being taken for underdeveloped areas around the world might well be employed in deteriorated areas of the advanced countries. The United States has its own abandoned-mine communities, which received so much attention during the depression years when "re-habilitation" was one of the more constructive methods chosen to try to "prime the pump." We have had our Arthurdales, Norrises, and Greenbelts, which were depression-born efforts to pull many of our own deteriorated areas out of the doldrums. We know the opposition which this type of governmental activity generated, but we also can thank these experiments for much of today's slum clearance in which the government is sharing costs with private industry. We probably also can thank the Greenbelt experiments for the greater thought which has gone into the Levittowns of the private speculative builders in the last decade.

Despite the movement of industry into the suburbs, there is as yet little emphasis on bringing industrial activity to existing man power. Abandoned communities still exist in Northern Minnesota, Michigan, and other areas which are largely dependent on welfare grants. Here lumbering has deforested the area, leaving sandy wastes unsuitable for agriculture, and then moved on. Our Indian areas possess man power far in excess of the work available. This again emphasizes the "vicious circle" of accumulative downward deterioration in regional areas of wealthy countries.[13]

One or two instances where imaginative industry has seen these pools of potential man power and profited by it are the projects of the Simpson Electric Division of the American Gauge & Machine Company of Chicago on the Lac du Flambeau Indian reservation in Wisconsin, and of the Bulova Watch Company on the Turtle Mountain Indian reservation in northern North Dakota.[14] Both have taken advantage of the exceptional manual dexterity of the Indian people to bring small and intricate assembly jobs to their home areas. This may prove to be a far better solution than the momentarily popular effort to transplant surplus Indians from their rural areas to city slums.

National pride has kept such countries as Italy and France from acknowledging the need for widespread community education within their borders. If we recognize the broadest interpretation of

13. Gunnar Myrdal, *Rich Lands and Poor, op. cit.*

14. Bureau of Indian Affairs, *Annual Reports*. Washington: Government Printing Office.

community education with which we are becoming increasingly concerned—that of a re-education of all of us to prepare for the adequate use and mastery of the technological changes which are rushing upon us—we must grant that today's better education is still doing little more than "conserving the cultural heritage of the past" in an era when sensitivity to potentials is imperative.

Community education as we know it today is not a new concept. As Scanlon's chapter sets forth, steps have been taken by a superior culture to extend its "benefits" to less-developed people in almost every "civilization" in history. Often the beneficiary has been forced to accept the new way of life. That drastic enforcement of cultural change has not vanished from the earth may be seen in the repetition of many of its aspects in the cultural changes which have been instituted by Communist dictatorships. Even today they do not hesitate to uproot and transport thousands of people if it is believed that such action will speed the acceptance of a new way of life or destroy dependence on a traditional social pattern. The Free World, on the other hand, is developing a new approach to community education, which depends on the understanding and acceptance of the desirability of change by the people who will be affected, so that their conscious and enthusiastic participation in making the change is assured.

## What Community Education Is About

The collaborators on this yearbook are familiar with all the different designations which have been attached to the basic ideas with which we are concerned, both within the activities of our own government abroad and with the jockeying for leadership among the agencies of the United Nations in order to accomplish what is basically the same thing, a multiple approach to community improvement. All of the various specialties must participate in this endeavor if success is to crown their efforts to reverse the "vicious downward spiral," referred to in the beginning of this chapter, and inaugurate in its stead the kind of "constructive upward spiral" which now characterizes the industrial growth of the leading nations. Nothing is static. Whether community life is deteriorating or developing, the purpose of community education is to arouse and give the direction to community self-help that will spur a steadily broadening economic and cultural development.[15]

The most pressing needs and problems of each community represent the starting point for a program of community education, and a developing program of self-help should be keyed to the expressed needs of the people.[16]

Where endemic diseases are undermining the vitality of the people, a community health campaign in which health education is linked with curative medicine and sanitary engineering may take precedence over anything else. In bringing this about, the first step should be to acquaint the people with existing agencies of government designed to deal with these problems.

Through vast rural areas of the world, the need may be for guidance and help in improving agricultural practices, whether these involve the introduction of superior strains of plants or livestock, familiarizing the people with modern modes of enriching the soil, eliminating animal or plant diseases, or counteracting the wastage of natural resources through improvident agriculture or through deforestation which leads to erosion and its interference with water conservation.

Provision of universal, free, and compulsory schools where these do not exist may be a basic objective; but community education must reach all sections of the community, adults as well as children and women as well as men.

Isolated communities will wish to build roads to link them with more advanced areas and many of them have the surplus man power to do the work if some outside help or direction can be supplied.

Community education is designed to "help people achieve the social and economic progress which will enable them to take their place in the modern world." But low living standards cannot be raised by educational means alone. Education must be integrated with economic development schemes, sometimes including the development of local industries.

Community improvement depends on self-help which may involve the development of increased and better participation of people in their local community affairs, revitalization of existing

15. Gunnar Myrdal, *An International Economy, op. cit.*

16. *Fundamental Education: Description and Program.* Paris: UNESCO, 1949.

forms of local government, or the initiation of some effective form of local administration where this does not yet exist. This should involve the organization of schemes for training local leadership.

Whether self-help programs of community education and development are the result of bilateral or international governmental agencies, active and continuing assistance from the national as well as the local governmental agencies will be necessary. In many instances departments of government exist whose responsibility it is to extend help to local areas, and it is essential that their representatives be alerted to the kind of active co-operation they will be called upon to render.

As for methods of communicating these newer ideas, it is necessary for workers in community education to be adequately supplied with a variety of supplementary media of instruction such as film strips, films, disc recordings, posters, flannel boards, and museum techniques. Use of puppet shows, simple dramatic expression, local folk dances, and recreational activities should all become part of any program seeking to help people develop what is best in their own culture, as well as helping them adopt new ideas that will aid them in building a new and better future.[17]

This statement of objectives is neither detailed nor complete, for space does not permit elaboration. It is drawn from material prepared by UNESCO in describing fundamental-education objectives in 1949–57;[18] by United Nations Bureau of Social Affairs discussing community development in 1955–56;[19] the American Technical Co-operation Administration;[20] and from the work of some nongovernmental agencies.

## What Are the Requisites for Change?
### WORLD WAR II AND THE MANUS

Rapid adaptation of a primitive group to sophisticated techniques was at one time considered very unlikely, despite evidences that

17. *Visual Aids in Fundamental Education* (Paris: UNESCO, 1952); *Radio in Fundamental Education* (Paris: UNESCO, 1950); "Museum Techniques in Education," *Educational Studies and Documents*, Series XVII (Paris: UNESCO).

18. *Fundamental Education: Description and Program, op. cit.*

19. Bureau of Social Affairs, "Social Progress through Community Development." New York: United Nations, 1955.

20. Philip M. Glick, *The Administration of Technical Assistance: Growth in the Americas.* Chicago: University of Chicago Press, 1957.

the Sioux Indians of the United States had made a complete cultural change in response to the coming of the horse in about 1770, transforming themselves from forest dwellers to plainsmen in about 50 years, as a result of having this new mode of transportation. Now Margaret Mead,[21] in her recent report on the Manus after World War II, clearly documents a complete social transformation from the Stone Age to the twentieth century in less than two decades, as a result of contacts with the Western world through hundreds of thousands of U.S. Army Air Corp personnel who used the Admiralty Islands as a staging area during the war in the South Pacific. Mead believes that the complete acceptance of the Islanders as equals by the Americans, in all man-to-man relationships, while possibly dictated by convenience on the part of the military, was of great influence in initiating the change. In the many years of contact between the Manus and the Germans, Australians, and Japanese who had successively controlled the Islands, they had always been treated as inferiors. Here among the Manus was clearly evident "the desire for national and personal respect, status, prestige, and importance in the world, which experience shows not to be readily accorded to 'backward,' weak countries or their citizens." And here was evident the easy, unself-conscious acknowledgement of this desired "status" by representatives of an alien culture who possessed, and cheerfully shared, many material advantages previously unknown by the Manus, or seen only as possessions of the representatives of a "superior" culture. Scanlon touches on a similar cultural revolution which took place in Turkey under the leadership of Mustafa Kemal following the breakup of the Ottoman Empire after World War I.[22]

### WORLD WAR II AND THE NAVAJO

Within the United States we have numerous small enclaves of American Indians, where the use of a tribal language persists among themselves even though they have been completely surrounded by English-speaking people for several generations. The largest tribe of

21. Margaret Mead, *New Lives for Old*. New York: William Morrow & Co., 1956.

22. Ahmed Yalman, *Turkey in My Time*. Norman, Oklahoma: University of Oklahoma Press, 1956.

which this was true is the Navajo, which in 1940 numbered over forty thousand. Less than 20 per cent of these Indians had any knowledge of English[23] at this time, and the group as a whole resisted the efforts of the government to enrol its children in federal schools. When the second world war came, only about five thousand Navajos were admitted to the armed services. Because of language limitations and ill health, thousands of enthusiastic volunteers were rejected. When the Navajo veterans returned to the reservation, they had become so completely convinced that knowing English and being able to read and write English was essential if one was to get on in the world that they wrought a transformation in reservation thinking in a matter of months. As a result of this psychological change, special curricula were set up by the Indian Service[24] for adolescent Navajos who came from their hogans without any knowledge of English. With this new, intense concern with the need for education, these illiterate, non-English-speaking, adolescent Navajos learned, according to some of the older leaders, more English in three months than their parents had learned in three years at the older boarding schools. It proved possible to teach these young men and women the basics of an elementary education, including English, and, in addition, to train them in a vocational skill. More than 70 per cent of those who took these courses are today successfully employed and living happpily away from the reservation.

OPERATION "BOOTSTRAP" IN PUERTO RICO

Puerto Rico came under the American flag in 1898 as a result of the Spanish-American War.

It is doubtful that most Americans at that time knew anything about Puerto Rico or were conscious of its annexation. We had promised to free Cuba when the war was won. Puerto Rico had not been mentioned. Our administration of the island was no worse than that of the Spaniards but probably little better. Most decisions relating to its administration were made by the American Congress which knew little about the island's problems and probably cared

23. *You Asked about the Navajo!* Washington: Bureau of Indian Affairs, Department of the Interior.
24. *Annual Reports on Special Navajo Program.* Washington: Bureau of Indian Affairs, Department of the Interior.

less. Decades of varying policies preceded the first attempt under the impact of the great depression to do something really constructive about Puerto Rico.

Accomplishments under the Puerto Rico Reconstruction Administration were valuable, but limited. However, they paved the way for the remarkable social and economic revolution which followed the new extension to Puerto Rico of "self-determination." First, there was the privilege of electing the governor and legislature. More important, however, was the granting to Puerto Rico in 1952 of an entirely new governmental status within the American union —that of an independent Commonwealth. Full self-government, and freedom from many federal taxes exacted of citizens on the mainland were features of the new status.[25]

The experiments of the preceding decade undoubtedly paved the way and trained the leadership for the new constructive growth which began under the Commonwealth. Freed to undertake its own salvation, Puerto Rico launched a variety of projects calculated to halt its economic deterioration and inaugurate an upward spiral of economic and social improvement. As a first step, the government set out to bring industry to its unemployed population, thus providing many new jobs and diversifying the economy. To make the island commonwealth an attractive industrial location, property taxes on industrial development were reduced or eliminated for a definite period of time. This attracted many American firms to open branch factories in Puerto Rico. There was no encouragement offered for a firm to remove its main operations from the continent. Advantage was taken of the climate to invite investment in hotel and other tourist attractions to lure American vacationists to Puerto Rico. A basic attack was launched on the causes of ill health, and a program of health education, infant and maternal care, slum clearance and rehousing of thousands of peasants was undertaken. Community education on a large scale was begun.

Step by step that aspect of the rehabilitation program which affected the common people was based in large part on community self-help, with a minimum of government subsidy, but plenty of good community leadership. Again as in the case of the Manus and

25. Earl P. Hanson, *Transformation: The Story of Modern Puerto Rico.* New York: Simon & Schuster, 1955.

Navajos, progress from the lowest levels of economic degradation to an increasing status of economic self-sufficiency has proceeded through self-help under guidance.[26]

### LAND FOR THE LANDLESS

In the Middle East today, various efforts are being made to provide land for the landless. In Iraq thousands of acres of "Crown Lands" are being provided with irrigation and made available to landless nomads with some financial assistance and instruction in its use and development provided by the government. This has been possible for several reasons: Today's population of Iraq is nearer five million than the thirty-five million believed to have occupied this area when the old irrigation systems of Babylon were in use; the "crown" has mollified the sheiks whose nomadic retainers had been permitted to roam the area, by assigning parts of the newly irrigated lands to these sheiks and their dependents; and lastly, a determined portion of Iraq's oil-royalty millions have been placed at the disposal of an Iraqui-designated international advisory board to finance the rehabilitation of these lands.

In Iran a similar pattern of improvement is under way. However, opposition from the old landholders is greater; but oil money is being employed in the execution of a seven-year-plan of building roads and railways, in expanding agricultural extension work, erecting schools and hospitals, and improving nutrition.

In Egypt the ousting of King Farouk was accompanied by a pledge on the part of the Revolutionary junta to reduce individual land-holdings to about two hundred acres per person. Former landowners were reimbursed with state bonds to pay for the confiscated land. Surplus land was sold to the fellahin at a moderate cost with payment spread over twenty to forty years. The famous Aswan dam proposal was expected to permit the irrigation of new land equivalent to about 25 per cent of the existing agricultural land of the country. This was to play a great part in relieving the present intolerable poverty of the agricultural workers. If the present rate of population increase continues, the food supply would no more than keep abreast of the soaring population. However, a lowering of the birth rate has frequently accompanied a rise in the standard of

26. *Ibid.*

living—Puerto Rico is the most recent demonstration of that tendency.

In the Philippines the late President Magsaysay, while still Secretary of National Defense in President Quirino's Cabinet, began to open up government lands on the island of Mindinao for settlement by the land-poor Huks who surrendered and agreed to cease their revolt against the government. Little permanent progress has yet been achieved in this project because of the difficulty in subjugating the land and the shortage of funds.

In the French territories of North Africa, prior to the recent upheaval, work was under way to provide irrigation for large blocks of land which were to be made available to the Arab population, in an endeavor to redress some of the economic imbalance between them and the French Colons.

Other instances might be cited, but these are typical of many present-day efforts to give the impoverished farmers access to land to which they can gain title.

### URBAN REHABILITATION

In all that has been said above, no mention has been made of urban rehabilitation which should be an essential element in any program of community education. The neglect is not from choice but from lack of data. With all the recent work in community education, little or nothing has been done for city populations, in either the less-developed areas or in the more advanced countries. To the extent that slum clearance has made progress in our own and some other countries, it has been largely a government-administered program. Little emphasis has been placed on self-help or community participation. Indeed, it is doubtful whether in much of the work which has been done there has been enough community participation to insure effective use and desirable maintenance of many of the new facilities made available, whether they be skyscraper apartments in New York City or simple two-story duplexes of adobe in some of the new villages of Egypt.

The Manus and the Navajos changed when faced with totally new experiences which swept aside the normal frustrations of colonial administration, traditionally approved behavior, and similar self-restraints within which the people normally operated. Interestingly

more careful study of all the factors involved could have prevented the ill advised action.

There is a good deal of evidence that the emotional appeal of learning how to read and write has been considerably exaggerated, as well as the reputed speed with which nonliterates achieve literacy. While it is undoubtedly true that many simple people, whose lives have depended on careful observation of the details of the world around them, have little difficulty in rapid initial memorization and recall of written symbols, this falls far short of reading fluently and with comprehension. The older view that literacy per se will lead automatically to a correction of other social ills has little foundation in fact. However, literacy is one tool in community development which can simplify the spread of information leading to improvements.

Illiteracy is normal in societies in which written records have never existed; and it occurs in literate societies where schooling has been denied to part of the population. The psychological attitude or conditioning toward reading as a skill may differ greatly in these different environments. Men and women in a nonliterate milieu have usually created a successful system of communication without writing and frequently require exposure to a variety of new experiences to become convinced that reading and writing have any advantages. On the other hand, an illiterate surrounded by the products of literacy—newspapers, printing on packaged goods, advertising signs, other people receiving letters—may be entirely conscious of its advantages and, in given circumstances, avid to acquire the skill.

Regardless of which illiterate we are considering, the acquisition of functional literacy takes time. In most Western countries where literacy is taken for granted, it is generally agreed that it takes about *four years to teach children* to read with speed and comprehension and that any less training is liable to be insufficient to maintain functional literacy into adulthood. Gray's recent UNESCO study,[31] in which the experiences of many countries and many languages all over the world have been assembled, supports a conclusion that a

31. William S. Gray, *The Teaching of Reading and Writing*, pp. 152, 170, 176. Paris: UNESCO, 1957.

minimum of 150 one-hour lessons, spread over several years, are required to bring *interested adults* to a point where they can easily comprehend written materials involving about 2,000 different words. This learning experience is only an excellent beginning for a "continuation of training which will carry them to higher levels of efficiency in reading." Gray's report in chapter v of this yearbook deals further with this matter.

PAPER SHORTAGE A SERIOUS HANDICAP

Establishing literacy in a nonliterate culture is a monumental and expensive undertaking. Developing a phonetic alphabet and teaching people how to read a few simple sentences is comparatively easy but will not create a literate populace. From the standpoint of the individual, there is little point in learning to read, unless he sees that reading will improve his prospects in life and that there is interesting or valuable reading matter available. This involves the printing and distribution not only of primers and readers for instruction but also informational pamphlets, secular and religious literature, and some form of news periodicals. Some countries of Asia, for example, which for many years have had a written language limited to the cultured few, (i.e., China and India) are now finding it difficult to extend such learning to the many because of the difficulty in securing the paper on which to print books and magazines. There is today a shortage of paper even to meet the needs of our own and other western countries.[32] The United States, with 10 per cent of the world's population, is today consuming approximately 70 per cent of the paper produced annually in the world. Asia, with 55 per cent of the world's population, is receiving less than 3 per cent of the paper that is being produced. Both areas are short of needed paper supplies, and to furnish the paper to meet the Asian and African shortage will require the development of completely new sources and kinds of raw materials, as well as new manufacturing plants.

What has been said about the requisites of effective literacy applies with equal force to experiments, here and there, to teach people how to read by lessons broadcast by radio or instruction by projection on a screen. The key incentive to learning how to read is the desire to read something which is immediately or continuously

32. *Paper for Printing Today and Tomorrow.* Paris: UNESCO, 1953.

available. Without that incentive, the instruction is relatively value-less. Even in Western Europe, we have instances in France and else-where of graduates of the common school being found illiterate at a later date, because they were peasants engaged in agriculture and without daily papers, magazines, or books to provide a continuing exercise of the skill.

## MULTIPLICITY OF LANGUAGES COMPLICATES READING PROBLEM

Pretty generally it is agreed that, although literacy teaching is only one aspect of community education, it is an essential element in any program that aims to offer "a ladder of upward intellectual and cultural mobility to all those who show the ability and desire" to move toward the expanding concepts of the present century. However, the problem is still further complicated by the vast num-ber of languages and dialects which are spoken throughout the world. A relatively limited area such as Ghana reports over 100 mu-tually nonunderstandable languages.[33] Experience around the world has established that literacy is most easily attainable in the vernacu-lar of any area.[34] A new language is very difficult to teach to any group of people who are not exposed to a continuous need to speak it.

The assumption that any kind of education operating on a limited budget is going to be able to produce a printed literature for a wide variety of primitive languages within a limited period of time is fallacious. It is doubtful that the cultured man power is available to translate even a small number of informative pamphlets into lan-guages of limited use. When the world was small and the peoples of these underdeveloped areas had limited contact with adjacent tribes speaking a different language, the language problem was not par-ticularly serious. As the contacts of trade increased, "languages of commerce" grew up. Swahili,[35] an African language which Moham-medan traders and slavers on the east coast of Africa picked up and spread, gradually incorporated many native terms from diverse lan-guages until it became a lingua-franca for the area. Along the east

33. Richard Wright, *Black Power: A Record of Reactions in a Land of Pathos.* New York: Harper & Bros., 1954.

34. *The Use of Vernacular Languages in Education.* Paris: UNESCO, 1953.

35. *Ibid.*

Asian coast Pidgin evolved as a simplified combination of English and native dialects;[36] and throughout the islands of the South Pacific Neo-Melanesian, an adaptation of Pidgin, has begun to supplant or supplement the tribal languages of the islands. The British in east Africa accepted Swahili. As schools for native peoples were opened, they offered instruction in the native dialect but, after a few years, switched to Swahili so that the area of mutual comprehension would be expanded. More advanced students who showed promise were offered the chance to learn English and, later, were often sent abroad to England or the United States for advanced education. Such advanced training was usually limited to the children of chiefs or leaders.

Pressure is now coming from the native peoples themselves for instruction in English as the second language, by-passing Swahili entirely,[37] on the ground that today's commercial employment is largely limited to those who understand and can speak and read English.

## The Problem of Adequate Staffing

### ANNUAL APPROPRIATIONS AND STAFF SECURITY

All governmental and international programs appear to suffer severely from the apparently inevitable budgetary requirements of the "annual appropriation." For the United States this delays the initiation of a program until funds have been made specifically available through Congressional appropriation. As a result, the means are usually lacking which would permit field workers to take immediate advantage of that contagious community enthusiasm which can result in immediate and creative action. Any commitment must be conditional, which allows enthusiasm to cool and other factors to divert attention from once evident needs.

With the utmost care in selection, it is difficult if not impossible to judge how effective a new employee is going to be until he has been on the job for a while. For this reason, the initial contract is usually limited to one year. If the man (or woman) has been successful, it is desirable to offer a contract renewal for a longer period

36. Margaret Mead, *op. cit.*

37. *Reports of UNESCO Staff Visiting African East Coast in 1952.* Paris: UNESCO, 1953.

of time, so as to profit from his acquired knowledge and experience and keep the program advancing in the confidence of the people with whom he has been working.

Here again, the problem of annual appropriations becomes of key importance, for the language of the appropriation bill may preclude contracts which commit a government agency for more than a year at a time. Also the casual attitude of congressmen toward the speed with which appropriation bills should be acted upon frequently leaves the employing administration, which is desirous of renewing a contract, without any legal assurance that funds will be provided to continue the project. Therefore, in both Technical Assistance and the United States bilateral programs, the offer of a renewal may be delayed so long, while waiting for the agency furnishing funds to act, that the employee may feel forced to begin negotiations for a return to his home base in order to be sure of continued employment. Many good men have been lost to overseas projects because of these delays.

A further problem involved in the staffing of many projects under the UN and its specialized agencies grows out of the fact that many of the less-developed countries are ones in which age and maturity have much greater prestige value than is true with the Western nations. Given a choice, many of these recipient countries will select for exchange professors or TA advisers, men of middle age or older. While this may be complimentary at the moment, it is these very mature and successful people who may encounter greater difficulty in re-entering home employment after several years of overseas activity, during which they have aged further and slipped out of their place in the economic or cultural fabric at home.

The budgetary uncertainties of the United Nations Technical Assistance Program are further complicated by the fact that the Agency is a voluntary co-operative activity dependent for its annual budget on the results of an annual "pledging conference" at which representatives of all interested nations meet to make commitments for the following year. These commitments must then run the gamut of the fiscal authorities of their respective countries. In the beginning, the United States which helped initiate the program, pledged to match every dollar from other countries with two dollars, American. Thus the exact amount of the American contribution remained uncertain for a considerable period of time each year. Sometimes the American Congress added to the confusion by deciding to appropriate only half of the American TA commitment at one session and postpone action on the remainder to the following spring. Another year the entire UNTA program was thrown into confusion by the "discovery" that some of the foreign pledges were being made in "soft currencies" (local currencies) which were not readily convertible into dollars, francs, or sterling. These funds were like the "counterpart" funds or local currency which the U.S. itself has been accepting in payment for agricultural surpluses being sold abroad to some countries and were expendable only in the country of issue. In a number of cases these countries had pledged funds considerably in excess of the funds needed to finance Technical Assistance projects planned for their own countries. As a result unexpended balances were accumulating. The United States suddenly decided that it would not match these balances until they had been actively absorbed into some aspect of the TA program. This decision resulted in a sudden and unexpected reduction in Technical Assistance commitments and the cancellation of authorized or active projects with the consequent embarrassment to the sponsoring agencies and some unfortunate ill will toward the United States. A recent policy decision by the U.S. Congress calls for a gradual reduction of the American share in Technical Assistance to one-third of the total.

Other participating nations have their own ingenious ways of delaying their pledged funds which has caused the TA Board to set aside a portion of all money it receives as a cushion to insure the continuation of its basic programs regardless of these vagaries.

#### REINTEGRATION OF INTERNATIONAL WORKERS BACK HOME

The reference above to the reintegration of technical-assistance specialists and exchange intellectuals into American employment reveals quite a serious embarrassment to both the bilateral and international programs, and it is matched by similiar difficulties on the part of the nationals of all countries furnishing such overseas staff members. In order to get both national and international programs launched, the Truman administration, in May 1945, through Executive Order 9721, provided that federal agencies might loan employees for work with TCA or any of the UN agencies, placing them in leave-without-pay status with re-employment rights limited to three years to the job which they had vacated or one of equivalent status. This was an extension of the principle of the Roosevelt order initiating Inter-American co-operation. Many American colleges have made similar gestures to their staff members. However, many individuals have accepted international employment without any assurance of job protection. A great many returned specialists have found that it requires from six months to a year to secure positions of status equal to those they left; many have not been able to return to the agency which originally released them because they have "overstayed" their released time; a number have found that they have lost their "seniority" rights and have been passed over when promotions were considered (the section of Executive Order 9721 guaranteeing seniority and promotions expired three years after the order was promulgated); and some have found that new jobs are not easy to find for a person who has been "out of circulation." Today, throughout the nations which are furnishing expert help for overseas technical assistance, the men who go abroad are, in general, finding themselves at a decided disadvantage in securing re-employment on their return.

Suggestions have been made among the United Nations agencies that some agreement should be reached by the major Western nations, at least, by which an international civil service is set up for such technical-assistance work. The pattern for such a security agency might be the colonial and foreign office civil service set up by Great Britain in the days of Empire, which furnished an assured career in foreign specialized employment for men especially trained for such work, followed by a substantial retirement annuity. The world is now entering upon a widespread and increasing program of technical assistance and foreign exchange which requires for its success a much more specific training in the behavioral sciences and languages than is usually provided in the core college course, as well as specific education in medicine, nursing, agriculture, livestock management, literacy teaching, linguistics, governmental administration, banking, irrigation, engineering, dam building, and a host of other specialties. For a beginning it may have been adequate to pluck a man or woman here or there whose past training and experience appeared to fit him to do a reasonably good job in some underdeveloped area over a short term. Now that such programs are growing in importance, special training is needed for this work. This need is further developed by Harlan Cleveland in chapter xiv. There is sufficient similarity between these jobs in various areas so that there is reason to believe that experience gained in one area may be a definite asset in undertaking work in another area. Men and women who are willing to devote all or a large portion of their professional lives to this new international service need the assurance of civil service protection and retirement, for the longer an individual spends in overseas work, the harder time he may expect to have in reintegrating into normal employment in his home land.

### TRAINING FOR OVERSEAS EMPLOYMENT

The history of the United States in meeting the need for overseas technicians has been to approach the problem on a more or less amateur basis. For example, when we recruited teachers for service in the Philippines, it is doubtful that anyone concerned with the program conceived of these jobs as differing greatly from rural school teaching in the United States. A few of those who went to the Philippines may have known Spanish, which was the only European language of the archipelago (and not in universal use), but one would be safe in asserting that no American accepting service in the Philippine school system had ever heard of Tagalog, the indigenous language of most of the island of Luzon, or of any of the many other indigenous languages of the provinces, whose people knew little or no Spanish.

Similarly during our organization of the Inter-American program, though there was an attempt to secure the services of persons who spoke Spanish, it is doubtful that we even attempted to find a Kechua-speaking teacher or agriculturalist for work in the Andean area, where several million Indians about whom we became concerned speak only Kechua and no Spanish.

Overseas-training will not call for the kind of language-teaching in our high schools and colleges about which current magazines and newspapers are becoming concerned. In many areas of the world French, German, Spanish or even Russian are of little more help than a good knowledge of English. People going abroad may well be called upon to use Arabic, Hindii, Urdu, Thai, Japanese, Tamil, Singhalese, Malay or any one of two hundred or more other languages, many of which do not yet possess an accepted written form, but each of which nevertheless is spoken by several hundred thousand and upwards to millions of people. This calls for the kind of language instruction offered by the American Military and Foreign Services special schools during the war. Britain and other European nations have operated such schools for many years. Russia has recently initiated comparable plans to equip their foreign service nationals for successful work abroad. In view of the fact that few persons during high school or college can possibly anticipate the language which they may ultimately need, such language training demands the establishment of government-sponsored language institutes in several key cities of the United States, where persons going abroad for various periods of time in technical-assistance work, or employment overseas by American business, can receive intensive short-term training with the opportunity to gain pronunciation skill from a native of the area to which they are going.

Great Britain for many years operated a foreign-service training program consisting of several years of work at home and abroad. This was a graduate program and began with the careful selection of candidates for training, which involved an extensive inquiry into the school and university history of the candidate and required the personal evaluation of his previous headmasters and professors and a detailed account of academic and other attainments. Special stress was laid on health, bearing in mind the toughness of demands especially in the tropical territories. A good deal of emphasis was also placed on athletic achievement and attainment of distinction in competitive games, which probably was important in view of the hard field work frequently encountered in grim climates.

Digestion of this mass of references was followed by a series of oral interviews but not by written examinations. A large majority of the applicants were rejected each year as a result of a careful "weeding out" process. The successful candidates entered a year of post-graduate study at either Oxford or Cambridge and, often, a period of six months at the London School of Oriental Languages. The course involved about an hour a day of study on the future working language of the area for which the candidate was being prepared and a similar amount of study of civil and criminal law. Courses in social anthropology, practical surveying, first aid, primitive housing (applied directly to the areas to which the students might be sent) with practical suggestions for improvements and bridge-building. Following the completion of the campus courses, the students were required to engage in twelve to eighteen months of field experience under competent leadership. Successful completion of such probationary experience led to junior-grade permanent appointments. The program as a whole offers valuable suggestions as to elements which should be incorporated in training for service abroad today.

## Operating Principles

### THE PEOPLE SERVED MUST IDENTIFY THEMSELVES WITH PROJECTS

Experience has taught us that, in order to bring about constructive change, it is necessary to obtain the active participation of the people themselves. They are the best judges of their immediate problems; and only with their assent and understanding can lasting progress be made.

Sometimes such effort at social improvement is the result of internal leadership, as was the case in many devastated Philippine[38] rural areas following the evacuation of the Japanese after World War II. Former rural leaders who had been in hiding in the wooded mountains came down to disordered villages to help with reconstruction. Village inhabitants had been content once again to look to Manila for financial support and leadership. Manila had been almost bombed off the map, and the national treasury had been looted, so that the former national leadership and financial support were not available. At this point, local leaders proposed that the communities themselves decide what were their greatest needs and then combine their resources of man power and money to solve their own problems. Thus were school buildings rebuilt, sanitary water supplies restored, roads regraded, agriculture and livestock-raising resumed, and community law and order and recreation reorganized. The sequence of activities varied from place to place, but the important thing was that each community began to pull itself up by its own bootstraps and, in doing so, frequently planned a future far richer

38. J. C. Laya, *Little Democracies of Bataan*. Manilla: Inang Wika Publishing Co., 1951.

than its past had been. Pedro Orata (chap. vi) offers a vignette of his own experience in his home area of the Philippine Islands during this era.

At other times the impetus for community improvement has come from teams of nationals, similar to the Mexican Cultural Missions.[39] These teams moved into local areas, to stimulate consideration of local needs and to furnish the technical knowledge required to solve the major problems which came to light in frank discussions with the people.

In still other cases, the leadership may come from foreign specialists, made available through the UN Technical Assistance program at the request of member states of the United Nations. The activities of the multinational "teams" working in the adjacent "laboratory" villages of CREFAL,[40] the UNESCO Fundamental Education training center in Mexico[41] or similar teams in training at the Arab States FE Center in Egypt[42] are cases in point. The reader is referred to chapter xii for further information about the UNESCO training centers.

Regardless of the origin of technical leadership, it is essential that specialists familiarize themselves not only with the conditions in the community but with the people themselves. They need to win their confidence and jointly, with them, determine what needs to be done and how best to proceed.

LEADERSHIP CAN HELP COMMUNITIES USE EXISTING SERVICES

Once a project has been selected, the specialist should guide the group leaders of a given community, making a careful analysis of the project, and should help them plan a desirable sequence of steps looking toward its resolution. It is highly important to be able to show group leaders how to take advantage of existing governmental or other services which are available and then urge their co-opera-

39. Lloyd H. Hughes, *The Mexican Cultural Mission Program.* Paris: UNESCO, 1950.

40. *Learn and Live (Technical Assistance Plan for CREFAL).* Paris: UNESCO, 1951.

41. *New Horizons at Tzentzenhuaro (Balance Sheet of a Fundamental Education Center in Mexico).* Paris: UNESCO, 1953.

42. *Fundamental Education for the Arab World.* Sirs-El-Layyan, Egypt: UNESCO, 1952.

tion in mobilizing a community labor force to perform the necessary work. The less developed the country, the fewer are the national agencies which can help. However, in many areas where there is need for community development, national road agencies, national health agencies, school leadership, and sometimes national credit agencies already exist. They need to be informed of the project and their assistance secured. When this is not possible, various international agencies, bilateral programs like United States Technical Assistance or the Colombo Plan, private funds like the Ford or Rockefeller Foundations, philanthropies like the Save-the-Children Federation or the Mass Education Movement, or the foreign mission funds of some churches are in a position to extend limited aid.

### LOCAL INITIATIVE AND SELF-GOVERNMENT

Lastly, as has been frequently discovered, it is often necessary to re-establish some form of local initiative and self-government. For generations rural masses have been accustomed to rule from above, as in the case of the Philippines. Therefore, it has proved difficult at first to interest local people in their self-improvement. Efforts to bring about change and improvement have met the inertia of belief that anything they might do to bring about material or economic improvement would be taken from them in higher taxes, higher land rents, and higher interest rates on necessary operating loans. Methods of overcoming these beliefs have differed, but it has been necessary for community leaders to persuade the workers themselves that they would profit from such changes as they would help to bring about.

While community education seeks to transform the life of the least successful citizens of an area, it is necessary that, if help in such regeneration is to be permitted to come from international, bilateral, or foundational guidance or direction, its terms must be so couched that *it does not threaten the governmental integrity of the participating state.* The work of all these outside agencies today is contingent upon acceptance. If revolutionary results are to be obtained, therefore, the recipient government must be aware of the possibilities of community-improvement programs and be prepared to lend assistance where possible.[43]

43. *Social Progress through Community Development, op. cit.*

In the selection of projects for community improvement, effort should be made so to design them that *the entire populace identifies itself* with the undertaking and works toward its successful completion. It is also important that leadership for such projects be channeled through long established or acceptable local agencies. This is frequently an involved process, for many local leaders are older men who have not kept up with new thinking and who are more concerned with maintaining the status quo than in making it possible for newer and more desirable procedures to be introduced. If ignored, these leaders, whether secular or religious, can bring about the failure of even the best of projects by discouraging participation by the older members of the community. Many times, however, older leaders, if included in the preliminary planning, will grow to realize their own inability to cope with many of the newer problems and will propose the selection of younger men for active direction of the project, or at least will accept the selection of such younger leaders.

In Mexico, many community-improvement projects have made excellent headway, because opportunities for leadership have been offered to younger men. Many of these men had participated for several summers in the labor contracts which the Mexican government arranges for its Nationals in the United States. These men have learned different ways of doing things by direct experience and are often glad to put this experience to work for their home communities.

In Afghanistan the resistance to fundamental education by the mullahs in the provinces, which in some instances had resulted in driving out trained Afghan teachers, was partly corrected when the government established a school for mullahs in Kabul. Subsequently, these trained young religious leaders were sent into the villages to further community education.

FUNDAMENTAL EDUCATION IMPORTANT FOR WOMEN

As noted earlier in the chapter, fundamental education must be aimed as much at women as at men.[44, 45] Many of the adverse con-

44. *Fundamental Education: Description and Program, op. cit.*

45. "The Scope and Nature of Fundamental Education," *Fundamental and Adult Education Quarterly*, IX (April, 1957), 51–59.

ditions under which the common people of underdeveloped areas suffer are conditions which are largely under the control of the women. The man is often engaged in field operations, the produce of which is sold commercially. Whether or not there is a home garden which produces food for family consumption may depend entirely on the women. Care in matters of health almost always revolves upon them as does school attendance.

In one area, a national program of improving rural conditions was launched, which involved the distribution of young chickens so that a small flock might be raised. It was assumed that the flock subsequently would produce enough eggs to provide each child in the family an egg a day to improve its health. No particular emphasis was placed on the children's need for better nourishment, and it was soon found that the women were carefully collecting the eggs and taking them to market where they were used as currency to buy other needed things. While the project was ultimately helpful, it failed to accomplish its original purpose.

In another area, where an outside agency concerned with health-improvement dug wells for a village to eliminate the need to depend on irrigation-ditch water for drinking and bathing and so to eliminate the infectious round of bilharziasis, the women were found after a year or so to be using the well water for their own use but continuing to supply their men-folk ditch water, because of an "old wives' tale" that well water would render the men impotent.

Community-education teams originating from outside a given district must be staffed with women as well as men. Any program which is clearly designed to improve the health and general conditions surrounding children will usually enlist the co-operation of mothers. The need for women on the staff is, therefore, apparent.

### A PROGRAM OF EVALUATION NEEDED

With all that is being undertaken in various parts of the world in the field of community education, there is very little valid evidence of success, or recorded causes of failure. Experiments burst into publicity shortly after their inauguration with claims for success. There is no doubt that most communities throw off their lethargy for a period under the spotlight of attention. Unfortunately there has seldom been a basic study of conditions "as they were" against which to measure the claims for improvement. Mead's Manus studies offer the first thorough "before and after" comparison which has yet been made, but the availability of initial data was accidental. Again, with the Navajo there is the good fortune of a thorough-going and basic "status study" by Kluckholm and Leighton made just prior to the war crisis.[46] Some of the recent changes are being documented in annual reports of the Bureau of Indian Affairs.

What is needed, however, as has been proposed to UNESCO and the United Nations on numerous occasions, is a consistent pattern of preliminary analysis, against which constructive comparisons can be made as a community-education project progresses. The analysis might serve significantly also as a contrast, a number of years after the excitement has passed and the community affected has settled into a new routine. We need to know whether the community is on an upward spiral or has relapsed into an earlier pattern of progressive stagnation. It is important that this kind of evaluation be done so that we may learn more rapidly the keys to success in rehabilitation. Too often we have been content to wait for delayed evidence that our efforts at community development have not been fruitless.

46. Clyde Kluckholm and Dorothea Leighton, *The Navajo*. Cambridge, Massachusetts: Harvard University Press, 1946.

# CHAPTER II

# Historical Roots for the Development of Community Education

DAVID SCANLON

If community education is viewed as a cultural transformation which leads to self-improvement under either the leadership of foreign specialists or nationals working in depressed areas within their own country, then the history of community education can be traced from the ancient Egyptians to the present time. It is also possible to see emerging specific patterns based upon changes in agriculture, health, industrialization, and literacy. Historically, community education has been primarily concerned with rural areas. It has been the means by which the advances of technologically superior societies are introduced to less-developed societies.

The term *fundamental education* was introduced by UNESCO in 1946. There are other terms that describe in large measure the same process. Gandhi introduced *basic education* to describe the organization of education around basic handicrafts. *Social education* was later introduced in India to describe the various adult programs concerned with such basic problems as literacy, hygiene, and economic self-improvement. *Mass education* was used, particularly by the British, to describe a movement designed to "promote better living for the whole community. . . ."[1] However, it apparently was felt that the term *community development* more adequately described the process, for the *Mass Education Bulletin*, published by the University of London, changed its name to *Community Development Bulletin*. Other related terms used to describe similar processes include the *Pronoia dia tis Ergassias* or National Development Program of Greece; the *Paysannats Indigenes*, a rural economic program in the Belgian Congo; and the multipurpose *"Centres of Attraction"* found in French Africa.

1. "What Is Mass Education?" *Mass Education Bulletin*, I (December, 1949), 2.

Cultural transformation by force has been the traditional pattern when either a nation was conquered by a technologically superior power or, in more recent times, when a Fascist or Communist dictatorship has arisen. The degree of transformation may differ from the total change brought about by the Incas to the more evolutionary change that occurred with the expansion of the Roman Empire. We have also seen how rapid internal transformation can lead to a democracy, as in the case of Turkey, or be merely used as a technique for strengthening dictatorship, as in the Soviet Union.

Fundamental education, as envisaged by UNESCO, is based upon the premise that it is necessary to wait until one is invited to work with people on a partnership basis. The practice of going to a country and forcing change is, fortunately, no longer acceptable. The failure of the Anchau Development Scheme in Nigeria was a typical example of a well-intentioned community-development project that was carried out without the full participation of the people and, as a result, did not meet the expectations of the planners.

A second basic difference in present viewpoints from projects in the past is that the change that is being effected is for the people themselves. It is viewed as the foundation on which advanced development can take place. It is for this reason that community education is being developed in practically all of these countries which have recently gained their independence.

### Early Forms of Cultural Transformation

#### TOTAL CULTURAL CHANGE BY MITAMAE SYSTEM OF INCAS

The Incas were among the first to use community development as a means of bringing conquered territories into close economic, social, and political relationship with the mother country. After conquering a territory, technicians were sent to the area to show the newly conquered people how to grow better crops. Builders were sent to help with the construction of new buildings. Roads were built through the new province, linking it to the vast network of roads in the empire. In addition to sending technicians to the area, the Incas used a system called Mitamae which kept a loyal and trusted population in all sections of the empire. The Mitamae was used in two situations: first, whenever a district became overpopulated, a number of people would be sent to an outpost of the empire to start a new district; second, whenever a province was conquered, approximately half of the conquered population would be sent a hundred miles away, and another conquered group, which did not speak the local language, was sent in to take the place of the one which had been sent out. "In this way the Incas were able to break up the older cultures of the conquered people and impose Inca culture upon them, so that within a few generations they were completely assimilated."[2]

People were assigned to specific responsibilities, and there were technicians available to teach what was expected of them in the way of contributions to the empire. Some were trained to build and repair bridges and roads while others were taught agriculture. Where necessary, populations were transferred to the humid areas to grow coco-leaf. Young men who showed artistic ability were drafted into the Yanacuna, where they were trained as artists and craftsmen. As a totalitarian state, the Incas were extremely successful in cultural transformation.

ROMAN TECHNICAL ASSISTANCE IN AGRICULTURE AND COMMUNICATION

The expansion of the Roman Empire has been referred to many times as the first "technical-assistance" program. As Rome expanded, it was necessary to build roads, to open rivers for transportation, and to effect rapid transportation and communication with the center of the Empire. Military needs opened areas that had remained comparatively untouched by the Mediterranean civilization. In many ways a parallel can be drawn with the construction of military installations during and since World War II in many less-developed societies. With the military went Roman law, government, and business. In some areas, such as England, the occupation by Roman soldiers led to demands upon agriculture that forced the people to adopt intensive agriculture and the beginnings of scientific agronomy. In Gaul, because of its close geographical contact with Rome, new industries arose, and Roman colonists and businessmen migrated in large numbers, particularly in the southern region. The growth of new cities presented opportunities for men to become skilled workers in the expanding manufacturing area.

2. Ralph Linton, *The Tree of Culture*, p. 655. New York: Alfred A. Knopf, 1955.

In North Africa, the Romans found an area that had been extensively colonized by the Phoenicians. With the loss of former lands, the Phoenicians concentrated their efforts on the agricultural development of the territory. The most famous treatise on agriculture had been written by a Carthaginian, Mago, and had been used as a basis for the development of scientific agriculture. The effectiveness in agriculture was soon apparent. The rapid expansion of the cultivation of olive trees led to such harvests that by the fourth century "no province supplied such quantities of oil as Africa."[3] Rome used the area for colonization, particularly under the rule of Augustus. In those places where agricultural population was needed, the natives of the area were transported in a manner not dissimilar to that of the Mitamae system of the Incas.

The rapid expansion of plantations and the extension of the military to the south created a need for rapid communication. As a result, Roman North Africa was soon covered with an intricate road system. The construction of the roads was the responsibility of the communities. "From the Second Century onward, we find all the larger towns and several smaller ones active in providing the necessary communications within their territory. . . ."[4]

Roman irrigation in North Africa has remained effective until the present time. When, in 1950, the United Nations Educational, Scientific and Cultural Organization started its study of the arid lands, it sent a representative to the Mediterranean area to make an exploratory survey. The representative, Ritchie Calder of the *London News Chronicle*, found that over one hundred Roman wells had been cleaned out and "were functioning as well as they did two thousand years ago."[5] Over two hundred wells have been discovered in Tripolitania, and from the records of Roman occupation there are thousands more waiting to be discovered. The use of ancient wells and cisterns in a modern technical-assistance program is an interesting link between the present and the past in man's techniques in solving his basic problems.

3. Theodore Mommsen, *The History of Rome*, Vol. II, p. 338. London: R. Bentley, 1886.

4. *Ibid.*, p. 339.

5. Robert Brittain, *Let There Be Bread*, p. 23. New York: Simon & Schuster, 1952.

## ROAD-BUILDING, AGRICULTURE, HEALTH MEASURES
### BY MEDIEVAL MONKS

During the Middle Ages, community education, where carried on at all, was primarily executed by the various religious orders. As monasteries and religious orders were established in various countries, there developed a type of internal education among monks and priests connected with the orders. The traveling from one monastery to another in different countries brought about the exchange of ideas in basic skills—skills that would start in the monasteries and gradually spread to the community.[6]

The Cistercians were excellent agriculturalists. Under their supervision, waste lands were reclaimed, and marshes were drained. New crops were introduced, and as the Cistercian monasteries spread, so did their agricultural techniques. They were also responsible for the diffusion of knowledge of animal husbandry. Cattle-breeding and veterinary science were highly developed by the monks, and where a Cistercian monastery was established these techniques were passed on to the local people.

A prominent feature of monasticism and religious orders in the twelfth century, such as the Premonstratensians, Hospitalers, and Templars, was service to others. The role of health and caring for the sick had been an integral part of the philosophy of the early Christian community. Following the establishment of the first general hospital in Rome (approximately 400 A.D.) smaller cities made an effort to construct "hospital centers." *Xenodochia*, or refuges for strangers, were ordered placed along the routes of pilgrims by the Council of Nice. With the decline of the Empire, the monasteries became the centers of medicine in the Western world.

The concept of service led in the thirteenth century to the establishment of many orders with a variety of functions. Of particular interest is the Order of Friars, who were known as the Order of Bridge-builders.[7] Their function, as the name implies, was to build

6. In a sense the constant traveling by various monks and priests inside Europe could be compared to the effect of the crusades, in which people of many nationalities were brought together and caused an interchange of ideas.

7. Dana Carleton Munro and Raymond James Sontag, *The Middle Ages*, p. 327. New York: Century Co., 1921.

bridges for the convenience of travelers. However, by so doing, travel was made easier between various sections of the country and led to an increase in contact between the rural areas and the cities.[8]

## Education by Missionaries

### COMMUNITY CENTERS FOR INDIANS IN MEXICO

With the Spanish conquistadores in Mexico went the missionaries. Early missionary leaders were concerned with arts and trades for both boys and girls. Vasco de Quiroga was named *oidor* of New Spain in 1530 and showed a great interest in establishing centers for the Indians. The first hospital-pueblo, a community center which he called Santa Fe, was opened under his direction. All Indians were required to learn a trade and were given technical assistance in agriculture. When, in 1537, Quiroga became Bishop of Michoacán, he expanded the community centers, and all Indians in a center were bound in a social organization along co-operative lines.

### CALIFORNIA MISSIONS TRANSFORM INDIANS
### INTO LOYAL SPANIARDS

However, while the community-center concept was used extensively in Mexico, it was in California that the mission became most effective as an agent of cultural transformation. In California the Indians were encouraged to congregate in a pueblo. There, under the direction of the missionaries, they were taught the Spanish language, the fundamentals of the Spanish way of life, and the Roman Catholic religion.

The Spanish government supported the missions financially and assigned soldiers for the protection of the missionaries. The effectiveness of the mission program was very appparent to the Spanish government. The government had seen in southern California the cost and difficulty of conquering the local Indians. The missions were able to do what had been impossible for the military, namely, bring about the acceptance and support of the local people. In the Spanish budget the cost of supporting missions was included under frontier

8. The various craft guilds served as an important means of educating young men in the trades and skills of the period. Communities would occasionally invite guilds to establish centers in their towns and by so doing would extend the trade techniques to an ever-widening geographical area.

expenses. In a very real sense the success of the missions could well represent the success of Spain in the New World. The possibility of assembling enough Spanish colonists to build a strong area loyal to Spain appeared extremely doubtful. The next-best approach was to make the Indians loyal to Spain by making them Spaniards. The mission soon came to be "the kingpin of the Spanish frontier system."[9]

As originally established, the mission was to be a temporary measure. Once the Indians were considered to have sound understanding of Spanish civilization, were able to produce those goods and materials necessary for the new civilization, and were fully converted to Roman Catholicism, the mission would move on. The area would then be regarded as a parish rather than a mission.

Around the church which served as the center of the mission were the quarters for Indians who were considered neophytes until the mission was declared a parish. Workshops occupied a major portion of the mission, and here Indians were trained as carpenters, blacksmiths, soapmakers, and brickmakers. Storerooms and granaries were also found in the mission. Attached to the mission was the garden where training in agricultural methods became an important part of the education of the neophyte. Fruit-growing was introduced at the missions and soon spread throughout the area.

The California missions represented one of the greatest efforts to effect cultural transformation by persuasion, for the most part, rather than by force. The unusual feature of the California mission was its interest in and development of those activities, such as agriculture and manufacturing, that did not become an integral part of most missionary activities for several centuries.[10]

The greatest missionary effort took place during the seventeenth and early eighteenth centuries. "Certainly it is true of this century that further expansion was almost solely the work of the missionaries."[11]

9. John Walter Caughey, *California*, p. 86. New York: Prentice-Hall, Inc., 1940.

10. For a more detailed description, see Zephyrin Engelhardt, *The Missions and Missionaries of California*, 5 vols. (San Francisco: James Barry Co., 1915); and Bryan J. Clinch, *California and Its Missions*, 2 vols. (San Francisco: Whitaker & Ray, 1904).

11. Caughey, *op. cit.*, p. 87.

## HEALTH, EDUCATIONAL, AND AGRICULTURAL ACTIVITIES OF
### EARLY PROTESTANT MISSIONARIES

While the Protestant missionary movement was started in England in 1792, it has been to a disproportionate degree an American movement.[12] By 1825 the Protestant missionary effort was well established. Americans ships were becoming common carriers in world commerce, and, as transportation became possible, missionaries were soon found in most areas of the world. The wealth of the United States plus an increased concern about religion led to a rapid expansion of missionary effort.

The second-generation missionaries, those who followed the founding fathers, began to see an intimate relationship between poverty and spirituality. The importance of the village school had been realized even before the second-generation missionary, but the "new" missionary was concerned with all social and economic aspects of the society in which he was working. He saw as his obligation the training of the local people in better agricultural methods, better workmanship, and better economic management. It became apparent to many that in the side issues, health and agriculture, "there lay the very essence of the Christian gospel."[13]

As early as 1836, the first doctor was sent as a missionary to the Maoris in New Zealand. By the twentieth century, missionaries had become in many instances specialists—medical missionaries, educational missionaries, or agricultural missionaries. Centers were established where specialists representing these various services could work together on the problems of the whole community.[14]

### BUDDHIST AND ISLAMIC MISSIONARIES TEACH LITERACY

In addition to Christian missionaries, Buddhist missionaries have for centuries been bringing literacy to many sections of Asia. When

12. Loy L. Smith, *The Revolution in Christian Missions*, p. 14. New York: Abington-Cokesbury Press, 1941.

13. *Ibid.*, p. 31.

14. It is undoubtedly for this reason that the indigenous people in one area assumed that the UNESCO mission was a new religious group, for here was the familiar pattern of a variety of "experts" in health, education, and agriculture.

Europeans reached Asia, particularly the Far East, they found some established schools.[15] In Burma, the Europeans found that many men were literate. In Thailand, education in the basic three R's was primarily the work of the Buddhist priests who taught in villages without pay.

From Africa to the Philippines, missionaries of Islam and traders brought the Arabic alphabet and literacy. The Koranic school in various forms and levels was in most areas the only means of gaining literacy, although in many instances the missionaries did nothing more than teach the pupils to recite the Koran by rote in Arabic. "It has been said that Al-Azhar University in Cairo has trained and sent two thousand Moslem missionaries into Africa since World War II."[16]

## Impact of Industrial Revolution

### EARLY CO-OPERATIVES AMONG WORKERS

The social and economic consequences of the Industrial Revolution led to various movements which attempted to organize workers for mutual improvement. Robert Owen had established "Villages of Co-operation and Union" and a farm at New Harmony, Indiana. The Reverend George Ripley had founded the Brook Farm Colony, and the followers of Charles Fourier had organized scores of phalanxes operating on the principles of Owen's co-operative villages.

In the north of England a group of weavers had formed the "Equitable Society of Rochdale Pioneers." In 1844 the Society opened its own store and shortly after bought and ran a flour mill. From the Rochdale Pioneer movement there developed the co-operative Society which became one of the largest single food-distributing businesses in the world. The techniques and methods of the co-operatives, consumer education, and marketing procedures were invaluable in working in societies where capital was limited and community development depended upon co-operation.

15. J. S. Furnivall, *Educational Progress in Southeast Asia*, p. 13. New York: Institute of Pacific Relations, 1943.

16. Gloria A. Wysner, *Africa Today*, p. 14. Edited by C. Grove Haines. Baltimore: Johns Hopkins Press, 1955.

### NEIGHBORHOOD GUILDS AND SETTLEMENT HOUSES

The rise of cities with the accompanying slum conditions led to institutes, neighborhood guilds, and settlement houses that were concerned with helping men improve their trade and with stimulating "self improvement." Among the earliest of these, opened in England, were the Mechanics Institute (1820), People's College at Sheffield (1842), and Brighton Working Men's Institute (1849).

Toynbee Hall, opened by Samuel A. Barnett to help the poor of London and run by university students, was visited by Stanton Coit, who remained for two years studying the organization and function of the Hall. Upon his return to the United States, Coit formed Neighborhood Guilds on New York's East Side (1887). Five years later, the Neighborhood Guilds were called University Settlements.

At the same time that Coit was opening the Neighborhood Guilds, four graduates of Smith College met in Boston to establish a residence group in a "working class" neighborhood in a large city. The project developed into an association with representatives from Bryn Mawr, Smith, Vassar, and Wellesley. Two years later the first college settlement sponsored by the association began its work on Rivington Street in New York. During the same year Jane Addams and Ellen Starr founded Hull House in Chicago, and the Settlement House movement was firmly inaugurated in the United States.[17]

## Community Education in the United States

### EARLY INTEREST IN AGRICULTURAL EDUCATION

In the United States community education has been carried on primarily in agricultural and rural communities. The concern for agricultural improvement has had a long history in this country. One of the first schools for orphan boys, Bethesda School in Georgia, was opened in 1740 with agricultural education as one of its primary objectives.[18] A society for promoting agriculture was organized in 1785 in Philadelphia, and in the next twenty years a number of state agricultural societies were founded. The agricultural fair developed

17. See Stanton Coit, *Neighborhood Guilds*. London: Swan, Sonnenschein & Co., 1891.

18. Rufus W. Stimson and Frank W. Lathrop, *History of Agricultural Education Less than College Grade in the United States*, p. 89. Washington: Government Printing Office, 1942.

by Elkanah W. Watson, who started the Berkshire (Massachusetts) Agricultural Society in 1811, was the first "demonstration technique" used in agricultural education.

The increased interest in agriculture led to the formation of the United States Agricultural Society in 1852. Made up of members from twenty-three states and territories, this society sponsored exhibitions and educational agricultural activities. The United States Agricultural Society became a powerful organization whose influence contributed to the formation of the United States Department of Agriculture.

### LAND-GRANT COLLEGES AND AGRICULTURAL EXTENSION

With the establishment of the land-grant colleges in 1862, various agricultural societies, particularly the Patrons of Husbandry, urged the extension of agricultural-education facilities in rural areas. It was pointed out that this could best be accomplished by using the agricultural colleges as centers for this expansion program. With the passage of the Hatch Act in 1887, which established agricultural experimental stations in connection with land-grant colleges, a major step was taken in bringing the best agricultural practices to the farmer. The Chautauqua movement had illustrated techniques of adult education that were adapted by Pennsylvania State College in 1892 and applied to its extension work. Iowa State College in 1906 authorized its agricultural department to "give lectures and demonstrations on the growing of crops and fruits, on stock raising, dairying, land drainage, and kindred subjects, including domestic science."[19] In 1905 a committee on extension work was started by the American Agricultural Colleges, and two years later the Committee reported that thirty-nine agricultural colleges which had not previously been engaged in extension work were now doing so.[20]

One of the common features of the early extension program was the Farmer's Institute. The institutes ranged from two to five days and were designed for both men and women. For the men there were discussions and demonstrations of farming techniques; for the women, programs were arranged in domestic science.

19. Alfred C. True, *A History of Agricultural Extension Work in the United States, 1785–1923*, p. 49. Washington: Government Printing Office, 1928.

20. Edmund de S. Brunner and E. Hsin Pao Yang, *Rural America and the Extension Service*, p. 7. New York: Teachers College, Columbia University, 1949.

and encouraged people to buy drills for the boring of deep latrines. From the government they received many varieties of fruits and vegetables and showed villagers how they could be introduced in their communities. Ramai rice, the most productive in the world, was introduced by the young men. With the co-operation of officials, better marketing procedures were introduced so that Lanao products could be distributed in distant cities of the Philippines. In commenting on the work at Lanao, Laubach wrote, "With the literacy campaign as an entering wedge, the larger program was natural and almost inevitable."[25] While literacy, of itself, may not have great value to a people, it becomes, as demonstrated by Laubach and by subsequent work in other countries, a necessary prerequisite if people are to move into more advanced stages of cultural change.

FOLK HOUSES AND TECHNIQUES OF AGRICULTURAL
REFORM IN TURKEY

Under the leadership of Mustafa Kemal (1923–38), Turkey made one of the most dramatic cultural transformations in modern times. One of the most effective means of bringing about cultural change was through the use of the halkevis (folk house). The halkevis served as a cultural center for the community. Concerts, lectures, plays, and dances were held, with special rooms providing adult-education classes in cultural and practical subjects. All folk houses had a ninefold program: "(1) language, literature, and history, (2) fine arts, (3) dramatics, (4) sports, (5) social assistance, (6) adult classrooms, (7) library and publications, (8) village welfare, and (9) museums and exhibits."[26] Each program was designed to be a part of the total cultural transformation of the area. The language and history division was used to help gather words, investigate root words, and collect national fables and folklore. Such work was invaluable to the literacy movement. The dramatic division presented plays and pageants designed to foster encouragement and support for the ref-

25. Frank Laubach, *Toward a Literate World*, p. 52. New York: Columbia University Press, 1938. For a description of the extensive work carried on by Dr. Laubach, see the work cited and also Marjorie Medary, *Each One Teach One: Frank Laubach*. New York: Longmans, Green & Co., 1954.

26. Donald B. Webster, *The Turkey of Attaturk*, p. 187. Philadelphia: American Academy of Political and Social Science, 1939.

ormation.[27] The social assistance division was concerned with opening clinics and founding "health museums."[28] The folk schools and courses division offered classes in such areas as sewing, embroidery, health, and farm machinery. Lessons were given for illiterates, and folk reading rooms were maintained for the newly literate. The library and publishing division opened libraries and issued special magazines for the people of their area. Technicians and advanced students from the halkevis held special classes in the rural areas. So-called "peasant evenings," fairs, and holidays were used as a means of propagandizing for the new way of life.

The need for agricultural reform and development was felt to be such a pressing problem that the army was used as a basis for agricultural courses. All young men who came from rural communities were given agricultural instruction. In addition, instruction was given in the responsibilities of farmers under the Village Law (March 18, 1924). This law established a considerable degree of autonomy for local villagers, and part of the educational process was education in democratic techniques of local government.

It was soon found that the agricultural specialists were scattered in too large an area to be able to consult frequently with the farmers and to give the necessary demonstrations. It was also impossible for the six agricultural schools, then in operation, to produce the large numbers of specialists needed immediately. In 1936–37, eighty-four literate former noncommissioned officers who were considered potential rural leaders were gathered together at Eskisehir, where they lived under conditions similar to those prevailing in their rural villages, working the typical day from sun up to sun down. Under the direction of instructors who had been trained in both the normal school and the agricultural college, they were shown scientific agriculture without the prohibitive cost of expensive machinery and tools. Basic techniques in agriculture, animal husbandry, and methods of construction were learned. Model schoolhouses were built to illustrate building techniques and to suggest a needed project that could be built by villagers under supervision. The experiment proved successful and was used extensively to train additional workers for village development.

27. A similar movement may be found in the puppet shows presented by the UNESCO center at Patzcuaro.
28. Webster, *op. cit.,* p. 188.

To illustrate what could be done in agriculture, large experimental farms were established. Irrigation projects were constructed. Kombinats, centers from which agricultural machinery is distributed, were established and training was offered in mechanics for the maintenance of the machinery.

## CULTURAL TRANSFORMATION BY CULTURAL MISSIONS IN MEXICO

The end of the armed revolution in 1920 saw the beginning of Mexico's educational revolution. *"Tierra y Libro*—Land and Books— was a battle cry of the Revolution as deeply felt, as expressive of the needs and aspirations of the masses, as that other and more famous refrain—*Tierra y Libertad."*[29]

Under the leadership of José Vasconselos, a movement was started for the education of the masses and the redemption of the Indians.[30] There was general agreement that the few federal rural schools in operation were poorly equipped and taught by teachers who were not trained to meet the challenge of the rural community. A group of selected supervising teachers was assigned the task of creating what was hoped would be a social revolution in the rural areas. Significantly, the selected teachers were called *missioneros* or missioners. The missioners were to visit rural Indian centers of the Republic, present community studies of the needs of the area, help stimulate interest in literacy, and assign rural teachers to the areas of largest Indian population.[31] In addition, the missioner was expected to encourage and develop local industries, organize a type of industrial fair, assist the representatives of the Secretary of Agriculture in studying local lands, and make recommendations in terms of agricultural development. It was assumed that the missioners would learn the local language and train teachers from among the local Indians.

The missioners had little except the revolutionary spirit to help them. Their main responsibility was to encourage the people and show them how to improve their economic position and conditions of health. There were no funds for anything except the salaries of

29. Eyler N. Simpson, *The Ejido: Mexico's Way Out,* p. 230. Chapel Hill, North Carolina: University of North Carolina Press, 1937.

30. For an excellent analysis of this outstanding leader, see Patrick Romanell's *Making of the Mexican Mind.* Lincoln, Nebraska: University of Nebraska, 1952.

31. George I. Sanchez, *Mexico: A Revolution by Education,* p. 66. New York: Viking Press, 1936.

the teachers. The people were expected to construct the building and furnish the basic materials. The community donated the land for the school. Known as "The House of the People," the school had classes for children in the morning and classes for adults in the late afternoon and evening.

Unfortunately the missioners were few in number. They were not properly organized and were scattered over great distances. To remedy this situation, the Secretariat of Education adopted a program that developed into the Cultural Mission, one of the most effective means of solving the problems of rural Mexico. Each Cultural Mission was a "normal ambulante," or traveling normal school, and each consisted of specialists in the fields of rural education, soap-making, tanning, music, physical education, and nursing. The functions and methods of the Cultural Mission varied from area to area and have changed in various periods of Mexican history.[32] However, it was during this early period of the 1920's that the basic experimental work was conducted and upon which later programs were built.

The Cultural Missions were given the responsibility of the cultural and professional betterment of the teachers in service and the "development of popular enthusiasm leading to the cultural, economic, and social improvement of the communities in which the missions operate."[33] In addition, the mission was expected to serve as: (a) a community center and clearing house for educative materials on areas related to the economic and cultural needs of the people, (b) a social welfare agency designed to bring about an improvement in the social and economic practices of the people, and (c) a center to supplement the work of the normal schools by offering normal school courses.

When a mission was sent to an area, it usually selected a rural school which would serve as its headquarters during the eight weeks the mission would remain in the area. The school served for demonstration purposes while the mission remained in the area. The members of the mission devoted the first ten or fifteen days to studying the community in terms of its social and economic problems. This

32. See Lloyd H. Hughes, *The Mexican Cultural Mission Programme*. Paris: UNESCO, 1950.

33. Sanchez, *op. cit.*, p. 73.

tatorship every medium was and is being used for cultural transformation.[40] Illiteracy has been reduced from approximately 60 per cent to between 5 and 10 per cent. From a primarily rural agricultural society, the Soviet Union has developed to a stage where the number of its graduates in engineering are causing serious concern in the United States.[41]

If the Soviet Union were to be transformed to an industrial society, one of the major problems to be overcome was that of illiteracy. Literacy was important to develop the huge number of specialists needed for industrialization. Of equal importance to the Communist leaders was the political education of the population. By control of the means of communication, the literate individual could be more easily indoctrinated with the new political philosophy. In 1919 Lenin issued a decree "On the Liquidation of Illiteracy among the Population of the RSFSR," and three years later there was organized the First All-Russian Congress for Liquidation of Illiteracy. From this Congress and a subsequent meeting held in 1923, there was formed the Down-with-Illiteracy Society. School children helped with the literacy movement by (a) taking polls of the adults in their community who were illiterate, and (b) sometimes teaching adult classes. Nurseries were organized so that illiterate mothers could attend classes.

In factories a "Red Corner" was established and became the center of educational and political orientation. Most of the shops had an organizer for literacy who was responsible for carrying on the literacy drive in his particular area. Once the worker was literate, he joined an evening institute where he learned additional skills that would help him improve his trade. In smaller villages educational work was carried on in cottage reading rooms. In larger villages the "people's houses" served as a center not only for literacy but also for classes taught by local teachers, doctors, and agriculturists.

Wall-newspapers were used in schools, factories, collective farms, and offices. New literates were encouraged to write articles for the wall-newspapers and for local newspapers.

40. See George S. Counts, *The Challenge of Soviet Education.* New York: McGraw-Hill Book Co., 1957.

41. *New York World Telegram and Sun,* October 31, 1955.

In the agricultural communities mutual-aid societies and co-operatives were organized. General agricultural, wood-working, and hand industry were the typical type of co-operatives found in many areas. As the collectives were formed, experts in agriculture were sent as instructors for those working on state farms.

The basis for change in the early period of the Soviet Union was campaign and slogans. Once a campaign such as the "Down with Illiteracy" campaign was started, it was carried on zealously by party members and supporters throughout the entire country. Failure to participate in the campaign placed the individual in apparent opposition to the party and the state.

Villages were collectivized by the state power. To build the mills, canals, and hydroelectric stations, and to expand population centers in the east, labor was mobilized and distributed to those projects and areas under development.

While development was taking place on the farms and in industry, there was carried on an extensive campaign of political orientation to the new state. Every facet of education from the lowest literacy school to the university held compulsory classes in Marxism-Leninism. The degree and difficulty of the philosophy presented were carefully prepared to fit the background of the students. In addition to the formal classes every medium from the calendar to the theater was used to build loyalty to the concepts of the new state.

### MOTIVATIONAL BASIS FOR COMMUNITY EDUCATION

It is difficult to assign specific motives for many community-education programs. The technical-assistance program of the United States illustrates the variety of bases for community education. To some Americans, community education as carried on by the government in less-developed countries is desirable as a humanitarian movement to help those people with problems of health, literacy, and economic development. To other Americans, community education is a political weapon in the "cold war"—a means of building allies. To still others, community education is a technique of building future markets for business investments and future trade. The variety of reasons offered for American technical assistance can be found in many other examples of community education.

From the Buddhist missionary in Asia to activities carried on in nineteenth-century America, representatives of various religious societies have introduced elements of community education. The establishment of Hampton Institute and the Penn School were typical of the missionary effort for the rural American Negro in nineteenth-century America, while in England Toynbee Hall and the settlement-house movement represented a concern for the people in the slums of cities. The eighteenth-century missionary work in Mexico and California represented a dual motive. On the one hand, the work of the missionaries was basically concerned with religion, but at the same time the Spanish government was interested in the expansion of the missions as a means of political control of new territory. In more recent times, the work of Frank Laubach is indicative of the vast effort being made by missionary programs.

Undoubtedly the humanitarian and philanthropic motives have been found in many programs. The work of James Yen in China and the activities of the Peabody and Slater Funds in the United States were typical of the humanitarian and philanthropic motives.

Cultural transformation has been the goal of many political leaders and parties for centuries. Political leaders in Mexico, Turkey, India, China, and the Soviet Union have used community education in an effort to change the basic cultural pattern of the people in their areas. The extent to which it has been organized and the method of organization have depended upon the political philosophy of the country. In the Soviet Union and contemporary China, cultural transformation has been an integral part of the political doctrine and, as a result, has received the full attention of every apparatus of the state. Improvement is not the concern of the individual for himself alone but rather his responsibility as a contributing citizen of the country. India is also concerned with cultural transformation but is following the basic principles established by Gandhi. Basic and social education in India has become an important part of the economic development of the country. A secondary and yet important function of social education in India is to inculcate a sense of citizenship for the country on the part of the many groups living in the state. This function, that of building citizenship, was also used in Turkey and Mexico and has been developed to a high degree in Communist China and the Soviet Union.

REALIZATION BY INTERNATIONAL AGENCIES AND WORLD POWERS
OF THE ROLE OF COMMUNITY EDUCATION IN
UNDERDEVELOPED SOCIETIES

Since the close of World War II there has been great concern
on the part of Western nations for the less-developed societies.
UNESCO and the other United Nations agencies such as the World
Health Organization, the Food and Agriculture Organization, and
the International Labor Organization have developed programs and
projects designed to help the people in less-developed societies find
solutions to problems of health, agriculture, and economic development. United Nations technicians can be found from North Africa
to the Philippines.

In 1949 President Truman in his Inaugural Address called for a
new program that would make available to the less-developed societies the "benefits of our scientific advances and industrial progress."
In addition to the humanitarian motives of the United States technical-assistance program, there has been the belief that in the present
ideological struggle people who live on the edge of starvation are
more susceptible to international communism than a prosperous nation. In this sense, by helping people find a way to a more healthful
and economically productive life, the breeding grounds for potential
communism would be eliminated. In the wave of nationalism following World War II which has led to the emergence of many newly
independent nations, it was believed that technical assistance could
help strengthen governments which were friendly to the West and
yet were faced with serious economic and health problems.

In recent years the Soviet Union has sent technicians to countries
that had been oriented to the West. In addition to Russian technicians
in China, Richard Hughes of the *Sunday Times* of London reports
that there were technicians from East Germany, Poland, and Czecho-
slovakia.[42] While technical assistance within those countries closely
allied to the Soviet Union has been going on since World War II,
the offer of aid to Asian countries such as India and Burma suggests
that the Soviet Union now realizes the potential of technical assistance in less-developed societies. The Soviet Ambassador to Cairo is
reported as stating that his government will offer industrial and agri-

42. *New York Times*, March 31, 1957.

cultural equipment to all Arab and Asian countries that request it.[43] In addition, the Ambassador states that his country would send "economic missions, scientific missions, agricultural missions, and any other kind of mission you can imagine that will help these countries."[44] This offer was repeated at the Asian-African Solidarity Conference in Cairo.[45]

Thus while the specific terms used to describe "community education" may be of recent coinage, the process, cultural transformation, has been used for centuries. While there is a wide variation in the methods and the auspices under which it has been functioning, the purposes have, for the most part, remained constant.

Community education has been mainly concerned with rural areas. Unfortunately, little has been done in the urban centers. The improvement of agricultural techniques, road-building, literacy, health, and the opening of the less-developed societies are the major interest of community education today, as they were in the days of the Romans.

Fortunately, there is a great body of knowledge in the behavioral sciences today that can be of assistance to those who are engaged in community education. In the fields of social psychology and anthropology there is ample evidence to suggest that the failure or success of a community-education project may well depend to a large degree on the attitude of the community-education worker and his knowledge of the culture of the people.

43. *New York Times,* June 3, 1956.
44. *Ibid.*                                        45. *Ibid.,* January 5, 1958.

# CHAPTER III

# Cultural Factors in Community-Education Programs

MARGARET MEAD

## The Changing Climate of Opinion

The sciences which deal with human behavior are peculiarly interwoven with the political and moral climate of opinion within which they develop and are peculiarly sensitive to changes in that opinion. To understand the extent to which cultural anthropology can attest to a scientific background for the practice of community education, it is necessary to visualize the changing world situation which has obtained since the latter part of the nineteenth century, particularly the decisive changes introduced by World War II. The behavioral sciences have been developing rapidly owing to the introduction of new models and new methods, and the questions which they have been asked to answer have altered drastically. Moreover, the living materials available to these sciences have assumed new forms, such as societies in the process of rapid transformation, studies of brain-washing, a proliferation of cults, or factories completely converted to automation. Also, these studies of new situations of change have made it possible to reinterpret some of the less-satisfactory cultural records and psychological experiments of the pre-World War period.

Up to World War II, community education, whether it was imposed by military force, transplantation of populations, monastic orders, or gentle doctrines of local participation, was primarily something that was done *to* or *for* some people *by* some other more advanced people desirous of raising the cultural level of the less advanced. Implicit in these various endeavors was the idea of raising the cultural level of a local population within limitations but not raising it as high as that of their mentors. The assumption was made that, along with backwardness, illiteracy, low agricultural skill, superstitious and magical practices about health, and inferior forms of

66

social organization, there went various other forms of inferiority which could be remedied. Depending upon the nature of the assumptions about the people to be benefited and the people who did the benefiting, the level to which the recipient population was to be raised would be differently conceived. So, slavery might be seen as a temporary and appropriate state for a recently Christianized savage, whereas manumission would become the correct procedure, once the slave, or his children, had received a "Christian" education. Contradictions between regulations which rigorously segregated natives and Europeans might be justified by the general state of hygiene, skin infections, and living habits of the bulk of the population; and yet members of this same group, wearing clothes and carrying pocket handkerchiefs, might be admitted to university or court circles in Europe. The prevalence of racial theories of inferiority could be invoked in order to give more opportunities to the hybrid members of a population, to limit the opportunities offered to their full-blood relatives, or to ban whole populations from opportunity.

Throughout these varying devices, by which people temporarily occupying positions of superiority explained their positions, there ran corresponding variations in the remedies proposed and the rate of change believed to be possible. When the emphasis was on the soul, a few years or even a moment of conversion might entitle the simplest savage to a place in heaven. If the emphasis was historical, then possibly many generations of "experience with free institutions," for example, would be demanded before any sort of equality with the present advanced state of the donors could be expected. If nutrition and health were heavily invoked, then often it would be regarded as hopeless to do very much with adults, undernourished and diseased from childhood, but great hopes could be held out for a change in one generation. But, however conceived, there was a consistent degree of patronage from those who tried to educate toward those whom they educated and whom they conceived of as *in need* of education, for the sake of church, or state, or for their own welfare. These needs were usually seen as unrecognized by the recipients, who therefore had to be induced to admit them by a great variety of methods, preaching and proselytizing, demonstrations, "finding local leaders," permitting converts to buy little pigs cheaper, or near-coercion in sending the younger generation away to school. Even those efforts which relied on community co-operation were instigated from outside or above, and the local community had to be "stimulated to want" change.

In a historical context, it is not surprising that the older literature concentrated on negative elements, such as how to overcome resistance to changes in living habits, and how to combat the dangerous effects of social disorganization and individual breakdown. In explanation of these unfavorable results of induced change, several theoretical positions have been used, such as the intractability of habit, the painfulness of new learning, and the primacy of early childhood learning, on the psychological side, and the importance of the whole pattern of culture, on the anthropological side.

The effects of the type of psychological thinking characteristic of the first half of the century, with the enormous new knowledge about childhood and with the growth of animal experiments on learning, inevitably weighted the scales in favor of early experience, endangered by later disruption. And without taking the extreme position taken by Laura Thompson in the 1940's at the close of her study of American Indian acculturation, namely, that the American Indian still lives in a primordial pattern of relationship to nature and his fellow men, most anthropologists still emphasized the contrasts between older patterns of culture, whether they were considering the peasant peoples of Asia and northern Africa, the dwellers in small European enclaves in the Balkans, the Hebrides, the aboriginal primitive—that is preliterate—peoples of North and South America, Africa south of the Sudan, Oceania and the Arctic, or the immigrant groups—Poles, Algerians, South Italians, Slavs, Japanese, Tamils—who moved in large numbers from one country to another and resisted, at least in the migrating generation, the culture of the country to which they moved. In both these theoretical assumptions—the potency of earlier over later learning, and the potency of an achieved cultural whole over new patterns—there was the assumption that adults not only learned differently from children but also could not be expected to learn as much, or as completely, something that was new.

Community education is primarily concerned with teaching adults. Thus, nonliterates are taught to read; poor farmers to farm better;

mothers who let flies cluster on their babies eyes to put their babies under netting; peasants who keep their money under the mattress to use banks; people who had no form of co-operative corporate action to work on committees, organize boards of directors, take and delegate responsibility. When the emphasis is upon changing the immediate physical circumstances, there is usually less attention given to the children in the scheme than where community education and community development are seen as laying the groundwork within which the next generation can be brought up differently, fed, clothed, disciplined, and taught in a way which their parents have not been. But whether the goal is to change poor farmers into good farmers, to teach adults to read the 1,300 commonest Chinese characters, or simply to introduce the adults to the idea that their children should be allowed to go to school instead of tending sheep, pigs, or younger children, it is today still a form of education directed toward adults. A few experiments, based on a recognition of the role children in the United States have had in changing the attitudes of their foreign-born parents, have been tried where the school was the focus of change, but this was primarily just another way of pressuring adults into doing something good for them. From the New Deal experiments and the related experiments in India, Mexico, the Middle East, and Greece, in which fully formulated democratic participation patterns were artificially, although devotedly, stimulated, to the lack of faith of the Soviet leaders in the re-educability of adults of the wrong mentality and the resulting penalization and liquidation of millions, to the more recent Chinese Communist attempt at an intensive reformation of adults, the mid-twentieth-century community-education movements have worked with a concept of an adult, preformed in conservative ways, unanxious to change, who formed an obstacle to social advancement.

It is important to note that there were also groups of those interested in the welfare of the peoples being subjected to this process who formed a countermovement, stressing a people's right to maintain their historical culture, no matter how backward; the superiority of a whole, traditionally patterned way of life, however simple, over the fragmentation of "modern mass society"; the beauty of handicrafts as compared with machine manufactures, or natural

dyes over chemical dyes; and the security given to the individual
by the rituals of kin and clan, planting and harvest, which he lost
when he became a resident in a Westernized city. Under this heading
fall attempts to provide scripts for small indigenous languages, to
revive ancient languages, to revive or nourish languishing handicrafts, to encourage the simple life of the village as leading to
greater faith in God, to maintain native costumes and folk dances—
activities which have been instigated from the point of view of
religion, art, and the humanities, as opposed to the technological
emphases of the agricultural expert, the sanitary engineer, and the
economic planner. The contrast between these points of view comes
out sharply in the discussions about alteration of ancient scripts,
like Chinese, Japanese, and Arabic. The advocates of change and
improvement point to the need for simplified orthographies which
do not implicate an immense system of reference to a historical
literature available only to scholars. The opponents of change point
to what has happened in Turkey, for example, where, with the
changes in the written language, the young Turk gained access to
the science of the West but lost his connection with his old tradition.

So the advocacy of any set of principles "basic to community
education," which must also be referred to the behavioral sciences,
must be put in this setting of the moral and political attitudes toward
change, the experiences of one-sided change on which our theories
were built and the particular state of the sciences of psychology
and anthropology.

World War II created a new over-all political position as people
in every part of the world began to realize the advantages and the
accessibility of those "goods," material and immaterial, toward the
desire for which so many different agencies had attempted to direct
them in the past. Whether it was powdered milk on the shelf of a
remote country store in the southeast of the United States or the
availability of atabrine in New Guinea, where only quinine had
been available before, or the presence of planes, field hospitals,
outdoor film showings, in a thousand ways, through the behavior
of individuals, the experience of organization, and the presence of
machines and other goods, the peoples of the world learned to aspire
to the products of Western science. Literacy centers turned from
attempting to bribe or seduce a few "leaders" to turning away

the queues that formed at their doors. Naked savages, the pig fat washed off, and speaking through two interpreters, marched into government centers in the highlands of New Guinea, saying they had built a hospital and a school and would like to have a doctor and a teacher tomorrow morning. Villagers in remote islands of Indonesia set to work to build roads and bridges, in intended imitation of modern techniques but without the necessary technical knowledge for such work. In mountain and jungle the people who would formerly have been the resisting, conservative objects of community education became its initiators.

There has also been a shift in the availability of energy to instigate and carry through the changes involved in introducing literacy in a population of which 50 or 90 per cent are illiterate. In the past, the exigencies of church, or state, or party, and, individually, the moral commitment of monk, missionary, official, extension agent, or party organizer were the channels through which energy was mobilized. When the efforts were unsuccessful and conservatism and "resistance" defeated these aims, the situation in which "long contact with the oppressed whose lot one is powerless to ameliorate breeds a subtle contempt" became one more reinforcing factor in separating the improved from the improvers. Today, the energy is provided by those who in the name of their village or tribe, their class, their sex, or their nation are demanding literacy, medicine, technical skill, and new social institutions. The resistance which they meet to their demands, in turn, tends to invest those who they think should help them with an aura of resentment, which is also potentially divisive.

It is possible to trace the history of education from an emphasis on learning, in which the student sought out the teacher, to the emphasis on teaching which came with a greater complexity of skills than parents and apprenticeship could handle. From the primitive pattern of taking a present to the man one hoped would teach one or one's children, we have shifted to forcing children and adults to learn and attempting to equip the schools with techniques and sanctions to make them do so. Community education developed as one facet of this second pattern. Just as universal childhood education has been directed toward making other peoples' children acquire some, but not all, of the skills available to the children of the privileged and powerful within a society, so community education has been devoted to making the adults of other countries, other regions, or other classes learn part, but not all, of the skills available to the donor nation, region, or class. As the shift has come between the desire of the donor group to educate, to the desire of the other groups to catch up, a new inequality between the two groups has been introduced. But this time it is not an underestimation of the recipients, as too inferior to be able to learn all that the more advanced group has to teach. The new interpretation of the relative positions of donor and recipient has come from phrasing the state of the donor culture as static, and that of the recipient group as dynamic. The people of underdeveloped countries are to work very hard to catch up, and no allowance is made for the fact that the donor cultures, whether they may be those of the Western world or the entrepreneurial core of business and governmental leadership in India, for example, are also changing very rapidly so that most of the adults in the advanced groups hold beliefs as hampering to their functioning in regional or national planning as is a belief that painting blood and feathers on a carved wooden image will improve the crops in local community development.

So, instead of equipping the personnel of community-education efforts with the most advanced projections of what medicine or communication is likely to become in the next half-century, too often they are given sixteenth-century phrasings of religion and nineteenth-century schoolbook models. This, of course, has not been universally so; many programs have drawn on the most advanced *techniques* of education, use of film strips, films, radio, giant projection screens, and teacher-selection devices. But too often this tapping of the rapidly moving sections of our own culture has been limited to techniques—twentieth-century electronics devices to teach nineteenth-century methods of child care, anthropomorphic representations of germ theory to teach people who are fully ready to grasp the implications of the most modern psychosomatic medicine, medieval pre-Columbian religious geography to people who then have to reconcile the medieval concreteness about heaven and hell with their experience of modern submarines and airplanes.

It is within this climate of opinion and of historical and contemporary practice that the behavioral sciences began to make contributions to the theory and practice of social change. Just as World War II marked the shift from people who had to be thought of as resisting change to people who were expecting and demanding too much change, so World War II also provides a convenient boundary line in the development of scientific theories of change.

### Pre-World War II Anthropological Approaches

The cultural anthropologist, working with the peoples who were having various types of experience with the attempts of outsiders or factional leaders to change their traditional cultures in the directions which government, missionaries, and modernizers wished to go, was specially sensitive to the disruption produced by such changes. It was his scientific task to try to record, and reconstruct when possible, the untouched pattern of the life of an American Indian, or African, or South Sea tribe before "contact." Contact was the word for the dramatic meeting of peoples with highly developed cultures and peoples who, because of the accidents of history, had preserved ways of life which were primitive and lacked a written language of any sort. Every change—the introduction of a mission or a school, indentured labor which took the men away . to work—further complicated the anthropologist's task and "spoiled" his material. Furthermore, he saw the effects of induced change and so was particularly ready to identify the incongruences and destructiveness of this external grafting of new upon old.

During this period the use of the science of cultural anthropology made two contributions to community-education programs: (a) It helped break down the image of a great mass of savage, illiterate, superstitious peoples clustered in jungle, mountain, and desert, whose major characteristic was their ignorance of our culture, and establish the fact that each of these peoples of the world had a historical tradition of its own, a cherished way of life, a "cup from which they drank their life," as old as our own. (b) It helped establish the importance of differences among peoples and a recognition that methods of education for change must be developed in connection with the special attitudes of the different groups. It was concerned about whether a group preferred to follow conspicuous leaders or men behind the scenes, what would trigger wider change, which deeply rooted religious beliefs were significant for some particular change, where appeals to pride or fear of the death of children or the destruction of fertility of the land were appeals to values of central importance in a given culture. It served to focus attention on the need to study not only the situation and needs of the community, such as a rift between returning soldiers and a village population or which diseases were endemic and which sanitary practices would have to be changed, but also the need to study the culture of the group, whether they were Navajo or Burmese, Mexican Indians or village Greeks. Emphasis was placed upon the wholeness of the cultural pattern and the disruptive effects of a change which threw one part of the pattern out, as when firearms led to the disappearance of the buffalo, or the introduction of factory-made cloth destroyed the weaver's handicraft and status, or mission teaching upset the authority of the garden magician, or the acceptance of a new religion led to a lopsided development of black magic, or the introduction of sheep as men's property upset the previous balanced matrilineal ownership of land and agricultural products, or the mission teaching about forbidden degrees of marriage wrecked a social system based on cousin marriage, or the elimination of pagan holidays led to a change in food consumption and so to undernourishment, or the introduction of a head tax necessitated all the young men going away to work. Anthropologists pointed out that each of these changes was related in a special way to a particular culture and that if an agency wished to introduce a change, start a school, or build a hospital, a knowledge of the whole cultural pattern of the particular tribe or area was necessary.

From the pre-World War II anthropological work came, then, the following principles:

1. Each human culture is unique and, although cultures in the same area of contact will show important similarities, each must be respected as embodying the whole way of life of a people within which they were able to perpetuate their society. Although cultures may be arranged on a scale in regard to any single feature or clusters of features, no scale has been found which would make it possible to arrange them in rank order when the whole pattern is considered. The recognition of each culture as comparable, in this way, with every other culture provides a basis on which cultural change, community education, or community development must proceed with

mutual respect for the cultures of each group involved in the process of change. As a later insight, it was recognized that the culture of the donor group, involving as it does a complete pattern, must also be taken into account just as much as the culture of the recipients, and in the culture of the donor or teaching group there will be found traditional and irrational elements comparable to those found among the people of the less-developed area. So we have the very different history of the relationship of Catholic Spaniards or Portuguese and Protestant Northern Europeans to both African slaves and indigenous American Indians; frontier Czarist Russians lived on quite different terms with Lapps than did the Danes; the colonial attempts of British, Dutch, and Americans established very different forms.

2. There is no evidence that there is any difference in the capacity to learn, to innovate, and to transmit culture among any of the existing human stocks, all of whom are members of one species, capable of fertile matings, and possessed of the same general range of capabilities. Thus, differences in race should not be regarded as having any significance unless they have been given social significance. If an Australian aboriginal child has accepted an estimate, held by whites and aborigines, that all aboriginal children are inferior, this will influence his achievement in school; or if Negro American boys have given up hope of competing successfully in the labor market, this may show itself as an apparent loss of capacity for intellectual maturity. Comparably, if a people living in a tropical climate have defined their rate of possible activity as low because of the climate, this may keep their activity low; and moving them to a cooler climate may step it up. Again, there is no evidence that the culture of ancestors with whose culture one has had no contact will have any influence on a child reared in another society. "Gallic" wit, "Negro" rhythm, "Anglo-Saxon" stolidity, "Oriental" mysticism are examples of the kinds of cultural characteristics which have been mistakenly attributed to race and expected to survive several generations after cultural transmission is interrupted.

The recognition of these principles meant, in practice, that when anthropologists were asked to advise on programs of change, they insisted on a complete cultural study being made of the people selected for study. In the course of such studies the anthropologists were reimpressed with the disruptive effects of the change which had already occurred, the loss in tribal unity, in a sense of dignity, in motivation, in a sense of security in the individuals, as well as the economic and social confusion which accompanied the fragmentation of the old culture. The advice with which they came up was: *know each culture in detail, make changes as slowly and carefully as possible, and work on equivalences between old and new cultural forms.* For example, study the shaman before you introduce a physician, the local midwife before you introduce a public health nurse, and provide a pig as a substitute victim before forbidding headhunting. These findings based on a quarter of a century of active interest, research, and applied anthropology still permeate the thinking of many anthropologists and are responsible for other members of community-development teams, especially the economists, seeing the anthropologist as the defender of the old, the one whose task it is to put a carefully calibrated brake on change by providing details of probable resistance on the part of any given people. The other part of the anthropological role, as specialist in the full content of the local culture, has been given a great deal of lip service but less recognition.

The anthropologist's emphasis upon the disastrous effects upon individuals of cultural disorganization and rapid change permeated the mental health field and has become part of the background thinking of psychiatric and educational work with individuals who are seen as needing to be judged in the light of the cultural contact situation within which they have been reared and are trying to function.

## The Situation during World War II

World War II presented anthropologists with a whole series of challenges in which speed was an important consideration. The older recommendation that an intensive and complete study be made of the whole culture of any group before any advice could be given was impractical. During this period there was a demand for answers to questions about the organization of partisan units behind enemy lines, the selection of personnel from little-known Asiatic groups, the provision of food for evacuated or just-liberated peoples, the design of programs of block organization in large cities, guides for GI's in Moslem countries, instructions for pilots downed in the New Guinea bush, orientation courses in how to establish liaison between

American and English staff officers, strategy for getting bills for re-inforced flour through a U.S. state legislature, methods of persuading American-trained doctors to use local substitutes for absorbent cotton—a hundred and one diverse requests, all of which demanded a knowledge of the culture of some particular group. This stimulated the development of new methods for generalizing anthropological theory to meet such situations.

For the demand that a complete study of the local culture pattern be made, new principles were advanced:

1. In preparing to transmit to members of another culture, or to individuals within one's own culture who embody another version of that culture (members of another region, class, sex, generation, or occupational group), it is first important to recognize that there will be a cultural difference, grossly perceptible when one group is European and the other Eskimo or Indian. It is also important to note that this is much harder to perceive between groups with the same physical appearance within the same national unit. This cultural difference, furthermore, will be systematic and will be found to run through many different aspects of life: the way parents treat their children, employer-employee relations, and how audiences deal with actors, or how teachers manage their pupils. For the need to know a large number of small details which seem unrelated, it is now possible to substitute higher-level generalizations which subsume the details from which they were abstracted.

2. In preparing to transmit any practice or theory from a donor cultural group to a recipient cultural group, one useful device is to strip the new practice or idea down to universals, attempting to provide only the core, which is free from particular emphasis. For example, in teaching nutrition, kinds of food, number of meals, and ways of preparing foods carry a great deal of cultural baggage from the particular historically developed habits of the donor group who have developed the science of nutrition. Instead of insisting on particular culturally limited style of food use, students can acquire knowledge of the nutritional content of food, ways of assaying it, and ways of assaying the biological status of those who subsist on it. It is possible to teach principles of the conservation of vitamins during preparation or principles of combinations of different nutrients within given periods of time, as a day or a week, so that they can be

reconstituted within the pattern of the recipient group. These have been called "stripped universals"; they are sometimes called "culture-free," but this is misleading, for they bear the imprint of a high development in Western culture, and they are simply stripped down to the point where they are cross-culturally viable, applicable to a diet of dates, fish, or legumes, to cooking in earth ovens, clay pots, or pressure cookers, to three meals a day or five. Although the emphasis to date has been on members of teams who go out to teach how to strip techniques down in this way, we may expect that the sophisticated spokesmen of the recipient groups will also demand that those who come to teach them consider what and when to strip. For example, the vice-chairman of a Council of Navajo Indians, making plans for enlisting in their attack on tuberculosis the help of a school of public health, said, in his sanctioning speech: "Medicine covers a wide range, at one end the white man has more knowledge about drugs, while at the other end, the Navajo has more knowledge about treating special types of mental illness; in the middle group we must work together!" The request that the campaign against tuberculosis should be free of local American preoccupations, such as the perils of "kissing babies," would be a logical corollary of such an attitude.

3. In the reclothing of such a stripped universal in forms appropriate to the receiving culture, it is not necessary, nor even desirable, to place this responsibility on a foreign specialist in that culture. A more reliable method is to provide for ways in which the recipient group, themselves, work with the bare principles, the new materials, the new techniques and, acting as members of their own culture, incorporate the new ideas within the traditional patterns. These principles accord, of course, with the more widely recognized desirability, which has been stressed by the social psychologists and community organizers, of a people always participating from the start in any program which involves their own lives.

4. After the world-wide repercussions of World War II, it is necessary to contemplate a kind of culture change which will make some members of every culture world-mobile in one generation, speaking some of the world languages—English, Chinese, or Russian—in which the principal scientific and humanistic achievements of mankind are available, and for which translation is available at inter-

national conferences. (Although this was stated as a principle in the handbook which we prepared for UNESCO in 1950, it was still at this time regarded as unfortunate that this would mean such very rapid change, as rapid change was still regarded as much more disruptive than slow change.)

## Three Case Studies

Today we have, for the first time, comparable and careful studies of peoples who have been changing, both through practices initiated from within and programs of change induced and directed from outside and above. This makes it possible to evaluate different kinds of effort. I can draw on my own years of anthropological work to give time depth and, at the same time, illustrate several kinds of total situations. All of these are examples of drastic contact between very primitive groups and modern Western society. Contact with traditional high but unindustrialized societies, such as Indonesia, or contact between the urban educated and the peasant and the proletarian in both Western and traditional societies present less drastic but comparable problems, such as the consequences of induced change and of spontaneous change, what kind of learning can be expected of adults, what kind of models are needed, what are the conditions for transformations rather than piecemeal change.

### THE SAMOANS OF AMERICAN SAMOA, 1925–

In 1925 the Samoans of Eastern (American) Samoa were a politically sophisticated people, with a culture in which religion was subordinated to social organization, with a simple technology, an adequate food supply, and few indigenous diseases. They were organized into autonomous local groups, who combined in purely ceremonial ways into larger units, and they had the good fortune to be missionized by the formally congenial London Missionary Society, Congregationalists who were not given either to extremely complex ritual practices or to evangelistic types of religious intensity. After a century of contact, during which they were Christianized and became literate in Samoan, they had for a quarter of a century been governed by the U.S. Navy as a part of a Naval Station, where the emphasis had been placed on good medical care, formal good relationships, and keeping the islands free of civilians whose activities might have disrupted the even order of events. Within this regime, the felicities of which were largely a matter of historical accident, the Samoans had developed a stable new level of culture. They grew copra which the government marketed for them, and the funds were available for village projects such as a whale boat, piped water, a roof for the church. They had preserved their own house forms, open pavilions with thatched roofs and coral rubble floors; but for the traditional bark cloth they now had cotton sheets, mosquito netting, and European-type pillows; the new bedding was still wrapped in a pandanus mat and stored in the rafters. Kerosene lanterns had replaced strung candle nuts as a source of light; they had charcoal irons; matches, soap, starch, kerosene, sugar, tea, ink, pens, pencils, paper, cloth; hand sewing machines had been added to the usual consumption goods. The guest house of the chief of each village boasted enough European furniture, cutlery, and crockery to serve a correct European meal to a visiting missionary or government officer. They were 98 per cent literate in Samoan, and a few individuals in the local police, the local pastorate, and nursing and medical corp knew English. There was no pidgin; people who knew only a few English phrases spoke them correctly. They were completely Christian, and practices abhorrent to missionaries and government, such as the power of life and death which a head of a household had had over members of his household or the public defloration of a bride, had been discontinued. The space into which promising young men could move had been widened by the jobs provided by the mission, the educational system, police and medical care, clerical jobs in the port, the foreign mission field among the peoples of New Guinea. Occasional trips away from the islands as entertainers or stewards on yachts provided a little overseas adventure. Very occasionally a member of the American Navy took a bride from the islands or married and attempted to stay there.

Their Christianity was an effective compromise between their aboriginal ideas of human relationships and those of the missionaries. Premarital chastity was expected of the groups of school girls who lived in the pastors' houses or in boarding school; otherwise one did not become a church member until after marriage. Combined with the high level of literacy was the Samoan disapproval of precocity; each class waited for advancement until its slowest member had completed the work, and this effectively blocked roads to higher education. The training of the nursing, medical, pastoral, and teaching groups had been adjusted to a simple level of literacy and a simple clear pattern of practice well integrated within the economy of each village, which provided for their daily subsistence.

Analysis of this system showed that from many points of view it was ideal; older, more burdensome technologies—like making bark cloth—had lapsed; where the older technology was adequate and simple, like the use of the earth oven, banana leaves as dishes, and the older forms of house and furniture, it had been kept. Their literacy was fully adequate to the new social and technical skills which they were using. Ability to read the Bible and to read government orders, combined with a knowledge of the necessary social etiquette of entertaining European visitors and wearing European dress while at the same time preserving their own basically democratic and formally hierarchichal system, gave them a sense of dignity vis-á-vis the Western world.

But the weaknesses in the system are also warning signs in any technical-assistance program which relies on this type of local and protected cultural syncretism. The introduction of medical care has greatly increased the survival rate, and the birth rate did not suffer the decline which sometimes comes when a primitive people lose their zest for living, so the population increased beyond the economic capacity of the fishing, agriculture, and copra-growing potentialities of these tiny islands. During World War II, some five thousand U. S. troops were stationed in Samoa, wage labor on a large scale superseded the former type of co-operative household and community activity; after World War II, the departure of the big Navy installation and the installation of a very modest civil administration in keeping with the climate of opinion of the modern world, left the islanders with a feeling of impoverishment and isolation. Whereas the few individuals who had gone abroad before World War II had made very good adjustment, the group of young Samoans who followed the Navy to Hawaii found adjustment as wage laborers in a modern city much more difficult; the pride which had sustained them in their contacts at home became a source of touchiness and liability to insult in the more complex environment. In 1956, the Navy, in a recruitment program, found 84 young men who were able to meet their tests—including English, which had been a school subject for many years—among the 150 who were anxious to leave the islands.

The compromise adjustment between aboriginal Samoan life and the core of Western religious and medical ideas, combined with literacy, was not adequate to deal with disaster—where the Red Cross had to step in—with the inroads of a large group of servicemen and a money economy, with an increase in population, and with immigration as workers into a more complex society. One element had been missing, the expectation that Samoans would become mobile members of a world community, with all adults able to meet the requirements of life in a modern urban industrialized society—if necessary—and some members prepared for a university education and participation in the world intellectual and political scene.

### A PLAINS INDIAN TRIBE IN 1930: THE "ANTLERS"

The Samoan situation represents a high point of historical good fortune, a bountiful food supply, a healthy people, and a fortunate congruence between the style of the mission and governing group and the local culture. Most culture contacts between very primitive peoples and modern cultures have not been so felicitous but have produced compromise cultures, much less stable than the Samoans' and more vulnerable to outside pressures. Such a culture was that of the group of buffalo-hunting North American Indians, whom I have called the "Antlers" because when I studied them in 1930 there was so much that was painful and damaging to report.[1] These Indians had led a seasonally divided life, hunting in small groups in the winter, planting and harvesting in villages in spring and fall, and engaging in a large buffalo hunt in the summer. The scale of the buffalo hunt was itself a result of the post-Columbian importation of the horse, so that a very recent flamboyant cultural development was ushered in by the introduction of firearms, the coming of the fur trader, and the extinction of the buffalo. As American settlement pushed westward, a part of the Antlers' original territory was assigned to them as a reservation, thus permitting them to remain in a

---

1. Whereas in writing about the Samoans I had only to change the names of individuals to protect their privacy when I reported intimate details of their personal or political lives.

familiar environment. Under government administration and financing and mission pressure, they gave up their old way of life as a hunting, raiding, and only partly horticultural people and became nominally Christian, adopting the square frame house which the government provided, a slender standard of furniture and modern dress, and began farming. The earlier forms of political organization in which the position of chiefs had been validated by distributions of property, including horses taken in raids, buffalo robes, and meat obtained by hunting, was gone. The dress which became standardized, although based on factory-made materials, marked both men and women as Indians and sharply distinguished them from their white American settler neighbors. The earlier religious ceremonial had shrunk to a few observances for love magic and sorcery, and a Peyote cult, in which mystical experience is obtained by eating mescal, incorporating some Christian and some aboriginal elements, provided the religious framework for life. A few individuals had been sent East to school and came back speaking good English to act as interpreters for the group.

But the land on which the Antlers had lived, a generous section of which had been given to each adult male, was some of the best farming land in the United States. Settlers continued to press west looking for land; meanwhile, the pattern of farming for which the government had provided houses and equipment had never really taken hold among a people where horticulture had been women's work. So a new way of life developed, in which the Indians leased their farmland to white settlers and lived on the rent, supplemented by the gardening and food gathering of the women, while the men devoted their time to social gatherings which preserved an attenuated but recognizable stamp of the old culture. The children were sent for a few years to large government boarding schools, where several tribes were mixed together, where they did a large amount of manual work with equipment they would never see again, learned the barest rudiments of English, and returned to the reservation to forget most of what they had learned. A way of life defined as Indian had become standardized, based on federal protection and federal subsidy, setting a permanent barrier between the Antlers and the people of the wider society. There was no definition of any future to which they could aspire, and there were still old men to tell of a more glorious past. Under the guise of preserving their identity, their culture, and their land, they had been immobilized, no longer able to adapt constructively to new events and new inventions as they had when the horse had been introduced just a few generations before.

Then came a genuine land rush. Under the original federal grants, individual Indians now owned and could sell their land; there was a reversal of the federal policy which had sent their children to boarding schools, which meant the children had to attend local schools. So at the period when I studied them, the thin, economically unstable adjustment was disintegrating—malnutrition, disease, gambling, family instability, and drunkenness were becoming ever more prevalent as their economic resources diminished with the sale of more and more land. This disintegration has continued, until in 1953 the withdrawal of federal protection left the "reservation" entirely without any police protection at all. Their situation was vividly described as follows in September, 1957:[2]

"The landless adult Antlers of today do not realize that it was the government which built the good houses their fathers used to live in and that their fathers owned the land because the government for twenty-five years would not let them sell it. They think wistfully of their fathers as greater men than they are and look back on their fathers' time as a kind of "Antler golden age," which has vanished because, they, the sons, are mysteriously a lower order of men.

"No wonder they think so. Today, large fertile areas of their reservation have passed into the hands of white owners, and good corn is growing on them. Some land remains to Antler individuals and the tribe, but the Antlers, with a few magnificent exceptions, do not farm that either. They lease it to white farmers and, themselves, live below subsistence level on the lease money. The good frame houses that the government built for their fathers in the Antler golden age still stand on the reservation. Some of them are in excellent repair, painted, curtained, and cheerful; these have passed into the hands of non-Indian farmers along with the land. Others are grey for lack of paint, have front steps missing and doors broken; these are the ones which remain in Antler ownership. Most of those who do not live in these decaying farmhouses live in rickety little homes in the joyless town which is the center of the reservation. Their land, if worked by

2. Adapted for purposes of preserving anonymity.

*lish* (now called Neo-Melanesian), based on Melanesian grammar and a predominantly English vocabulary. The Germans discouraged the native from learning German and helped to standardize *pidgin English* as a language. The Protestant missionaries tended to learn one small local language and then, as new linguistic groups were converted, to teach mission teachers a limited literacy in this language in which there was nothing to read except the Bible and a hymnal. The Catholic missions worked in *pidgin English* which gave a territory-wide type of literacy but, again, kept the natives in a linguistic enclave.

With World War I, the German territories in New Guinea and the Bismarck Archipelago fell to the Australians and was established as a mandate under the League of Nations. A regime consciously designed to protect native rights was introduced, a few schools were established, more stringent rules in regard to indentured labor were set up, medical patrols were combined with training local medical assistants in simple first-aid skills, and a fairly stable situation prevailed for the years of the mandate, which ended with the Japanese conquest of the islands in World War II.

Here again was a regime which was consciously benevolent, protected native lands, prevented traders from giving credit for which land could be seized, and prevented overt physical cruelty from white man to native. There was a native constabulary—as in Samoa—and natives became skilled as supervisors of labor, captains of small schooners, etc. But the gulf between the level of any white man and any native was fixed and appeared absolutely uncrossable. Where the Germans had brought Samoan wives with them, and sometimes had married or taken natives of the territory as mistresses, a rigid racial line was now drawn, under which old settlers with a quarter of Samoan ancestry were made to smart. Natives might become teachers or catechists, but not ordained members of the clergy. No native sat at the same table with a white man (except possibly in some remote missions) or walked beside a white man down the street of a town. A caste system developed, based on both racial differences and the primitiveness of the villages from which the laborers came and to which they returned—villages where people sat and slept on the ground, wore hardly any clothes, chewed betel constantly and spat out the acrid saliva, ate lice out of their hair, and had very recently been cannibals, headhunters, and grave robbers. Government control meant a cessation of warfare, the partial elimination of diseases like hookworm and yaws, paths cleared between villages, taxation, sometimes a rearrangement of the houses of a village, and the maintenance of courts in which quarrels could be resolved. Mission influence meant the substitution of a very rudimentary concrete type of religious belief and a few rituals for earlier beliefs, usually with a fair amount of local black magic surviving, clothing for the upper part of women's bodies in church, as well as a contempt for their own past savage ways and for un-Christianized natives.

Between 1928 and 1938, I studied five of these New Guinea peoples, and in 1953 I returned to restudy one of them, the Manus, who, under the stimulus of World War II conditions, were reported to have wrought a transformation in their culture. In 1928, the Manus were just half a generation from warfare and the practice of selling victims to cannibals, not yet Christianized; they had incorporated only steel, a little cloth, beads, and tobacco from the white man's world. In 1946, under the combined influence of a very gifted leader named Paliau and a typical New Guinea Cargo cult—in which the return of the ancestors bringing them at once all the wealth of the white man is promised in return for the destruction of all native property—the Manus transformed their culture into a crude but recognizable version of the twentieth century. They had redesigned their social organization, set up a crude democracy within a group of thirty-three villages now politically unified into a movement, emancipated women, set up skeleton schools, hospitals, courts, customs, and banks. They then clamored for teachers, doctors, and an administration-sponsored local government scheme for which they would not have been expected to be ready for years.

This movement was conceived in a desire to have political and social equality with the white man, in the newly acquired belief that the native was capable of acquiring full equality with the white man, that just as the American Army had made the African "all right," so that he spoke and thought as well as dressed and ate and moved like a white American soldier, so the natives of New Guinea, having come late into their social inheritance, could also become full and complete participants in the modern world. It is clear from old records that this sudden desire for imitation was not unique but has happened many times before in history, when a people have met another people whose level of civilization is perceived to be higher. But gradually the honeymoon has faded off into discouragement as the eager imitators found that the newcomers admitted them as souls into their heaven but not as guests at their table, as workers but not as husbands of their daughters; on the national level, their chiefs might be invited to a coronation, but, in between, they were people with whom one did not mix or marry.

But the Paliau movement of the Manus took place after World War II in the new climate of opinion in the world; Paliau was taken to Port Moresby and told about co-operatives and baby clinics, instead of being executed for treason or goaded into an armed uprising. The policy of the party in power in Australia, which had continued the mandate, as a trust, was in favor of encouraging native leadership, community development, literacy. So, in spite of tremendous difficulties, a break with the mission, and conflict with local white men, the new society has survived, and the New Way has swept everyone along with it, grandparents as well as grandchildren.

The detailed analysis of this extreme and successful transformation, which was possible because I could study the same village and the same individuals whom I had known as children, suggests that their success was due to a variety of circumstances, some fortuitous and unrepeatable, others which can be incorporated into world-wide programs. The fortuitous events were exposure to large-scale models of Western society, in the American, Australian, and, to some extent, Japanese armies, the special gifts of Paliau, and the peculiarity of the local culture of the Manus people who formed the core of the movement. Manus culture was extraordinarily pragmatic, experimental, oriented toward flexible, skeptical, intelligent response to the external world, and the Manus found American ways of thought particularly congenial. As in Samoa there had been a fit between the Congregationalist form of religion and the Samoan form of village autonomy, on the one hand, and the Naval hierarchical formality and the Samoan hierarchical formality on the other; so here also was a specially good fit.

But leaving aside the historical accidents, the Manus success can also be laid to its initiation by the people themselves; to the completeness with which they changed the whole pattern of living habits so that old parts were not there to compromise the new; to the fact that the whole people moved together, preventing the usual break between generations; and to their sudden sense of their own capacity to do anything that the white man could do.

Their future is not only dependent upon world events completely beyond their control, such as the advance of Communism in the Pacific, changes in the political climate of opinion in Australia, and shifts in the price of wool and of copra, but also by two more immediately relevant conditions. The first of these is emphasis on their local identity, as Manus, rather than upon becoming citizens of New Guinea, participants of the Commonwealth, and in the world. This emphasis can be laid at the door of the administration which tried to "contain" the Paliau movement and so made it local and chauvinistic. The second inimical condition is the refusal to teach literacy first in Neo-Melanesian (as pidgin English had now been renamed in accordance with the new climate of opinion), as a basis for literacy in English. A combination of circumstances, namely, the attitude of Asian and African members of the United Nations toward any *lingua franca* which can be regarded as a "slave language," the attitude of Australians sensitive to any bastardization of English, the old guard in the missions who invested heavily in local languages—these attitudes resulted in an insistence that English (for which there are neither teachers, texts, nor any local readiness) be taught immediately in the schools. Experiment has shown that English can be very easily incorporated if the children, who already speak Neo-Melanesian, learn to write in it, just as the enormous experience in Indonesia, during the Dutch administration, showed the value of becoming literate first in a language which was spoken. As Manus, rather than as citizens of New Guinea, bound to their own territory and interested in "becoming more" rather than going on to higher education and a role in the country, foiled in their hope of becoming literate in a world language in which they might listen to broadcasts and read books and magazines, these people who have themselves taken a giant step into the world may also be thrown back into a partial, self-defeating adjustment.

## Our Present State of Knowledge

In the post-World War II period, anthropological theory has been able to draw upon the new climate of opinion, in which the "haves" of the world were recognizing as never before their obligations to the "have nots" and in which the demand from those who lacked literacy, medicines, agricultural techniques, community organization, and the facilities for dignified participation in the larger world exceeded the eagerness of those who were able to impart the knowledge and techniques which were demanded. We have had the benefit of anthropological restudies of communities studied a quarter of a century before, of the reports of many kinds of technical-assistance teams, of the experience of the newly freed colonial countries, of the extraordinarily diverse experience of Israel, and to a lesser extent, of the methods used in the countries which have recently come under the sway of Soviet Communism. These experiments and experiences have been utilized in new ways in response to the theoretical position called "action research" developed by Kurt Lewin which recognized the advantage of a continuous interaction between theoretical and experimental work and attempted to apply the theory so developed, so that records of what happened when the attempts were made become part of the developing body of theory. Furthermore, post-World War II anthropological field research has been specifically directed to some of the problems of purposive and controlled change, so that the results have been more relevant than was the case when anthropological work was done within the framework of pure science alone.

From the anthropological field research and analysis of the last decade a new set of principles is emerging:

1. The comparability of all human cultures, which has been one of the basic assumptions of cultural anthropology, is not only a statement which exacts respect from all those involved in the processes of change but has more profound implication. Each viable human culture, whether that of a handful of Eskimos or of a nation of fifty million people, must be seen as a system which contains provision for all "normal" human beings who are born within it, with the recognition that, as we make technical and ethical advances, more previously discarded individuals, such as the blind, the deaf, the cerebral

palsied, will be included within the communication system of the culture. Furthermore, as the range and kind of individual differences discernible in populations of any size are assumed to be of the same order, a language or any other part of the whole system of a culture which has been developed by one human group can be learned by every normal member of another human group. So children of any stock learn as their first language any language with equal proficiency, the stupid child learning less well than the bright, of course, but no language as a system presenting greater problems than another to the naïve learner.

2. Rapid change which is pattern change, in which a whole culture is transformed, may be less traumatic than slow, uneven change, which separates generations, the sexes, members of the family, work life from home life, manners from material culture, and results in fragmentation of life and faulty adjustments. Groups, primitive or peasant, who have a clear, coherent cultural tradition may be able to change their entire way of life in a very few years, carrying the entire community, grandparents, parents, and grandchildren with them, and take on a new way of life, provided they are presented with living models of the new culture. (This has been true of the rapid transformation of the culture of immigrants moving to the United States who were scattered as single families within the American scene.) Just as remaining in a familiar habitat within a large community practicing the old culture holds back change, so the more complete the change, in material and nonmaterial ways, the more rapidly is needed adjustment facilitated.

Rapid change can have the advantages over slow change that are found as between someone who moves to a new country but only picks up the language slowly and haphazardly, as compared with someone who makes a tremendous effort to acquire the entire pattern of the new language and a large vocabulary immediately after arrival, which will in turn faciliate his making a living and participating in the life of the new country.

But because it is the across-the-board change in pattern which is the essential here, a smaller change, if it is across the board, is more desirable than a larger but more uneven type of change. It would be better for a primitive, jungle-living group to develop a pattern roughly comparable to that of a handicraft society, in which a

# CHAPTER IV

# Psychological Factors in Community Education

LEONARD W. DOOB

The psychological factors in community education and the principles in which they conceivably can be embodied are too numerous even to be catalogued here. Two forms of limitation, therefore, have been deliberately adopted. First, the material is presented didactically and crisply. The presentation thus lacks documentation; anecdotal references to personal observations in East and South Africa, where perchance the writer has carried on field work, are offered merely for illustrative purposes. Secondly, only the high points of what are arbitrarily believed to be the most relevant aspects of modern psychology are suggested. No better defense for the choice can be offered than the fact that some decision has had to be made.

The analysis can begin by considering the plight of the outsider, such as the educator, the observer, or the traveler, who has a role to perform in some society or group unlike his own. After he has accepted the fact that people there differ from his peers at home, he is in a mood to perceive shades of variability. That variability can be noted in two complementary ways. In the first place, people differ markedly from one another. In a city in East Africa there are Africans who have studied in European or American universities, who are practicing a traditional profession like law or medicine, who attend church every Sunday, who drive cars, who drink moderate amounts of whiskey on appropriate occasions, and who are faithful to a single wife. In the country which begins outside the city limits are other Africans belonging to the same extended family who have never been to a Western-type school, who till the soil without help from a wheel, who have faith in a pantheon of gods or spirits, who use animals for transportation, who brew their own beer for nutritional and spiritual purposes, and who are partially

97

supported by a principal wife and her co-wives. Secondly, the outsider soon discovers that practices and ideas from the outside are accepted with different degrees of unanimity and enthusiasm. In some African societies, for example, all people know the value of the money issued by the European government, almost everybody appreciates the value of a latrine, a large minority reveals the value that they place upon shoes by wearing them, relatively few subscribe to the value of premarital chastity in a Christian sense, and virtually nobody accepts the value of progress in the affairs of men or nations.

Such diversity is baffling, and immediately punctures easy generalizations about the society and the manner of its changes. Beneath the surface of the diversity, one's scientific faith nevertheless affirms, principles are discoverable that can render the discrete phenomena more intelligible. The principal aim of this chapter, consequently, is to indicate the issues which arise when, as in this instance, psychological principles are sought.

Why search for principles in a volume on community education? It would seem self-evident that the educator, confronted with the unique problems of another society or of a special group in his own society, can solve them more efficiently if he has principles to guide him. Later, he can incorporate his own experience into generalizations which he can bequeath to his successors or to himself if he moves on to another area or problem.

How does one search for principles? First, a universe of discourse is located. Then the effort is made to isolate the significant concepts or variables within that universe. By means of the concepts the principles are tentatively formulated. Finally, attention must be paid to questions of methodology, since information is needed both to utilize and to test the principles.

The universe of discourse of this chapter is quickly located simply by recalling that community education seeks to change people. Psychologically, change means learning. The citizen of an underdeveloped area who has an Oxford degree has learned more about Western civilization than has his cross-cousin who lives in the bush. Everyone in the African societies mentioned above has been taught the value of a currency system, but no one has been able or willing to acquire the idea of progress. In these terms, the aim of community education is to motivate a group of people, especially adults, to gain certain skills, to acquire certain knowledge and attitudes, and eventually to behave in certain specified ways by providing them with the most effective learning opportunities to do so. Let it be clear that a sentence like this last one would accomplish more than a verbal transformation. For immediately after diversity is viewed as a function of differential learning in the past and community education as the mode of learning new behavior in the present and the future, it becomes possible to utilize psychological concepts and psychological principles that have proven efficacious among rats and human beings, children and adults, or Africans and Americans and in connection with problems as apparently different as maze-learning and psychotherapy.

A generic term is needed, before proceeding, to contrast and compare behavior which is traditional within a society or group and that which is advocated or changed by community education. Luckily no neologism or tricky jargon has to be paraded. *Form of behavior* is sufficient. The adjective *old* can be appended to refer to traditional forms, and *new* to refer to those involved in community education. To this innocent distinction the *dramatis personae* can be quickly added:

*Leaders:* People who discharge the formal role of teachers or the informal one of models. The teacher deliberately attempts to achieve educational goals by means of suitable techniques; in contrast, the model may be unaware of the example that he sets and hence of the influence that he possesses. *Inside leaders* are indigenous teachers and models in the old society; *outside leaders* are people from another society, including those interested in community education who—deliberately or otherwise—introduce new forms of behavior.

*Learners:* Infants, children, adolescents, or adults who may be or are being taught or impressed with the old or new forms.

Factors affecting learning and, hence, community education can be conveniently and pragmatically grouped into three categories. First, there is the setting in which learning occurs: What are the surroundings or external stimuli which affect learners? Then there is the form of behavior to be learned, unlearned, or relearned: What kinds of dispositions and skills must learners possess, what sorts of action must they take? Finally, there are general predispositions

within learners: What types of people are to be affected in particular surroundings in order that certain forms of their behavior
can be altered?

An identical procedure is followed under each of the three headings. First, the concept or variable indicated by the numbered
subheading is delineated and very briefly illustrated. The appropriate
psychological principle or principles (if any) are then named and
stated. Virtually every principle is utilizable in other contexts besides the one in which it is first formulated.

To the task at hand, then; the introduction is over.

## Social Setting

(1) *Attitude toward Leader.* The first feature of the social setting
likely to affect learners is the group of leaders in whom the old
and new forms are embedded. Learning depends in part upon the
learner's attitude toward the leader. Three more or less distinct
components of that attitude can be distinguished:

*a) Recognition:* Is the leader recognized by potential followers
as a model or teacher? The role of educator from the West may be
ignored in the old society, for he may be considered a visitor who
has nothing to teach. The missionary's competence in biblical but
not in social questions may be revered.

*b) Affection:* Is the leader liked or disliked? It is possible to
recognize the competence of a man without feeling any warmth
toward him, and the reverse can also be true.

*c) Identification:* Does the leader attract learners because they are
interested per se in what he has to teach or because they would
master his teachings in order to become a person like him? Again,
the competence of a man may be rated high and he may be loved
dearly, but his students may or may not seek to emulate his
personality.

Before a principle is associated with this first factor, let the
complexity of the problem be indicated. For illustrative purposes,
each of the three components of attitude can be simplified by being
assigned either positive or negative values. Eight different combinations then result. At one extreme might be an adolescent who is
studying to become a minister of the gospel as promulgated by a
missionary-teacher. He respects that teacher as the font of theo-

logical and ethical wisdom, for certainly no one in his tribe knows as much about Christianity and its doctrines. He has deep affection for him, and hence he listens attentively and studies industriously. He also prays that some day he will be like him in deed and word, and hence he seeks whenever possible to imitate his ways of behaving and his general manner of life. With such a combination, the outlook for learning is good.

At the other extreme could be a tribesman who has complete confidence in his own traditional religion. He does not recognize the same missionary as a potential teacher but considers him an interloper who would destroy some of the adolescent initiation rites in which he himself firmly believes. He does not like him as a person, for he seems to behave differently from the way people should. Obviously he feels no identification with the man. Such a person will not be converted; the learning outlook for him is dismal.

Between the extremes are other combinations. The Zulu factory-worker may thoroughly detest his European foreman, and he may have no desire whatsoever to adopt his philosophy, but his hostility and rejection do not prevent him from appreciating the man's competence as a mechanic; hence, the component of respect, however grudgingly bestowed, produces efficient learning. Or the same Zulu may follow the advice of his father who lives on a Reserve, not because he considers him competent or not because he himself wishes ever to return to that Reserve, but because he genuinely likes the old man and would not contradict him.

Here, then, is an illustration of interacting variables, the outcome of which is difficult to predict. The very first principle, consequently, must recognize this state of affairs:

Principle 1. Interaction. Factors affecting learning, and hence community education, operate in conjunction with one another; the effect of a single factor can be specified only under particular circumstances, when other things are declared to be equal, or as probable tendencies.

Principle 1, in effect, insists: "Beware; do not oversimplify; try to take everything into account." Such a principle, however, admits the possibility of producing principles that are more positive in nature. Concerning leaders, the teachers and models in the learning situation, the following can be said:

*Principle 2. Attitude toward leaders.* Learning can occur only when the relevant competence of teachers or models is recognized; it is greatly facilitated when learners admire them and/or identify with them.

(2) *Leaders' Attitudes.* In Principle 2 reference is made to "leaders" and not to a single model or teacher, since learners undoubtedly associate not one but many individuals with the old and new forms of behavior. To obtain attention and co-operation, the agricultural officer of a colonial area who seeks to introduce methods of preventing soil erosion, for example, may be competing not only with other European officers who urge different improvements like better houses and more schools but also with inside models like parents, children, clansmen, and neighbors who favor old methods of planting and plowing. The learner, consequently, may be in a state of conflict, and conflict can affect his readiness to learn.

Whether or not conflict arises or has an appreciable effect depends in part upon the learner's conception of the leaders' attitudes toward the old and new forms of behavior. That conception, like any view of what occurs in social life, may not necessarily be a true reflection of what the leader privately feels or publicly advocates, since it may not be based upon adequate information. Again there are many possibilities. The child who likes his parents and who is sent to a trade school has a firm basis for believing that they approve of what his teachers are doing; he is not torn between what he considers to be the wishes of two forces toward whom he has positive feelings. The cultivator who is convinced by the agricultural officer that chemical fertilizer will make his corn grow tall but who also knows that his tribal chief considers chemicals contrary to the traditions of his ancestors is in an unhappy situation if he also loves and respects the chief. The learner always knows what his teacher seeks, at least with respect to the formal content of the curriculum; but he may not be aware of his attitude toward fundamental values that are not discussed in the classroom.

Since attitudes toward change of inside leaders are likely to be known, the role of these leaders in community education can be crucial:

*Principle 3: Leadership.* Changes are more easily learned from inside than from outside leaders.

There is always the possibility that outsiders may not be looked upon as models or teachers and that, since whatever they know about people has been acquired through observation rather than as members of the society, they may not be able to devise skilful pedagogical techniques. In contrast, inside leaders are perhaps more likely to influence followers by the example which they set and the intimate knowledge of their contemporaries which they undoubtedly possess. On the basis of such knowledge, as has been indicated in this book, they may be better able to devise efficient means to achieve ends which they themselves have been taught by outsiders who are promoting community education. Let them be convinced that they and their countrymen would benefit from a change in diet; let them learn the principle that is involved (e.g., that they need more protein and fewer carbohydrates in order to reduce the incidence of kwashiorkor); then they can perhaps determine which foods are likely not only to contain more protein but also to be acceptable in that society.

In passing, it is well to mention that Principle 3, like all these principles, is true only when "other things" are roughly equal. It is assumed that the inside leader possesses prestige; if his prestige is in fact low, the principle may not apply, for under such circumstances an outsider who inspires awe may be a more effective teacher. Likewise, the assumption must be made that the inside leader can be converted. In fact his conversion may be more difficult to produce than that of marginal people who may be attracted to a change in order to improve their own status and relieve their own strains. The extra effort required to obtain his co-operation, however, becomes necessary when the immediate and ultimate influence of the marginal people is small.

(3) *Channels of Communication.* Unlike the outsider, the inside leader usually has ready access to a channel of communication to people. Without some kind of channel, learning materials cannot be presented and no influence can be exerted. The outsider, on the other hand, may have no way of reaching people, of getting them to listen. A school or demonstration area can be established, but it may not attract specialized groups in sufficient numbers; in many African countries, for example, relatively few girls attend Western-type schools.

The easiest and perhaps most frequently traversed channels of communication are those within the nuclear family. For this and other reasons, great importance is attached to early experiences:

*Principle 4: Socialization.* Forms of behavior acquired at an early age within the family are likely to resist change.

A basic challenge to community education is contained in this innocent, somewhat banal principle. Freud and his followers have obviously made the Western world fully conscious of what men everywhere had previously intuited and often well expressed, viz., the importance of childhood. The fact that all psychoanalysts, including Freud, attempt to help their patients, however, indicates their explicit acknowledgment that change later on in life is possible under particular circumstances. Community education, consequently, is merely setting for itself a difficult goal, not a hopeless one.

The channel of communication to adults in underdeveloped areas often depends upon the permissiveness of the resident outsider. Any form of segregation or color bar always means the elimination of certain learning opportunities. Clearly Africans who are barred from joining a European club cannot be expected to acquire the niceties of behavior which membership entails. Less obvious is the fact that the kind of general aloofness which most Europeans display toward Africans decreases informal interaction between the two groups and, hence, prevents Africans from learning the details of European family and social life. What occurs in the classroom or demonstration center affects directly what is taught there; what occurs outside these formal areas can affect the attitude toward European civilization as a whole and therefore the will to learn in the formal situation. The reasons which outsiders have for facilitating or inhibiting channels of communication constitute a separate problem; community education must operate with these channels as given or else seek to alter them.

A potentially important characteristic of a channel of communication is the amount of "feedback" which it permits: Is the communicator able to obtain information about the predispositions and reactions of learners as he communicates information to them? Sometimes it is necessary only to listen in order to improve his techniques; but the big gap which often exists between the outsider and learners may make him feel that he need pay little attention to them and that, instead, he can follow teaching plans formulated beforehand in London, Brussels, or Washington. A methodological principle, therefore, must be stated:

Principle 5: Feedback. Planning and execution of effective educational programs require provision for obtaining continuous information concerning the predispositions and reactions of people.

(4) Incentives. The social setting offers incentives to change or to remain unchanged. Some of the original incentives may be evoked by the teacher or model. "I like him," the learner says in effect, "and therefore I will learn this—because he does it"; or "because he wants me to"; or "because in this way I can become more like him." Other incentives involve the consequences of learning or not learning the new forms. When Africans decide to acquire a trade or join a profession associated with the West, they may or may not receive encouragement from their family group and from the Westerners with whom they have contacts.

Principle 6: Social support. Important incentives to change or not to change are provided by the groups to which the individual belongs or to which he aspires to belong.

This principle calls attention to the continuing influences exercised by groups. Forgetting, for example, is likely to occur unless some group provides or demands that the new form be exercised sufficiently frequently. Many East Africans who once doubtless spoke English fairly fluently as students at Makerere College in Uganda appear to lose their fluency in later years unless their occupation or other contact with Europeans requires them to make use of the language.

The schoolteacher who would attain in the classroom some of the goals of community education may create an atmosphere friendly to the acquisition of a learning goal; but at home the learner may face hostility to the new form. Once more, social conflict can lead to conflict within the individual. The atmosphere within a group and hence the social support for the old and new forms, however, may change. The first converts to the new form may be difficult to obtain as a result of the enmity poured upon them from inside. As converts become more numerous, they feel less lonely, and eventually a point may be reached at which the incentives for change, being provided by a large and influential group, are stronger than those to remain unchanged.

The possibility that the atmosphere and social support may be different in the learning situation from conditions at home raises a very general problem, viz., the extent to which the two situations resemble each other not only with respect to social support but also with reference to other social and psychological factors:

> *Principle 7: Transfer.* Forms of behavior learned in one situation are likely to be utilized in another situation when both situations provide similar incentives and opportunities to employ similar forms.

Principle 7 warns that there is no automatic transfer of forms of behavior; in fact, transfer in most social situations is difficult to achieve. The proponent of community education often must choose between two alternatives. On the one hand, he knows—as does any teacher—that learning is likely to be promoted in an isolated situation like the classroom where students are relatively free from distractions and other competing influences. On the other hand, forms of behavior learned in such an atmosphere may not be easily transferable to the home or market place where a different atmosphere prevails and other incentives operate. For the latter reason it may seem necessary and desirable to insure transfer by having a program in community education pursued in the context of the home or literally in the community itself. Otherwise, there is probably only one way of being psychologically certain of transcending a learning situation and producing transfer, viz., by motivating the learner so strongly that, like a newly ordained minister, he can surmount almost any kind of opposition in any social setting and hence function with the minimum of social support. But, fortunately or unfortunately, such a spirit is rarely created.

Transfer refers not only to new but also to old forms of behavior: Will the latter be utilized in different contexts? Principle 7 states that the old forms will be exercised when appropriate incentives and opportunities to utilize new ones are not provided. Conceivably, therefore, community education can proceed more rapidly when competition from old forms is eliminated. In theory, if a group of people could be removed from their old environment and shifted elsewhere to a milieu in which little if anything reminded them of their old way of life, they might tend to forget the old forms relatively rapidly. They *might* forget, it is said, but the presence of their peers by itself would probably reinstate some of the old forms. In the preceding chapter, Margaret Mead cites the example of the Manus, who have successfully and happily entered the Western world by radically changing their way of life in a hurry. Before the technique of such a transformation can be confidently utilized in other societies, however, it is well to continue to observe the Manus and to discover whether the forgetting of the old is as complete as now appears on the surface to be the case.

## The Form of Behavior

Critical features of the social setting in which community education occurs have been sketched. What is learned is affected by teachers and models, by channels of communication, and by incentives. Now an analysis must be made of the specific form of behavior to be changed. Learning to believe in democracy, for example, involves different problems from learning to install a window screen.

(5) *Significance.* The verbal labels attached to a form of behavior usually give important clues to its significance. The labels do not necessarily correspond to one employed by an outsider. What is called abject poverty by a foreigner with higher standards may be considered relative luxury by the people themselves. Ways of preparing food can involve not only dietary considerations but also methods of demonstrating loyalty to ancestral ways. To a visitor from the West, a hospital is an institution in which sick people receive medical care, but to some Africans it is a strange place from which people never return—and indeed relatives, whose fears prevented them from seeking medical help until the disease was hopelessly advanced, may have died after finally being confined there.

Similarly, the significance of the difference which is perceived between the old and new forms plays a role in the learning process. In many African societies, it has been observed again and again, the difference between traditional polygyny and the form of monogamy espoused especially by missionaries lies not so much in the number of wives and children as in the number of economic units at the disposal of the male. Since misunderstandings can occur, it seems necessary to state:

*Principle 8: Externalization-internalization.* An imperfect correspondence almost always exists between the external form of behavior observed by an outsider and its internal significance to the people concerned.

Principle 8 is obviously useful at the start of a program in community education, since it urges the outside leader to know his learners by becoming acquainted with the significance which they attach to traditional forms. At the end of the program, the same principle also warns against prematurely assuming that the effort has been successful or unsuccessful. Missionaries have often learned that outward conformity does not mean inner attachment to the principles of a religion, or that years later truly religious actions are demonstrated by people who at first appeared externally to be unconverted heathens.

It is necessary to inquire in passing whether there are sweeping differences between the ways in which people in underdeveloped and developed areas attach significance to their varied activities. Many investigators, including this writer, for example, have the not completely undocumented impression that nonliterate peoples are less apt to compartmentalize their behavior, and, hence, like an extremely devout person in our society, they are inclined to perceive or postulate connections between most of those activities. With our present knowledge we are probably not in a position to establish such a wide-sweeping difference; and so for the moment it must be sufficient, as will be done in the next section of this chapter, to single out the modal tendencies in a given society without establishing whether other peoples also reveal them.

Principle 8 indicates possible sources of misunderstanding between new leaders and old learners. It is well also to formulate a principle suggesting that the significance which is attached to old and new forms can often be dramatically altered:

*Principle 9: Patterning.* Relatively minor changes in stimulus patterns can have relatively major effects upon the significance that people attach to those patterns and upon their ensuing behavior.

Involved in such changes are the responses evoked by the alterations in the pattern and their interaction with responses previously aroused. The reaction to a new blemish, for example, is more devastating when it is added to a pattern previously called beautiful than to one previously considered neutral or ugly. Since most programs in community education involve complicated patterns of stimuli, it follows that minor changes in phrasing, in symbols, or in sponsorship can make a previously acceptable or unacceptable program evoke the opposite kind of response.

(6) *Drives.* Whatever difference is perceived between the old and new form is eventually evaluated. The evaluation consciously or unconsciously is made in terms of the satisfactions offered by the two forms. A term is needed to refer to this factor of satisfaction which has the connotation of motive, impulse, need, want, or desire. Here *drives* are said to be or not to be satisfied. It matters not which term is employed, provided that the one selected conveys the following dicta concerning the components of motivation: (*a*) some are instinctively determined but then profoundly affected by environmental or social conditions, and others tend to be rather exclusively social in origin; (*b*) they vary in importance within each personality; and (*c*) many of them must be reduced or satisfied to some extent if people are to survive biologically or psychologically. The incentives provided by the social setting, then, evoke or do not evoke appropriate drives.

At least four factors seem to determine how old and new forms are judged in terms of drive satisfaction or dissatisfaction:

*a*) *Confidence:* Before a person is willing to learn, he must, in effect, believe that he himself can achieve the learning goal, that indeed the problem at hand is solvable. He may be living close to starvation, for example; but, if he also feels that his condition is divinely ordained, and hence is as unalterable as death, he may not co-operate with a program which would prolong his life.

*b*) *Demonstrability:* The learner has had demonstrated to him the satisfaction which the old form can bring, perhaps he knows or thinks he knows the degree to which the new form will bring satisfaction. It would appear that there is a solid foundation for some judgments; people know whether they have had enough to eat, or whether their shelter is adequate. In addition, their general habits of thinking are likely to play an important part in determining what sorts of evidence they will accept as demonstrating satisfaction. Judgments concerning food satiation or concerning protection from the elements differ, as do the reactions to a practical demonstration. The European veterinarian in Africa believes that the death of a few cattle, when herds are being dipped for prophylactic purposes, is inconsequential in the long run; whereas a cattle-loving African, when his senses are confronted with such evidence, may lose confidence in the entire procedure.

c) *Anticipation:* Besides noting present satisfactions and dissatisfactions, the learner anticipates the satisfactions which old and new forms will bring in the future. The basis for the anticipation may be actuarial, wishful thinking, or externally imposed, but in any case the conception of the future affects the evaluation of the present.

d) *Importance:* Some drives (usually but not always primary or unlearned ones) make more insistent demands upon the individual and, when aroused, require virtually immediate satisfaction. People whose source of food or whose system of basic values is threatened are more likely to seek change than those who conceivably can lose a trivial material or nonmaterial luxury; but, if the threat is removed, the former are less likely than the latter to risk the possible changes which innovation may bring. What is said to be important socially to a society as a whole, however, may not be important psychologically to all of its members, but must be important to some of them. Crop cultivation may determine the survival of a society which does not import food from the outside, but as an activity it *directly* affects only cultivators and distributors, not people like clerks who are otherwise engaged.

These four factors give rise to a very general principle:

*Principle 10: Drive satisfaction.* Learning is likely to occur when learners have confidence that they can solve the problems associated with unsatisfied drives; when the utility of the forms of behavior to be learned is demonstrable and/or anticipated; and when the drive, if important, is relatively unsatisfied in the present or, if unimportant, appears satisfiable in the future by means of the new form.

Certainly Principle 10 is awkward and complex, but again interacting variables do not emit a pleasant, simple generalization. In addition, the key words—the four factors—are left undefined, since their values must always be specified in a given situation. The combination, however, is thought to be fruitful because on its high level of abstraction it would embrace other time-worn generalizations as well as apparent exceptions thereto.

In this light, for example, the conservatism of old forms—as suggested by Principle 4, socialization—can be more realistically appraised. People cling to old ways but only if they are satisfied or if they anticipate a continuation or a rebirth of satisfaction therefrom in the future. New forms are resisted but not always; anticipations which spring from fantasies can render novelty more alluring than demonstrated experience. In the previous chapter, it has been said that a demonstration of a proposed reform is usually better than a discussion, but—it may now be added—only when fantasy is less potent and, of course, when the demonstration itself is truly effective.

Philosophy and social science are strewn with theories trying to account for the relative ease or difficulty with which material and ideational changes in behavior are adopted. At the outset, it has been indicated, the nature of the drives must be considered; material changes, for example, are likely to involve basic drives which may be more insistent than the drives supporting ideas and values. Demonstrability and anticipation are also relevant. In community education, many material proposals can be demonstrated: With new methods, the grain grows taller, the incidence of disease declines, the effort required to achieve the same end is palpably less. In contrast, the efficacy and desirability of ideas are difficult, if not impossible, to demonstrate. When Africans were asked by this writer to comment upon the proposition that "life in heaven will be better than life on earth," again and again they pleaded ignorance because, they said, most seriously, "No one who has ever been there has returned to tell us." People may cling to old ideas not only because their utility in the past has been fuzzily demonstrated but also because their anticipations can be equally fuzzy: Who knows, they say in effect, what will happen to me here on earth or in the future life if I abandon the beliefs of my fathers?

Note must be taken, too, of the relation between Principle 10 and other principles, notably Principle 3, pertaining to leadership. Learners are likely to have more self-confidence when they see that their own leaders or peers can perform a task than when they observe outsiders succeed. In East Africa many Africans are inspired to improve methods of cultivation by watching the progress of neighbors who have been trained by Europeans rather than by noting the better crops grown by Europeans whose accomplishments they believe they cannot conceivably duplicate.

(7) *Skill.* In addition to perception and motivation, the principal factors considered so far, learning requires the achievement of crude or delicate co-ordination through patience, repetition, trial and error, and, often, sheer ingenuity. In a society that has not previously invented or borrowed the wheel, the skill needed to manipulate a wheelbarrow is undoubtedly less than that involved in driving a motorcar. The examination to be passed to qualify as an unskilled miner is less complicated for an African than the one confronting the potential schoolteacher. It is fair to say, therefore, that some aspects of community education have an advantage over others because they can be more easily learned, provided it is recognized that the advantage is not completely inherent in the form as such but depends also on the previous experience of the learner. If a man has learned to drive a car, then he can more easily master the operation of some power-driven earth-moving equipment than an individual whose mechanical techniques have advanced no farther than a bicycle. In the realm of ideas, however, the gain from one's background is much less clear. A resemblance between an old and new doctrine may promote antagonism toward the new rather than the learning of it, as when a missionary seeks converts among those already converted by a slightly different sect from the West.

The chief principle which appears as a result of this discussion of skill is one already enunciated, viz, number 5, feedback. A program of community education must be adapted to people's skill, and that skill can be ascertained only if there is feedback through some channel of communication. An additional generalization with implications far beyond that of skill can also be adduced:

> *Principle 11: Initiative.* Changes are more easily learned when the initiative thereto comes or seems to come in part or completely from the people themselves or at least from their own leaders.

An assumption here is that learners are the best judges of their own learning skills and that outsiders are likely to misjudge them. In addition, as people in a democratic society are wont to assert, the factor of motivation may be linked to skills: People usually wish to control their own destiny and hence function more effectively when they feel that they are doing so. Some who are quite content to have their parents or a group's leaders act for them do not demand the initiating role for themselves but for superiors with whom they identify.

A challenge to community education is to find such identification. In chapter i, for example, the active participation by people in a program is extolled. For if people participate, they become identified: What I do is part of me. Here is another reason for having people and their leaders work out the details—the means—of a program whose end is indicated by an outside teacher.

## General Predispositions

In one sense the predispositions of potential learners have already been considered: They bring to the learning situation tendencies which affect their perceptions, which make them prone to react favorably or unfavorably to the new form, and which enable them with ease or difficulty to comprehend and master one problem at hand. These are predispositions, however, that are evoked by the specific form of behavior which is to be unlearned or learned: A particular teacher is liked or disliked, his teaching is perceived in one way and not in another, a strong drive is or is not evoked. In addition, there are predispositions which affect all or virtually all learning, and these are the subject of the present section.

(8) *Adjustment.* The first predispositional factor is that of adjustment. The concept, it must be quickly added, is bewildering and ambiguous, but no better one can be produced to refer to the general state of the organism. It is important to ask whether people are content, whether they are satisfied with their general lot, because an effort is thus made to discover the presence or absence of a learning mood. Of course, standards of contentment and satisfaction are relative, but on the basis of their own standards people react favorably or unfavorably to their milieu. General discontent, it is now recognized, frequently, but not always, facilitates susceptibility to some new doctrine like communism or revivalism.

The concept of adjustment calls attention to the fact that human personality is organized. Sometimes fairly important drives may be unsatisfactorily reduced without general dissatisfaction occurring.

In contrast, the frustration of what might appear to be a relatively unimportant drive can lead to general maladjustment and then to an explosion, or—in a different kind of person—to desperation or apathy. For this reason, those interested in community education cannot be advised to single out as learners either the content or the malcontent in the society. The fact that maladjusted people do seek some kind of solution to their problems, however, demands a guiding principle:

> *Principle 12: Related consequences.* A change in one form of behavior is likely to have effects upon related forms.

Principle 12 is deliberately vague, for it would suggest only that learning has its repercussions. What appears to be a trifling change in a society eventually gives rise to a whole series of major changes —if this is so, why is it so? Such changes occur within people. Initially they accept one change when it seems to reduce their misery. Then, when their type of roof or manner of eating is altered, they discover new maladjustments which in turn require more learning. One thing leads to another: What begins as a modification of roofing or eating may end as a radical modification of their philosophy of life. In addition, a change learned under one set of circumstances may also have virtually unforeseeable consequences upon behavior which occurs under different circumstances as a result of intervening events. The fruits of being literate may become evident to the African not when he resides in the bush where the ability to read is of no great moment but when he moves into a city where that ability qualifies him for a Western-type job.

The changes accepted by some people in a society, moreover, may demand changes in social relations without necessarily producing maladjustments in all the people who are involved. The opening of a new mine or the development of a cash crop in an underdeveloped area depends upon a group of specialists who thereafter use their earnings to exchange for whatever seems to satisfy their primary and secondary drives. Other people who then, directly or indirectly, provide them with food may be rendered happy or miserable by the new responsibilities.

(9) *Modal Personality.* Among the general predispositions related to community education is what is often called the national character of a people, their basic personality, or their modal person-

ality. Perception and motivation are always selective processes, and there are within each person broad predispositions which function frequently and in numerous situations. The well-integrated artist, businessman, or sportsman again and again observes, judges, and learns in accordance with his dominating interests. What is true of the individual is true of many people who have been subjected in the past to fairly similar influences. It thus becomes possible to detect in a group or a society modal tendencies. Just as the artist in our society is affected by his art and his artistic prejudices, in the same way most people in a society whose livelihood depends precariously upon fish are likely to observe fish and to be ready to learn some kinds of new fishing techniques but not others. Not all the inhabitants are equally observant or equally prone to adopt certain methods, but each probably reveals a modal tendency in those directions.

When people from societies with different modal personalities meet, which is always the case when community education occurs in underdeveloped countries, misunderstandings occur as a result of their different modes of perceiving and evaluating the world about them. One such loss must be singled out:

> *Principle 13: Linguistic differences.* Almost inevitably misunderstandings and difficulties arise when material from the language of one culture is translated into the language of a different culture.

The outsider interested in community education, consequently, must continually remind himself of the fallibility of translations and interpreters. Even when students know the outside language as a second language and not as a mother tongue, their expression of attitude and the accuracy with which they recall material may be affected by the language in which a communication is conveyed to them.

(10) *Modal-learning Method.* Modal personality refers to people whose traits are organized in particular ways and who therefore behave in a manner different from people in other societies. A component of this behavior may be a modal learning method. For people everywhere have a tendency to differ with respect to the ways in which they acquire knowledge or even co-ordinate their movements. Some plunge recklessly ahead, others are cautious, almost regardless of the problem at hand. Some demand immediate encouragement, or

at least rewards which they can receive in the not very distant future, whereas others can work tirelessly to attain very distant goals. Some learn more efficiently when surrounded by their peers; others demand solitude and quiet. Some seek answers to puzzling problems in books, others look to sagacious peers who will listen to their questions. It seems clear that these modal modes of learning differ from time to time not only within the same person and from person to person within the same society but also from society to society. One society's effective pedagogical techniques, consequently, are not necessarily effective elsewhere. This factor gives rise to no new principles, but attention must again be directed to Principle 5, feedback (any leader must have a way of becoming acquainted with the learning modes of students), and Principle 3, leadership (the inside leader is likely to pick almost automatically the most suitable learning mode).

(11) *Modal Reactions to Adversity.* Another component of the modal personality is a modal reaction to adversity. Available to human beings who cannot attain their goals are innumerable alternatives which psychoanalysts and psychiatrists have catalogued at length: aggression, rationalization, repression, displacement, masochism. Doubtless each person at some time displays all the processes, but gradually he learns that it is more effective or satisfying to react generally in one way than in another. When faced with most adversity, therefore, he usually blames himself or someone else, is quiet or nasty, grows confident or insecure. On a large scale the same is true of a society: Its members, faced with some common adversity like a famine or an epidemic, may demonstrate a variety of reactions, but most of them are likely to react in a traditional and hence rather stereotyped manner.

Other factors could be isolated which distinguish societies from each other, but they would serve only to reinforce Principle 8, externalization-internalization: Whatever differences exist between the basic personality of the society from which the outside leader comes and that of the group from which learners are recruited are likely to have critical effects upon the understanding between the two and the learning of the latter. It is no longer necessary to debate the point that differences between diverse cultures are not absolute and that, given time and patience, they theoretically can be diminished, perhaps even abolished. At the moment of contact, however, the difference must be taken into account. It may be confidently stated, for example, that all peoples seek both immediate and future rewards. The cultivator in any society expects his hunger to be assuaged when he eats food, and he knows that he must wait for a harvest after he puts seed into the ground. But the extent to which the future plays a role in people's lives, the extent to which they are willing to make momentary sacrifices for the sake of future gains probably varies from society to society. It seems possible that one of the pivotal points of Western education, perhaps of Western society in general, is an emphasis upon such sacrifice.

One final misunderstanding resulting from basic differences between peoples must be highlighted:

> Principle 14: Symbolization. Learners who are attracted to another culture are likely to attach particular significance to what they believe to be its important symbols.

The misunderstanding arises when new leaders do not attach the same significance to those symbols as learners. Many Africans who aspire to live like Europeans, for example, find symbols for that form of life in the Europeans with whom they have contact. Since almost all the European models are in the white-collar category, the Africans demand similar positions for themselves at a time when their society may more urgently require artisans and technicians. If forms of behavior with great symbolic significance are denied to learners, their resentment is likely to be great. It is often reported that Africans object to a curriculum especially designed for them, since it signifies, they think, the colonial view that they are not fit to receive a real European education.

*     *     *

The psychological factors related to community education can be conveniently summarized by bringing into existence an "undereducated man" who will be a distant relative of that famous, methodologically useful entity called "economic man" and who as an abstraction can be postulated to exist whenever and wherever there is material or spiritual poverty. The Arabic numbers below correspond to those used throughout the text to refer to the factors:

A. Community education reaches undereducated man in a social setting. There he has or can learn to have (1) certain attitudes toward old and new leaders: He affords them a certain degree of recognition and affection, and he may or may not identify with them. He believes that these leaders have (2) certain attitudes toward the old and new forms of behavior. He has been affected in the past, and he will or will not be affected in the future by available (3) channels of communication. Through formal and informal channels he is provided with (4) incentives to change or remain unchanged.

B. Community education proposes certain learning goals, which means for undereducated man specific or general changes in forms of behavior or the learning of new forms. Each of these forms, old or new, makes certain demands upon him. But first he reacts to them: They have (5) significance for him; and he perceives, too, differences between the old and the new in his own manner. In a sense, like his relative with whom the economist does intellectual business, he must make a decision between competing forms. These decisions he makes in terms of (6) his drives, but, unlike that relative, he draws upon unconscious impulses as well as rational ones. Consciously or not, he must wonder whether he has confidence in his ability to solve the problem at hand; whether satisfaction from the old or the new form has been demonstrated or whether he can anticipate varying satisfactions in the future; and whether the form of behavior, new or old, is important to himself and to his group. Moreover, each new form makes a demand of (7) his skill, which may or may not be adequate.

C. Community education would also tap certain general predispositions which are frequently and generally evoked and hence transcend the particular parts of any program that is advocated. Undereducated man reveals (8) a certain degree of adjustment to his environment and his fellows. With them he shares (9) a modal personality, (10) modal methods of learning problems, and (11) modal ways of meeting adversity.

## Problems in Method

From the viewpoint of the educator, the factors related to community education can be divided into two categories: those which he himself can control and those to which he must conform or adapt his program if that program is to be successful. In the first group are the ideas and practices which he would have people learn and the learning methods which he would employ to bring about the learning. These he controls in the sense that he has a choice of objectives, and, after a selection is made, he utilizes whichever methods seem best suited for the people at hand. In the second group are the people themselves, for their specific and general reactions to the social setting and to the material to be learned must be apprehended and taken into account. Therefore, no matter what his own predilections or training has been, he must acquire empirical information about the social setting, the specific tendencies, and the general predispositions of the potential learners.

Before the educator leaves home, he may have access to reports by others who have preceded him in the area. These reports must, of course, be evaluated, since no one observer can ever produce completely unblemished truths and since the data and conclusions in any report cannot automatically be applied to a new program. Then, at his destination he must always collect additional information more concretely related to his pedagogical problems. A methodological treatise must point out the pitfalls which evaluation and collection entail.

Here only the outlines of such a treatise can be most broadly sketched. Clearly it is necessary to perform the traditional task of the anthropologist: There should be some over-all understanding of the people's culture and the structure of their society. In addition, insight must be gained into their feelings, attitudes, and capacities. In effect, community education can progress most efficiently only when there is complete knowledge of the society and its people. Thus stated, the research objectives sound fantastically unattainable, as indeed they are, but knowledge short of them is imperfect and must be ever appraised by using them as criteria.

All relevant field methods seek to solve some aspect of what in general terms may be called the problem of *sampling*. First, there is the sampling involved in observation: Is the investigator viewing a representative sample of the society's activities? He cannot watch all the activities of everyone or even of a single person. He cannot be present to observe all the changes in time or all the phases through which a society goes. Perhaps he has been brought there by reports of adversity, in which case he will not be experiencing instances of prosperity. He cannot observe without being himself observed in part or completely; his presence may make people self-conscious in certain respects, and hence atypical.

Then sampling is involved when selected people become special informants. Every field worker knows that the individuals who are most co-operative, and perhaps, too, those who are least co-operative, are likely to be unrepresentative. Modern methods of obtaining scientific samples are easier to formulate than they are to follow under field conditions, since often the attributes of the universe are not known or it becomes extremely difficult and tedious to run down the people who must be interviewed if the method of randomization is to be realized.

Finally, an interview with informants involves sampling problems similar to those which arise in connection with observing the society as a whole: The questions asked and the tests administered do or do not elicit in somewhat standardized situations typical samples of his behavior. A projective technique like the Rorschach test, for example, evokes a host of responses, but those responses are obviously limited by the nature of the ink blots on the cards and are affected by the informant's particular mood and reaction to the examiner. Whether or not typical responses emerge under such conditions is a question of deep concern to anyone employing the technique. If the investigator seeks to know how people feel about aspects of community education, how shall he proceed? In the last analysis, observation may be the most valid test, but in the interim he may need to know something about the people's internal feelings. If they follow a custom which makes them wish to please rather than inform an interrogator, then atypical responses will be obtained. The problem is to discover some kind of technique which in the situation at hand elicits representative replies.

Underlying the sampling problems is a basic issue: What is the universe being sampled? Clearly, not every universe in the society can be investigated, for then not enough information about any one of them is likely to be gained in a limited time and with limited resources. The decision must be pragmatic and must be based upon the program being promulgated. It may be, for example, that the program applies only to certain occupational groups or to a limited aspect of behavior, like health. Perhaps, then, the investigation can be *largely* confined to the relevant occupation and to behavior related to health. Note, however, the adverb *largely*, which would suggest that a pragmatic division is arbitrary and hence can be perilous, for the repercussion on other groups or on other behavior may turn out to be highly relevant. In a sense the educator must continually goad himself with the thought that the last scrap of information will never be in; that what he thinks he knows about the people and the society he knows most tentatively; and that therefore he must be ever ready to revise his notions of them and hence to alter the methods which he employs in contact with them. Such saintly open-mindedness should characterize leaders everywhere, but in a strange community the quality seems even more essential, since there the outside teacher, being a foreigner, cannot find within himself, as he often can at home, the psychological information that he needs.

# CHAPTER V

# World Literacy: Its Status and Problems

WILLIAM S. GRAY

Implicit in the discussions of this yearbook is the assumption that literacy is an essential aid in promoting individual and group welfare. It is conceived also as a ladder of intellectual and cultural mobility for all who have the ability and desire to move upward with the expanding concepts and activities of current life. In the discussion that follows, we shall first view recent progress in extending literacy and the size of the task still faced. The remainder of the chapter will consider selected problems involved in promoting literacy within the framework of community education. In the past, literacy has been defined as "the bare ability to read and write." As will be pointed out later, this conception has gradually expanded during recent years in harmony with the demand that the mastery of these arts should reach a functional level.

## Recent Literacy Developments

Although efforts to extend literacy began as soon as the arts of writing and reading developed, progress was very slow for thousands of years. Since about 1450, however, it has increased continuously but more rapidly at some periods than others. By 1910, illiteracy had been reduced to a relatively low level in most countries of western Europe, in the major part of North America, and in certain other areas. Encouraging efforts to extend literacy were also being made in an increasing number of countries in both the Orient and the Occident.

The close of World War I ushered in a period of greatly increased effort to extend literacy.[1] It was stimulated by radical political and economic developments which called for increased understanding

1. Karel Neijs, *Literacy Teaching for Adults*, p. 1. South Pacific Commission, Paper No. 72. Noumea, New Zealand: South Pacific Commission, 1954.

on the part of individuals and groups. As a result, national literacy campaigns were organized and carried on with unusual vigor. Those in Turkey, Russia, and China are notable examples. Many of the so-called literate countries also greatly increased their efforts to reduce illiteracy within their borders. In the United States, a National Advisory Committee on Illiteracy was appointed in 1929 with the approval of President Hoover. The Commission reviewed critically the materials and methods used in promoting literacy and recommended programs of action.[2]

Paralleling the foregoing developments, new approaches to literacy training were developed through work with groups which had previously been deprived of such opportunities. The pioneers of this movement included Jimmy Yen, who taught Chinese illiterates while they were in a strange country without means of communication during World War I; Frank Laubach, an American missionary, who began in the twenties to teach the Moros in the Philippines and has since directed literacy campaigns among almost three hundred groups who had previously had no experience with a written language; Lorenco Filho, who for many years directed literacy campaigns in Brazil among thousands who could neither read nor write; and Jaime Torres-Bodet, who promoted "the each-one-teach-one" literacy campaign among both children and adults in rural areas of Mexico.

The experiences of these and other inspired leaders showed clearly that people in most underdeveloped areas were in urgent need of help in solving both their personal and their group problems. Also, these early experiences led to the conclusion that any literacy program which merely develops ability to recognize words falls far short of an effective stimulus toward the attainment of personal and social goals. Moreover, they showed that it requires far more time to attain functional literacy than had previously been assumed, that the each-one-teach-one procedure was wholly inadequate in developing reading interests, attitudes, and skills to serviceable levels, and that there was an urgent need for better instructional programs,

2. William S. Gray, *Manual for Teachers of Adult Illiterates*. National Advisory Committee on Illiteracy, Bulletin No. 2. Washington: Department of Interior, 1930.

more abundant supplementary reading materials, and well-trained teachers.

At the close of World War II, the plight of millions of people in underdeveloped areas stood out in tragic relief. Intensive studies showed that they were not only illiterate but were also victims of poverty, superstition, malnutrition, endemic diseases, archaic methods of farming, lack of opportunity for self-government, and exploitation by nonresident landowners. They felt insecure, dissatisfied, and, in many cases, had developed hostile attitudes. They had learned during the war that better conditions existed elsewhere. They were eager to improve their conditions but lacked the necessary knowledge and skills.

In efforts to meet these needs, many plans developed, such as "Basic Education" in Thailand; "Mass Education" in Indonesia, China, and British Africa; "Social Education" in India; "Community Education" in the Philippines; and "Fundamental Education" in various parts of the world under the direction of UNESCO. Without doubt, the most spectacular efforts to promote literacy today are being made in connection with such programs.

## Extent of Illiteracy Today

If world literacy is to be attained, what is the size of the task faced? Fortunately, two recent UNESCO reports[3, 4] present data on which estimates can be based. Attention is directed first to the lack of schooling for children. The fact has long been recognized that the hope of a literate world in the future depends in part on the extent to which boys and girls of the current generation receive adequate schooling. The size of the task still faced in providing schools for all children was dramatically stated as follows on the basis of data available in 1955: "Of every 10 children in the world, 5 do not go to school. Of the 5 who go to school, 4 are in the primary school and one is receiving postprimary education."[5] It is true also that

3. UNESCO, *World Survey of Education: Handbook of Educational Organization and Statistics.* Paris, France: UNESCO, 1955.

4. UNESCO, *World Literacy at Mid-Century: A Statistical Study.* Monographs on Fundamental Education—XI. Paris, France: UNESCO, 1957.

5. William S. Gray, *The Teaching of Reading and Writing: An International Survey,* p. 29. Monographs on Fundamental Education—X. Paris, France: UNESCO, 1956. (Also Chicago: Scott, Foresman & Co.)

many of the primary schools include so few grades that the children
who attend make only limited progress toward functional literacy.
Table 1 presents a summary view of the extent of adult illiteracy
today. It focuses attention on the gross amount throughout the
world and its distribution among continents and their major areas.
The literacy status of specific countries is indicated in the UNESCO

TABLE 1

ESTIMATED POPULATION AND EXTENT OF ILLITERACY IN THE WORLD
AROUND 1950, BY CONTINENTS AND REGIONS[7]

| CONTINENT AND REGION | ESTIMATED POPULATION | | ESTIMATED EXTENT OF ILLITERACY | |
| --- | --- | --- | --- | --- |
| | Total (All Ages) (millions) | Adult (15 Years Old and Over) (millions) | Per Cent of Adult Illiteracy | Number of Adult Illiterates (millions) |
| World total. . . . . . . . . . . . . . . . . . . . . | 2,496 | 1,587 | 43–45 | 690–720 |
| Africa. . . . . . . . . . . . . . . . . . . . . . . . | 198 | 120 | 80–85 | 98–104 |
| Northern Africa. . . . . . . . . . . . . . . | 65 | 40 | 85–90 | 34– 36 |
| Tropical and Southern Africa. . . . . | 134 | 80 | 80–85 | 64– 68 |
| America. . . . . . . . . . . . . . . . . . . . . . . | 330 | 223 | 20–21 | 45– 47 |
| Northern America. . . . . . . . . . . . . | 168 | 126 | 3– 4 | 4– 5 |
| Middle America. . . . . . . . . . . . . . . | 51 | 30 | 40–42 | 12– 13 |
| South America. . . . . . . . . . . . . . . . | 111 | 67 | 42–44 | 28– 29 |
| Asia. . . . . . . . . . . . . . . . . . . . . . . . . | 1,376 | 830 | 60–65 | 510–540 |
| South West Asia. . . . . . . . . . . . . . | 62 | 37 | 75–80 | 28– 30 |
| South Central Asia. . . . . . . . . . . . | 466 | 287 | 80–85 | 230–240 |
| South East Asia. . . . . . . . . . . . . . . | 171 | 102 | 65–70 | 68– 72 |
| East Asia. . . . . . . . . . . . . . . . . . . . | 677 | 404 | 45–50 | 180–200 |
| Europe. . . . . . . . . . . . . . . . . . . . . . . | 393 | 293 | 7– 9 | 22– 25 |
| Northern and Western Europe. . . . | 133 | 102 | 1– 2 | 1– 2 |
| Central Europe. . . . . . . . . . . . . . . | 128 | 96 | 2– 3 | 2– 3 |
| Southern Europe. . . . . . . . . . . . . . | 131 | 95 | 20–21 | 19– 20 |
| Oceania. . . . . . . . . . . . . . . . . . . . . . | 13 | 9 | 10–11 | 1 |
| U.S.S.R. . . . . . . . . . . . . . . . . . . . . . | 186 | 112 | 5–10 | 6– 11 |

report. Unfortunately, the data on which the estimates were based
are not altogether comparable because various standards were used
by different countries in making literacy surveys. The literacy tests
used varied all the way from answering such questions as, "Can you
read and write?" to the reading of a short passage for its meaning
and the writing of a brief letter.

On the basis of the entries in the table, from 43 to 45 per cent of
the world's population fifteen years old or more, are illiterate. This

7. *Ibid.*, p. 15.

is somewhat lower than previous estimates, due either to rapid progress in eliminating illiteracy or to greater accuracy and inclusiveness
of recent studies. In summarizing the data in the table, its compilers
reported that "about 75 per cent of the world's illiterate population
live in Asia, some 14 to 15 per cent in Africa, about 6.5 per cent in
the Americas, and the remaining 4 to 5 per cent in Europe, Oceania,
and the U.S.S.R."[6]

As indicated by the foregoing estimates, elementary-school facilities are needed for at least one-half the children of the world, and literacy programs for an equal proportion of the adults. In addition,
provision should be made for millions of young people and adults
who at some time learned to read and write but are not as yet functionally literate. A conservative estimate indicates that from 60 to
65 per cent of the adult population of the world is in need of literacy
training.

## Role of Literacy in Community Education

In the effort to meet the basic needs of individuals and groups,
widely different views have been advanced concerning the role of
literacy in community education. At one extreme is the traditional
view that the ability to read and write is an indispensable aid in promoting individual and group welfare. At the opposite extreme is the
view that literacy training has little, if any, place in meeting the fundamental needs of adults in underdeveloped areas. A third view assumes that efforts to meet the personal and social problems of a
group and the spread of literacy are intimately related and that each
can be achieved best through co-ordinated effort. It is claimed, for
example, that many compelling motives for learning to read and
write arise as other steps are taken to solve personal or group problems. As the skills of literacy are acquired, they are applied eagerly
in achieving goals to which the learners attach great significance.
According to this view, community development is the broader undertaking within which literacy training is provided as an essential
means.

The next question faced relates to ways in which literacy aids in

6. UNESCO, *World Literacy at Mid-Century, op. cit.,* p. 16.

achieving the goals of community education. A review of reports from many parts of the world justifies two significant conclusions. The first is that the initial purposes served by literacy vary widely among both individuals and groups; for example, to keep in touch with members of one's family, to learn how to raise better crops, or to read religious literature. The second is that, as individuals rise in the scale of literacy, its values increase rapidly, varying in nature with the conditions faced by groups and with the interests and intelligence of individuals. Many discussions of the major purposes served by the ability to read or write appear in the literature. The outline that follows includes purposes or values that were emphasized most often in a world-wide study[8] of reasons for wanting to attain literacy among groups engaged in programs of community education.

To meet the practical needs of daily living such as being alerted to danger, finding one's way about, keeping posted on current events, keeping in touch with relatives and friends.

To improve health, promote good sanitation, improve child care, raise better crops, increase economic status, and learn how to do and make things.

To promote a growing understanding of one's physical and social environment, the personal and group problems faced, the issues involved, possible solutions.

To develop an understanding of local traditions, institutions, and prevailing practices.

To cultivate the attitudes and ideals that make for worthy membership in a family, community, nation.

To increase understanding of other places, countries, people, times.

To deepen interest on the part of students in their expanding world.

To broaden their cultural background and to enrich life through a growing acquaintance with the group's literary heritage.

To help satisfy religious aspirations through the reading of sacred literature.

To (secure) enjoyment and pleasure.

Although the foregoing list is incomplete, it shows clearly that ability to read and write may open up almost unlimited opportunities for individual development and group progress, assuming that appropriate reading materials in sufficient quantity are available.

8. William S. Gray, *The Teaching of Reading and Writing, op. cit.,* pp. 151–52.

## Levels of Literacy

Thus far no general agreement has been reached concerning the level of literacy essential to achieve the goals sought through community education. In early efforts to extend literacy, "minimum standards" were adopted as an aid in encouraging enrolment and because extended programs of training were not then possible. In the course of time, however, the concept of "functional literacy" was accepted and defined as the ability to use reading and writing in meeting the practical needs of daily life. But the level of competence essential required more explicit definition.

One proposal assumed that a person is functionally literate who is able to read and write as well as children who have had four full years of schooling. Whereas this proposal represented a distinct step forward, it did not provide the level of competence needed by many groups, such as members of the armed forces. Furthermore, it did not enable adults to secure without great effort the information, pleasures, and rewards that are normally expected through reading. As a result, many who had attained the proposed standard did very little, if any, reading and writing, and the skills which they had acquired disintegrated through disuse. Again, when applied universally it was assumed that the standard was equally appropriate for all groups and cultures. Experience shows clearly, however, that the level of literacy needed must be adjusted to the varying needs, aspirations, and cultural patterns of the group served.

In harmony with this view, it has been proposed that "a person is functionally literate when he has acquired the knowledge and skills in reading and writing that enable him to engage effectively in all those activities in which literacy is normally assumed in his culture or group."[9] According to this proposal, it becomes the responsibility of those directing literacy training in specific areas to determine experimentally both the level of competence needed and the length of the basic training programs. In doing so, the procedure adopted by Flores[10] in determining the level of literacy for good citizenship in

9. *Ibid.*, p. 24.

10. Gerardo Flores, "A Study on Functional Literacy for Citizenship in the Philippines," *Fundamental and Adult Education*, II (July, 1950), 24-29.

the Philippines is suggestive. He assumed that a good citizen should be able to read with understanding such materials as newspapers, bulletins, advertisements, tax notices, and letters, and to write an ordinary letter. Through the use of carefully planned tests given both to school children and adults, he found that the equivalent of six years of schooling was essential to insure satisfactory attainment on the part of at least three-fourths of the trainees.

## For Whom Should Literacy Training Be Provided?

Implicit in the facts presented in chapter i are certain principles which may serve as helpful guides in determining to whom literacy training should be given. For example, as long as ability to read and write is not essential to personal welfare and effective group participation in a given culture, universal literacy is not imperative. In such areas it may be provided only for leaders and for those who aspire to literacy. But when a culture adopts new patterns of living and faces common problems that can be solved best through the aid of reading and writing, literacy becomes more or less imperative on the part of all its members. In such cases, every effort should be made to stimulate keen interest on the part of all adults, excepting possibly those with serious handicaps, in enroling in literacy classes. Even in the case of the least competent, it may be necessary for their own safety and welfare to teach them to read and write their own names and to read such signs as "stop" and "go," the names of streets and buildings, and house numbers. Successful techniques have been developed for conducting literacy campaigns in both urban and rural communities.[11] Description of recent campaigns in northern Nigeria, Spain, Uruguay, India, and Morocco appear in a recent issue of *Fundamental and Adult Education*.[12] One of the impressive lessons taught by past efforts to extend literacy is that short-term campaigns, which provide no systematic follow-up activities or are unrelated to other educational efforts of a community, are usually ineffective in establishing functional literacy.

11. Frank C. and Robert S. Laubach, *How To Make the World Literate*, chaps. vi, vii, and viii. Syracuse 10, New York: Robert C. Laubach, School of Journalism, Syracuse University, 1957 (private distribution). Also, Karel Neijs, *op. cit.*, pp. 51-58.
12. *Fundamental and Adult Education*, Vol. X (January, 1958).

## Directing Agency and Staff

If literacy is conceived as an aid in achieving the purposes of community education, those responsible for literacy training should work in close co-operation with the directing agency, be it a community-education team or some other group. In the early history of this movement a member of the community-education team assumed the responsibility of conducting literacy classes. This plan was effective if he was adequately prepared to do so. As the demand for literacy training increased, it became evident that an inspired literacy officer who had vision and technical insight was needed to organize and direct literacy programs.

In an effort to determine the nature and scope of the staff needed, an experimental study was made by those in charge of the UNESCO Group Training Scheme for Fundamental Education, Mysore, India.[13] As a result, the following teams were organized which worked under the direction of the central administrative agency: the "basic survey and evaluation" team which made an initial study of needs and conditions and evaluated the progress of the literacy program and the results achieved; the "audio-visual" team which studied the use of such aids in arousing interest, in providing adults with needed information, and in increasing the efficiency of teaching; and the "literacy" team which prepared literacy materials, secured and trained teachers, and set up literacy classes. Reports from other centers emphasize the need also for supervisors, specialists in preparing adult reading materials, and staff members qualified to do needed research. As indicated earlier, the literacy training given should be tied in with the broader adult-education programs that aim to promote alert, productive, civic-conscious, and healthy citizens.

The importance of keeping the literacy organization as simple as possible has been emphasized repeatedly by different leaders. On the basis of wide experience, Karel Neijs concluded that the basic principle[14] involved assumes "careful planning for the utmost effect within the limits of the existing possibilities and means." He main-

13. J. B. Bowers, "The UNESCO Group Training Scheme for Fundamental Education (Mysore)," *Fundamental and Adult Education*, VII (January, 1955), 27–31.

14. Karel Neijs, *op. cit.*, p. 50.

tained also that the program should be effectively "adjusted" to the "social environment," "economic circumstances and possibilities," and "psychological conditions and demands"; properly correlated "with the existing organizations and plans for educational and socio-economic work"; and should utilize "the best possible scheme of handling finance and staff resources." The various organizational problems involved in observing the foregoing principles are discussed at length in Neijs' reports.

## Relation of Literacy Programs to Public Education

In early efforts to promote literacy as a part of fundamental education, attention was focused chiefly on the needs of adults. Very soon, however, children began to attend literacy classes because they, too, wanted to learn to read and write. In time experience showed that the teaching procedures most appropriate for adults were ill-adapted to the needs and modes of learning of children. Accordingly, special classes for children were organized which made use of activities, materials, and methods better adapted to their background, age, and learning ability. A foundation was thus established for the development of a school system which prepares children and youth to fall into step with the expanding cultural pattern.

Inherent in this conception were so many promising implications that it was adopted by many countries which were either developing or expanding primary or elementary schools. As stated in the *1950 Yearbook of the Philippine Association of School Superintendents*, the activities of the school "go far beyond the limits of the school compound and reach the homes, the occupations, the leisure activities of the people, and all the other aspects of social living. Its subject matter is not the books but the life which the children and adults live."[15] The basic principles that have guided the efforts to develop effective community schools were summarized as follows in a recent report by the Bureau of Public Schools in the Philippines: "(1) adherence to democratic principles and processes; (2) utilization of native mores, traditions, cultures and the corresponding approach to community needs and problems from the grass-root level; (3) the

15. "Education in Rural Areas for Better Living," *1950 Yearbook of the Philippine Association of School Superintendents,* pp. 21–22. Manila: Bookman, Inc., 1954.

concept that the community school program is designed mainly for the furtherance of the common welfare; (4) active participation of the community, the school, other governmental entities and lay organizations in the pursuit of local as well as national objectives; (5) a better understanding of the function of the school through the actual participation of adults in its activities; and (6) development and enrichment of the curriculum by the effective utilization of resources, needs, and problems of the community as well as those of the nation and the world."[16]

Within the farmework of such principles, the specific program and procedures vary widely in different countries and territories.[17] As effort is made to teach children to read and write, use is made of materials that meet three important requirements: They must appeal strongly to the interests and motives of children; they must facilitate progress in developing essential attitudes and skills; and they must provide the understandings needed to enable children to acquire status and participate effectively in the life of the group.

In developing both the literacy program and the school system of a community, it is not enough to provide merely for the literacy level essential on the part of all of its members. In addition, provision should be made to prepare capable individuals to fulfil broader functions than those expected of the group as a whole. The need is urgent, for example, for civic leaders and for specialists in such fields as health, agriculture, teaching. Of large significance also are opportunities for intellectual and cultural mobility to any level to which individuals may rightly aspire. In many countries such provisions are made through the adult divisions of public school systems, YMCA's, and other educational agencies. In less well-developed areas, literacy programs must often be sufficiently extended to enable young people and adults to secure admission to institutions at home or abroad which supply the educational opportunities they need.

16. *The Community Schools of the Philippines*, pp. 21–22. Manila: Republic of the Philippines, Department of Public Education, Bureau of Public Schools, 1954.

17. Victor Montoya Medinacely, "The Teacher's Function in Community Work, Bolivia," *Fundamental and Adult Education*, IX (April, 1957), 85–89.

## World-wide Similarity in Basic Reading Processes

Anyone who studies the problems of literacy on a world-wide basis is immediately impressed with the fact that languages differ widely in form and culture. Questions arise, therefore, concerning the extent to which the basic processes involved in reading, and the related attitudes and skills, are similar or different. It has often been assumed that they differ so widely that there are few, if any, common guides to literacy instruction. As a result of early eye-movement studies of reading, evidence was secured which challenged the validity of this assumption. It seemed advisable, therefore, to investigate the problem further as a part of a recent world-wide study of the teaching of reading and writing by UNESCO.[18]

Accordingly, eye-movement records were secured from mature readers of fourteen different languages, each of whom read the same passages which had been translated and printed in their respective languages. The languages involved were so selected that they included most of the variations in the form and structure of the written languages in current use. It may be assumed, therefore, that the findings are universally applicable.

Observation made while the adults were reading, and answers to questions relating to what they read, indicated clearly that all of them read with their minds intent on meaning. Analyses of the eye-movement records showed that a mature reader of any language follows the lines in a series of alternate movements and pauses. He recognizes words quickly and accurately at each fixation, often in units of two or more. At times he makes a regressive or backward movement to scrutinize an unfamiliar word more thoroughly, or to verify or secure a clearer grasp of meaning. Otherwise he proceeds rapidly and rhythmically along the lines, making accurate return sweeps from the end of one line to the beginning of the next. These findings supply clear evidence that the basic perceptual processes involved in reading are similar for all languages independent of differences in their written form and structure.

But reading involves far more than the fluent, accurate perception of words. It is equally essential that young people and adults under-

18. William S. Gray, *The Teaching of Reading and Writing, op. cit.,* chap. iii.

stand and interpret what they read. The next step, therefore, in comparing the processes involved in reading was to identify the needs and purposes for reading in different cultures and the interpretive skills needed. To this end reports were secured from groups in many areas of the world where programs of fundamental education were in progress. Space will permit only a very few examples.

A group of natives in South Africa stated that they read to observe danger signals on the highways and at work, to locate streets and buildings, to follow directions, to keep in touch with members of their families when away from home at work, to keep up with the news, and to read little books on "how-to-do-it," healthful living, best foods to eat, and better ways of farming. In addition, reports from Thailand indicated that adults read to learn how to do their work better, to conduct their businesses more effectively, to keep in touch with developments in their country, and to find valid answers to personal and social problems. In reports from India special emphasis was given to the fact that all people must learn to read thoughtfully and critically if they are to be good citizens and help build a democracy adapted to their culture.

A study was made of the steps essential in achieving these and many other purposes. The findings are very illuminating and convincing. They showed that if literacy training is to help the individuals of any culture meet their keenly-felt needs, it must promote the development of the following attitudes and skills: a thoughtful reading attitude; a clear grasp of the meaning of the passages read; thoughtful reaction to the ideas apprehended and the fusion of these ideas with previous experiences. This last step is the heart of the learning act in reading. It enables the reader to correct wrong impressions and to acquire new or clearer understandings, rational attitudes, and improved thought and behavior patterns. Of special significance is the fact that all of these attitudes and skills are essential at all literacy levels. Furthermore, if reading is to function regularly and effectively in the lives of young people and adults, they must acquire the disposition to use reading in securing needed information and in solving personal and social problems.

Unfortunately, most of the literacy training in the past has carried the reader only to the threshold of the values inherent in reading. This has been due, in part, to the limited amount of training given but more largely to the almost exclusive emphasis on word recognition.

## Basic Problems in Teaching Adults To Read

As revealed by the foregoing findings, reading should be conceived primarily as a quest for meaning. In planning instruction and in teaching adults to read, the following aims should be emphasized:

To stimulate compelling motives for learning to read.
To cultivate a thoughtful reading attitude.
To develop accuracy and independence in word recognition.
To promote ability to secure a clear understanding of what is read.
To cultivate the habit of reacting thoughtfully to the ideas apprehended.
To make use of the ideas acquired in clarifying thinking, in acquiring rational attitudes, and in solving personal and group problems.
To increase speed of reading for meaning.
To promote ability to read aloud to others.
To broaden reading interests and to establish the habit of personal reading.

In efforts to achieve these goals, the instruction should be adapted to the characteristics of adults as learners. Many of the adjustments essential have been discussed at length by Neijs.[19] Among the points emphasized are the fact that adults are mature in respect to motivations, experience, will power, and ability to reason. They possess shrewdness and common sense, are usually "word mature," and possess a "practical command of language." They have fixed habits and established ways of viewing life. As learners, they are extremely sensitive and often preoccupied and tired. They resist knowledge which has no meaning to them and resent instruction which follows the pattern and technique used in teaching children. To be most successful, a teacher should study the characteristics of his group and adjust teaching procedures to them.

During recent years the value of the use of audio-visual aids in teaching adults has been repeatedly demonstrated. The use of posters, pictures, objects, and demonstrations are very helpful in presenting new ideas. Filmstrips are now used effectively in presenting and mastering new words. They are used also in presenting background information, in providing a single focus of attention in teaching, and in presenting various types of practice exercises. The

19. Karel Neijs, *op. cit.*, pp. 7–15.

radio is also being used in directing literacy classes. In Colombia, South America, for example, guidance in learning to read and write has been provided through simultaneous broadcasts to groups of adults in "Radio Schools." Furthermore, television is now being used in promoting adult reading skills.[20] A series of experiments in the use of television as an aid in directing learning activities among adults has been in progress in Memphis, Tennessee, in which reading materials and techniques prepared by Frank C. Laubach have been used. These experiments have been made possible through the co-operation of the Literacy Department of WKNO-TV, Channel 10, and through grants-in-aid by the Memphis Section of the National Council of Jewish Women.

## Organization of Literacy Instruction

In the past a single literacy course of about 24 lessons and lasting for about three months was usually provided. Experience has shown clearly that such courses are far from adequate in developing functional literacy. As a result, literacy programs are now being greatly extended and divided into a series of successive units or courses. A practical advantage of a relatively short beginning course is that many adults can be induced to enrol who otherwise might hesitate to register for a long period of training. The attractiveness of a beginning course is also greatly increased if it aims to achieve quickly certain relatively simple goals which illiterate adults prize highly.

Further help in dividing a literacy program into a series of closely co-ordinated courses is secured from wide experience in teaching illiterates and from the results of research. They show that both children and adults pass through similar stages in learning to read. For example, those who make satisfactory progress acquire early a thoughtful reading attitude, a sight vocabulary of words used most frequently in simple reading materials, ability to understand, interpret, and make use of the ideas read, and word-attack skills that are learned through the study of the simple vocabulary used.

With the foregoing attitudes and skills as a background, rapid progress is made next in developing the attitudes and skills needed to read accurately, independently, and thoughtfully any materials

20. Edmund N. Fulker, "Using TV To Improve Adult Reading Skills," *Adult Leadership*, VI (October, 1957), 113–14.

expressed in the language of everyday usage. In this connection, much emphasis is given to the further development of word-attack skills and the stimulation of independent reading. During a further period of training, adults acquire ability to read and interpret more difficult types of material essential in meeting personal and group needs within the culture and that contribute to a full, well-rounded life.

Reports from teachers in many parts of the world indicate that some adults are not prepared to learn with reasonable ease and rapidity when they enrol for literacy training. For example, many adults in remote communities have never discovered that printed or written words represent meanings. Other adults have limited oral vocabularies, do not express themselves well, possess a narrow background, and are hesitant to participate in group activities. To overcome these and many other personal limitations and handicaps in learning to read and to write, preliminary training and experience are provided before formal instruction in reading and handwriting begins. If the learning experiences are carefully selected and adjusted to individual needs, many adults make rapid progress in learning to read who might otherwise fail.

On the basis of the evidence now available, a literacy program may be organized in terms of the following stages or periods with respect to reading:

Stage    I—Preparing for reading

Stage    II—Establishing initial reading interests, attitudes, and skills

Stage    III—Promoting rapid progress in ability to read any material within the range of familiar experiences and the everyday vocabulary of the group

Stage    IV—Developing competence in ability to read all the kinds of material and for the various purposes normally expected of literate members of a culture

Examples of literacy programs organized on this basis are described in a recent UNESCO report[21] and in a bulletin describing a reading program in India.[22] Training in handwriting is co-ordinated with the

21. William S. Gray, *The Teaching of Reading and Writing, op. cit.*, chaps. vii–ix.

22. *Literacy Teachers' Guide*, UNESCO Group Training Scheme for Fundamental Education, Yelwal, Mysore, India, 1955.

various stages in the reading program. The length of each stage and many of the details of training provided vary with the characteristics and conditions faced in given communities and with the needs of groups and of individuals.

## Methods of Teaching Adults To Read

Of the various problems faced in organizing literacy programs, none has been more widely and vigorously discussed than the specific methods to use in teaching adults to read. In order to secure needed insight concerning the best procedure to adopt, UNESCO[23] made provision in 1952 for a study involving three steps: to identify the methods used today throughout the world; to evaluate them in the light of all the evidence available; and to prepare suggestions for teaching reading in the light of the conclusions reached. As a result of the first step, hundreds of methods were identified which varied significantly from each other. An analysis of their basic characteristics showed that they belonged to one of two general types; those which focused attention at the beginning on letters and their sounds as aids to word recognition; and those which made use from the beginning of words or larger language units and focused attention chiefly on the meaning of what was read.

As the two approaches were studied in historical perspective, it was found that each of them had been modified at times in order to eliminate criticisms or to improve their efficiency. Of large significance is the fact that each has gradually assumed some of the characteristics of the other. Thus, "phonic methods" have made increasing use of words to introduce the sounds of letters and "word and sentence methods" have directed attention much earlier than formerly to word elements and their sounds. These trends suggested that elements of the two contrasting methods are essential in an effective approach to reading.

In an effort to secure added insight, a comparison was made of the results of all experimental studies that could be found of the merits of different methods of teaching beginning reading. A total of more than fifty different experiments carried on in several countries were identified. The data were analyzed and the initial findings submitted

23. William S. Gray, *The Teaching of Reading and Writing, op. cit.*, chaps. v–vi.

for criticism to specialists in reading in many different countries. The final conclusions follow: (*a*) Because most of the methods in current use have not been compared experimentally with other methods, final conclusions cannot be drawn as yet on the basis of objective evidence concerning their relative merits. (*b*) The use of a given method is not equally effective among all members of a given group. This implies that there are factors other than the method used that influence progress in learning to read. (*c*) Contrasting methods, such as those which begin with major emphasis on phonics and those which focus attention primarily on meaning, promote the development of different types of attitudes and skills. (*d*) Progress in reading is most satisfactory when both meaning and word-recognition skills are emphasized from the beginning.

The foregoing findings imply that the methods used in teaching adults to read should promote the development of all the attitudes and skills needed in efficient reading. To this end the content of early reading lessons should relate to things and activities of great interest to the learner. The pictures and verbal text must be so organized that they stimulate purposeful reading. Until students have made considerable progress, teachers should promote through the use of guiding questions the thoughtful reading of sentences or longer units. The first reading of a lesson should be followed by rereading and discussion that promote broader interpretations, thoughtful reaction to the ideas read, and a clear recognition of their significance and use.

Paralleling the foregoing steps, vigorous effort should be made to promote the skills of word recognition. This involves sufficient rereading and practice to insure instant recognition of all the words of high functional value used in the early reading lessons. Equally important is training in the auditory and visual discrimination of words and the gradual mastery of various aids to word recognition, such as meaning clues, word-form clues, structural analyses, and phonics. Because of wide variations in the form and structure of words, specialists in each country should identify the specific procedures which are most effective. As adults gain competence in recognizing words independently, the useful words should be read and reread in context until they can be recognized without conscious effort. Experience shows clearly that we interpret best, not when we are struggling to identify words, but when we recognize them instantly at sight. The good reader is also well equipped to attack words independently whenever the need arises.

## Learning through Reading

If literacy is to serve as an effective aid in achieving the goals of community education, the training given should insure growth through reading as well as promote skill in reading. This means that much of the material read in literacy classes should aim to enrich the experiences of readers, cultivate new interests, and provide needed information, such as how to raise better crops, to avoid disease, to select and prepare food better, to rear children more effectively, and to improve the sanitation of the community. In addition, for example, varied types of materials are essential to meet the needs of specific groups; passages of sacred literature for groups taught by missionaries; versions of religious poems for groups in India; historical accounts of great leaders for groups in South America; the history and traditions of the culture or country to which a group belongs; and descriptions of people in other lands and their way of life. The nature and scope of the various types of material needed are discussed more fully in chapter xi of this yearbook.

As informational materials are read by a group, many types of guidance are essential. Of primary importance is the arousal of interest in the new materials presented, the recall of related experiences, and the introduction of new items of information that will enable the students to understand the passages to be read. If new words and concepts are introduced in the lesson, they should be used in the preliminary discussion until their meaning and significance are clear. Experience shows that it is also helpful to write these new words on a blackboard or felt board, thus providing an initial acquaintance with their form. If familiar words are used with new or unusual meanings, the latter should be made clear. Before the discussion ends, the class should be asked to suggest the types of information and the answers to questions they would like to secure as they read.

When the foregoing steps have been taken, most members of a class are prepared to adopt an inquiring attitude as they read and to seek for a solution of the problem raised. A first reading should result in a reasonably clear grasp of the new items of information presented. Whether or not further help is needed in understanding what is read can be determined through discussion and answers to questions. The next step is to consider the new ideas acquired in the light of the needs and problems faced by individual readers or by the community. Stimulated by questions from the teacher, the members of the class should reflect on the significance of the various ideas read, discover important relationships among them, and consider carefully their value and implications.

Finally, they should face pointedly such questions as the following: What new ideas have we learned today? What answers do they provide to our problem? What new ways of doing our work or carrying on community activities do they suggest? Through such guidance new literates gradually acquire the attitudes and modes of thinking essential for continued growth through reading.

## Supplementary and Follow-up Reading

From the very beginning of a literacy program, provision should be made for stimulating interest in independent reading. To this end a good teacher places pictures on the walls with labels attached and provides interesting picture books, comic strips, and copies of newspapers for the reading table. During each class period he refers to them and stimulates curiosity concerning their content. He also reserves time for looking at the newspaper in class and guides the students in securing ideas from the pictures, advertisements, the weather report and headlines, and, ultimately, from the simpler news items.

As adults acquire a vocabulary of one hundred or more words, simple sentences, news items, and stories should be prepared within the range of the known reading vocabulary, duplicated and distributed for home reading. As growth in ability to read continues, simple books which inform and entertain should be available for independent reading. Two values of great importance attach to such reading. It provides repeated contacts with the vocabulary introduced in the primers and readers; this is essential in promoting instant recognition of words and fluent reading habits. It also starts young people and adults on lifelong habits of personal reading.

Of great importance also is the need of a wide variety of material which can be read independently after the period of formal instruction is over. Much of the literacy training in the past has been ineffective because the new literate had little or nothing to read. As a result, the reading skills developed soon disintegrated through disuse. It is imperative, therefore, that provision be made in each community for reading materials adapted to the levels of reading ability, interests, and needs of its literate members. Some of the materials provided should supply needed information and help solve the individual and group problems faced. Equally important are materials that entertain, that acquaint the reader with the history of his group and his cultural heritage, that aid him in his search for values, and that satisfy his spirtual needs. Next to lack of an adequate supply of reading materials in a follow-up campaign is failure to provide reasonable balance in the types provided. The nature and scope of the essential reading materials are further discussed by Dale in the chapter on "Reading Materials."

## The Teaching of Handwriting

Reports from many countries indicate that most adults who are illiterate are as eager to learn to write as to read. Although many of the purposes for writing are common the world over, they also vary widely among cultures and individuals. Before attempting to teach handwriting to any group, a careful study should be made of the chief purposes that handwriting serves in the community and the motives that prompt specific individuals to want to learn to write.

A survey of literacy programs reveals the following common aims in teaching adults to write: to deepen interest in learning to write well; to develop the skills involved in writing clearly, legibly, and with reasonable speed; to guide adults in the use of handwriting until it serves effectively their practical needs in daily life; and to promote interest in a high level of attainment in handwriting. The training given should parallel and be closely integrated with the activities involved in learning to read. This is due to the fact that the processes of symbol recognition and symbol writing reinforce each other. Furthermore, the need for both reading and writing arises early in the efforts of a group to achieve the goals of community education.

The essential tasks in teaching handwriting are co-ordinated with the stages of a sequential, carefully planned reading program out-

lined earlier. During the reading-readiness period the teacher becomes acquainted with the characteristics and writing needs of students and introduces a few simple motivating activities, such as writing one's name. During the initial period in learning to read, the basic
skills of handwriting are introduced as adults seek to achieve a cov-
eted goal, such as ability to write a friendly letter. During stage
three, these skills are further refined as training is provided in the
use of handwriting in meeting practical needs, such as writing other
types of letters, filling out forms, keeping records. During stage
four, any further training needed by individuals in quality and speed
of writing is closely associated with efforts to engage in more ambitious writing projects, such as preparing minutes of meetings or a
brief history of one's community. The basic principles involved and
the problems faced in organizing handwriting courses and teaching
adult illiterates to write are discussed at length by Gray, [24] Neijs,[25]
and others.[26]

## Measurement of Literacy Competence

Only limited progress has been made thus far in developing instruments for measuring progress among adults in learning to read and
write. As long as "minimum standards" of literacy prevailed, the
learner's competence was usually measured by noting the accuracy
with which he read passages from the primer used and by his ability
to write his name or one or more simple sentences. As the concept of
functional literacy developed, more exacting measures were adopted,
for example: (a) "Reading with understanding a passage in the vernacular." It "should be self-contained, so that it conveys a complete
meaning. The subject matter of the passage should be within the
understanding and experience of the candidate. The language should
be in the idiom familiar to the candidate . . ." (b) "Writing a letter
to a specific person containing specific information." It "must be
framed in the customary form, contain the sender's address, and his
personal signature. An envelope should be prepared according to the

24. William S. Gray, *The Teaching of Reading and Writing, op. cit.,* chaps.
ix–xi.

25. Karel Neijs, *op. cit.,* chap. v.

26. *UNESCO Group Training Scheme for Fundamental Education, op. cit.,*
chap. ii.

accepted method and inscribed in such a way that the addressee is sure to receive it."[27]

During the last decade several efforts have been made to develop objective tests for use in the placement of adults in literacy classes[28] and for measuring their attainments and needs in reading.[29] As a result of these and related efforts, certain guiding principles have emerged: (*a*) Instruments and techniques for placing adults in literacy classes, for measuring their progress and needs in acquiring literacy, and for evaluating the effectiveness of existing literacy programs are greatly needed. (*b*) The minimum level of attainment in each culture is that required for effective participation in all the activities normally expected of its literate adults. (*c*) The tests used should place primary emphasis on a clear understanding and interpretation of what is read and on the functional use of handwriting. (*d*) The test exercises in each essential aspect of reading and handwriting should represent a continuum from the simplest level to that beyond the prescribed level of functional literacy. Such measures are needed in following the progress and needs of adults from one stage to the next.

Several sources of help are now available as guides in further efforts to develop needed tests. Examples of reading tests, a list of reading tests for children in various countries, and measures of progress in learning to write have been listed by Gray.[30] Of major importance is the effort of UNESCO to provide help and guidance in this field. A recent article[31] presents generalizations based on a series of surveys and studies. Among other items, it describes the work of Irving Lorge of Teachers College, Columbia University, who has

27. *Report of a Conference of Provincial Representatives To Discuss the Adult Literacy Campaign, Northern Nigeria,* June, 1950, p. 6. Nigeria: Zaria, Gaskiya Corporation, 1950.

28. *Reading Placement,* pp. 1–4 (*Home and Family Life* series). Project for Literacy Education under the Sponsorship of the Federal Security Agency, Office of Education. Washington: Educator's Washington Dispatch, 1949.

29. *Adult Reading Test,* Forms 1 and 2. New York: Institute of Educational Research, Teachers College, Columbia University.

30. William S. Gray, *The Teaching of Reading and Writing, op.cit.,* pp. 179–87, 201–8.

31. "The Defintiion and Measurement of Literacy," *Fundamental and Adult Education,* IX (January, 1957), 3–8.

co-operated with UNESCO in the study of techniques for measuring literacy. He has recently completed a report entitled *Literacy Testing*. It considers the basic problems involved in measuring literacy, presents examples of literacy tests, discusses what is to be tested, and considers procedures in constructing and standardizing such tests. As soon as published it will be the best guide available to those working in this field.

Although tests to determine the attainments and needs of adults are essential in a sound literacy program, other types of evidence are also needed. For example, teachers should seek constantly for evidence of growth in favorable attitudes toward reading, in interest in and the kind and amount of personal reading done by individuals, in the use of reading and writing in meeting daily needs, and in growth through reading in the interests, understandings, and patterns of behavior essential in achieving the purposes of fundamental education. On the basis of all the evidence secured, teachers and administrators can determine not only the progress and needs of individuals but can also identify elements of strength and weakness in current literacy programs. Through the use of such procedures, literacy programs can be continuously and progressively improved.

### REFERENCES

AHMED, MUSHTAG. *A Survey of Reading Materials for Neo-literates in India.* Research, Training, and Production Centre, Series No. 27, Jamia Millia. Delhi, India: Jamianagar-Indian Adult Education Association (30 Fiaz Bazar).

GUDSCHINSKY, SARAH. *Handbook of Literacy.* Summer Institute of Linguistics, University of Oklahoma, Norman, Oklahoma, 1953.

HOWES, H. W. *Fundamental Adult Literacy and Community Education in the West Indies. Educational Studies and Documents,* No. XV. Paris, France: Educational Clearing House, UNESCO (19 Kleber Avenue), 1955.

KIRLEW, MARJORIE. *The Literacy Project and Teachers Manual for the Literacy Project in Jamaica.* Kingston, Jamaica: Jamaica Social Welfare Commission (undated).

NEIJS, KAREL. *The Construction of Literacy Primers for Adults.* Noumea, New Caledonia: South Pacific Commission, 1954.

RODRIGUEZ, BOU ISMAEL. *Manual para la ensenanza de lectura y escritura a adultos analfabetos.* Rio Piedras, Puerto Rico: Universidad de Puerto Rico, 1953.

SHARMA, T. R. "Construction of a Hindi Handwriting Scale for Primary School Children," *Education and Psychology,* IV (January, 1957), 24-31.

SPAULDING, SETH (editor). *Communication through Educational Materials*. Rangoon, Burma: Burma Translation Society (37th and Merchant Sts.), May, 1955.
TRONCOSO, AUREA NIRA JIMENZ, *Illiteracy*. Patzcuaro, Michoacan, Mexico: Regional Fundamental Education Centre for Latin America, October, 1954.
UNESCO Education Clearing House. *Literary Teaching: A Selected Bibliography*. Educational Studies and Documents, No. XVIII. Paris, France: UNESCO (19 Kleber Avenue), 1956.
WALLIS, ETHEL E., and GATES, JANET B. *Outline for Primer Construction*. Glendale, California: Summer Institute of Linguistics, Inc. (Box 870), 1948.

# REPRESENTATIVE PROGRAMS

# CHAPTER VI

# The Grassroots Approach to Education for Community Improvement

PEDRO T. ORATA

## Narrowing the Gap between Educational and Social Progress

One of the paradoxes of our time is that education is not always the unmixed blessing that many people believe it to be. Under Spain for some four hundred years the Filipino people developed a profound distaste for labor with the hands, an attitude which has hindered very greatly the economic development of the Philippines.

During fifty years under the United States of America this attitude has persisted in spite of every effort to encourage vocational training. When Spain left the Philippines at the turn of the century, there were only a handful of schools, mostly secondary and higher. These were exclusively for the sons of the rulers and those of a few influential Filipino families. Now, one of every five inhabitants— men, women, and children—is in school, a ratio next to those of the United States and Hawaii. Literacy has gone up from 5 to nearly 70 per cent. If the standard of living actually varied as the opportunities for schooling and the advance in literacy among the Filipinos, as Frank Laubach and other pious believers in the miracles of literacy have often claimed, the Philippines would not today be classified as an "underdeveloped" area. But the fact remains that, in spite of the tremendous strides in education, the annual per capita income of the people is less than $150.00. The reason is not the lack of vocational and technical courses in colleges and universities.[1]

The fact is that the gap between educational and economic prog-

1. The enrolment in public and private schools in 1955 totaled 4,287,220, distributed as follows: Preschool, 9,051; elementary, 3,444,608; secondary (including vocational), 650,993; higher (including technical), 182,568. (Population, United Nations 1956 estimate: 21,849,000.)

ress is very wide. Where the school is modern, many of the homes are backward. The schools teach scientific methods to children, but many of the parents remain superstitious in the extreme. There is gardening in every elementary and high school, and there are agricultural schools and colleges in every province where modern methods of cultivation are taught; but over the fence next to the school and on the two million farms all over the country, primitive methods of agriculture are employed. The result is that, whereas Hawaii produces 258 piculs of sugar per hectare, Java 256, and Puerto Rico 117, the corresponding production in the Philippines is only 91 piculs. In rice, it is the same: Spain produces 141 cavans, Italy 120, and Formosa 62 cavans per hectare, but the average in the Philippines is 27 cavans. In corn, Canada produces 62.5 cavans and the United States 43.6 cavans per hectare, as compared with 12.4 cavans in the Philippines.

In hygiene and sanitation, in infant mortality, in life expectancy, a similar comparison may be made. In spite of advanced health instruction in the schools, the Philippines lag behind countries which are below average in educational facilities. Moreover, in most other areas of life in the Philippines practice is far behind theory. Instruction is very far ahead of practical application. The paradox is that, while the resources are rich and varied, they remain undeveloped or, still worse, they are often selfishly exploited. While there is much to be done, idleness is rampant. There are too many people trained for jobs that do not exist; or, to put it another way, there are far too many intellectuals where life calls for men able and willing to work.

It is to bridge over the chasm that exists between the community and its schools that the community school has been designed. Since 1949, the objectives of the public schools have been re-examined and reoriented in order to stress both the education of children and the improvement of standards of living; that is, to provide simultaneous education for children and adults. Correspondingly, the role of the teacher has been redefined in order to include, on one hand, teaching books, imparting information, and developing fundamental skills in reading, writing, and arithmetic, and, on the other hand, helping children and adults improve their ways of living. In these community schools the teacher performs a double role, namely, as teacher of children and as leader of adults. So far, the community-school approach has been fairly successful, but many problems remain to be solved: (*a*) how to relate subject matter and practical activities; (*b*) how to adapt field assignments to the age and developmental levels of the children; (*c*) how to avoid overemphasizing activities to the neglect of the fundamentals; (*d*) how to counteract the charge of exploitation of children.

To meet these problems, the curriculum of the community school has been divided into two interrelated parts: the school subjects, such as the three R's, the social studies, science, drawing, handicrafts, agriculture, home economics, and music, on one hand, and out-of-school activities, or extension work, on the other hand. In the 1957–58 revised curriculum for the elementary school, "work education" is one of the six subject areas, requiring 80 minutes a day; and in the high-school curriculum, "work experience" is required of everybody in the first two years in the amount of 4 out of 16 units, and 12 out of 34 units in the case of the students who elect the vocational course in the third and fourth years. At every level, methods of teaching are calculated to develop skills, impart useful information, inculcate attitudes, and provide a maximum carry-over from learning to living.

To illustrate what is meant by a community school and to provide specific examples of how principles, to be discussed later, are applied in practice, we shall now describe a few incidents. These will make clear the manner in which the features of the approach were applied. These were taken from the writer's notebook. Accordingly, the narration is presented in the first person.

## Examples of Community Improvement

### FROM MINUS TO PLUS

In many of the homes in towns and cities as well as in the villages, sanitary latrines are not used. In rural areas, people commonly use the backyard or the seashore as a latrine, and many families follow this practice rather than construct a latrine which cannot be flushed. When I was a boy I used to carry a shovel with me with which to dig a small hole in the ground and fill it in afterward. But one cannot do this in cities and other crowded places. Since then, a campaign has been going on for simple but sanitary latrines. Progress is being made, but the process is slow.

In my village of Bactad, the fences in front of the houses are well made and artistically designed, but the backyards are often filthy and unsightly. Many of them are dumping grounds for manure and other refuse and have been so for years.

We conceived of a positive measure, as is our way, to deal with such problems. We thought, first, of getting rid of the bushes near the bank of the canal which were regularly used as latrines by some of the villagers, and, secondly, of making fishponds on the ground where the bushes grew. One of us, a teacher, Segundino Obra, made the first fishpond. The next one was built by Mr. Reyes, the husband of another teacher. Then more fishponds were made, including three that were made by the family of my sister. We saw to it that every one of the families bordering the lots in question had their own fishponds, and we helped those that could not or did not have much inclination to do so to build one. The idea behind this help is really self-help. Everyone who has a fishpond in the place would be inclined to keep it clean.

### WAR ON LOOSE PIGS

It is commonplace that no food-production campaign can be successful if pigs, goats, and other animals are let loose to destroy crops, to scatter waste, to make filth, and to spread disease. In our town, as in most places, the municipal council from time immemorial has passed ordinances carrying penalties for those who let their animals run at large. Such an ordinance in due course becomes a dead letter, for reasons known to everybody. What happens usually is this: The mayor and the members of the council, as human beings, are influenced by human motives and incentives. They naturally do not want to offend the sensibilities of influential people who, regardless of ordinances, choose to let loose their pigs and use the town plaza and even schoolyards to pasture their goats and horses. One exception made invalidates the ordinance, the result being that nobody cares whether the ordinance exists at all.

In the villages, this is what happens. The rural policemen, who are supposed to enforce municipal ordinances, do not receive salaries from the government. At the end of each harvest season they go from house to house to ask for "donations" in rice and similar produce. If they are strict with law enforcement, most particularly the enforcement of the ordinance against loose pigs, the chances are that, since nearly everybody has one or more pigs, they will be told, "No mercy on pigs, no rice."

What are we doing in regard to this problem?

First, we tried this in Bactad, which we have since found successful. The Bactad elementary school appointed two squads of "special catchers of stray animals" among the larger boys, each squad supervised by a male teacher. I, myself, am a member of one of the squads. Segundino Obra, one of the teachers, is a member of the other squad. We receive our official appointment from the mayor of Urdaneta as "special catcher of stray animals," with the instruction to report to him from time to time "the results of operations."

Second, all the pupils of the school, from the first grade up, are "informants" and have to report stray animals to the particular squad assigned to their zone. When the squad receives the information from any of the four hundred pupils who act as "intelligence observers" for the whole village that a pig, goat, buffalo, or horse is found loose outside their own yard, they go to the spot, day or night, to catch the animal.

Third, the purpose of the project is education rather than to enforce law. When the offender appears to claim his animal, he is asked to read the ordinance, or the ordinance is read to him. He learns of the provisions of the ordinance, and he therefore begs to be given back his animal with the promise not to let it loose again. Before the squad allows him to take back his pig or goat, an inquiry is made as to why the animal was let loose in the first place. If it is found that the family cannot construct a pigpen because it lacks either the manpower or the material, or both, the squad volunteers to help them make the pigpen. The construction of the pigpen is then made a community project, to which the pupils and adults who wish to do so may contribute material and labor, in the sensible belief that it is more economical in the long run to contribute than to suffer the consequences of loose animals. So far, there has been no second offense, and the response has been most successful.

Fourth, the problem of loose animals is presented to all the grades. The pupils are made to see evidences of destruction of plants and property, of fences, fishponds, and similar establishments, and to calculate the approximate amount, in pesos and centavos, of the damage caused by stray animals. They are made aware of the impossibility of raising good home gardens if animals are allowed to destroy them. They are led to become indignant and to report the presence of loose animals anywhere in their vicinity.

Fifth, the owners of pigs, goats, and other animals are being educated to see the value of the waste from such animals through the making of compost fertilizers. This is yet a new idea, which may take time to penetrate the minds of the people, but it has possibilities which cannot be gainsaid. If and when the people begin to appreciate the value of waste products for their own vegetables and fruit trees, they will naturally want to keep their own animals at home so that they can add their waste to the compost pit in the backyard.

We have far to go in this direction, but it is reassuring to see other communities in Urdaneta following the lead of Bactad. The central school has already appointed eight squads of intermediate pupils under male teachers to catch stray animals in different parts of the district. Many pigs have already been caught. The menace to themselves and to the community of stray animals is explained to school children from the first grade up through observation outside and discussion inside the classroom. Opportunities for such instruction are regularly utilized in connection with social studies, arithmetic, reading and language, character education, health education, geography and spelling, and, of course, the national language. The children do not hesitate to report to the special catchers the presence of loose animals in their neighborhoods.

### FLOWING WATER

Clean, fresh water flows through road canals in one section of the village of Bactad. And what a joy to see the faces of men, women, and children who expressed delight and relief when they saw the water flow. For the first time everyone took to sprinkling the dusty street, and since then the large clouds of dust stirred up by the traffic no longer settle on the faces of the people or on plants and trees along the road. Vegetables and fruit trees have become more vigorous as a result of being watered daily. The stagnant pools that used to disfigure the street sides are no more; mosquitoes and flies are much fewer, fewer indeed than in the rest of the district and in other villages. If fire starts in any house, there is water ready to put it out, whereas previously the people had to depend upon wells which were not readily accessible. The day before we left Bactad to go to Manila, a fire started in a lot in front of my sister's house. It was promptly put out with the water from the canal.

Better sanitation, more effective fire protection, and greater food production are the results of the flowing water in Bactad, which has since been the subject of admiration and envy by people from other towns and villages who passed through or visited Bactad. Last week I visited the village of Bantug, in Asingan in this province, and there, too, was flowing water in a part of the village. As I passed through the street with the principal, he introduced me to the people we met: "This is Dr. Orata whom we have been expecting for many weeks and who was responsible for the flowing water in Bactad and, indirectly, our own flowing water."

Inspired by this example, the students of the Urdaneta High School resolved to bring water to the high-school ground and farm. One Saturday morning at seven o'clock, 105 Junior and Senior boys, plus 7 male teachers and I went to San Vicenta, about one kilometer from the high school, to build a dam in order to raise the dykes on both sides of the canal to prevent the water from overflowing and to clear and deepen the irrigation canal to the high-school grounds. We worked for four hours, barefooted and in shorts and shirtsleeves. It was refreshing to see the boys work joyfully and hard, in part, no doubt, because their teachers worked with them. I, myself, enjoyed using my own shovel from beginning to end. It was a real vacation from paper work!

Within the hour after the dam was constructed, the water, in gushes, flowed through the canal to flood the high-school grounds, thus disproving what was generally claimed, that the ground was too high to be irrigated. Once more, the stagnant water in the canal originating from the near-by artesian well was swept away and in place of it flowed clear, fresh water. As soon as the water started to flow, the people along the road—men, women, and children, all were happy—began to sprinkle the road. Fire—dare it come now?

Less than a week later there was a move started to bring water into the district of Urdaneta. Since it was possible to have water flow into Bactad and into the high-school grounds, water from somewhere could certainly be made to flow into the canals of the

Urdaneta district. Indeed, it was possible, as was shortly afterward shown when Mayor Sison, the district supervisor of Urdaneta, a few others, and I went to make a survey on the spot where the water could be diverted by a dam in a near-by brook. When the news was known, without being asked to volunteer, three hundred students in the high school, central school, and Badipa elementary school raised their hands, saying: "I want to work, sir." The mayor promised to have the dam constructed in a short time, as there was pressure from the people to bring the water to the canals in the district to sweep away filthy and stagnant pools, to provide water to sprinkle the streets or to put out fire, and to water vegetables and fruit trees.

### WE BUILD A COMMUNITY BATH- AND WASHHOUSE

From my bedroom window here in Bactad, I can see the public artesian well where the people have learned to congregate to wash clothes, to scrub dirty pots, and to bathe themselves and their animals. Where filth and confusion prevailed for years, there is now cleanliness, beauty, orderliness, and privacy.

How did this happen, and how much did it cost? The story is very simple. Two years or so ago, my wife and I with a group of friends visited parts of rural France. There we found situations and problems very similar to our own. The people did not have electric light or piped water. They lived in some degree of isolation just like our village folk in the Philippines. But they did have a community bath- and washhouse, which was nearly always in the center of the village, near the rural church and community market. It was a concrete place in the shade, where the women took turns doing their washing.

When we returned home in September this year, I was once again confronted by the unsightly artesian well in the village of Bactad. Early in the morning there was a horrible confusion as women fought to be near the source of the water in order that they might do their washing more easily. The well was used indiscriminately for bathing, for washing clothes, and for scrubbing kitchen utensils. The most disgusting feature was the stagnant pool that had been accumulating for years as a result of water flowing into the field. Pigs, chickens, and other animals used to wallow in the mud, and, of course, mosquitoes bred there in thousands.

What could we do to follow the example of the French villages? We gathered together a few of our village people, including some teachers, and described the community bath- and washhouse we had seen in rural France. They all liked the idea, and, when we proposed that we should build a similar one near the artesian well and the school, everybody agreed to do his part. My wife and I gave the cement and the thatch roofing. Mayor Sison gave the sand and gravel, while the people provided the needed bamboo and palm leaves and did all the work. A high-school shop teacher, Antonio Laberinto, who lives in Bactad, designed the building and supervised the work. Segundino Obra and Saturnino Tabingo (village mayor), together with Nicholas Almoite, organized the people in the different zones to contribute material and labor.

It took less than two weeks to finish the construction; it took six bags of cement, one truck of sand and gravel, 350 sheets of thatch roofing, fifteen pieces of bamboo, five buri leaves, and a half-kilo of nails. All in all, counting labor, the bath- and washhouse cost about forty pesos, or twenty United States dollars.

First, we separated the waste water from the clean water—the waste water being directed to a canal which carried it into the rice fields, and the pure water, especially at night when the artesian well is not in use, was turned into a large fishpond a few meters from the well. The fishpond is fenced around and vegetables are planted on its raised sides.

The filthy stagnant pool has dried up, and where the pigs and poultry used to wallow there is now a flower garden which is cultivated by girl students of home economics. The women no longer scrub their pots and pans there, for they, too, admire beautiful things and want to preserve them.

Then the women no longer need to fight for the source of water because the washhouse has separate taps and gives room for three or four women to wash clothes at the same time. The washhouse is strictly private, and the women enjoy being left alone. They can wash at any time of the day, rain or shine. The washhouse is fitted with utensils for scrubbing or pounding the clothes, and arrangements are provided for rinsing and hanging them.

There is no more bathing in public. Men, women, and children now use the private bathroom for the purpose and line up to take

their turn. The habit of bathing privately is being formed quickly
now that a private bathhouse has been provided. Heretofore, many
laws had been passed prohibiting bathing in public, but, like many
other measures, they could not be enforced because there was no
alternative.

There is an educational value in all this. The pupils in all grades
shared in surveying the problems and needs, in making the plan and
carrying it out, and, later, in appraising the results. Questions such
as these came up: Why do people bathe and wash clothes in the
open? What is the danger to health of the foul water which has accumulated near the artesian well? What can be done with the good
water, especially at night? Where should the waste water go? What
can be done to help in building the bath- and washhouse? The pupils took an active part in the construction of the building—they carried the sand and gravel in small containers; they separated the large
stones; the home-economics girls converted the ground around the
well into a flower garden; the older boys helped split bamboo or dig
holes in the ground for the posts. After the building was completed,
all the classes took time to see it and to be shown how the various
parts were to be used—the taps in the washhouse, the towel rack in
the bathhouse, the brooms and water containers in both. Then came
the problems of maintenance—who would be responsible for cleaning the floors and not allowing water to accumulate? Of course it
was decided that those using the place should themselves thoroughly
clean up afterward. The pupils volunteered to take care of the
canals so that they would not get clogged and took turns doing so.

Before the women were allowed to use the facilities, they were
gathered together by Mr. Bravo, the school principal, who advised
them that they should leave the place as clean and tidy as they would
wish to find it. He proceeded to show them how. They readily
agreed that unless they took great care of the house themselves, it
would not last long, and "what a shame that would be." All this was
part of the technique for educating them to make intelligent use of
their own resources.

EXPERIMENTING WITH COMPOST FERTILIZER

The other day I advertised in school, as well as outside, that we
would buy buffalo, horse, or cow manure for ten centavos a petro-

leum can (four gallons). No offers were forthcoming until the price was raised to fifteen centavos. Even then we got only thirty pesos worth, or two hundred cans, from a village of two thousand inhabitants where every family had at least one buffalo, and this at a time of scarcity, when many people were very much in need of cash with which to buy rice.

The people have learned the value of manure and compost. The pupils of Bactad school were the first to use buffalo, horse, cow, pig, or chicken manure in their school garden, but now most families preserve all the refuse from animals and plants in compost pits. Late in 1952 I saw a batch of soya beans in the Bactad school garden, the east side of which was twice as productive as the western. Nobody seemed to be able to offer any explanation until Mr. Obra suddenly had an idea and said to me, "You remember that the last time you were here we built a compost pile there (pointing to the place south of the plot of soya beans). When the heap decayed, there was a pile of it which we put here where you find the vigorous soya beans." Only then did we realize that compost was good fertilizer. It was the first time I had actually seen the difference between fertilized and nonfertilized plants. Up to that time, like Mr. Obra, I had believed in what I had been told about composts; now I knew from experience.

We decided to show that plot of soya beans to the adults and to the school children. Everyone agreed that the compost must be responsible for the difference in production between the two sides of the plot. Visitors came from other schools and communities, and they marveled at the strange sight. They, too, readily agreed that it was the compost that was responsible for the difference, but they soon forgot.

The Bactad pupils, however, did not forget; they immediately went to work making compost and using it to fertilize their plots. In the next harvest they reaped the benefit of their efforts and could not fail to notice how much bigger their crops were than before. Since then they have been using compost in their gardens, and I have seen fathers, mothers, and older brothers and sisters carrying compost in baskets on their heads to the school to help the children in their garden. They, too, remarked on how much bigger the crops were as a result of the use of compost fertilizer and green manure.

I do not know how many people outside Bactad actually try to use manure or compost in their lots and farms, but I do know that when I tried to buy animal manure at fifteen centavos a can, many people preferred to keep it and use it themselves.

I must admit that in offering fifteen centavos a can I had in mind more than securing fertilizers for our new orchard of pineapples and fruit trees. I wanted to make the people of Bactad realize even more the value of manure. When my wife took me to task for offering fifteen centavos, I replied that if some of the children and their parents saw that I was willing to pay fifteen centavos a can, they might come to appreciate more the value of manure and compost. If so, the difference of five centavos would be worth it.

When I think of it now, our village is much cleaner than the rest of the district and the near-by villages, it is freer from mosquitoes and malaria, and food production is on the upgrade.

GARDENING TAKES NO VACATION

On the morning of the twentieth of December, I was surprised to see several pupils and one of the teachers, Francisco Tablada, all working as usual in their plots in the school garden, although the Christmas vacation had already begun, and in most places the school gardens are deserted at this time of the year. I asked: "Why do you and the pupils work in your garden as usual during vacation?" As if asked a superfluous question, Mr. Obra replied: "This morning a businessman came to see our garden and offered to buy the fifty-eight plots of pechay (cabbage) of my third-grade class for one hundred pesos. He would do the harvesting and we could take our vacation after he paid us. I consulted my pupils and their answer was a unanimous 'No.' They did not want to sell at this time because they said, 'At the rate offered, we would get only four centavos per head, while later on we could get at least five centavos or probably more.'" And Mr. Tablada explained: "Every teacher has his own plot, and we raise the same vegetables as the pupils do. We also sell our plants, besides having what we can eat."

In other words, the pupils have found that gardening pays. Since 1951 the pupils have been selling their garden produce. According to Mr. Obra, the pupils earn each year from four and a half to six and a half pesos, with an average earning per pupil of more than five pesos. This is quite a sum for them, considering their ages—nine to eleven—and the fact that their plots are small (one by five meters for the Grade III pupils and one by ten meters for the Grade IV pupils). This amount is more than enough for all incidental expenses during the year, including pocket money for the movies and for candy and soft drinks. Not a few of them give a part of their earnings to their mothers, especially during the months preceding harvest when rice is scarce and many families go without food a part of the day.

In order to get the best price for their plants, the pupils have to grow them scientifically. They do not spare themselves in making compost at their homes and in using compost to fertilize their plots. Toward the end of the school year all the plots are planted with beans. When the plants are in flower they are plowed under as green manure. When school starts in June, the pupils are assigned their plots—the old pupils invariably choose the ones they had the year before—and they immediately start bringing their compost. A planting calendar is drawn up which enables them to raise three crops during the year, including vacation time.

The pupils do not regard their school grade in gardening as important. What they are after is the money their vegetables will bring, and this is determined by the quality of the plants. This in turn is conditioned by many factors, such as the quality of the seeds, timing of preparing the seedbeds and transplanting, preparation of the plot, fertilization, irrigation, weeding and cultivation, and harvesting. The pupils observe all the principles of scientific gardening because they know that this is the way to get the maximum production and income from their plots. That is why gardening goes on all the time without vacation, for they know that the slightest relapse means reduced production and reduced income. This year my nephew declined an invitation to spend his vacation in Manila because he preferred to tend his garden.

Incidentally, the pupils are learning business methods and the value of co-operation. When their crops are about ready for harvest they send one or two of their classmates to the market to find out the price per head of "pechay" or cabbage, as the case may be. They argue about the price that they should accept. When a buyer comes to Bactad—several come during the harvest time—the pupils have a price below which no one sells. I saw pupils refusing to sell their produce because of a difference of one centavo per plant. They preferred to take their produce to market the following morning even if actually the difference meant only the twenty centavos per plot, which would have been required for transportation. They saved this by walking the four kilometers (one way) to the town market in Urdaneta.

EIGHT YEARS LATER

It must not be concluded that the people of Bactad have changed their habits generally as a result of a few years of working together to improve their lot under the leadership of schoolteachers. The fact is that they are the same as people in other villages. Many of them refuse to co-operate even now, preferring to stick to the old ways of doing things. Occasionally there are loose pigs and goats, especially after ten o'clock in the evening. While many have asked for vegetable seedlings which are raised in the school nursery, there are still many vacant lots remaining untouched in spite of the continuous and intensive campaign for increased food production. Many people still throw their rubbish, including dead animals, into the flowing canal instead of putting it in the compost pit.

In the high school, it is the same. Some of the teachers pay lip service to community education, but they do not lift a finger to change their bookish methods. The fact is that the students are far ahead of the staff in realizing the value to themselves of working half of the day and studying the other half. There is all the emphasis that is needed on work experience, but in awarding honors to the students the teachers confine themselves to the results of examinations.

But, there are gains that have stood out like sore thumbs. At the beginning, many parents and town officials objected to the work-study program or made fun of the pupils working to help clean the town square or the streets in preparation for a festival. Last year, to our great surprise, the officials of the town of Urdaneta, from the mayor down, and professionals and businessmen were seen working to clean the canals around the school and municipal building. They had formed a civic club, called "The Tarantados Club of Urdaneta," whose purpose was to improve Urdaneta physically, socially, and morally. Armed with shovels, rakes, bolos, brooms, and wheelbarrows, and dressed to work in "maong" (of which overalls are made), the members of this club work the last Sunday of every month to clean the public places of Urdaneta.

Many parents did not like their sons and daughters to work for pay, on the ground that they were sent to school to study. But last year there was no one raising any objection to the pupils of Bactad earning from their gardens from five to ten pesos a year (which is enough to buy what they need in school and to go to the cinema occasionally); or to the students of the high school making as much as one hundred pesos (more than the amount of their tuition) by doing any kind of work, from building latrines to repairing furniture. The girls as well as the boys earned money, and they were happy in doing so. Furthermore, they were no longer ashamed of being seen at work. We saw two boys carrying the chairs that they made on a bamboo pole instead of paying someone to deliver them. The Bactad pupils who sold their cabbage in the market walked back and forth to save their pennies.

Beauty contests are no longer on a cash basis, as they used to be, but on a merit basis. In order to win, the contestants have to satisfy certain requirements of physical merit (including sound teeth) and attitudes, instead of depending upon rich parents and relatives. Town fiestas are no longer the expensive events they used to be. The people, particularly the young boys and girls, are beginning to learn the value of money. They realize more than ever before what it takes to make money.

Teachers and extension workers (agriculture, health) have learned to work together. Extension workers who can stay only a few hours at a time depend upon the teachers to follow up the work started by them, as the teachers have learned to depend upon the extension workers to show them the intricacies and technicalities involved in the work of improving sanitation and food production.

Much remains to be done, but it is very much easier to start a project now than before, an indication that the people have learned to depend upon the teachers, extension workers, and leaders among themselves. There is more food, such as fruit and vegetables, in the home lots and in the market; children are visibly healthier (many prefer calamanci juice to commercial drinks) and they are happier;

there is more self-employment now than eight years ago; peace and order have not worsened as is the case in many places. In spite of these improvements, or perhaps because of them, the standards of achievement in the fundamentals have not suffered. On the contrary, there is ground for the belief that they are higher now. The gap between the school and the community in Urdaneta is not so wide as it was, and it is becoming narrower every year, thanks to the vigilance of teachers and community leaders.

Education for community development is a slow process, but it can be speeded up with a little imagination, foresight, persistence, and hard work. The Filipino people are not indolent, as has often been charged; they are good workers by any standard. This we know from our experience of less than ten years in Urdaneta.

## Guiding Principles

The present writer has taken an active part in the community-school movement from the beginning. His interest in the idea started in 1936 in the Little Wound Community School on the Pine Ridge Reservation at Kyle, South Dakota.[2]

Returning to the Philippines in 1941, he tried to introduce the idea of the community school, but his effort was interrupted by the war. In 1945, as chief of the Curriculum and Research Division of the Department of Public Instruction, he went much further and, through articles in the press and a weekly seminar organized to discuss the problem of curriculum reorganization for the postwar period, he was able to rally the support of some thirty of the young educators of the Philippines, who have since become leading supporters of the community-school movement.[3]

2. Pedro T. Orata, *Fundamental Education in an Amerindian Community*. Washington: United States Department of the Interior, Bureau of Indian Affairs, 1953.

3. See the following articles in the *Quarterly Bulletin* of the Philippine Association of School Superintendents: "Learning of the Problems of the Community School," Vol. I, No. 1 (September, 1951); "Exploring Ways of Community Development," Vol. I, No. 2 (December, 1951); "The First National Training Program in Community Education Leadership," Vol. IV, No. 3 (March, 1955). See also: V. Bernardino, *Improving the Community School Program* (a report of the second education conference in Bulacan; Malolos, 1951); Dalmacio Martin, *Curriculum Development for the Elementary* (Community) *School* (Baguio, 1954); Juan C. Laya, *Little Democracies* (Manila: Kayumanggi Press, 1951); and Juan C. Laya, *New Schools for Little Democracies* (Manila: Kayumanggi Press, 1952).

Late in 1948, the writer joined UNESCO but continued his interest in the community school through his writings and participation in two projects, one each in his home village and in town in the province of Pangasian. In these projects, the objective was to make the community school really effective in helping to raise the standards of living of the people by improving sanitation and increasing food production without lowering educational standards. Besides maintaining standards of achievement in the three R's, it was important to avoid the exploitation of children, which is the strongest objection of both educators and laymen to the community-school approach. After eight years of successful operation, the approach to these two projects would seem to merit wider application. As leaders in this approach, the writer and his colleagues—the mayor of Urdaneta, the principals and teachers in the schools, the district supervisor, and others—used the following as guiding principles of operation:

1. Start with the simplest and most obviously felt need, e.g., for running water, and lead gradually to other and more remote needs which may grow out of it, such as the application of compost fertilizer.

2. Do something to show immediate results, and later on talk about principles and their application to more urgent problems.

3. Work with the people and live with the problem, and if there is any digging to do, do it first; dress as the people do and go barefooted where shoes are a handicap, as in walking over rice paddies.

4. Start the project but withdraw as quickly as others are willing to take over; be absent occasionally, so as to give others a chance to lead.

5. Work on only one or two manageable projects at a time, but see to it that they are well managed and, especially, that the people who work in them feel that the success is due to their efforts.

6. Work on projects that require no more than available resources in manpower, material, and tools, leading on to more ambitious ones only if people are ready and willing to make contributions.

7. Relate activities to knowledge and skills and lead people to the understanding and application of principles.

8. Work on projects that will benefit all the people and give

each person a chance, commensurate with age and capacity, to do his very best to contribute to the success of the undertaking.

9. Secure the help of other agencies, such as the Bureau of Agricultural Extension and the Department of Health, but do not give up if they fail to show interest.

10. Appeal to the profit motive. For example, show that gardening and poultry-raising pay dividends if done scientifically and on an intensive commercial basis. This has been particularly successful with school children who, heretofore, let their plots grow weeds after the grading period was over.

There are other principles, but these will suffice to show reasons for doing the things that were done during the last eight years.

### Improvements Attained through Community-School Approach

1. Each project was educational through and through as well as practical and productive. The importance of flowing water was brought out through observation, reading, and discussion before a survey was made of the possible source of water. The high-school students were led to realize the danger to the bean crops in the adjoining fields if water should overflow the dykes. Also, they were encouraged to accept the responsibility of raising the dyke on both sides of the canal to a requisite height, of filling holes in the dyke, and of taking further steps to follow up their initial work from then on.

2. The students were made to feel the responsibility of using the water to irrigate, to sprinkle the streets, and to put out fires; and the teachers, once again, saw to it that their resolutions were carried over into appropriate action. Constant reminders of important responsibilities were presented by teachers, just as there have to be frequent drills with flash cards and on the blackboard for arithmetic classes. They were also made to realize that the water is public property and no one, not even students, can have a monopoly of it.

3. The participation of adults was secured in each case, since it was clear that it was the joint concern of all the people that water should flow freely into the community.

4. The projects were related functionally to lessons in science, in arithmetic, in geography, in physics, in economics, in art and

literature (the beauty and freshness of flowing water), in horticulture, in piggery and poultry raising, in home economics, not to name such other subjects as health and character education.

5. As already mentioned, the only way to start is to start, and the place to start is right here with what little we have. In no case did we wait for experts to come, for money to be appropriated, or for certain things to be done. Our only capital was ourselves, our health, our determination to succeed, and our own resources—land, artesian wells, canals, and shovels. We did not have a budget. We studied our needs, made plans, and went ahead the best we could to achieve our objectives.

6. There was sufficient local talent to guide us. Our mayor was the best type of resource person. Most fortunately, he was interested in the same things as we, namely, the improvement of Urdaneta and its many barriors. His pet projects were peace and order, food production, road construction, and irrigation. Then, there was Isidro Bravo, principal of the Bactad elementary school, whose knowledge about food production is tremendous and varied and who exemplifies his theories in his own yard. Isidro Fabia, principal of the Urdaneta high school, never wavered in his determination to give his 1,500 boys and girls a chance to work and earn money. The teachers of the Bactad high school and those of the central school of Urdaneta co-operated with us wholeheartedly. In some situations it was possible for us to utilize outside help, such as the three instructors from the Central Luzon Agricultural College.

7. School children and high-school students may be relied upon to render community service, be it digging ditches, constructing latrines and compost pits, or catching pigs. They know that their communities leave many things to be desired in sanitation, in food, in leadership, and, given a chance, they would help correct these deficiences. Some of us were afraid of criticism emanating, it was claimed, from the private schools, but the words of encouragement from officials, parents, and the students themselves were more than we could have expected. There need be no fear so long as one is rendering useful service, and we saw nothing dangerous in causing water to flow over stagnant pools, irrigating a dry farm, building a road, making fishponds to take the place of open toilets, giving

students a chance to earn their tuition fees, or constructing sanitary latrines, compost pits, and pigpens, or even catching stray animals and later helping the owners to build corrals for them.

8. We found the educational and positive approach most effective and satisfactory. Heretofore, the only approach to the problem of hygiene and sanitation has been through ordinances and community lectures. The head of the sanitary division of Urdaneta has been here twenty-six years, and he has long given up in despair. We found the district and the villages filthy—they still are—but at last sanitary latrines are being constructed, stagnant pools being drained or swept away by flowing water, and drainage systems under the kitchens being installed. We heard this remark from one private citizen: "The happiest person among us is the president of the sanitary division. The things which he has been advocating for twenty-six years in Urdaneta are being done at last." No one chooses to be without a latrine or to get along with one that smells bad if he can help it. We provided a service to build such latrines, and people are making use of the service. One person told me this: "I could have provided these things before, but whom could I have relied upon to build them? I do not know how to construct a latrine or to drain our pagbabasaan, and I do not have the time even if I knew how; but now that the high-school boys can do them for me at so cheap a price, I would indeed be a fool if I did not ask for the service."

9. Community health is everybody's business. If the people in the next lot use the open spaces near the fence as their latrine, that is the business of the people in the neighborhood if not all members of the whole community. Or, if there are loose pigs roaming around, we must not wait for the policeman to catch them. Again, if a family cannot dig a canal in front of their house, we could not fold our hands and wait if we want the water to flow freely. We have adopted the policy that we should as a community, or as groups of individuals, do something to help construct latrines, catch pigs, dig canals, or build dams with or without pay. We would even contribute material and labor, as indeed we did, to do these things for persons who need our assistance, in the belief that it would be far more expensive for us in the long run to tolerate the objectionable conditions.

10. We have proved once more that the longest way round is the shortest way to the goal. For instance, we chose a round about way to bring the water to the high-school grounds. We could have chosen another way which would have required one-tenth the time and effort spent upon it. But, the shorter way would have given us only water—whereas, the longer way, because it passed through a road with houses on the sides, gave us water to sprinkle the road and the plants and to put out fires. Furthermore, it swept away the ugly and filthy stagnant water that resulted from the use of the artesian well near the high-school building.

11. We tried, in every situation, to live by the principle that a good leader must be a good follower. There is not a single activity in which we, the leaders, acted in the capacity of overseers. When there was digging to do, we had our own shovels and used them. The leader must be willing and able to do what he asks his followers to do. He must live among them and with the problems. I stayed in the village most of the time, going to town only when I needed to work in the high school. In the same way, our mayor, our principals, teachers, and adult leaders all tried to exemplify this kind of leadership.

12. We believe that the surest and most effective way to kill a project is premature publicity. We declined requests to be visited. Individuals, groups, even whole schools or classes wanted to come to see our "wonderful project." We replied that there was nothing wonderful about it. "We are just beginning," we told them. We shunned picture-taking as a rule, and did not invite newspaper men. Truthfully, there is nothing unusual, much less spectacular, in Bactad or the high school. We have far to go.

# CHAPTER VII

# Lessons Learned through International and Bilateral Programs for Community Education

## I. Technical and Scientific Developments

WILLARD W. BEATTY

Technical and scientific developments since 1940 have made possible a dramatic new attack on social and economic handicaps from which more than half the world's people have been suffering. The efforts of socially and economically more advanced communities to transmit their culture to dependent or conquered areas is nothing new. But the modern approach to such acculturation appears to differ for several significant reasons: first, the dramatic effectiveness of new drugs, antibiotics, and pesticides in arresting or controlling disease or the agencies of disease transmission; second, the phenomenal increase in productivity of new hybrid seeds, new chemical fertilizers, and new techniques of planting or cultivation available and adaptable to various areas of the world; third, the new speed of intercommunication and transport introduced by radio, television, and air travel; fourth, the new techniques of international and bilateral co-operation which enlist the participation of governments and the people of their local communities in seeking community improvement through guided self-help.

Dramatic as has been the growth of technical assistance through the United Nations and its specialized agencies, in which most of the nations of the world are participating equally in the give and take of international co-operation, equally challenging has been the rise of bilateral-assistance programs such as the American Technical Co-operation Administration, the Colombo Plan of the British Commonwealth, and the more recent offers of technical aid from the Soviet countries. Each of these programs, international or bilateral, has been based upon invitations from the recipient countries and has involved a co-operative attack upon a locally recognized social or economic problem, with the full participation of local counterpart specialists and the understanding and collaboration of the people of the community being served.

The last twenty years has seen a reorientation of the foreign-missions programs of many of the Western churches, with increased emphasis on education, health, and economic improvement. Also, there has been a significant rise in overseas work in community education and development by such nongovernmental agencies as the Ford and Rockefeller foundations, the Save the Children Federation, CARE, and others.

### AMERICAN IDEALISM

For the United States this concern for the well-being of disadvantaged people is entirely in keeping with the best impulses of our past. The Emma Lazarus inscription on the base of the Statue of Liberty is an appropriate expression of the idealism of many fellow Americans of that period toward the poor and humble of the world:

> Give me your tired, your poor,
> Your huddled masses yearning to breathe free,
> The wretched refuse of your teeming shore,
> Send these, the homeless, tempest tossed to me;
> I lift my lamp beside the golden door.[1]

There were, of course, dissenters; especially when such idealism interfered with the profits of the wealthy or the jobs of the laborers. But, by and large, the impulsive reactions of the American people have tended to be more generous, especially in the abstract, than those of the average citizen elsewhere.

President Wilson's Fourteen Points, with their introduction of the anticolonial concept of self-determination,[2] Roosevelt's Four Freedoms, and our "Lend Lease" program[3] during World War II, which generously placed our material resources at the service of our allies; the Marshall plan[4] "to assist in the return to normal economic health

1. Emma Lazarus, 1886.
2. *The Columbia Encyclopedia.*     3. *Ibid.*
4. *Memoirs of Harry S. Truman,* Vol. II, p. 114. New York: Doubleday & Co., 1956.

in the world, without which there can be no political stability and no assured peace . . . [a] policy . . . directed not against any country or doctrine but against hunger, poverty, desperation, and chaos," were likewise reflective of the best of American impulses. So were the Truman Doctrine,[5] to assist Greece and Turkey control internal dissension and prevent a "take over" by a Communist minority, and his Point IV Program[6] proposed in his 1949 inaugural address:

More than half of the people of the world are living in conditions approaching misery. Their food is inadequate. They are victims of disease. Their economic life is primitive and stagnant. Their poverty is a handicap and a threat both to them and to more prosperous areas.

For the first time in history humanity possesses the knowledge and the skill to relieve the suffering of these people.

The United States is pre-eminent among nations in the development of industrial and scientific techniques. The material resources which we can afford to use for the assistance of other people are limited. But our imponderable resources in technical knowledge are constantly growing and are inexhaustible.

I believe that we should make available to peace-loving people the benefits of our store of technical knowledge in order to help them realize their aspirations for a better life.

It is American ideals like these, clearly expressed and carried into action, that account for the "reservoir of Good Will" toward the United States as reported by Wendell Willkie on his return from a globe-circling tour.

### TECHNICAL CO-OPERATION IN LATIN AMERICA

Prior to 1940, about 65 American religious agencies had been operating 1,600 projects, involving 1,360 schools, 120 hospitals and clinics, 43 demonstration farms and agricultural projects, and some 94 miscellaneous projects, including social service centers, in Latin America[7] in which about 2,100 full-time people were employed and for which between eight and ten million dollars were spent annually.

In 1939, the United States government set up its first organized and systematic technical co-operation program with Latin America

5. *Ibid.,* p. 106.              6. *Ibid.,* p. 227.

7. Philip M. Glick, *The Administration of Technical Assistance,* p. 4. Chicago: University of Chicago Press, 1957.

in implementation of a phase of Franklin Roosevelt's "Good Neighbor Policy,"[8] enunciated in his first inaugural address. The new program provided for the loan of persons in the employ of the United States for temporary services to give advice or guidance, on request, to the government of any American nation.

As a result of potential involvement of the nations of the Western Hemisphere in World War II, President Roosevelt by executive order set up the Office of the Co-ordinator of Inter-American Affairs.[9] Mr. Nelson Rockefeller was appointed to this position and, shortly thereafter, secured a charter under the laws of Delaware for a government-owned corporation called the Institute for Inter-American Affairs which was authorized to conduct co-operative programs with Latin American governments in promotion of public health and in agricultural development. In 1944, a similar corporation was organized, called the Inter-American Educational Foundation, with authority to give similar co-operation in elementary and secondary education.

This Latin-American experience preceded the establishment of UNESCO and prepared the United States to undertake the Point IV extension of technical co-operation on a world-wide basis following President Truman's inaugural address of 1949.

President Truman's Point IV proposal was only an extension at world level of the program of educational and economic assistance to Latin America described above.

### NONGOVERNMENTAL AGENCIES

The official national and international programs now receiving so much attention were preceded by the work of nongovernmental agencies in most of the underdeveloped areas. Often such help was inextricably joined with religious proselytizing. This greatly complicated for the recipient the already difficult acceptance of new concepts of disease and new techniques of agriculture, both of which were matters often deeply imbedded in his pagan religious beliefs. Not only was he being asked to try new ways of working but also to abandon the religion of his fathers and his social associates for new and strange gods.

Surprising as it may seem, American missionary work was prob-

8. *Ibid.*, pp. 6–7.                    9. *Ibid.*, pp. 14–15.

ably more widespread over the globe than that of any other country and, even in some British possessions such as India and Ceylon, was tending to supplant in some areas the work of Anglican missions.

Thus, it is reasonable to find various adventures in community education being undertaken by American missionary leaders in India considerably prior to independence and partition. Village betterment work was not limited to foreign experts, however, for several native programs of community education and development laid foundations for the tremendous activity now associated with India's plans for national development. Neither is it surprising to find American agencies, including the Ford and Rockefeller foundations, together with financial support from the U.S. Technical Cooperation Administration supporting such activity on a generous scale for thousands of villages and millions of India's village dwellers.

THE UNITED NATIONS SPECIALIZED AGENCIES

UNESCO was the first of the UN specialized agencies to define a program of guidance toward the improvement of conditions in the underdeveloped areas of the world. The necessary programs to meet the needs of the people suffering from disease, malnourishment, archaic agriculture, peonism, and illiteracy were defined by a committee of the First UNESCO General Assembly in 1946, and the title, "Fundamental Education," was adopted to describe the proposed attack on these conditions.

It early became clear that technical leadership in health, agricultural improvement, redesign of handicrafts, and in community reorganization would have to come from the respective specialized agencies, WHO, FAO, ILO, and UN Social Affairs. UNESCO, in setting up its pilot projects in fundamental education and in establishing the training centers at Patzcuaro in Mexico and Sirs-el-Layyan in Egypt, enlisted participation of these agencies. In this pioneering work of UNESCO, it was discovered that illiteracy was only one of the difficulties from which the rural illiterate suffered.

It thus became clear that effective work in fundamental education, as then defined, demanded either a team approach so that the needed attack could be directed toward that aspect of community concern which could most readily enlist local co-operation, or the training of multipurpose community workers so that versatility could respond to the community needs. Experience in Latin America by Torres Bodet and others favored the team approach which had typified the Mexican cultural missions. The early UNESCO training-centers were likewise organized to promote the team approach.

As each of the specialized agencies swung into action, the need for trained field workers in its own specialty became evident, if it was to satisfy the demands of its member states. Efforts were initiated to prepare local leaders of limited skill as agricultural extensionists, first-aid and health educationists, and similar partly trained community leaders.

Approaching the problem from the side of community organization, the United Nations Social Affairs Division also found the need for its local leaders to possess multiple skills and, adopting the title "Community Development" for its new work, plunged into a technical-assistance program. In fact, "community development" has become the accepted UN overriding descriptive title for the multipurpose attack on local community needs. This has resulted in a redefinition of fundamental education by the Committee on Coordination of the Economic and Social Council of the United Nations.

> Community development may sometimes be initiated by a broad program of popular fundamental education . . . in this case, fundamental education is a first phase of community development, which should lead as soon as possible to a composite program involving other technical services. Where a composite community development project already exists, fundamental education will take its place among other technical services in a narrower and more specialized role. . . .[10]

The importance of the integrated concept originally underlying fundamental education has been recognized by a conclusion of the recent UN *ad hoc* working group[11] appraising the FE centers in Mexico and Egypt. The assertion is made that "the Centers may become interagency institutions of increasing value in the growing pattern of rural development in the two regions."

10. UN Economic and Social Council, E/2931 (October 18, 1956), Annex III, p. 18.

11. UNESCO Executive Board, 44 Ex/7 Annex, p. 3. Paris: June 11, 1956.

## SELF-HELP AN ESSENTIAL FACTOR

Reference has been made frequently to the fact that many non-governmental agencies had been at work in the foreign-assistance field for many years before such assistance became a concern of governmental or international agencies. Most of this earlier work consisted of *doing something* for these disadvantaged people. Sometimes it was to distribute used clothing; sometimes to send food packages; sometimes to furnish health services; sometimes to demonstrate agricultural technology. A majority of these efforts have been primarily eleemosynary, inviting the acceptance of gifts and services from the donors and doing little to promote self-help.

A new point of view is beginning to animate such agencies today. There is a growing recognition that while much of the world is poor, ill fed, and otherwise badly off, there are, nevertheless, tremendous pools of unemployed labor in many of these centers which, if engaged in self-help, might do a great deal to improve the conditions under which they live.

Anyone who has visited the poverty-stricken villages of southern Italy or Sicily, as an example, where literally hundreds of men lounge around the market place doing nothing but wait for the weekly government pittance, while streets disintegrate, bridges wash out, buildings leak, and fields go untended, must realize that a new point of view is desperately needed. Most governmental approaches begin with the assumption that money must be found with which to employ men in jobs. In the lack of enough money for constructive labor projects, at least a little can be doled out to save them from starvation while they remain idle.

The main thesis of this volume is that social improvement must depend largely on self-help. Readiness for self-help is a psychological condition. Unfortunately, governmental action is seldom organized to permit self-help, much less to promote it. The major contribution of the community-education programs described in the volume has been to inspire people with confidence in their own ability to achieve progress through the investment of unemployed man power in the improvement of local conditions.

### MAJOR DEVELOPMENTAL INVESTMENT

It is, of course, clear that there are other important areas of technical assistance in which considerable money is involved. The assistance being given to Afghanistan, Pakistan, and India in the damming of rivers and the developing of vast new areas for irrigated agriculture to provide increased food for the increasing millions of these nations does involve vast sums for expensive machinery and for skilled man power. Most of the unskilled man power is drawn from the locality and paid for by the nation being served. In this class belongs the Aswan High Dam proposed by Egypt for technical aid from the United States, Britain, and the World Bank. There was evidence, resulting from the Bank survey, that such a dam would serve to increase greatly the arable area of Egypt and at the same time furnish power for Egypt's evolving industrial development. Available evidence appears to show that it was not only feasible but economically desirable. The decision not to furnish assistance in this case may have been a tragic mistake.

It is increasingly probable that major developments of this kind, like the Volta River project which Ghana has recently proposed, may prove to be sufficiently sound economically to invite the kind of private investment which is often proposed when a "foreign aid" program is discussed in the United States. Much help for projects of this kind is already supplied as a business proposition by the International Bank for Reconstruction and Development (usually called the World Bank) and the American Export-Import Bank. The recent administrative proposal of an International Development Fund, both as a part of the American bilateral program and as an underwriting source for major projects under the UN, appears to be inevitable, if great reclamation projects like our own TVA, Columbia-basin, and Missouri-basin development plans are to be made available overseas. Projects of this type are quite different from the self-help programs to which this volume is devoted but may become equally important in the long run.

## II. *The American Bilateral Programs in Community Education*

### WILLFRED MAUCK

#### THE INTER-AMERICAN EDUCATIONAL FOUNDATION

Bilateral programs of technical co-operation, as sponsored by the United States government, date from 1943. Technical co-operation programs in health and agriculture were already in progress in many Latin-American republics. But activities in education had been largely confined to higher education. The conviction that there was an urgent need for work in elementary and secondary education, in vocational education, and in teacher-training led to the establishment, within the Office of the Coordinator for Inter-American Affairs, of the Inter-American Educational Foundation (which later became the Education Division of the Institute of Inter-American Affairs).

Generally speaking, the purpose of the Inter-American Educational Foundation was to develop educational activities within the scope of community education as defined in chapter i of this yearbook.

When the president of the IAEF outlined to his staff the general purpose of the organization, he was speaking to educators. They greeted the outline with a mixture of enthusiasm and awe: Enthusiasm, because they recognized the possibilities of such a program. Awe, because as educators they were immediately conscious of three sobering factors. First, they were about to sail uncharted: there were no adequate precedents to guide them in international co-operation in community education. Second, they had much to learn about the needs and how they could best be met, before they could do work which would satisfy them or their Latin-American collaborators. And, third, there was going to be no time to acquire that knowledge before starting to work, for in the pressure of wartime it was required by the Congress of the United States that the work start immediately. The ship was going to have to be built during its maiden voyage.

It is important that all this be understood, for it explains many of the successes as well as many of the difficulties encountered by the bilateral programs as time went on. And, since the experiences, good and bad, of the bilateral programs were studied by the engineers of the later multilateral programs, it is well to know what lay behind them.

It would be difficult to give a brief description of bilateral programs in community education which would present a true comparison with the multilateral programs. One reason, of course, is the fact that the bilateral programs are older by several years; therefore, the mass of data to be compared is enormous. But the chief reason is that the multilateral and bilateral programs have not proceeded along parallel lines.

In the earliest days of the multilateral programs, community education emerged as a somewhat vague concept, but as a single concept, nevertheless. It was intended that a program should be evolved which would give simultaneous attention, under unified direction, to elementary education through the schools, to out-of-school literacy for children and adults, to basic improvement of agriculture, home life, and hygiene, and to arts and crafts.

ORGANIZATION OF BILATERAL PROGRAMS

In the bilateral programs of the United States, on the other hand, separate and virtually independent programs were established in: (*a*) education, (*b*) agriculture, and (*c*) health and hygiene. There was *ad hoc* co-operation among these programs in isolated instances, but until the establishment of the Foreign Operations Administration in 1953, the United States programs of technical co-operation in Latin America and, to a large extent, in the Near East and African areas were carried on through functional divisions, each working more or less independently.

The work in education was chiefly concerned with major aspects of community education as the term was coming to be understood, but not entirely. The work in agriculture and health included much that was soon to be defined as fundamental education but with only occasional instances of co-ordination with what the education division was doing. And even after 1953, when the work of the Foreign Operations Administration, and the succeeding International Co-operation Administration, was reorganized to provide a unified "country" approach to technical co-operation, the stress was laid on the co-ordination of all efforts toward a unified approach to economic development. The term "fundamental education" has been seldom used, nor was the UNESCO concept consciously adopted in the administration of the bilateral programs.

This section of the present chapter is, therefore, concerned chiefly with the bilateral programs in education, making only occasional references to the contributions of the agriculture and health divisions to such problems as were included in the UNESCO programs of fundamental education.

From the beginning, the bilateral programs in education adopted certain basic assumptions. First, it was assumed that the improvement of social and economic conditions anywhere in the free world would be of benefit to the United States. That was considered to be sufficient justification for pouring United States money and effort into co-operative programs. Whatever political advantages to the United States might be hoped for by the Department of State and the Congress, it was always the conviction of the administrators of the co-operative program that their sole concern must be the professional job to be done and that, if that job were well done, the political advantages would probably follow anyway. That relieved the personnel of the programs from the burden of keeping political considerations in mind.

Second, a decision was made at the start that our concern would be the strengthening of national education systems below the higher-education level. While that did not exclude work outside the schools in community betterment and adult education (in fact, such activity was conceived as being part of the mission of the schools of a community), there was little enthusiasm for adult-literacy campaigns. There was much interest in such campaigns elsewhere at the time; but the administrators of the bilateral programs had little faith in their long-range benefits and preferred to approach the problem of literacy by the much slower but supposedly more realistic route of promoting the literacy of the coming generation through an improved and expanded school system.

Third, it was recognized that the scope of work undertaken and the speed of progress must be determined on the basis of resources available in each country, and not on the basis of United States experience. Technicians going to the field were, therefore, strictly instructed to inform themselves early on the actual state of the education system, the existing and foreseeable resources at the disposition of the national government and the communities for bringing about improvement, the minimum realizable goals which must be set, and then to determine the best means of using available resources in order to reach those goals. This injunction to make haste slowly was perhaps the most difficult part of the technician's assignment.

Fourth, the principle of "co-operation, not assistance" was adopted early. It was accepted as an axiom that we could not do a job for another country. All that we could do effectively would be to give as much co-operation as possible to national efforts at self-improvement.

This was true with respect to finances. Although, in the very beginning, it was sometimes necessary for the United States to contribute the major share of the funds to start a program, provision was always made for the assumption of an increasingly larger part of the financial burden by the other government so that, when a program should come to an end, there would be little or no financial shock to the other government in carrying on the work alone. The first year sometimes showed the United States carrying virtually all the costs; within a few years the contribution of the other government would have increased to 60, to 80, or to 95 per cent.

The principle was observed, also, with respect to technical participation. The ideal sought was the initial appointment of at least one national technician to work side by side with a United States technician in the same field of specialization, all planning and execution of projects to be by joint decision and action. Then more national technicians, as they were trained, would be added to the staff, until at last the United States specialist could be withdrawn, and all the work carried on by nationals.

"Co-operation, not assistance" was also meant to imply that technical co-operation is a two-way street, that United States educators had much to learn which would benefit American education, and the technicians were exhorted, before going to the field, to lose no opportunity of learning something new and making it available at home.

And the principle of "co-operation, not assistance" also implied that our work was to be primarily technical. It was believed that, as a general principle, the programs must not involve the use of United States funds for capital outlays: the building and maintenance of schools was assumed to be the responsibility of the national government, or of the communities.

There were exceptions, most of them legitimate. Sometimes, the ability to move ahead with a program required that certain facilities be made available immediately, and if national resources did not permit their construction at the moment, some of the joint funds, including some United States dollars, were put into a construction project. For example, it was decided at one point that much of the rural-education work in Bolivia would be centered in and around the normal school at Warisata. Before the technical work itself could be carried on effectively, however, the unfinished school had to be completed. The use of some joint funds, to supplement the moneys which the Bolivian government could throw in directly at the moment, was considered to be a legitimate means of pushing the entire program along.

Occasionally, there was use of United States funds for construction which could not be so readily justified, but instances of that are rare. Even when the legitimate use of such funds took place, it was usually for certain dollar costs which would have been most difficult for the national government to defray because of a tight exchange situation.

Bilateral programs, like the multilateral ones, have been entered into, of course, only at the request of the other government. These requests, at least in most of the course of the bilateral programs, have not been blanket requests to assist in fundamental education, as has often been the case in the multilateral effort. They have been, instead, very specific as to the area of co-operation. That often made it impossible to plan a concerted attack on all fields in community education from the beginning.

Sometimes the request itself was for co-operation in some field which the United States administrators of the program did not regard as the most fundamental need of the requesting country. For example, it was felt in the office of the Institute of Inter-American Affairs that the most urgent need of a certain South American republic was the improvement of its elementary-education system, especially in rural education. Although the government of the republic had little interest at the time in rural education, and not much more in urban elementary education, the request was complied with; and it is believed that a satisfactory job was done. The vocational school which was created on the edge of the capital is thriving, now wholly staffed and administered by national technicians, and it is busily extending vocational training into other parts of the republic. But the interesting thing is that the success of the vocational-education project caused a new minister of education, who did have a keen interest in elementary education, to request that work be started in that field also. Most of the energies of the co-operative program in that country are now devoted to the elementary schools and to the training of elementary teachers.

### THE "SERVICIO" SYSTEM OF BILATERAL PROGRAMS

Here it would be well to mention one contribution made by the bilateral programs to the entire area of technical co-operation—the *servicio* system. The Institute of Inter-American Affairs did not invent the *servicio* system, but they put it into widespread use.

"*Servicio*" is a Spanish word which, for the purposes of this description, might be translated "bureau," though no translation into English can give an exact idea of its meaning. A "*servicio* co-operative," or co-operative bureau, is a special office set up within a government ministry to plan and execute a co-operative program. Its staff and administration are appointed by the minister concerned; but either the director of the *servicio* may be a national of the country itself or the minister may appoint as director the chief of the United States educational mission. In the latter case, the United States director may administer his own staff of American technicians, as such, and be responsible to Washington for such administration; but with respect to the *servicio* staff, which is composed chiefly of technicians of the country concerned, and with respect to the program funds contributed by the two governments, he is responsible to the minister and is practically a member of the ministry's staff.

As intimated in the last paragraph, the funds which are made available by the United States and by the co-operating government for program expenses are deposited to the credit of the *servicio*. Thereafter, they lose their respective national identities and become a single, joint fund. They can be disbursed only on project authorizations signed by the minister (of Education, for example), the director of the *servicio*, and the United States chief of party. Where the chief of party is also director of the *servicio*, he signs twice, but in different capacities. His signature, as chief of party, signifies his agreement to the project on behalf of the United States; his signature as director of the *servicio* signifies his acceptance of responsibility to the minister for carrying out the terms of the project and accounting to the minister for its administration.

Once a project is signed and funds thereby made available, the execution is the responsibility of the *servicio* itself. Most of the technicians in the *servicio* are "nationals." Sometimes the corresponding American technicians are members, but, in any case, they must act as if they were, for the project is not theirs, but the *servicio*'s, and is carried out in the name of the ministry, by joint action.

It is customary in many countries for the minister to agree with the *servicio* on some geographical area within which the *servicio* may concentrate most of its work and where it is given special latitude for "laboratory" work in education. There may be, for example, a normal school and a group of surrounding elementary schools, where an improved curriculum may be devised, tested, put into practice; where a specially selected group of teachers may be trained in the new methods and curriculum, and later sent out to other parts of the country to train others. Warisata, in Bolivia, already mentioned, is one good example of such a laboratory area; so are the Central Normal School, near Asunción in Paraguay, and Danli and Comayagua in Honduras.

### TEACHER EDUCATION IN BILATERAL PROGRAMS

The core of each bilateral-education program is teacher education. Since the goal to be reached is not that of creating some impressive monument in stone or brick but that of helping to create an improved and self-perpetuating educational system, the emphasis must necessarily be on the evolution of effective machinery for training those who must carry on the work in the future. No project undertaken can make a true contribution to the program unless it contributes in some way to an improved teacher-education system.

Still, that offers a rather broad scope of activity. A teacher must have some curriculum for which to be trained; the development of an improved curriculum, closely geared to the needs of the communities to be served, rather than one handed down from past generations, or worked out to satisfy a theory untested by realities, is a prerequisite to determining just what kind of teacher education is needed. The new curriculum generally requires improved teaching methods, different from those which have been used almost unquestioned for some generations. Teaching by rote, for example, gives way to class participation, a practical "activity" program, and the use of texts and simple teaching aids. New teaching materials, springing from the new curriculum, have to be developed; and they are being developed largely by collaboration of the teachers themselves. Old, rigid forms of school administration have to give way to newer forms with enough flexibility to enable the system to grow, and this may entail a long and painful process of persuading national authorities to relax old habits of strict centralization. All these may be involved in a program, since all of them are essential to the development of effective teacher training.

### COMMUNITY EMPHASIS ON BILATERAL PROGRAMS

By different paths, the bilateral programs arrived at the same conclusion as the multilateral programs did, regarding the educational needs of a community, especially in the less-developed areas of the world. We came to believe that, in many lands, the school must become the generative force for community betterment; there is frequently no other organized entity in the commmunity that can be made into such a force, unless it be the church.

It was, therefore, recognized very early that, within the school itself, much of the educational content and activity must be concerned with the environment. In rural schools, for example, there has always been a constant effort to include in the curriculum a good deal of content dealing with agricultural life and with personal, home, and community health and hygiene. School gardens have been used to promote better methods of simple agriculture and even to introduce new products which the parents find it profitable to grow in their fields. School clubs have often been used to initiate whole communities into the importance and mysteries of home cleanliness, of privies, of the care and proper restraint of domestic animals, of the potentials of simple home crafts. And this has led naturally to a sort of extension work among the adults and to training of teachers in their new responsibilities of making the school a potent factor in improving personal and community living.

By the same token, it has been found possible and useful to train whole communities to the idea that the school in the village is their school, and that there is much they can do to make it better. The writer has visited communities which, a few years before, traditionally regarded the school as something belonging to the government, far away—as something with which they had nothing to do. If the building decayed, one waited until some inspector concerned himself with the matter and succeeded in bringing help from the capital city. But, once the program had made an impact, virtually the entire man power (men, women, and children) of these communities might be seen working hard on Sundays and on long summer evenings, making adobe bricks and putting them in place, raising roofpoles, constructing rude blackboards under the direction of the teacher. One may see women, and even some men, lingering just outside school doors or windows to hear some lesson inside on home improvement or the care of sheep and goats.

By and large, however, education work in the American bilateral programs has dealt mainly with the public elementary and vocational schools themselves and with the training of their teachers. Until very recently, little has been done in the field of higher education (except for that part of it which deals with teacher education). Except for one early program in Chile, the level of secondary education has also received comparatively little attention until recent years (again, excepting teacher-education institutions of secondary-school level). The reason is fairly obvious: Higher education and secondary education were not in such difficult straits, nor do they reach such a large part of the population. Efforts were, therefore, concentrated for some time on those areas where the most people needed the most help—on the elementary schools and the development of vocational training.

Even before the functional programs in health, education, and agriculture became more closely co-ordinated through the development of "country programs," there was a fair amount of collaboration among the divisions which contributed to the objectives of fundamental education. The Agriculture Division was chiefly concerned with its programs on the farms and in the agricultural schools; but it responded to many requests from the Education Division for assistance with the school gardens, with school club work, especially of the 4-H type of project, and with obtaining seeds and garden tools. Similarly, the Health Division worked with the Education Division on developing hygiene instruction in the schools, providing for school inoculation programs and training technicians in carrying them on, giving instruction in school communities on the building, maintenance, and use of latrines, on DDT programs for village and farm homes, and on supplying health films and animated cartoons devoted to community instruction.

### ADVANTAGES AND DISADVANTAGES OF BILATERAL PROGRAMS

It may be useful to consider some of the advantages and disadvantages of the bilateral approach and what steps have been taken to minimize some of the disadvantages themselves.

One of the most obvious potential weaknesses of the bilateral approach is the self-interest which is traditionally attributed to the foreign policy of any state. The disinterest of an international body is generally assumed; but what is the motive of an individual power nation? Is there some deep purpose of cultural imperialism, if not worse, behind it?

Now, professors of international relations are prone to say that the foreign policy of any country is necessarily based, in the long run, on national self-interest. It is undoubtedly true. And if the self-interest is selfishly interpreted and served, the potential disadvantage to any foreign state in participating in a bilateral program of co-operation, even in the field of education, is obvious. The benefit or harm which can result must depend upon just how enlightened is the self-interest which prompts the offer of co-operation and how objectively the program is carried out.

The writer is convinced that, thus far, the bilateral programs have succeeded in steering clear of the disaster of imperialism in any form. The very first of the assumptions made by administrators of the bilateral programs at the start was that justification for the co-operative programs lies in the benefits which must accrue to the United States from improved conditions of life among these peoples who are our friends or our potential friends. At first, it may have been the defensive aspect of the problem at which we were looking: Unless living conditions of our neighbors improved, there was danger to us in the unrest and suffering which would develop and the added probability of an unproductive burden for emergency relief; it would be better to help prevent an emergency from developing. But as time went on, the more positive approach became apparent; improved conditions among our friends made for stronger friends, for greater prosperity for all, for more security for us as for them.

Self-interest, of course; but a self-interest without sinister implications!

Throughout the history of the bilateral programs, the writer has been impressed by the attitude of the technicians sent to the field and of the specialists in Washington to whom they were responsible. It has been as decorous a professional attitude as one could wish. The personnel were wholly absorbed in a professional task, which happened to be carried on outside the borders of the United States instead of inside those borders. Aside from their constant awareness that they were invited guests in a foreign land and must conduct themselves as such, there was nothing in their actions to show that they were not engaged in educational work in Iowa or New Mexico or Tennessee.

Co-operative programs have generally been entered into only with extreme caution and on the basis of requests which, we were satisfied, were genuine and sincere. Technicians have been chosen with care, for professional capacity, temperament, flexibility of mind, and often from portions of the United States having problems and conditions bearing some resemblance to those which they will meet abroad. Their orientation has been stern with respect to avoidance of even the feeling of superiority and omniscience and with respect to the principle that they are being sent abroad only to lend such support as they can to the efforts of other educators to help themselves.

If all these safeguards are maintained in the future, the danger of bilateral programs developing into adventures in cultural imperialism will be slight. The danger that they may be suspect, and the danger that lies in any relaxation of professional watchfulness, will necessarily remain.

The use of the *servicio* device, however, is an added safeguard. For under it, it is the ministry of the co-operating government which is really carrying on the work, largely with its own technicians, reinforced as need determines by the experience and collaboration of the Americans—and only to that extent.

Another disadvantage which is often argued is that, under the bilateral programs of the United States, the foreign technicians who come into a country to work are all from a land where educational problems and conditions are quite different and where there is a level of expenditure for educational purposes which seems lavish to nationals of economically less highly developed nations. It is suggested that American technicians, previously unacquainted with many of the problems they are to face, are in no position to judge what needs to be done or can be done with available resources. And the argument is usually reinforced by comparisons with UNESCO missions, made up of technicians from many lands, some of which have problems and modes of life very similar to those in the countries which are their hosts.

The fact that almost all the technicians sent abroad by ICA are citizens of the United States and heirs of its educational experience alone is contrasted with the cross-fertilization of national ideas made possible in a UNESCO mission. In light of these facts, there is no preponderance of evidence that either system has a clear advantage over the other. If the UNESCO approach provides a greater richness of diversity in ideas which may be applied to a given situation, the bilateral approach perhaps makes for less confusion: There are, practically, only two systems to compare and perhaps to reconcile. There are only two languages to be brought into understanding with one another. The balance of advantage or disadvantage depends on the particular problems to be met.

It should be kept in mind, however, that the bilateral programs are not carried out by United States technicians alone, or even to a major extent. In the first place, even the specialists appointed and paid by the United States are not all American citizens. Use has been made in the past of American-employed specialists from Latin America, Canada, and other lands. Most of them had had at least part of their formal education or professional experience in the United States. There is likely to be a considerable increase in the near future of the use of noncitizens of the United States on the American payroll of specialists in the bilateral technical co-operation program.

But, more important, the technicians paid by the United States are a small minority in the bilateral programs. Most of the personnel, whether under the *servicio* system or otherwise, are nationals of the other parties to the co-operation agreements. The *New York Times* of December 29, 1957, reports that as of June 30, 1957, there were not more than 2,361 United States nationals serving abroad—in all countries of the world—as technicians in the bilateral programs (not in education alone). But in a single co-operating country, there may be as many of its own nationals engaged as the United States supplies to its total world-wide program. No bilateral program is considered to be an "American" program: It is a Brazilian or an Iranian or an Ethiopian program, in which a few United States specialists are collaborating.

Programs of the UN specialized agencies are supported by funds contributed by many nations; each bilateral program is supported by funds contributed by two nations only. In both cases, the amount being devoted to programs of technical co-operation is pitifully small in comparison with the needs. Both the internationally contributed funds and those supplied by the United States government alone are somewhat precariously based; perhaps the funds made available by the United States for bilateral programs have a somewhat more stable expectancy of continuity than the others have. Of course, this is written before the 1959 budget of the United States has been presented.

### RELATION OF BILATERAL TO MULTILATERAL PROGRAMS

A comparison of respective advantages of the bilateral and the multilateral approach, however, need not imply that the two systems are competitive, or that, even in the United States, there must be a choice between using one or the other. Each has its place, each its special advantages. The important thing is to promote every opportunity for collaboration between them, for it is the goal to be reached and not the road to the goal which is paramount.

Technicians in the bilateral programs have participated very actively in conferences of UNESCO, for example, to give the benefit of such of their experiences as may be useful to the multilateral bodies and to draw on the wisdom of UNESCO technicians for their own guidance.

In many countries there are periodic meetings of UNESCO and ICA staffs. There is a wide exchange of documents and information. The ICA has employed technicians who gained their experience in multilateral programs, and perhaps an even wider use has been made by UNESCO of specialists who earned their spurs in the bilateral programs.

The Institute of Inter-American Affairs, now a part of ICA, is concerned with Latin America. Collaboration between the Institute and the Organization of American States has been especially close. The Institute was consulted constantly in the making of plans for the Inter-American Normal School sponsored by the OAS; the OAS participated most actively with the Institute in a joint conference on vocational education.

UNICEF and ICA have joined forces in many places in the school-lunch program, the international organization supplying milk, for example, and the ICA missions providing for storage and distribution in the name of UNICEF.

Many ICA officials, in the midst of efforts to obtain their own appropriations from Congress, have urged increased support also for the multilateral programs.

There is more to be done than either type of program can do alone at present. There must be no rivalry; only a seeking of means by which the combined efforts can be made most effective.

### III. *Helping the Asian Villager Help Himself*

#### HORACE HOLMES

##### THE ASIAN VILLAGER'S NEED FOR HELP

Hemmed in by tradition, often limited by religious taboos, and always operating near the brink of economic ruin, the Asian villager finds it difficult to embark upon any program that changes his usual ways. He, like any other careful person, is unwilling to exchange something that works, even poorly, for something that he is not sure will work at all. The villager, schooled by experience, taught by his father and his father's father, cannot be expected to experiment with new and unproven things.

Faced with the problems of drought, floods, insects, and diseases, about which he knows little, one is amazed that the villager has been able to keep faith in himself; to struggle constantly, and to continue to hope. He does not hope for much—only that tomorrow will be better, if not for himself perhaps for his children.

The typical villager has honor, integrity, and the will to work. He loves and has the love of his family. He is generous with the little that he has. He is jealous of the few rights that he possesses.

He worships his God in the manner that he chooses. He offers his friendship unstintingly. He resents being looked upon as an inferior. He wants to be respected as a decent human being, not only in his village community but in the world at large.

We know the causes of many of the diseases that affect his plants, his animals, and even himself and his family. We know what can be done to prevent many of them. We know that it is possible for the same land and the same amount of water to produce more bountiful crops; for the same animals to yield more milk, meat, or fiber so that the villager can get a higher return for his efforts. But this new knowledge must be applied with judgment and discretion; it must be understood; it must be fitted into the patterns of living in such a way that the benefits will be real and permanent and the results meaningful and understandable.

To the villager, this means that he must slowly, step to step, fit the new and proven things into his system of farming and way of living. Before doing so, he wants to be shown that the new seed does produce more than that he has relied upon throughout the years. He is willing to try, in a limited way, those new ideas that make sense to him, and to determine for himself whether or not the change is good. Once he becomes convinced, he needs no further urging.

He needs a dependable source for seed, fertilizer, insecticide, and other essential supplies. He frequently needs credit in order to buy these things. He certainly needs the seed before planting time and the insecticide before the insects have destroyed his crop—not when planting time has passed or after his crops have been ruined, as is too often the case.

Not all of the villager's problems are confined to the fields. While bringing about practical improvements in his crop and livestock-production methods is of tremendous importance, these alone are not enough if he is to make most progress.

He needs to improve his home, his living habits, his health and that of his family. He needs to understand the rights, privileges, and responsibilities of citizenship. He needs to participate more effectively and with greater understanding in those undertakings designed for the betterment of his village and his country. His children need to be better prepared so as to lead useful and constructive lives and to be able to understand, appreciate, and participate as respected and responsible citizens in the democratic processes now being opened to them.

The villager desperately needs practical and competent help in solving some of his many problems. He does not want a lecture: He has already heard too many speeches. For excellent reasons, he does not have faith in promises. He wants someone in whom he has confidence to come to his village and help him.

### PROBLEMS OF THE ASIAN VILLAGER

While villagers in most countries have their own peculiar problems due to climate, poor soil, fluctuating markets, floods, droughts, incidence of disease, and a host of other reasons, yet the basic problems of low productivity, ill health, and ignorance do not stop at national boundaries. They are common to much of the underdeveloped world.

Within each country there are wide differences; some areas being much more prosperous or progressive than others. Within practically every village some cultivators have managed to do much more than their less fortunate neighbors. There is a growing awareness that something can and must be done to bring about some improvement. "We want progressment," a villager explained recently. There is no doubt that they do, and they are willing to work for it. Many efforts have been made and continue to be made to find some practical solutions for some of those problems.

Certainly most leaders recognize that a healthy village economy is essential for the well-being of all the citizens. In those countries faced with a rapidly and constantly rising population, the lack of essential food and fibers is a constant threat. Increased production is necessary not only to achieve a better standard of living but even to maintain the present low standards. In order for all to have more, more must be produced.

For many years, efforts have been made to develop agricultural research, colleges, and agricultural departments and to improve the irrigation system, so necessary in many areas. Some of this work has been excellent. In some areas many improved varieties of crops have been developed; improved methods have been devised for the control of insects and other pests. Much has been done to improve livestock, to control animal and plant diseases, to make better use of legumes and fertilizers, or to utilize village waste. While the extent and quality of scientific research has not been uniform, there is a wealth of knowledge in some areas that can aid the villager to make better use of the resources at his command.

Demonstration farms have been set up by some governments as a means of showing the farmers the utility of some of the scientific practices that have been evolved. Subsidies have been offered for the distribution of seed and fertilizers and for the improvement of cattle or for the sinking of wells.

As the services aimed at improving village conditions have been expanded, so have the number of departments dealing with them. In many instances, the villager is at a loss to know to whom to turn. He does not recognize his problem as being in the field of plant pathology, agronomy, or engineering, but only that some disease is destroying his crop or that he needs better seed or needs to get water to his field. Even in those countries where much scientific progress has been made, there is often a lack of practical application to the farmer's problems. The villager cannot operate on generalities or vague instructions. He wants to know what he can do where he is; he wants a demonstration.

### IMPROVEMENT IN INDIA

The British, unlike some colonial powers, did train some native scientists, teachers, and administrators. This has given India a decided advantage over other former colonial areas where such an enlightened policy was not followed. It was natural that strong and intelligent efforts would be made to improve the rural areas and that, with the coming of independence, even greater attention would be given to efforts to improve village life.

One of the more significant programs aimed at village improvement was initiated by a British civil servant. In the early thirties, Mr. Brayne, an official of the British government assigned to the Punjab, worked long and hard to improve village conditions in his area. He stressed all types of improvements. These included health and sanitation measures, building schools, organizing credit societies, and developing local government. Also included were a number of improved agricultural practices, such as use of improved seed, use of village waste for fertilizer, the improvement of cattle, controlling insect and disease pests, and a host of others. Many of the things that are taking place in the Indian villages today were stressed by Brayne and the Indian workers associated with him. Subsidies were given to induce villagers to make the improvements; administrative pressure was applied to enforce compliance. Most of the improvements that were carried out were not maintained or continued. This was not because many of the things that were advocated were not useful; most of them were. The program was imposed from above. It was designed to do things for people or to them, rather than helping the villagers to analyze their own problems and then assisting them to help themselves.

There is no question but that the work of Brayne and his group a quarter of a century ago has contributed much in content, if not in method, to the village-development program operating in India today.

The Firka movement in South India, designed as a village self-help program by co-operative means, has reached many villages in that area. While this program did not become a nation-wide activity, it did generate ideas of self-help and certainly did much to develop leadership among village people. It instilled into village people the belief that something could be done to better their condition.

The work of Spenser Hatch and his dedicated group at Trivendrum, in South India, emphasized self-help. Here much was done to find ways by which people could earn additional income through handicrafts, poultry, beekeeping, and such. Improved marketing procedures were demonstrated and proven. This work showed what could be done by working intensively with a small group. They trained a number of people who later found a place in the nation-wide program.

The work of William Wiser and Charlotte Wiser through "The India Village Service" has been of great significance in the development of method. This operation, quite unlike the work of Brayne, concentrated upon developing the voluntary participation of village people. There were no subsidies and, of course, no administrative pressures. The India Village service, a voluntary organization, had meager financial support. The available assets were an indomitable spirit, an unusual understanding of people, infinite patience, and an unquenchable desire to be of service. From the standpoint of actual content, Brayne and his group evolved more subject matter. From the standpoint of method, however, the work of the Wisers stands out as one of the most significant contributions to the present-day development program.

It was Mahatma Gandhi who developed the real spirit for re-building India's villages. He gave the power, unity, and will to village people to do something about their conditions. He stressed the dignity of the individual as a person, he taught the code of non-violence, he gave hope to hundreds of millions of oppressed people that life could be better, and that they themselves could make it better. Gandhi rose to a position of great stature, not just among the Hindus but among Muslims and Christians as well.

All of these forces, acting independently, were nevertheless in operation when India obtained her freedom from the British in August, 1947. Some of the leaders felt that, with the British gone, all that was needed to improve the villages was to mechanize the agriculture and proceeded to try to do it. Others thought that the answer lay in the starting of co-operative farming, while still others favored communal farming. Some far-seeing leaders very wisely felt that the problems were quite different from those of the West, where man power is scarce and other resources plentiful, while in India the limiting factor is not scarcity of labor but scarcity of land, lack of water, and low production on the little land that is available to the average cultivator.

The fact remained that the country was free, that a new day was dawning, and that conditions did not have to remain as they were. Many people felt that, with the departure of the British, life would be easy; others had great fears. But within the heart of everyone there was hope. There was a responsible and responsive government dedicated to bringing about an improvement in the villages. And there was Gandhi's spirit which demanded that whatever be done must be built on the basis of human dignity and love.

### LEADERSHIP BY GOVERNMENT TO IMPROVE VILLAGES

The New India took over a government that was a going concern but now entrusted to men of her own choosing. Despite the terrific pressure involved in the change-over, the leaders did not forget their commitments that with freedom would come a chance for village people to improve their lot.

The partition of the country into two nations in August, 1947, was accompanied by streams of refugees in both directions. Two projects were started in an effort to provide homes and employment opportunities for more of them. One such project was at Faridabad, on the outskirts of Delhi. The skills of the refugees were utilized in the building of houses, factories, and, in fact, a new town. It was a thriving community during its building. Little, however, was done to improve the agriculture in the surrounding area so as to help support the town after it had been built.

A second refugee colony was built at Nilokheri, some seventy miles north of Delhi. This was a less ambitious urban-development program and a magnificent achievement for the purpose for which it was intended. It utilized the skills and ingenuity of the refugees in the building of a place for themselves in their new country. Here an effort was made to improve the agriculture of the surrounding countryside. Nilokheri also suffered some economic "bad weather," but it does stand as a symbol of what a resolute people can do when faced with an emergency.

A third experiment, quite unlike the other two, was carried out by the government of the United Provinces. It was not designed to provide homes for refugees but to find some solutions to the problems of poverty, disease, and ignorance in the villages.

This experiment, later to become known as the "Etawah Project," was successful. The government wisely selected men in whom they had confidence and gave them enough freedom and support to enable them to find their way. It had the highest possible backing of government. Both Mr. Nehru and Mr. Pandit Govind Ballabh Pant, the then Chief Minister of the United Provinces, were keenly interested and gave much time and attention to it.

The government of the United Provinces employed a small American group with a carefully selected group of Indian administrators and technicians to try to develop a pilot project aimed at finding ways to solve some of the village problems.

The early conception of the job left much to be desired. Replanning an Asian village, though desirable, is not of top priority to a people who are struggling to have enough to eat. Similarly, the introduction of modern American machinery, even though important under American conditions, may have little to offer to the Asian farmer whose problem is not the lack of labor but the lack of land, water, and essential supplies with which to grow crops on the little that he occupies.

Etawah had not been selected as the place for a pilot project at the time that the writer became associated with the effort. There was a recognition of the problem and firm conviction on the part of the responsible government officials that something must be done. There was the concept of a "project" rather than an effort to do everything at once. This was fundamental. There was also the concept of the development of a "multipurpose village worker"—an adaptation of the American Agricultural Extension Service, which can be best attributed to M. L. Wilson, the former director of the Agricultural Extension Service of the United States. There were many ideas that proved to be wrong, but there were other basic ones that proved to be right. Etawah was selected only as a place in which to try out some of these ideas.

Albert Mayer, an American town-planner, had originally interested the government of the United Provinces in the idea of the rural-development project. He recruited a team, consisting of a town- and village-planner in addition to himself, an agricultural engineer, and an agricultural specialist, all from abroad. A suitable cottage-industries man was never found. A number of Indian workers were carefully selected to work with the foreign team. This group included an anthropologist, a professor of English, a professor of history and economics, and an experienced agricultural worker who had operated his own farm, a young but able teacher who later became a government administrator, and two engineers, one experienced in irrigation and the other in mechanics. All of these men were willing to go to the villages and work.

In addition to the training and experience requirements, those selected had a genuine interest in village people, respect for them as people, and a conviction that improving rural India is essential for progress. It was necessary that the team, American and Indian, work long hours and under difficult conditions in the villages. They were to pioneer in establishing a new and healthy co-operative relationship between government and village people.

Like similar efforts in many countries, the organization began to grow. Unlike most, however, rather than continuing to feed upon itself, those phases of the operation that were found not to be feasible were abandoned. The heavy equipment and staff originally planned for the project were shifted to the land-reclamation department of government where they could be used more effectively.

The village-planning idea was quickly given much lower priority than in the original concept. Except for several practical improvements within the reach of the villager, this function was transferred to the newly formed Town Planning Division of the United Provinces government.

These were fortunate decisions; it was the simplicity of the Etawah experiment that made it a logical pattern for the nation-wide rural-development program.

### GOVERNMENT CO-OPERATION WITH VILLAGE PEOPLE

Efforts were made to develop mutually acceptable programs with the village people concerned. These were designed to help alleviate the problems of hunger, disease, poverty, and ignorance. No programs were imposed. No one presumed to have the answers to the many problems, but the problems were discussed with the villagers and village leaders. The resources that were available, or that could be made available, were examined and evaluated. Help was asked where additional skills were thought to be necessary, and simple approaches, upon which there was complete agreement, were tried.

Improved varieties of crops that had been proven on the government farms were tested in the fields. Individual farmers volunteered or were nominated by the Village Development Council to make the tests so that others might see. The farmer was not asked nor urged to take any greater risk than absolutely necessary; usually only half of one field was devoted to the new practice. All tests were made with the co-operating farmer as a partner in the enterprise, jointly searching for something that could prove its worth in the village.

Careful records were made of yields. Neighboring villagers were asked to examine the results. Where the results were found to be favorable, villagers themselves decided the extent to which they wished to take up the practice. Experimental plots were located within walking distance of each cultivator. All were urged not to make up their minds on the basis of a single trial but to examine all the trials in the neighborhood before adopting or rejecting the idea. This appealed to the farmers' sense of fairness.

No preconceived program was initiated and stressed. No single program was advocated in each village. Village leaders were urged to concentrate on the things that were meaningful to them and for which they had the resources or could get the resources necessary for successful completion. Projects were encouraged that met a real need, were easily understood, and would require the minimum of external support. Villagers were urged to think through their problems and to evolve plans that they themselves could execute, that would give the desired results.

Such community projects as the building of approach roads, village drains, village clean-up, village schools, and organizing literacy classes were encouraged. Participation on the part of all persons was stressed. The village people, the specialist, and the officials joined in the work to be done. The idea that trained minds and willing hands should be part of the same body came to be accepted.

Early in the Etawah experience, the leaders in one of the villages decided to clear some of the village lanes, some of which had been blocked by crumbling mud walls for more than thirty years. A day was set to begin, but only a few small boys came. The village worker and the boys began the work; gradually others came. Late in the afternoon most of the villagers were involved. Work was continued until 2 A.M. the following morning and more than 800 feet had been cleared. When asked why the group worked so late, one of the leaders explained that they wanted to finish the job before interest waned.

This was followed by a number of improvements in the village, including the building of the first approach road to the village. In the villages of India an acceptable practice can actually be adopted faster than is the case in Western agricultural areas where farmers live on their individual holdings. The planting of an improved variety of wheat, for example, when found useful by several members of the village, quickly became a village-wide practice; and such villages soon became the principal source of improved seed.

## THE MULTIPURPOSE VILLAGE WORKER

The functions of the "multipurpose village worker" is a recent innovation in Asia. It is in part an adaptation of the American county agent system, as practiced so successfully in the United States, but especially designed to fit Indian village conditions. A high degree of specialization among the various sciences is necessary, as one does research or teaching; but to have a dozen different people, each with a different idea, approaching the farmer and all offering advice can be, and is, most confusing.

The farmer needs a source of factual information. When he needs fertilizer, insecticide, better seed, or someone to help control his livestock-disease problem, he needs access to the sources of information, and he may need help in obtaining the necessary supplies. The village worker is trained to play this part.

Lack of roads and transport, generally poor communication facilities, a high rate of illiteracy, and distrust of strangers on the part of the village people make it necessary that the person who is to be helpful live in the villages and have the full confidence of those whom he is to help.

Early in the Etawah experience the importance of this function was recognized, and a training school was designed to produce such persons. Before there were any village workers, the technical team, consisting of the agricultural worker, animal husbandman, education specialist, and others, learned the jobs of the village worker. It was felt that only in this way could they become competent to train and direct others for the job. It was peculiar to the Etawah experiment that the better-trained people actually went through the process of working with the villager before assuming more responsible posts. This was difficult for some, owing to the custom that an educated man doesn't work with his hands. But it soon became an accepted practice. The dirty hand became a badge of honor rather than a disgrace.

The specialist should be at least as well trained as the village worker in addition to the special knowledge required of him in his own particular field. Far too often the specialist is either ignorant of or indifferent to the practical problems and simple solutions that the village worker must know if he is to be successful. This is also true of far too many people who direct the program. Until a more practical grounding can be given to people in key positions, we will continue to have difficulty in keeping village-development programs properly geared to village problems.

The supervisors and specialists in the Etawah project had actual village experience. This should be a prerequisite for appointment or promotion of staff.

The rigorous practical training of village workers, specialists, administrative staff, together with the servicing of the village and those immediately above each worker paid real dividends in bringing about village improvement.

Training centers for village workers were set up in existing buildings. This was done to prevent the operation from becoming too costly. The teaching was based upon actual demonstration and practice. The teachers demonstrated the practical application of those things that they taught. They set up an example of practical work themselves and required of the students only those things that they themselves could and would do. The day started early, usually at 4 o'clock. It was full. There were no holidays and no Sundays. All religious groups worked together, ate together; all did manual work. Common prayers that were acceptable to the various religious groups represented by the trainees were led by the students. The food was so prepared as to be inoffensive to the vegetarians. All such matters were handled by the trainees through elected representatives. The ability to solve problems by democratic processes is vital to those who would provide leadership in village work.

The training course normally lasted six months. It was rigorous. At the beginning, many left before completing the course; some after the first day. The men who were able to survive the intensive training were well prepared for their work. It was strong medicine, but it was effective.

The early part of the trainee's course was devoted to developing proper attitudes, understanding village problems, learning skills, and demonstrating a willingness and an ability to work. Later on, more field work was given. Each trainee was expected to learn all of the usual farming practices and to be able to carry them out with skill and competence. A farmer has little respect for those who would advise him but who themselves cannot do the job as well as he himself can do it.

It is imperative that the village worker live and work in the villages. It is only when he has been accepted by the village people that he can carry on effective work. This system was followed from the very beginning in Etawah and has become standard procedure in the later programs that have evolved.

The villager's confidence can be earned and kept only on the basis of performance; this means that the village worker must be able to keep his promises to them. To do this, he must be assured of prompt and efficient servicing by those above him; this includes both technical services and essential supplies. Adequate and timely servicing of the village worker proved to be a major problem, even in the small Etawah project. It continues to be a source of major concern to those who are trying to carry on village-development activities.

### EMPHASIS UPON DEVELOPING PEOPLE

As the idea of community development, as it was now termed, began to spread, the shortage of properly trained and oriented staff became more acute. Not only was it necessary that each staff member have competence in his own field, but he also needed the necessary skills and temperament to help village people think through their own problems and arrive at practical solutions with the resources available to them.

This was a far different assignment from the training that most had received or the experience of most in a law-and-order type of government. "We have come not to be served, but to serve" became a slogan. Slogans, however, are much easier to adopt in theory than in practice, and many found and still find it difficult to live up to the high standards expected.

Prior to the beginning of the community projects as such, on the birthday of Mahatma Gandhi in October, 1952, there were fifteen pilot extension projects in India. In five of these, there was a training center devoted to the training and development of village workers. Technical assistance and some equipment were obtained from the, then, U.S. Point IV program to assist with the training, extension, and some other specialized fields. The Ford Foundation co-operated with the government of India in establishing and staffing these and later centers and in strengthening the supporting services.

The training and extension centers were designed to teach and actually demonstrate practical things that would help the villagers. The experience that was gained in these centers, together with the personnel trained, was invaluable in the larger effort that followed. The training combined theory and practical application to village conditions. Agricultural training was moved from the desk to the field, and many found that successful work in agricultural development meant much more than issuing orders or giving lectures. It was a healthy change.

Many of the problems faced by village people require technical skill beyond that mastered by the less-well-trained village worker. This is the role of the specialist. He forms the connecting link between the village worker and the research institutions whose function is to develop and test new methods and techniques in the various scientific fields.

The specialist, to be effective, must be able to adapt the findings of the research worker to the practical realities of the village. To do this, he, too, must understand village conditions and have the imagination and practical experience to apply the advanced knowledge to village problems.

### NEED FOR TECHNICAL HELP IN RELATED FIELDS

The demand for competent people to work on health, sanitation, illiteracy, and social-education problems became greater and greater as the work in the village expanded. All such people had to be trained. While there were many with technical knowledge in the various fields, reorientation to village conditions was and continues to be necessary. A number of institutes have been established to give such training and orientation. Short courses and in-service training have given the lower staff greater competence in dealing with these phases of village improvement.

Rather than the village worker displacing the usual departmental person, as some had feared, his work in the village has actually opened a channel for greater application of useful information and skills. The great challenge to the subject-matter departments is that of increasing the competence of the staff to fulfil the greater service demanded of them.

Administering such a co-operative and comprehensive program has its share of problems. It is much more difficult to carry on such a program in a co-operative way than it is to operate by edict. The result, however, can be much greater and certainly longer lasting.

From the original five centers for training village workers and the fifteen extension centers, the effort has grown to a total of sixty-six centers for training such workers. Other centers established for developing specialized personnel include special centers for training in public health, research projects in environmental sanitation, social-education organizers, women workers, centers for the testing of agricultural implements and hand tools, the training of village artisans, and special centers for training executive officers.

Extension departments have been established in a number of agricultural colleges, and a National Extension Service formed with appropriate subject-matter specialists both at the national capital and in most of the important states. The community-development program is a more intensive approach than the extension program. Grants-in-aid are given for the completion of certain types of work. To date, community-development agencies and the less intensive extension centers have been increased to a total of 2,360 blocks or centers, serving more than 161 million people in 299,000 villages. The quality of the work being done and the effectiveness of the administrative and technical staffs are highly variable. Certainly, the work in some areas is outstanding. There is justifiable concern about some. The recent evaluation report on the progress of the community-development program published by the government of India realistically appraised both the strengths and the weaknesses. This is healthy. Bureaucratic strangulation is an ever present danger; this could easily result in the loss of the vitality and freshness that has made this effort unique. This must not be permitted to happen. There is the equal danger that too much be expected of such an effort. It cannot cure all the ills of centuries in a few short years, yet complacency must not replace performances. It is a difficult task.

Villages cannot be "developed" and then forgotten. Development is a process, not a goal. As rapidly as one set of problems can be solved, there are others in a never-ending procession. Nor do the problems of poverty, disease, and ignorance remain solved. A continuing and effective co-operative leadership must be established and maintained between the villagers and those agencies of government that can and should help them. Training of staff must be continuous. Promotion of staff must be made upon basis of concrete performance. Changes in conditions and development of practical scientific methods of dealing with village problems demand alert and responsive action.

As villagers attempt to change gradually from the traditional patterns of agriculture and primitive living and adopt ways of farming and living that yield more satisfying returns, they, like any other people, need access to developing science. In this way, and only in this way, can they contribute their full share to the nation's growth and security.

The Indian example is only one of the many efforts currently being made to improve the lot of the villager. India's efforts, however, are of such magnitude and her early successes so striking that much of the world is watching with intense interest. Indian experience, like that in most other countries attempting to improve the villages, has clearly demonstrated that the villager wants to improve his condition and is willing to exert himself to bring it about. It has been shown that there is tremendous power in the active and free co-operation of village people when working toward goals that they understand and appreciate.

The challenges to the administrator of any village-development effort are many. He must keep pace with the awakened villager, making essential supplies available at the proper time and at a fair price. He must see that adequate credit is available to permit the villager to improve his operations on a sound, business-like basis.

His entire organization must provide timely and efficient administrative and technical support to the technician in the field, so that he can, in turn, fulfil more effectively the responsibilities entrusted to him.

He must maintain the human touch, the sympathy, the understanding, and the spirit of service so essential to keeping the trust and maintaining the interest and co-operation of the villager. He must favor no group or individual to the exclusion of others; he must keep faith with all who struggle to advance and, above all, with himself.

## IV. Community Self-Help Enterprise and the Private Welfare Agency

RICHARD P. SAUNDERS

THE PRINCIPLE OF MINIMUM EXTERNAL AID
IN COMMUNITY EDUCATION

After a generation of direct financial sponsorship for needy children and impoverished schools, one of the long-established children's aid agencies has recently discovered and is applying the significant concept of community self-help. Because the cash investment in its new ventures is relatively limited, though the community response in invested man-hours of self-help is often of major proportions, the "Save the Children Federation" of New York has used the phrase "tenfold self-help" to dramatize this newer activity. The phrase is not intended to express an exact mathematical relationship but a relative ratio of self-help to the external aid now being offered by the Federation in its work on behalf of underprivileged children in the United States and overseas.

It may be questioned that a private agency should enter a field in which substantial government funds are being channeled, through both international and bilateral national agencies. To those active in the field there appear to be several adequate answers: (*a*) The need is so vast and all available funds inadequate to sponsor more than token efforts here and there. (*b*) Official funds must be channelled through official bureaucratic agencies which lack the flexibility to meet needs at the time when recipient enthusiasm has been kindled and active response is ready. (*c*) Field workers of a private agency can be chosen because of their individual knacks for dealing with people, vested with the authority to make immediate field decisions, and supplied with funds with which to implement these decisions when interest and enthusiasm are high. (*d*) Field workers of a private agency may be permitted to take into consideration the likelihood that projects which do not conform to a preconceived formula may by this very fact possess transferable elements that may induce adjacent communities to initiate similar self-help activities without outside stimulus.

This plan is based on one of the Federation's operational principles—minimum external aid. The application of this principle is quite contrary to some of the current practices which are generally thought to be the best for village work. No Federation village worker lives in any of the villages in which he works. The frequency and duration of the visits depend upon the status of the work in a given village, but oftentimes there is a lapse of many weeks, and rarely does the worker remain in the village overnight. Very often, and perhaps usually, villagers have very sound ideas about changes they would like to see take place in their community, especially after having given careful thought to planning, as the result of a new hope that plans might actually materialize. In those cases where technical assistance in agriculture, forestry, health, and other matters is necessary, the Federation helps the villagers obtain it from the proper government agency. This help is often available, although the villagers do not know that this is the case. This approach has met with wide governmental approval, because officials see that no competitive organization is being created and that the villagers themselves, with supporting technical aid from outside, can make their villages better places in which to rear their children.

The idea of minimum external aid applies not only to professional counseling but to the amount of money grants or loans. When the work of the Federation began, it often contributed more than 50 per cent of the estimated project cost. At times this limit was exceeded, however, in the interest of getting the program under way. The situation has changed rapidly with the wider implementation of the self-help idea.

This approach is based on the fact that in nearly every community characterized by underprivilege there is a substantial reservoir of unused labor which constitutes capital when translated into an improvement program using locally available materials and other resources, such as special skills. Villagers as well as government officials have seldom looked upon the situation in these terms, however, since they customarily viewed the unutilized labor as a curse rather than as a potential asset. This was true in Stephani, Greece, whose leaders at first preferred to talk and argue rather than act, with the result that the surrounding villages were making progress and Stephani was not. After the Federation representative had driven through their village without even stopping, the people became irritated enough to do something. In the words of the field report:

The next day an irate village president visited our office demanding to know why they alone of all the villages of Dervenochoria had not been visited by the Federation. To go through their village and not stop even for a cup of coffee had been considered an insult. They had been burnt out during the war; they were poor; they were a desperate, unhappy village; why couldn't we help them the way we were helping their neighbors?

I agreed that they were indeed a very unhappy village and asked him what they had done so far to help themselves.

The President stopped, dumbfounded. They had no money, he insisted, as soon as he recovered his speech. How could they help themselves without money?

"Why don't they have any money?" I asked.

"Because they are all underemployed," he answered triumphantly.

That was a sad situation, I told him. But if they were all underemployed, then they must have plenty of time on their hands. Why didn't they use that free time to start the much-needed work on the road so that the bus line could reach them?

Oh, they were going to work on the road—tomorrow.

That was just fine, I said. As soon as they fixed the road so that we could visit them in the winter as well as in the summer, we would discuss the possibility of working in their village in the next financial year which would begin after six months.

The report tells how the road was built within a month, of the voting of an acre of community land as a school playground, and of the construction of five village fountains in place of one, to which the villagers contributed 1,000 days of free labor after the Federation had given $500.00 and the community had voted a like amount from its own funds. This was not exactly ten to one, but certainly moving in that direction through the use of underemployed labor.

CIVIC WELFARE EXPERIENCE AND COMMUNITY EDUCATION

The "tenfold self-help plan" is the result of a serious effort to serve children through community betterment over a period of years.

The twenty-six-year-old Save the Children Federation is aiding with village self-help projects in the southern mountains and among the American Indians in the Southwest as well as in eight countries overseas. Its village work is based upon the following concepts, first stated in the Annual Report of the Federation's President to the Board of Directors in 1954:

1. That groups of free people, of good will, reasonably intelligent and willing to work together for the common good can, by their own efforts, raise their standards of living socially, economically, and spiritually.
2. That from simple successes in group co-operation there develop the skills and courage to undertake projects of greater complexity and wider usefulness.
3. That natural leaders emerge and develop as the result of continuing co-operation.
4. That rich personal satisfactions accrue to those co-operating as they reach successive objectives by working together for the common good.
5. That professional counseling, such as the Federation endeavors to provide, can result in the inauguration and development of democratic action, or make it more effective, by aiding in the recognition and evaluation of community problems, and by offering encouragement and specific assistance when sound projects have been selected by the group.
6. That in the light of the Federation's function of serving children, the emphasis must be on the welfare of the children of the community.
7. That the counselor's task is to make himself constantly less necessary to the community until the community can continue unaided and the counselor has literally "worked himself out of a job."

This statement was intended to give summary expression to the social philosophy of the late E. George Payne of New York University, who attempted to give it application to the field of child welfare in his *Guides to Modern Child Service*, published in 1951.

The application of the concepts began with the organization of a staff of five professional workers in the southern mountain areas of the United States in 1953. The first overseas project was undertaken in Greece in 1954, with an appropriation of $200.00. Today the program constitutes the major emphasis of the Federation.

From the beginning it has been understood that, inasmuch as the Federation was undertaking a sociological approach to child welfare with a necessarily strong educational emphasis, its workers would be concerned primarily with the process by which people were brought together and then undertook to work for themselves, co-operatively and especially for the welfare of their children. The concern was with the achievement of human values and the means by which they were achieved rather than specific material outcomes. This does not mean that there was no concern for the material outcome, but due attention to values and process seemingly assures sound material outcomes in most cases. At any rate the Federation, from the beginning, has sought to help people make better villages in which to rear their children.

Against the background of such concepts and such an approach, the "tenfold self-help plan" has taken shape in what might be described as three stages: (*a*) improvement of community facilities; (*b*) emphasis upon increased family income; (*c*) establishment of a local child welfare fund.

In the first stage, the Federation followed what has almost become a conventional approach to many community-development programs. It contented itself with investing its funds and the time of its consultants in helping local people decide what they wanted done and in working out ways and means of carrying through these projects. Since it is a child welfare organization, the Federation in this stage focused most of its self-help efforts in the local school. In the Appalachian area of the United States, parents and teachers came together to discuss how the school building and school grounds could be improved, to draw up a plan, and then to work without compensation to make the improvements called for by the plan: repainting the school, grading the schoolyard so that a good playground might be possible, building and furnishing a school lunchroom, and the like. These contributed greatly to the welfare of the children, who profited from better nutrition, better light, and a more pleasant environment in which to spend the day. In Greece, too, most of the early projects called for the construction of schools, which were badly needed in view of the wartime devastation. In some communities the experience gained in working together on the school led to the improvement of other community facilities. But the emphasis was upon improvement of public buildings and not upon projects that were primarily income-producing.

Not long after the first village improvements had been made, it became obvious that if community improvements were to be undertaken or even maintained, there must be an improvement in the economic status of the village. The children could not be helped further unless the village could find means to continue the improved services. It was not enough to build new schoolhouses, to provide sanitary facilities or pure drinking water for the schools or even fruit trees which one day would provide this school with fresh fruit. Neither was it enough to awaken a strong desire on the part of the adults in a village to help their children in every way possible without helping them find a way to accomplish their purposes. It was obvious to all that continuing financial support by the Federation was neither practicable nor desirable.

Meanwhile the Federation had been experimenting with the loan of a part of the cost of a tractor in Peitransieri, Italy, which would enable the village to feed its children adequately for the first time, and for spraying equipment in Milesi, Greece, to save the olive crop after the winter wheat crop had been destroyed and only 10 per cent of the cherry crop harvested after a bitterly cold winter. In both cases there was a direct benefit to the children of the village, and in each case it was arranged that an indigenous organization should collect the loan and place it in a revolving fund which would become available to other villages under reasonable conditions. The amounts involved were small—$500.00 in the case of the tractor and $125.00 for the spraying equipment.

This kind of arrangement, while unquestionably useful and perhaps well worth exploring further, did not seem to be a solution generally applicable to the problem of increased economic well-being. There was one further experiment, however, at about the same time at Castiglione Messer Merino, Italy, where a loan for motors to power the knitting machines which had already been purchased had not only increased the income of the village substantially but had given employment to a considerable number of young women and made possible the establishment and development of a co-operative organization. Village leadership developed rapidly, and the status of women was transformed in the light of the fact that machine operators now make as much money as an adult male.

But failures as well as successes should be reported. In Korea seven of the first nine projects involving economic improvement failed, largely because they involved the raising of poultry and small animals in refugee camps where there was never enough food. The projects did not simply fail; the animals were eaten. But the Federation has had enough experience with its efforts to raise the level of income within a village to know that, in the beginning, spectacular results can be achieved with relatively little capital outlay. Yet, at this stage, the connection between the Federation projects and child welfare was not always as apparent as in the period when the school or the playground was the center of interest.

What seems to be a further step ahead emerged in the spring of 1957 during a conference of the Federation's overseas directors at Athens. The group went to Phokea, approximately thirty miles south of Athens, for a demonstration of village conference techniques, for better or worse, but with few facts at hand and the probable outcome altogether obscure.

Through informal discussion in the coffee house, the community was encouraged to discuss their hopes and plans. They wanted a dock. It would enable them to export their principal product, grape juice, to Salonika without the expense of transporting it by truck to Lavrion or Pireus. Questioning revealed the extent of the economic benefits that would be derived each year and the amount of work that would be involved. Their own figures showed them that for each day of work which they contributed to this community project, they would receive a return of seven times the value of a normal day's work. The validity of their own plan having been established, the village accepted with enthusiasm the proposal of the Federation to encourage the spirit of people who would freely and voluntarily work on such a splendid project. The Federation would make a small cash contribution. The contribution was met many times over by the work of the village people. In return the village people agreed with enthusiasm that 10 per cent of the economic gains would be deposited by them in a community-development fund and that a further 10 per cent would be earmarked to support services for children—including a clinic and visual-aid materials for the school.

The operating device of setting aside a portion of the increased income of the budget for child welfare purposes, specifically, was demonstrated for the first time at Phokea. The provision undoubtedly will result in some new and interesting relationships. Implicit in such an arrangement is a continuing concern on the part of the Federation for the further development of the village and especially its child welfare services. In this relationship, as in all other Federation relationships, it should be borne in mind that the SCF has no authority whatever, seeks none, and considers one of its greatest strengths the fact that it has none. This kind of relationship is diametrically opposed to the old adage that there must be authority commensurate with any responsibility.

The "tenfold self-help plan" represents not only the experience of the Federation but also has grown out of the broad experience of the Federation's program director, who, until joining the Federation a year ago, was actively promoting and studying self-help programs throughout the world. In the reporting of a visit to Hancock County, Tennessee, by the program director and an area consultant, the key concept is explained as follows:

We also explained to him [the treasurer of the Community Club] that the ideal project is one in which there would be an economic return, part of which would be reinvested for further economic development of activities for the community, so that there would be a growing income of which a proportion could be earmarked for the benefit of the children of the community. So this indirect type of project in the long run would be even more beneficial to children than the first activity [installing lights on the playground] which is essentially and exclusively for children.

Federation experience with this latest stage of its self-help program is still too recent to permit any broad generalization. It does call for greater initial outlay of funds in that it *requires more technical supervisory skill,* but it can become self-generating in a way that the pursuit of one isolated project after another seldom does.

BACKSTOPPING THE "TENFOLD SELF-HELP PLAN"

There are dangers in moving from working with relatively uncomplicated community projects centered around a school to those designed to increase income and provide enough of a margin for the establishment of a community child welfare fund. A high quality of professional counseling on a readily available, if not frequent, basis may be needed even more than in the past.

Better communication and in-service training are two of the main concerns of the Federation with respect to its village program. It is evident that the same basic principles apply to all of the societies in which the Federation is working and probably to most others. Many of the techniques also apply widely, but, inasmuch as practically every worker makes certain distinctive discoveries, means must be found to make them available to all workers and to those who are responsible for the development of policies and the over-all administration.

Already a number of publications have been prepared, in limited quantity, for the use of the Federation's professional staff and for the consultants who co-operate with the Federation in its program of helping people help children through community self-help projects.

### CONCLUDING STATEMENT

Experience with the "tenfold self-help plan" thus far indicates that it is community development in the finest sense of that term. It seeks to combine both social development and economic development. Socially, it stresses that people are more important than projects and that the aim of self-help is to make it possible for people to grow in the sense of achievement, in self-confidence, and in a deeper appreciation of one another as they co-operate. It seeks to leave in the "community memory" a pleasant association with the projects that have been undertaken and completed. It also leads frequently to the establishment of some social arrangement such as a local council or group through which many community needs can be met, or it gives a larger scope of activity to existing groups. It adds to a sense of personal growth by making an individual in some out-of-the-way place feel that he has some importance and that he can, with the help of other individuals, accomplish visible results which he may never have dreamed possible.

This plan has its economic facet too. It seeks to make the local community more independent economically, at least with respect to the pump-priming capital it needs for starting some new activity when the older one begins to pay its own way. Furthermore, it stresses those economic projects where group efforts pay rich dividends and where maximum use can be made of otherwise unutilized labor. Even when some project fails, an effort is made to learn from that failure so that a similar mistake can be avoided in the future.

The "tenfold self-help plan" is child welfare as well. It views the child not as a single individual to be vaccinated, taught the three R's, and fed two or three meals a day but, rather, sees the child as a person developing in a social context. As the adults about him move from a state of apathy about local conditions to one of active participation, the child is affected; as their sense of community grows, this becomes imparted to the child; as their attitudes toward change and better health practices modify, the child becomes the beneficiary; and as the family income improves, so does the physical well-being of the child, provided that this income is spent intelligently. In the light of its experience during the last five years, the Save the Children Federation believes that it has opened a new and fruitful contribution to community education and development by private welfare agencies.

CHAPTER VIII

# Community Education in the Trust Territory of the Pacific Islands

ROBERT E. GIBSON

## America's Purposes in Micronesia and Need for Education

In 1946 the United States agreed to administer Micronesia as a Trusteeship for the United Nations. The following year the administration began, and military government gave way to civilian administration under the Navy. On July 1, 1951, administrative responsibility was transferred from the Navy Department to the Interior Department.

Under the terms of the Trusteeship Agreement, the United States has accepted responsibility for furthering the economic, social, educational, and political development of Micronesia. Having assumed such obligations, community education, as defined in the first chapter of this yearbook, becomes a necessity. The need for Micronesians to be literate in order to achieve a fuller and more creative life is obvious if the United States is to live up to the responsibilities imposed upon it in the Trusteeship Agreement. If they are to become self-governing and to participate more effectively in the economic, social, and educational progress of their respective communities, then Micronesians must have a minimum of general education in order to understand the problems of their immediate environment and their rights and duties as citizens and individuals.

Micronesians suffer from such endemic diseases as yaws, filiariasis, dysentery, tuberculosis, hookworm, and other types of intestinal parasites. Their sanitation is poor; as they recognize this as the source of most of their chronic illness, there will be the incentive to improve it. Good health is correlated with a prosperous economy. There must be the wealth to command the services of skilled medical men to provide relief from disease. Community education must free

Micronesians from those pressures within their cultures which resist or restrict the public health services.

Economic development is paramount in these islands, where the population is rapidly rising and where the demands for services are increasing by leaps and bounds. Most of the people are dependent for their livelihood on agriculture and fishing. Their main exportable product is copra. Land is precious on the coral atolls, and the soil is infertile. Only the coconut, breadfruit, taro, bananas, and pandanus thrive there. American agriculturists are striving to help Micronesians improve the strains of the indigenous plants and animals, to introduce new breeds of both, and to show them how to improve the fertility of their soil.

Another of the problems which face Micronesians and with which those concerned with community education must come to grips is that of diet. The native foods provided fairly adequate nutritional elements. It seems that in the more primitive environment, where man relied upon the natural subsistence foods, he almost instinctively ate those foods that were good for him. In the more remote communities of Micronesia he is still sustained by the natural foods. This is no longer true around the district centers, where an urban society has congregated, the breadwinners of whom work for the American administration. Since they work eight hours a day, they no longer have time to tend the native crops and to catch the fish that provided them with their one-time subsistence foods. They must purchase imported foods, which come at a high price. They are forced to purchase the cheapest of these foods, which usually are not the most nourishing. The result has been some beriberi, which is the result of faulty nutrition. Here is fertile ground for the community educator. Americans must help these people solve the problems of diet both through education and through economic development. The people in the growing urban societies must be taught how to supplement their diet of imported foods with garden crops and fish. Somehow there must be such an integration of the economy that the salaried employee will be able to purchase native fruits, vegetables, and fish from fellow Micronesians to the mutual profit of both.

The impact of World War II on the islanders was devastating. For years there was almost no medical treatment or care, and schools were nonexistent. Trade was ruined. Many people had been displaced from their homes, gardens, and fishing grounds. Then came the Americans with their ideas of democratic self-government. All of these impacts have had a disorganizing effect upon the total life. In societies based on fixed relationships between groups and resources and on status determined by birth rather than individual effort, the concept of the more general distribution of economic and political power was at first disruptive. Where political chiefs, belonging only to the most noble kin groups, have had absolute authority over all life and lands, they do not surrender such power readily. Nor do the commoners accept their new political and economic status without some confusion.

Micronesian communities are in a state of ferment. A new synthesis is under way. Even remote communities are responsive to it. Americans can aid in this synthesis through the medium of community education and development programs. They will fail unless they learn the lessons that the sociologists have taught: that communities, like personalities, are living individualities and hence cannot be squeezed into arbitrary molds. Each community is held together by some authority at the root of which lie basic customs which cannot be ignored or opposed. The mores are changing through a combination of causes, but the extent of that change and the speed of it should be determined by Micronesians and not imposed by Americans.

The locus of authority in the organization of the Micronesian community has been for many hundreds of years in the hands of hereditary chiefs. There has been a monopoly of power in an autocratic organization. No doubt this system arose pragmatically as the most workable system where land was scarce and infertile and a good many people had to be fed. Competition for the land might have been ruinous. In a democratic society authority becomes diffused; leaders are responsive and responsible; and participation by all in policy questions is expected and encouraged. In our eagerness for more democratic political and economic institutions, we must not destroy those that have served the Micronesians well up to this time. A community is organized around the values that are most important for the common welfare. The most fundamental of these values become incorporated into the culture as established custom. As the social environment changes, new values arise about which there are diverse attitudes. This is happening all over Micronesia today. It is testing the strength of existing community organization and giving rise to the need for a new integration. The successful educator, be he American or Micronesian, must be alert to all this and must understand it well, if he is to assist the various Micronesian communities to effect a healthy synthesis. He must not only be a good educator, he must also be a student of sociology and anthropology.

## Examples of Community Education in Trust Territory of the Pacific Islands

Having set the stage with the above description of Micronesia, of America's purposes there, and of the need for community education in order to achieve those purposes, the rest of this chapter will be devoted to descriptions of ongoing processes in Trust Territory which are considered to fall within the province of community education and development.

### COMMUNITY EDUCATION AND DEVELOPMENT AMONG THE DISPLACED BIKINI PEOPLE IN THE MARSHALL ISLANDS

Bikini, an atoll in the Marshall Islands, first became known to the world at large in January, 1946, when the U.S. Navy Department announced that it had been selected as the site for an experimental explosion of two atomic bombs. In February the military governor of the Marshalls arrived, in order "to secure the islanders' assent to their evacuation from Bikini in the interests of U.S. National security." Their reply was that if the government required their atoll for scientific experimentation they were willing to surrender it.

The Bikinians were first resettled on Rongerik, an uninhabited atoll 150 miles east of Bikini. Here they arrived on March 8, 1946, without enthusiasm and with some disspiritedness, which was not easily dissipated. Homes had been built for them and enough food supplies left them to feed the entire community for several weeks. But, from the beginning, progress was unsatisfactory at Rongerik. Food resources were poor, and this resulted in an alarming decline in the physical condition of the former Bikinians. A board of investigation, after an evaluation of the situation in August, 1947, did not hesitate to recommend that the Bikinians be moved once more. Nothing was done for another six months. In the latter part of January, 1948, Leonard Mason, professor of anthropology at the University of Hawaii, was sent to Rongerik by the High Commissioner of the Trust Territory to investigate further. Mason had had previous field acquaintance as an anthropologist with the Marshallese people and their culture. His description of the near-starvation condition of the ex-Bikinians and of their heroic attempts to cope with the emergency at Rongerik brought about immediate relief from the Administration as well as the decision to resettle a second time.[1]

On March 14, 1948, they left Rongerik for Kwajalein Island, seat of the American Naval base. Here they remained until the following November, when they were resettled for the third time on Kili, an uninhabited, isolated island without a lagoon. The physical environment of Kili was as different to them from that of their former home on Bikini as if they had been transplanted to the other side of the world. Their new home has a dry land area of 0.32 of a square mile as compared with the 2.32 square miles at Bikini. There is no lagoon at Kili, while at Bikini there are 230 square miles of lagoon area. This lack of a lagoon or protected anchorage has presented serious problems. From December through March, landing conditions are unfavorable. There is a very heavy surf, which means that copra can be loaded or trade goods off-loaded only at rare intervals when weather is suitable. For a people accustomed to living from fish caught easily in the lagoon, the transition to life on an island without a lagoon has made provisions of protein in their diet extremely difficult. This lack of a lagoon has set up psychological barriers which have made it almost impossible for them to think of Kili Island as their new home. On the positive side Kili has a good rainfall and a rich, deep soil (for the Marshalls).

In 1950, just before the transfer of the administration from the Navy Department to the Department of the Interior, the Navy anthropologist, D. Phillip Drucker, wrote in a report to the High Commissioner: "The Island of Kili is potentially rich agriculturally and

1. Leonard Mason, "The Bikinians: A Transplanted Population," *Human Organization*, Vol. IX (Spring, 1950).

thoroughly capable of supplying the economic needs of the present inhabitants [the ex-Bikini population], if properly utilized. At the present time it is clear that the resources of the island are not being properly utilized in any respect. The causes are considered to be twofold: first, an erroneous belief that a return to Bikini is likely at any time; second, real lack of know-how of agricultural techniques suited to the southern Marshalls." Drucker suggested in his report that an American agriculturist and a Marshallese assistant be employed to teach the Kili inhabitants how to utilize the island to its maximum.

Mason had similarly written in 1950: "On the material side of their existence, Bikinians have made a good beginning at Kili, but a planned program of education is needed to aid the newcomers in adjusting themselves to their new environment, such as learning to handle small craft in rough surf, to cure copra by artificial heat during the frequently rainy weather, and to cultivate and process the strange foods to which they have been introduced."[2] Here is clearly indicated the need for community education.

In an attempt to meet this need, the writer, as director of education of Trust Territory, Jack Tobin, anthropologist, and Leonard Mason discussed, during the spring of 1952, with James Milne, a Marshallese student at the University of Hawaii, his interests in returning to the Marshalls to serve as Community-Development Officer on Kili after preliminary training. Milne indicated an enthusiastic interest in the project and spent that summer alternating between the University and the High Commissioner's headquarters, which were at that time in Honolulu.

Under the guidance of these three persons, he reviewed the literature of fundamental education and community development, explored through Mason's firsthand information about Kili the needs of the inhabitants, and studied ways in which their needs might be met. Time did not permit the learning of specialized skills and techniques that might have helped him do his job better.

Milne started as Project Manager (Community-Development Officer) in Kili in the fall of 1953. He had the advantage of knowing the people's language and their culture. This is important. Too often

2. Ibid., p. 13.

Americans in their relations with people of another culture have the tendency to interpret what they see and hear in terms of American culture and its values. There is a corresponding failure to comprehend what is really taking place. This was not true of Milne, who knew, respected, and had no desire to destroy the traditions and customs.

Shortly before the Project Manager had started his work on Kili, the District Anthropologist and the District Agriculturist went there for one week to attempt to discover: (*a*) the use which the Kili people make of their time between field trips, (*b*) the work pattern followed, and (*c*) the present attitudes toward Kili, and to uncover the bases of their discontent in an effort to help these displaced people solve their problems and make a successful and satisfying adjustment to their new life.[3] The agriculturist studied the utilization of tree crops and assessed the agricultural potentiality of Kili Island. All of this information was shared with the Project Manager before he came to the island.

The investigations revealed that the Bikinians had established their own political organization consisting of two communities similar to those they had known in Bikini. A Protestant church was regularly in operation, and the minister was a highly respected member of the community. An elementary school with two teachers and 39 pupils was functioning. A health aide was attending to the medical needs of the community. A work organization had been set up by the council. On four days a week the people were free to do any kind of work, make copra, fish, gather food, cultivate gardens, etc. But on the other two week days they worked for the community, doing such work as cleaning up paths, cultivating the communal taro patch, doing repair work on *benjos* (latrines), bathhouses, etc. There was one store on the island from which the people could purchase food supplies: rice, flour, sugar, etc., from their copra proceeds.

A year later the District Anthropologist returned to Kili to spend three weeks evaluating what had been accomplished under the leadership of the Project Manager. He reported a marked optimism among the Kili people. In his final summing up he said: "It cannot

3. Jack Tobin, "The Bikini People, Past and Present." Report to the District Administrator and the High Commissioner, October, 1953.

be overemphasized that James Milne is the key to the success of the Kili project. His guidance and technical knowledge are invaluable. His participation at this point . . . is absolutely essential if the project is to continue successfully."[4]

One of the Project Manager's first activities was to go by boat to Kusaie, a fairly large and prosperous island some three hundred miles away, and purchase several thousand taro plantings. This island grew the best breeds of taro in Trust Territory. While there he learned all the techniques of planting and cultivating taro from the Kusaieans, and when he returned he taught the Kilians all he had learned. The taro was planted before the stormy winter months in an attempt to insure a more adequate food supply for the coming year.

Breadfruit and pandanus plantings were increased, and in all these attempts to improve their agricultural productivity the technical aspects of the utilization of their natural resources were taught to the people.

In a search for other projects besides copra which would provide the people with a medium of exchange, the Project Manager greatly stimulated the development of handicrafts. The Kili people are adept at handicraft, but they had not been advised and shown the type of handicraft for which there was a market. The Project Manager had investigated the potential markets in Honolulu and Kwajalein and apprised the Kili people of the results. A Marshallese handicraft expert was brought to Kili from another island and taught handicraft techniques to the women. As a result of the research on available markets, the following types of handicraft were made: hats, square white handbags, table placemats, fine decorated mats, and wooden bowls.

The manufacture of large quantities of *jekmai*, a very delicious syrup from the sap of the coconut palm, was started, and soon considerable quantities were successfully exported to other islands of the Marshalls.

At council meetings, the Project Manager attempted to educate the people in the principles of nutrition as applicable to the local

4. Jack Tobin, "Kili Journal." Report to the District Administrator, September 19, 1954.

situation. He stressed the superiority of local foods to rice and flour and other imported foods.

Before he left the Kili Project at the end of 1954 to engage in private business, the Manager had assisted the people in obtaining a 40-foot Marshallese-type schooner with auxiliary engine. Their economy was developing to such an extent that there was need for regular and frequent communication with the outside, especially to transport local copra, handicraft, and other produce to market and to bring back trade products to Kili Island.

In order to insure the continuance of the Kili Project, another Project Manager (Community-Development Officer) was being trained in Honolulu under the guidance of two anthropologists at the University of Hawaii, Leonard Mason and Saul Riesenberg, both of whom had had extensive anthropological experience in Trust Territory. Riesenberg had been Staff Anthropologist for the Administration for one year. This student, Konto Sandbergen, was also a Marshallese who had had one year of education in Honolulu under a John Hay Whitney Scholarship grant. For the next year he carried on practically independent study under Professor Mason's direction in the field of community education and development. It is well to note here the nature of his training for leaders in community education and development, which does need a special kind of training in order to do a proper job. His reading was organized to cover certain general principles of community organization, the relation of the individual to his community, and participation in the culture of the group. Three or four hours each week the student reported to Professor Mason, and the two would go over the materials with considerable discussion on the more important points, always relating the materials to the student's own background in the Marshalls and, where information permitted, to the situation at Kili as the student expected to work with it. A second stage of the reading program involved more specific consideration of certain communities. The two went over the materials from Trust Territory files on Kili since 1950 and, with the student's own observation from field trips, tried to reconstruct as nearly as possible the community conditions there. Then the student read certain parts of the studies that Mason had previously made in the Marshalls in order to acquire more background on the nature of a small, relatively isolated community where resources are limited. Next, the student was encouraged to familiarize himself with specific community-development projects in the Pacific, notably Moturiki and the several projects in Papua and New Guinea.

Certain areas for concentration were established, as follows: agriculture (this meant improvement of what is there now and also included possible introduction of whatever crops might be judged suitable on the advice of agricultural specialists at the University); housing (improvement of existing housing with emphasis on greater use of local materials, e.g., thatch, or trade with other atolls for scarce materials); local government functioning, especially in regard to finance and co-ordination within the development framework; crafts (improvement of certain handicrafts for export to Americans or for trade with other atolls, e.g., sennit, a kind of rope made out of coconut fiber); sanitation (measures to prevent disease, to be co-ordinated closely with the work of the health aide, in respect to water supply, waste disposal, and housing); communication with the rest of the Marshalls (need for development of skills in boat-handling and navigation); and, last, education (divided emphasis on child and adult training with appropriate techniques and curriculum, all to be tied in with other emphases noted above).

The teacher and student discussed together many alternative possibilities for approaching each of the above problem areas, not so much in terms of the technical solutions (for these further information was sought from other experts at the University and the Hawaiian community) as the problems of human relations involved therein. This meant attention to the roles of individuals within the existing community, the significance of the present organization of the community, the fact of the relative isolation of Bikini in the past from the rest of the Marshalls.

All of this study and discussion was quite tentative. There was no attempt to work out any co-ordinated plan of attack, since there were still so many unknowns. The student and teacher were always cognizant of the fact that practical planning in this context must proceed on the ground with the participation of the people themselves.

Besides his close weekly contact with Mason, a series of meetings were arranged between the student and the head of the Botany Department at the University, who had carried out extensive studies of the plant life in Micronesia. The purpose was to find out how to improve the quality and quantity of what food crops were already available and, secondly, to consider what crop introductions might be feasible in the Kili environment.

Closely related to the food supply is the diet of the people. Consideration was given to the possibility of making a diet survey at Kili with the community's participation, partly as a means of educating the group to its own needs. In order to handle this problem more intelligently, the student worked with a nutritionist in the Home Economics Department at the University. He enrolled in a course on the elements of nutrition work, a basic introductory course for non-specialist students.

On the handicraft side, helpful assistance was received from a local agency dedicated to the encouragement of handicraft production in Hawaii.

Since instruction in bookkeeping would be helpful at Kili in keeping accounts in the store and council affairs, the student enrolled in a bookkeeping course.

In summary, the preparation of the Community Development Officer was of such a nature as to enable him to assess with some accuracy various elements of the community (housing, food, work effort, sanitation facilities, educational background, export products, and local resources and raw materials). By being able to make such surveys the Project Manager would have a useful device for developing within the community a realization of its inadequacies and assets.

During the first semester there was concentration upon general principles of community organization and individual and small-group participation in the larger community. The second semester was spent in learning about the more practical aspects of the problem where technical advice is needed to assist whatever community action is undertaken. Both these approaches are essential to any community-development program. Many of our technical-assistance programs in other countries have fallen short of established goals because the first approach was not given sufficient consideration.

Ths new Project Manager (Community-Development Officer), after his year of training in Hawaii, arrived on Kili in October, 1955. His first preliminary survey of the situation was a rather unusual document for a Micronesian. It showed a keen insight into the problems there and certainly was a favorable reflection on his preparation in Hawaii. He first made a study of the municipal government, which was composed of fifteen council members, headed by a magistrate, who served also as the community court judge. The financial situation of the local government next was investigated both from the standpoint of the total possible annual tax revenue and of the set annual operating budget. Here he noted that the treasurer's bookkeeping system left much to be desired. The training in bookkeeping in Hawaii came in good stead.

In regard to economic development on Kili, the new Project Manager noted that "there now exists a moral code against unwise harvesting practices which were very common during the early settlement." The land and taro patches had been divided among the extended family groups. There was a desire on the part of the *alabs* (leaders) to obtain more seed plants, poultry, and pigs to raise on Kili. It was also noted that "the people have learned to conserve uncooked edible taro tubers by preserving them in ground pits, a social pattern never before practiced." It was apparent at this time from the activities of the people that a large number of them were supporting the project. In the opinion of the new Project Manager: "The extent to which the people of Kili continue to support the development program is partly dependent on the reward (whether it be in the form of psychological, financial, or a material return) they will obtain from the work they themselves have been or will be establishing with the assistance of the Project Manager on Kili and partly upon the support extended the Project Manager by the Administration where it is needed."

In public health the Project Manager found the people to be in good shape. The health aide was out of some of the more commonly used drugs which should be regularly supplied by the District

Health Department. Sanitary conditions were fairly good. "Nevertheless," the Project Manager noted, "it could have been improved to a greater extent if both the materials needed for such improvement were available (nylon screens, water-soluble DDT, picks and shovels) and also if the community had continued to practice natural sanitary measures, such as use of proper toilet facilities and proper garbage disposal (dugout pits). There is but one usable toilet house on Kili and there is no dugout pit anywhere. It is obvious that a community-wide sanitation program will have to be encouraged if a healthier community and a prolonged period of health is to be maintained."

In commenting on the housing situation, the new Project Manager reported: "Almost the entire houses on Kili are badly in need of repair. . . . There are three cisterns, and all of them will have to be repaired immediately." Some of the materials for repairing these houses would have to be obtained from available surpluses at the District Headquarters.

So far there had been very little development of the marine resources at Kili. The former Project Manager had started a small fish pond, but, aside from the usual pole-fishing, spear-fishing, and torch-fishing, no other methods were being used. Since the waters around Kili abound in tuna, the new Project Manager saw the possibilities for the people to catch enough fish during the calm season to supply the demand. There was need "to establish a process whereby they could have a reserve supply of fish or other meats which they could draw upon during the rough weather."

It was noted that a tremendous economic and agricultural development had been accomplished during the past two years under the former Project Manager. Copra sales had increased considerably, and the handicrafts industry was bringing in a substantial income. The securing of a boat had provided for regular shipping and marketing. Konto Sandbergen believed that with solid plans for work and proper equipment to reduce the difficulties of production a higher production could be obtained. The 25,000 taro plants imported by the former Project Manager had taken root. The breadfruit plantings were doing well.

This first report showed only a very brief and preliminary observation of the elementary-school program but indicated that a closer
relation would be established later.

In September, 1957, Tobin revisited Kili for a final summing up
of the efforts there in community development. He met with the
Kili council, and this body stated that there were no serious difficulties on Kili and that the food supplies were adequate despite the fact
that the taro project had not turned out as well as was anticipated.
It could not be considered a failure, for the Kili people had learned
taro culture, a completely new technique to a people who had had
no taro on their native atoll. Enough were interested in taro and still
cultivating it to insure that they will continue and probably expand
the cultivation of this entirely new and important crop. Banana
plantings had increased noticeably and were doing well. Many new
plants were found throughout the island.

A large number of breadfruit trees in various stages of growth
were also scattered throughout the island. The seedlings brought
from Kusaie four years before were flourishing. The pandanus trees,
which supply food as well as leaves for weaving their thatches and
baskets, were also doing well.

The Kili people had learned how to run their co-op store. The
store was filled with staple items. The books were kept in excellent
condition.

Many Kili men had been trained as sailors to navigate the Libra,
the Marshallese-type schooner which was proving to be the key to
the economic and social welfare of the Kili people. With the help of
this boat they have been able to take the first steps to establish a settlement for some of their people on an atoll some forty miles away.

Animal production had increased, but the people wanted and were
willing to buy pigs, chickens, and turkeys from the Agriculture Department.

Their trade and transportation needs have increased to such an
extent that the forty-foot auxiliary schooner is no longer sufficient.
They want a larger boat with more cargo space and are willing to
purchase it themselves.

Tobin's final summing up was this: "Konto Sandbergen is doing a
good job, in my opinion, and has agreed to remain for another year,
after which he plans to apply for a scholarship leading to a law de-

gree." The latest monthly report from the Marshalls states: "Conditions have improved on Kili since installation of the Project. . . . The Kilians will be completely self-supporting within two years. . . ."

## Community Education in Yap

### LOCAL SCHOOL BOARD TRAINING

The Yap District of the Trust Territory is located in the western Carolines, some five hundred miles southwest of Guam. The Yapese are the most individualistic of all the Micronesians. They have great pride in their own culture and are the most reluctant to acculturate. In other words, they have to be shown. The community educator who attempts to impose his ideas on the Yapese people will get nowhere. But for one who "believes considerably in other human beings, in their capacity for growth, given a propitious set of circumstances, and in the tenet that human growth is best encouraged in any given environment as the people concerned participate both in purpose and activity in their own progress,"[5] working with the Yapese people can be most rewarding. Vincent Edson, the Educational Administrator in the Yap District has found it so, as he attempted a "grass-roots" approach to the problems of education in Yap. He started with the thesis that improving a culture means improving local communities and that education, broadly conceived, has a part in such improvement. His concept of education is not synonymous with formal schooling; nor is it equated with teaching and learning as primarily processes of memorizing subject matter. Rather, it accepts the view that there can be no higher educational act than that of the people of a community participating and co-operating to solve problems in community life.

One of the greatest problems in the functioning of elementary schools in Trust Territory has been that of the development of local responsibility. When the Navy first assumed the administration of Micronesia, it decreed the establishment of elementary schools on every island and atoll where there were children of school age. Public elementary schools were strange new institutions for a people who had for hundreds of years carried out the tasks of educating their

5. Robert E. Gibson, "Review" of *Moturiki: A Project in Community Development* by Howard Hayden. This review appeared in *South Pacific Commissions Quarterly Bulletin.*

young for the chief needs of life through a parent-child relationship or with the elders of the clan educating the young into the ways of their particular society. The universal, formal elementary school was a new creation, and one for which most of the people had no felt need. Since they were established first by the Navy, they are still often referred to as military schools or government schools. A sense of local ownership and responsibility is very slow in developing.

Edson and other educational administrators as well as Micronesian leaders are working hard on this problem. They realize that the chapter of the Code of the Trust Territory of the Pacific Islands describes very adequately the educational laws and regulations for each district in Micronesia, but the very way in which it is written purposefully leaves room for local interpretation and ingenuity. As far as Yap is concerned (and this is equally true of the rest of Trust Territory), after close observation it was concluded that the people were operating within the framework of a system about which they knew very little. It is very true that the Code provided for the establishment of a district as well as municipal boards of education, but if the present educational system is to become an integral part of the Yapese life (or an integral part of the life of the other peoples of Micronesia), it seems quite necessary that the idea of universal, free public education should not only become accepted but understood by the people and the boards who govern as well as by the educators. Boards especially must understand what public education is all about in order for it to become a real part of Yapese life.

The Educational Administrator, seeing the need for a program of educating his school boards directly and all the people indirectly, planned a series of meetings with his various local, municipal school boards to acquaint them with their own responsibilities and to bring about greater understanding of the purposes of this institution which Americans had set up. As explained by Edson:

Americans were responsible for the present system so we began with the "why" in our own cultural idea.

At the first meeting of each board, the "lesson" consisted of discussion— of why free education for all, especially of children? It was found that many understood and almost as many believed in the ideal. The Yapese had some basis for understanding because many board members remember, distinctly, educational facilities and ideals set forth by the Spanish, German, and Japanese administrations.

I cannot relate all the facets of these discussions that took place. Many questions were asked. The important thing is that the questions raised and discussed were not limited to our meetings. Many of the issues were discussed in the villages, at gatherings, and became topics for many conversations.

The next portion of our lessons was on organization. What was each group and individual in the educational organization to do? What was the responsibility of each? Was the present organization sufficient? Much confusion was evident concerning responsibility, power, and function of each group or individual.

Our next step was to discuss Trust Territory law regarding education. In this area it appeared that scarcely anyone really understood the Trust Territory code, such as that pertaining to attendance. Some people even believed that they were transgressing the law by sending their children to parochial schools. Some of the points of the Code in regard to education were not understood at all, even by the teachers. The questions and discussions concerning school law were too numerous to describe in detail. The most important conclusion regarding this part of our work with school boards is that Yap is now ready to make some school laws of its own. They will not be merely laws but rather standards made by the people who will be governed by them—standards and rules which the people will understand.

Financial responsibility was another topic of discussion with school boards. Even though Yap has done remarkably well in its local support of schools, the whole topic was one of common misunderstanding. We have been getting money because the Yapese are trusting and because they wanted to help. But the reason they wanted to help was limited almost entirely to their generosity and faith. Financial responsibility motivated by their own desires and needs rather than by the wishes of the Administration will develop as the schools become more truly their schools—answering their needs, understood by them, governed by them, and helping them to solve their own problems.

Our formal classes will not stop here. We have many more important problems to discuss. Here are a list of future objectives we have in mind:

(i) That Yap teachers and board members develop a handbook of policy and organization of the district educational program that will be a guide and learning tool for all. This handbook must not be an American creation; it must be a product of Yapese understanding.

(ii) That Yap district develop an education code of its own to supplement the Trust Territory Code. This Code must be more than a properly assembled group of laws; it must be a well-defined set of standards which express the desires and understandings of the people. It must be from the hearts and minds of the Yapese people—created and understood by them.

(iii) Yap teachers and board members must finally create, understand, and approve their own educational program.

SCHOOLS PARTICIPATE IN ECONOMIC DEVELOPMENT

Copra is the most important money crop in the Yap District. Every Yapese understands its importance and learns about it from childhood. All people on Yap participate in a certain amount of copra-making each year.

Scientific production of copra has never been emphasized on Yap, in spite of some experimentation and testing of products. There has been no realistic project undertaken which the Yapese have accepted as a change in method.

Each year a large percentage of the crop remains unharvested. Challenged by this waste of excess copra, the Education Department started a program which has come to be known as "Copra Week."

Copra Week provided funds for support of scholarships and school buildings. Three or four times in a year all schools are dismissed from classroom activities. Students go into various municipalities and work with the villagers in the task of harvesting and drying copra. All funds are turned over to the Board of Education to use for these purposes.

Each copra week has served as a successful school-community project. Besides raising money for good purposes, students and villagers have learned a great deal. They learned, for example, that the copra sold was not good copra. Often it came from nuts of an inferior quality. It was poorly dried and consequently often mouldy. While the project was worthwhile in its motivation, it was, nevertheless, an example of poor teaching because the educators were encouraging the perpetuation of bad methods of copra collection and drying.

Mr. Pieris, Director of Coconut Operations for Trust Territory, brought information to the Education Department on the "Improved Ceylon-Type Copra Dryer." The Education Department asked to be allowed to set up a project using this new type of copra dryer, thus bringing the information to the children of intermediate-school age. The Yap Trading Company, under the guidance of Mr. Pieris built a dryer on their property. The Agriculture Department furnished nuts for the first experimental drying. Students assisted in husking and chopping. The first batch was dried and sold for number-one grade copra. Prior to this, the copra collected by the students had always been grades two and three.

Following discussion with the Board of Education and the local trading company, it was decided that the students would participate in a weekly collection of nuts from one of the ten different municipalities. The nuts would then be taken to the dryer and, under the supervision of intermediate teachers and other departmental personnel, processed and dried in this new dryer.

The school processed some thirty thousand coconuts in twenty batches. Without exception every pound of copra sold for the number-one price. This rather thorough test which was given the dryer did much to convince the Yapese of its worth.

The Agriculture Department through the office of the District Administrator reprinted scale drawings of the dryer. The Education Department translated written instructions for building the dryer and a materials' list. The Agriculture Department then encouraged the building of dryers in different parts of Yap. Students assisted the people with the actual building during the weekends. Thirty dryers were started and many completed within a short time. Through these efforts more copra is being harvested, higher prices are being obtained, less labor is required per pound of dried copra, and there is continuous drying of copra despite wet weather.

Copra week still continues on Yap. By now many of the villages have a new-type dryer completed. In some cases they have not been sure that they were using it correctly. Students found themselvs actually instructing their elders in the drying of copra. The villagers talked to the students very happily about the innovation. An improvement has been made in Yapese life. The good feeling felt by students and teachers was not that they had done something but that they had co-operated in something—of value.

Thus community education in Yap has come to be regarded as the educational arm of community development. What still needs to be better thought out in most places is the detailed nature of that relationship, and this requires not only that the educator must try to meet halfway the agriculturist, the health worker, and all the rest but just as much that they must attempt to meet the educator the other half. In Yap you can see that this is being done.

In these and other projects, the possibilities of utilizing the techniques of community education and development as a means of bringing education to bear not only on the child but also on the family and on the whole community have been envisaged. In most cases, it will be noted, projects were carried out through the combined efforts of the community itself and of specially trained Micronesian leaders. There was adherence to the principle that program and planning should be adjusted to the needs of the situation itself. The people themselves of any community have the right of final judgment, and any outside expert in community education and development should defer to this final judgment of the people to be developed. At least he should give to their knowledge and judgment equal status with his own.

Such a viewpoint presupposes that the community educator or community development officer has the ability and inclination to learn from the people and does not seek to impose his judgment upon them. It also rules out detailed planning in advance for the very good reason that preconceived plans tend to make the officer carrying them out too committed to his own ideas of what the community needs. Preplanners are liable to define for themselves what the community's problems are. The next logical step is to provide the solutions and finally to manipulate the community into accepting both the problems and the solution.

In the opinion of those working in Trust Territory this is not good community education. What they have in mind is to make the community less dependent on the administering authority. They want to stimulate the people to the point where they are willing and able to identify and solve their own problems. Externally conceived goals will probably defeat such ends.

CHAPTER IX

# Lessons in Community Education Learned through Technical Assistance Programs

T. L. GREEN

## Agencies Involved

Technical Assistance in south and southeast Asia began in colonial days, even though its intentions were not those accepted today. In its modern form it is an aftermath of World War II. To trace its growth, even in broad outline, is too considerable a task to be attempted here, where only a few points can be mentioned.

Point IV projects brought the United States into the field very early. Almost simultaneously the specialized agencies of the United Nations began work on very diverse fronts—particularly in regard to food production, health, and education. In 1950 a meeting of the foreign ministers of the British Commonwealth of Nations initiated what is today called the "Colombo Plan."

The original Colombo Plan members were Australia, Canada, Ceylon, India, New Zealand, Pakistan, Malaya, British Borneo, and the United Kingdom. The United States, represented as an "observer" at first and already working in the area, became a full member in 1951, though American aid is handled through the United States Operations Mission offices in the various countries and not through the office of the Colombo Plan. Since then Cambodia, Laos, Vietnam, Burma, Nepal, Thailand, Japan, and the Philippines have become members. Also, working through resident representatives of the Technical Assistance Board, there are the many programs of the United Nations specialized agencies.

Historical relationships, together with certain attributes of the British Commonwealth, have perhaps given to the Colombo Plan a certain degree of informality of procedure which tends to emphasize the "family" situation, as compared with more rigid and formal relationships engendered by other agencies, which are either national or international. Despite these differences the various agencies work together smoothly in the conduct of technical programs which range far and wide, which are of very diverse kinds, and which are all joined in the common task of helping the peoples of south and southeast Asia to raise their standards of living in an area which includes a quarter of the world's population and which suffered great devastation as the result of war.

Nor must it be forgotten that such voluntary agencies as the educational foundations and the church missions have, in their various ways, been engaged in bringing about cultural change, in some cases over a long time and on a wide front.

## The Background

There are two important points which must be kept clearly in mind. First, while technical assistance is being offered to Asian countries upon a scale never before achieved, it is essential to remember that technology is not new in Asia. The compass and navigation, Ayur-Vedaic medicine and its *materia medica*, the great religious and military buildings, the production of glass, the first forms of printing, the metal craftsmanship, the vast water storage tanks and irrigation channels (dating back four and a half centuries before Christ in Ceylon), and the Moghul observatories are but a few examples of technologies with a long history. What we can offer today may well be different, but often it is a matter of degree, and not always of kind, as we too often tend to assume.

Secondly, there is the problem of rate or time, as a measure of the relation between aspiration and achievement. We are in danger of attempting too much too quickly, and in even greater danger of underestimating the difficulties of quickly inducing technical changes, and thereby of engendering a sense of disillusionment among Asian peoples[1] because performance differed from promise.

This factor of time scale must always be in mind when planning, performing, predicting, or conducting a post-mortem upon any project in social development in Asia. For, apart from all the potential brakes on progress, which are the outcomes of the techniques

1. T. L. Green, "Ceylon: Case Study for Evaluation of Education and Social Progress," *Year Book of Education* (London), 1954.

adopted, the tasks selected and the limitations of all involved in their execution, there is also all that is summed up in the phrase "the time-less East." Satellites may whirl overhead, turbo-jets cut time and distance schedules, and technologists show how to accelerate proce-dures—yet here in Asia we come, at some inevitable point, upon the bullock cart, the manual method, and the "patient peasant." As we set out to change them, let it never be forgotten that we ourselves have changed but slowly. Our farming and fishing communities are conservative and traditionalist, and our industrial revolutions were spread over a couple of centuries. Yet, made overconfident by our slow achievements, we often set out to change an Asian way of life almost overnight, seeking to jump from hand plow to bulldozer, without the intermediary shovel and wheelbarrow, forgetful of the fact that though human nature may be malleable, it is also enduring.

## Some Examples of Problems Encountered

With projects ranging from simple to complex, from short-term to long-time, and from social to technological, it is only to be ex-pected that a similar variety of problems would be encountered. Leaving aside the economic, technical, and even political aspects, which form a common background to all projects, there is a series of other problems the existence of which only becomes realized in functional terms on the job itself. It is this second group of on-the-job problems which is the significant background to those interested in the outcomes of technical assistance, as seen in terms of commu-nity education.

### ORGANIZATIONAL PROBLEMS

There are many kinds of organizational problems. Among these are two, closely related to each other and both with an immediate impact upon the educational and social aspects of a technical assist-ance project. These two are concerned with the distribution of re-sponsibility and the delegation of authority. Every technical expert, in introducing new techniques, finds himself involved in training those who work with him. Naturally the expert is concerned with the question of who will carry on when he goes; but he also wonders whether or not his successor will follow on the first group he himself has trained. He at once turns toward the schools and points out that technology demands technicians, who are themselves the product of education—particularly of science education.[2] The expert himself is the product of a situation in which, over the years, education has (to a considerable extent) become geared to social needs. Such conditions do not exist in any of the Asian countries, not even in Ceylon, which enjoys one of the best-developed educational systems in the area.[3] Our expert, working in irrigation, agriculture, forestry, mining, engineering, or even in social service work (such as training midwives or dental nurses) believes that, from his angle, education must possess a forward-looking, prevocational component—but to turn belief into action is full of difficulty! He, and his kind, work in diverse ministries—education is another domain.

Curriculum-planning is still largely a matter of unified control with directives which range from models deriving from the overlords of colonial days to the traditionalist throw-backs consequent upon a resurgent national sentiment. Interdepartmental planning in relation to education is minimal. In the attempt to achieve a new degree of collaboration, between those who should share a common responsibility, there arises the question of authority.

Feudalism, caste, and similar social controls have resulted in strongly authoritarian social structures in Asia. Their influence permeates the administrative world, so that it is seldom that one "authority" (e.g., education) is willing to delegate some of its powers elsewhere. Thus the field expert, engaged in a long-term plan, is often despondent about its continuance because he is devoid of the power to lay down the conditions essential for permanence.

### STAFFING PROBLEMS

These problems are mentioned here by reason of the fact that some experts are more successful than others in overcoming the problems they experience; in brief, there exist differentials of expertness. As seen by employing authorities, a major part of the staff problem is that of availability, but the position is accentuated by the question of suitability, for among those available some sort of selec-

2. T. L. Green, *Education and Technology in Southeast Asia: Oversea Education*. London: H. M. Stationery Office, 1954.

3. K. S. Arulnandhy, "Progress in Education in Ceylon since 1945," *Year Book of Education* (London), 1952.

tion is essential. What are the criteria to be used in this selection? Skill and experience go without saying, but what is often overlooked is that the skill has to be demonstrated under conditions of which the potential expert has no experience. One may, as an *ad hoc* judgment, suggest that the successful field workers are those who are not "culture bound." By the nature of their task, they are engaged in helping others change traditional culture patterns, and, unless they can adapt to new cultural conditions themselves, they have little chance of gaining the confidence and strengthening the determination of those they are inviting to forsake old and familiar ways for the unknown. Moreover, it is success at this level in human relations that is a prerequisite for success at the technical level, for the technician is inevitably mixed up with the people who are the participants in his processes. This is one of the most significant points in relation to community education: the winning of trust through the demonstration of ability to do what is asked of others under their conditions.

### ORIENTATION

To prepare experts for field work, orientation and briefing are commonly used techniques. Inevitably such orientation concerns itself with the material rather than the spiritual and with facts rather than values. The man who suggested the keeping of poultry, aware of the protein deficiencies in a village diet and of a waste product suitable as "feed," had made what appeared to be a logical proposal. In cultural terms it was doomed to failure. He had neglected the spiritual values of a particularly devout Buddhist group to whom the taking of life, even the potential life of an egg, was unthinkable. Or one may refer to an attempt to introduce individual latrines for houses in a village where the practice was to make use of the near-by seashore. It failed because the occasions of visiting the shore, at dusk and before dawn, gave to the women, living in seclusion, almost their only contact with other women outside their own family group. A house latrine would remove a world contact!

The need for orientation is not unrealized, nor does it remain unattempted. The questions to be determined are how may it best be done, and by whom? Orientation is of necessity concerned with theory; and experts, as practical workers, are not always sympathetic to a theoretical approach which often appears remote from their practice. The successful field worker orientates himself continuously, in the light of his experience—but his contract too often expires just as he has achieved the degree of cultural understanding basic to his success! Though I had spent six years in Ceylon, traveling widely among even the most remote villages, it was not until my sixth year in the country that I made close contact with the rich rituals of village life which, concerned with "bali" (invocation of planetary deities), the worship of Pattini (goddess of health), and the like, still appear to the villager to be more powerful than the cold comforts of modern hygiene! Indeed it is not insignificant to note that, on the first occasion of seeing a Pattini ceremony, I entered a village on the evening of the day when a project team left it. The team, involved in what was basically a health project, had labored long and hard; and by their standards, with no little success—for there were the records of talks given, films shown, innoculations performed, filters supplied, and latrines built. Obviously the villagers had cooperated, but they were taking no chances. Too courteous to offend those who had befriended them, they awaited the departure of their benefactors, then returned at once to the worship of old gods in the old way.

To tell a technician, come to teach a new skill, that he must learn what people think, and how and why, is to risk the charge of being either a romanticist or an academic, yet he must also know the people to whom he is trying to introduce the skill. This is a basic need for communication.

## COMMUNICATION

The problem of "communication" is both extensive and complex and too often neglected by those who are concerned with the practical issues of intercultural transfer. The technician who explains how to do a job is often exasperated by the performance of those he would teach. Like all who teach, he sees the fault in the learner— who is "slow," "lazy," "unintelligent," or "forgetful." Too seldom is the fault seen as one of communication, because the concern is with telling and remembering, rather than with communicating and understanding. The position may perhaps be more readily understood by the reader if an actual example is given.

I once watched a demonstration of the use of a large band saw to cut tree trunks into thick planks. The demonstrator, master of his technique and a burly, genial giant, not only handled the machine with skill but was able to drown its roar with his voice. Of the language of the men being trained he knew but a few words—enough to shout "stop," "start," "faster," and such dynamic imperatives. The learners themselves, young men from a village background, though doubtless possessed of the manual skills of their kind, were more than a little overawed by the immensity, velocity, and noise of mechanization. Explanation first went to them through the words of an interpreter, whose control of a foreign tongue argued an academic rather than a practical education. To me who lacked experience of using such a machine, though familiar with machines of many kinds and even skilled in using some of them, the verbal explanation appeared excellent. It was brief, clear, unambiguous, and logical. One by one the men answered the sequence of events, knew which knob or wheel controlled what—and all was set for action.

One by one they "had a crack at it." It was no mean thing either to step straight from hand work with a double-ended saw cutting through inches an hour onto the control platform of a monster machine able to tear its way through forest timber at inches per second! No one failed to get everything going. One by one they started the log trolley, aligned the timber, and set it on its path to the shining steel blade. All of them succeeded in getting the band in action, all brought the log to the saw teeth within a fractional distance of the desired line. But one by one all failed to complete the job—for slowly the harsh whine changed note, the feed trolley slowed down, the blade began to bind in the cut, and the saw stopped in a thin swirl of smoke!

First, above the roar of machinery and then in the silence of the shop, the demonstrator shouted instructions and imprecations. His first thought (that of all good technicians) was for his precious machine. His other thoughts, about the men on the job, are not sufficiently academic to bear quoting here! What he had not thought about was the cultural background which was influencing the problem of communication. He was, as he said, not only "dancing mad," but in a quandary. Back home he had taught this to mere kids, and they lapped it up. "Why couldn't these chaps do the same?"

Simply because, though they had heard, remembered, and repeated instructions, they had not understood many essential implications. A key point in sawing with the band saw relates to the velocity of the teeth. Below a certain minimum speed they tend not to cut but almost to burn their way forward. And recognition of that minimum speed is largely dependent, in the absence of a dial reading, upon recognizing that noise is an index of speed. The boy from a westernized mechanized background has acquired some inkling of this from informal common experience, from his toys, from his hobbies, from kitchen equipment, from laboratory experiment, from radio, from film, and from the machines which are part of his own world.

Once he had realized that his explanation and demonstration were incomplete, the instructor dealt with the question of speed and sound, in relation to the saw; and soon every hand present was able to do the job—because communication was complete.

Here is a problem of basic importance in the transfer of technique from culture to culture. It appears in many forms. Most often it is recognized only in terms of language differences, and it is thought that learning the language or using an interpreter will overcome it. To a great extent they do, but always there tends to be a hard core. Difficulties are not always easy to overcome, for a culture pattern which lacks a tool or a process obviously has no name for it—so that translation becomes difficult; and transliteration may carry no meaning.

Part of the problem of communication relates to a complex of belief and behavior which can be summed up in the word "attitude." Those who have seen machinery neglected and ill-used are well aware that many in the East have not yet developed that attitude which underlies maintenance. And all who have either invited or instructed others to participate in what appears to be either difficult or dangerous are aware that interpersonal attitudes, in which respect and trust are important elements, play an important part. It is those able to win the confidence of the people with whom they work who are most likely to be able to affect their way of living.

And it appears reasonable to believe that confidence can be commanded best by those who have confidence in themselves and their techniques.

I recall being present at the farewells between a team of experts and the villagers of a project area. One by one representatives of the government and of the village had their say. Much had been accomplished and a rosy picture of the future drawn. At that moment the team leader must have felt a word of warning desirable. Knowing only too well how much yet had to be done, and the many unpredictables likely to be operative, he summed up in words like this, "So, though we have done a lot together, there is still a lot to do. We have tried to show you how to do it. We hope that you will be successful—but we know how hard it is to be so. Why, even in my home, in that country far away over the sea, we have just this same problem—and we haven't succeeded in overcoming it yet."

At once an old farmer stood up. With the courtesy of his kind, and strong in the knowledge of his own position, he asked a pointed question: "If the master cannot solve this problem in his own village, among the people he knows, how does he expect to solve it in a village such as ours which he does not know?" If there should be a moral to be drawn from this incident, then it is (as pointed out earlier) that we must learn to be realistic, to seek the attainable.

One further point must be kept in mind by those who seek to understand the outcomes of technical-assistance programs. Not only can a country in south or southeast Asia be relatively advanced in one sphere and relatively backward in another but so also can it be involved in both reactionary and progressive, or conservative and destructive, processes at one and the same time and even in the same place. Political independence has stimulated both the search for economic advance and the resuscitation of a waning culture, and the science which is sought as *modus operandi* for the former may well be the death knell of the latter. At field level this situation may pose a problem which, however simple, is highly intricate.

Visiting a village school where conditions had been so favorable as to allow a foreign expert to organize a weekly discussion class for farmers, I came on an excellent example of cultural conflict. The school building was a one-room structure. In this, in the evening, three groups met; one at each end and one in the middle. At one end the farmers, the local agricultural inspector, and the foreign expert engaged in a lively discussion of new methods of rice cultivation. Asked why they attended, some replied that it was in order to learn new methods in order to get bigger crops, and, as none were literate, they were very glad to get help from the foreign expert, through the local inspector.

In the middle of the room a "literacy class" was in operation, composed of adults who had enjoyed little or no schooling. Their presence argued realization of a potential value in the ability to read.

At the other end a literate group of adults was engaged in lively work with books and a teacher making skilful use of a blackboard. At first sight, the writer thought it was a class in elementary science, engaged in learning a little simple astronomy. It turned out to be a study of astrology! When questioned as to why they attended, the predominant answer was: "I am a farmer and I want to learn about astrology so that I can sow at the auspicious time and get a bigger crop."

So brief a review of a few of the problems which face those working in the field in underdeveloped countries can do little more than present a bare outline of the situation. However, without even this, it would be a still more difficult task to attempt to assess the outcomes of a technical-assistance scheme in terms of community education. Even before attempting this, two other points must be noted—first, such an attempt unavoidably lies to some extent in the field of evaluation; secondly, aid programs are designed and executed in terms of economic development—that a social component is inevitably present is true, but the work done, whether in technological or any other field, is seen in technical terms. Moreover, to the extent that evaluation has been attempted, this too is in economic and technical terms, because, to those responsible for technical-assistance programs aimed at socioeconomic progress, action appears as a first imperative.

## Some Lessons Learned
### LOCATING THE PROBLEMS

A happy feature of the Colombo Plan, so well developed that the outsider can see it at once, is the degree of friendship and trust which underlies the co-operation between the members. This statement is not made to imply that such conditions are not found in other agencies; they undoubtedly are—but they do seem to be a particularly marked feature of the Colombo Plan. Their existence is of interest, not merely because they contribute so much to the forwarding of common aims but because they have developed between countries which have, at other times (and but recently) stood in very different relationships—those of overlord and colony, and even those of war itself. How they have come about is perhaps a problem for sociologist and historian, but that they have come about is significant both for the area and for the rest of the world. For long, many Asian countries have been subject to the directives of an overlord—so much so that "four hundred years of foreign domination" (as in Ceylon) has been seen as the root cause of many social and economic defects. Now, given the chance to shoot their own lines, such countries are able to realize that colonialism also had its rewards. Thus, while national aspirations are properly developed, there is lessening evidence of a desire to wipe the slate clean and ignore the past.

Another aspect of this new relationship is its quality of being self-generating, for good relations multiply and spread. In particular, they have led to a new feeling of self-confidence among peoples who, having accepted the appellation of "underdeveloped," might easily have been apathetic and lacking in self-determination. Arising partly from acceptance on a footing of equality and leading to a wider realization of such equality, they have conditioned the partners toward respect for each other's views. Moreover, they have achieved also another very important result, the engendering of a new respect among the Asian partners for each other's potentialities and achievements.

In terms of community education there is much to be learned from these new relationships, especially perhaps in what has become known as "the philosophy of the felt need." Inherent in this is the belief that the villager will co-operate in schemes only when he feels a need which such schemes appear likely to satisfy. To deny this would be foolish, for it has been demonstrated to be true on many occasions. As a basis for action, however, it appears to suffer from two defects. First, because, with limited experience and understanding it may often lead to a questionable order of priorities. Secondly, because the same factors tend to lead to recognition of only immediate needs.

With greater experience, and more particularly with a wider understanding stemming from research in socioeconomic fields, those from a relatively advanced country see priorities differently; especially do they see them in a different order and on a different time scale. Thus, while the development of a vocational guidance scheme is often seen as an immediate top priority, Western advisers might place a premium on an education of wide prevocational type and on efforts to extend and diversify the fields of potential employment. Then again, realizing that technology is the key to economic development, Asian planners have sought the opening of technical colleges, forgetting that the fruits of higher or specialized education can only be culled when a well-developed primary and lower-secondary education guarantees a continual supply of suitable students. Or, as a third case, there has been, time after time, a request for the complex development in many situations, long before the simple basic conditions have been satisfied.

One lesson then, and a particularly important one, is that the location of needs and the ordering of priorities are of extreme importance and no little difficulty. While this may well have been an outcome of almost any agency scheme, it has been the lot of the Colombo Plan to demonstrate that agreement in this sphere is most likely to be reached where good relationships have built a solid foundation of trust. A big factor in doing this is acceptance of partners in terms of equality, recognition that "know how" is not restricted to the westernized group, and that the Asian groups are allowed to participate at every stage of planning. This "give and take" has brought into being a very desirable degree of realism. Perhaps one should add that many countries which have had little or no colonial experience also benefit because they lack prejudice and have no back history of financial involvement.

### DEFINITION OF PROBLEMS

In referring earlier to types of difficulties, the question of language was mentioned. Experience of how these operate, in both linguistic and semantic terms, underlines the need for definitions which are clearly understandable to all concerned in a project. It has happened that, due to lack of a precise formulation, a government has duplicated a request for help; much more often, however, lack of clarity has resulted in an expert arriving in a country to find that the problem, as it appears to him, is not a little different from what it appeared in the job-description. Stemming from both linguistic and cultural causes, accentuated by an unavoidable lack of sufficient orientation and an obviously difficult readjustment, such contingencies are costly in time, money, and man power, even though they have seldom been very acute.

Those familiar with work in the field in community education will realize that here, too, many difficulties have a similar origin, namely, a lack of precise formulation. For example, work in this field has sometimes reduced itself to a drive for literacy by those for whom education has meant learning rather than living. A program aimed at family planning, which inevitably means family limitation, may not only encounter opposition to contraception, which is anticipated, but also founder because many Asian peoples see prestige in a large family.

In brief, we have learned not only the need to see and define a project in our own terms but also in terms which have meaning in the social context in which it is to operate.

### The Nature and Operation of Limiting Factors

The existence of factors likely to limit the progress of technical-assistance projects, and thus to slow down economic and social advance, can be postulated even by those with no field experience in this sphere. Critics of the rates of advance, however, even if aware of the existence of such limiting factors, are too seldom aware of their multiplicity, pervasiveness, and elusiveness.

Visiting a village, by chance and unannounced, I was impressed by the neat condition of the school and by the work being carried out at night under a community-development scheme. I learned that the schoolhouse had been put up by the villagers themselves, working co-operatively and supplying not only labor but much of the materials at their own cost. Here, it appeared, was one of the offshoots of other developmental work, an excellent example of what can be achieved when it is realized that a common need can be solved by joint action. Here, if ever there was one, the "felt need" could be seen in action.

Walking round the village at dawn I finally came to the "tank"— the artificial lake which alone allows life to continue in the dry zone of Ceylon. Its sluice gate could not be completely closed, so that there was a constant loss of water, due to a cause which the village blacksmith could have repaired. Its walls (the "bund") were in need of repair, and the tank was greatly silted up. Here was a felt need; but another story! When a group of villagers was asked why they did not co-operate to do the repairs and maintenance (though government regulation and ancient custom demanded that they should), they had a single answer—jealousy—because those with most land would benefit most and the landless not at all.

Here is evidence that among "felt needs" there are priorities, and it would appear that status-seeking and prestige operate as the differentials. Schooling (especially in Ceylon) means status, escape from the village level, perhaps even from caste itself. Thus, though it would be in the next generation, the villagers were prepared to co-operate to get a school but not to get more water on which they were all directly dependent.

Frequently what appear to be obvious needs for everyone in a village are the cause of factions and feuds, to which caste, religious, political, and linguistic differences add fuel. Many villages tend to be divided into high-caste and low-caste sections. Though there is a functional interdependence between them, social contact is minimal. Thus, to achieve co-operation in a project which requires total village action is often difficult. For example, in one village an attempt to organize a scheme for supplementary feeding for young children proved abortive, because the high-caste group, having insisted that the center should be in their area, did not want low-caste children feeding with their children. These problems of social distance are particularly difficult to understand, so far as the outsider is concerned. He knows just where a well should be dug; both he and the villagers know how great is the need for water; but they also know that a low-caste group may derive reduced benefit from it, because caste individuals, even today and on no small scale, cannot use the vessels for drawing water nor the receptacles and utensils for eating which are used by those of higher caste. Many times I have seen low-caste women, waiting sometimes for hours at a well, until a higher-caste woman would draw water for them in a special vessel. On one occasion, taking a meal at a village ceremony, I found that the drummers had to sit on the floor—not being considered worthy of chairs—and one indeed was of so low a caste status that, though allowed to sit on the floor, he had to extend his feet outside the door —in order to be technically out of the room.

One form of technical assistance in many Asian countries has been concerned with low-cost housing, particularly with improvements in design and materials. In Ceylon (as in the West!) housing is an index of status. Location in high-caste or low-caste areas is homologous with the areas of "good address"—or "much-sought-after locality" which typify Western town life. In Ceylon, to have a two-story house is a sign of status. Similarly, materials can be arranged in hierarchic order—mud-daub and wattle at the bottom, going up through "kabook" (a local soft conglomerate) to brick and stone at the top. Roofing goes up from "cadjan" (woven coconut leaves) through locally made tiles, on to Indian tiles, and finally to slates and artificially fabricated materials. Similarly, the larger the porch the greater the status, and one sees houses sometimes on which the porch seems as large as the house itself.

In connection with a social welfare center, which included a nursery school, the writer once built a small playhouse for children. Not all would play in it, for those from higher caste homes did not like the cadjan walls and roof! Though the bulk of research on intergroup attitudes shows that they are learned, it appears that such learning, under the influence of social pressures, occurs very early in Ceylon! In another instance, again in a village, I found that a Rodiya woman (the Rodiya are the lowest caste in Ceylon, indeed they are an outcaste group) had worked hard, saved money, and built a house, but was not allowed by other villagers to roof it with tiles. Moreover the glass panes were broken—glass windows are for higher social levels. Though these value-attitudes are changing, they still exist and often act as cultural barriers.

These cases perhaps illustrate why the housing expert often finds himself involved in unknown difficulties. He is concerned with techniques, but before he can apply them they are subject to a series of cultural controls of which he is probably entirely ignorant! This situation is most obvious in village life. In towns, education has begun to influence attitudes, and economics have begun to iron out caste differentials. Yet the fact that housing schemes, urban, semiurban, and rural, have been operated is evidence that cultural difficulties can be overcome. Often they have been perhaps ignored or unrecognized, but, whether action was indirect or direct, it carries an implication for the procedures of community education. What this is will be discussed in detail later.

Among limiting factors which are of cultural type, the question of the prestige-rating of occupations must be noticed. Hierarchic prestige-ratings of vocations are characteristic of all societies in which there is any marked degree of vocational differentiation and specialization. In the less-developed and more primitive societies, the hunter and the warrior have had pride of place, while in agricultural societies the farmer has come first. Although more complex, the same principle operates in more highly organized societies. Thus, in India and Ceylon, there are clearly marked occupational levels.[4, 5, 6] In Ceylon, however, although the farmer (goigama) rates highest in terms of caste, the operation of the economic factor and the low rating given to manual work tend to mask the farmer's status so that professional occupations (civil servant, doctor, lawyer) rate higher. Despite this anomaly the principle holds and has a significance for technical-assistance work.

In Ceylon there has been a very considerable program in technical education as part of the drive to produce technicians for a developing technology. One aspect of this program has been the setting up of workshops in schools and a training college to teach woodwork and metal work. Despite the obvious need for technicians, it has not proved easy to get all of the opportunities fully exploited, because

4. T. L. Green, "Education and Social Needs in Ceylon," *University of Ceylon Review* (Colombo), 1952.

5. T. L. Green and C. Wickremasuriya, "The Vocational Attitudes of Ceylonese Graduate Teachers," *University of Ceylon Review* (Colombo), 1952.

6. Bryce Ryan, unpublished data on vocational ambitions in Ceylon.

the manual nature of the work has had a lesser attraction than that deriving from academic training. In one school, where "carpentry" had been over the shop door, the response had been especially poor. Realizing that the carpenter held a very low social position, the label was changed to "wood work." This simple device alone resulted in a change of attitude which led to more pupils choosing the subject as an option.

The potter is held in even lower esteem than the carpenter, so that pottery, as a schoolcraft, is far from easy to develop. Wishing to buy some potter's clay, for the purpose of making biological models, I took a member of my minor staff to help in overcoming the language problem. This man was very helpful in selecting suitable clay and helped to carry it to the car. Back in the office he bluntly refused to be seen touching it—except when no other Ceylonese were around! On the other hand he was willing and skilful in making models out of a proprietary material which, under the magic of a tradename and a few additives, had lost its defiling significance, though its nature remained unchanged. Here again the scales were tipped by the mere avoidance of name which was emotionally charged in a negative manner for the people in a particular culture pattern.

A further example of what, despite the deep-seated issues involved, can be done by avoiding the use of emotive key words may be cited. In connection with the development of selective tests aiming at the prediction of practical skills, a colleague and I were engaged in standardizing a test battery. While it was described as a "Test of Practical Skill" there was considerable opposition toward its use among the parents and even the teachers, as well as among the pupils. This attitude was found to disappear the moment it was given a new name—"Test of Spatial Perceptual Abilities."

These examples, together with those presented in the earlier section on the types of problems encountered, have been offered in order to indicate an outcome of technical assistance which is of profound significance to the whole field of community education. This basically important lesson may be defined as the need to understand the cultural barriers operative in the fields of value and attitudinal changes. Community education, like technical assistance, seeks to introduce new ideas, new methods, new aims, and new standards. Some are accepted easily, others with difficulty, and some may be rejected; even more puzzling may be that reactions to any one change vary from place to place, even though the conditions appear to be identical. Only when we know more about cultural barriers and their modes of operation can we lift our attempts at cultural transfer from the *ad hoc* level to the rational plane. This we cannot do until we have developed a research component.

It may be that, instead of what some would consider as an atomistic approach on discrete elements in the social situation, we should accept the shock tactics of a holistic approach advocated by Margaret Mead in her study of the Manus[7] and in her stimulating and provocative chapter in this book (see chap. iii). Among the English, with a long colonial tradition and experience, rapid social change is looked at askance (see for example an English review of "New Lives for Old").[8] On the other hand, as an Englishman with a wide experience in community education, Elvin[9] has emphasized the need for a bilateral approach by asking whether "a decisive change in the conditions of ignorant and underprivileged people will only come if there is a change in their attitude of mind . . . and that . . . will only come if the approach is made through a visible material improvement?" If we are here involved in a cultural determination of attitude among students and practitioners in the fields of consciously directed social change, it emphasizes the need for such workers to be aware of the operation of cultural factors.

This awareness must come from research. While such research may range widely, it must certainly include a study of cultural factors, both in the role of barriers to change and as facilitators of such change. Similarly, it must be devoted not only to the project but also to the people. Indivisible as these may appear, such a distinction yet has meaning and is, indeed, demonstrated to some extent in the approaches of Hayes and Sower (*op. cit.*), first, in their con-

7. Margaret Mead, *New Lives for Old*. New York: William Morrow & Co., Inc., 1956.

8. D. F. Pocock, Review of *New Lives for Old, Journal of Education* (London), September, 1957.

9. L. Elvin, "Comparative Comments on Educaton in Relation to Technical Development," *Journal of Education* (London), September, 1957.

centration on an itemistic content (e.g., kinds of result, specific skills, etc), secondly, on effects rather than on causes, and, thirdly, on practical issues rather than on a theory. Their approaches were doubtless conditioned by a practical setting, for both were seeking answers to questions posed by practical field workers. Mead, as a research worker, was concerned with a theory of causes and, not being involved in any part of the techniques, has been able to see the position as a whole. It is this freedom from implication which is important in making judgments in this field. Curiously enough it may be that a narrow concern with techniques among technical-assistance workers has had its effects by placing them, to some extent, outside the value system, thus allowing the local group to exercise a greater degree of self-initiation in bringing changes in patterns of living. This point is often overlooked, though it received notice in an international study of evaluation techniques.[10]

However, even though technical field workers are concerned with practical tasks, one has but to make brief contacts with them to discover their interest in theory. Exhibited in many ways, this interest mostly takes the form of questions about motives, which are bound up with the cultural on which so much stress has been laid here, particularly emphasizing our need for more comprehensive studies in this field. If, from experience in the technical field we are led to a closer examination of cultural barriers, it will provide material of value in both technical assistance and community education. In applying such data, however, we must realize that cultural settings do not consist entirely of universals, so that what may be true in one setting may fail to apply in another, even an apparently similar one. The nuances of the social situation may be far more subtle than we appreciate. Research (and its applications) in this field should be envisaged along two major lines: first, in relation to the isolation and definition of the various cultural barriers in operation; and, second, in respect of the motivating factors and prestige elements which may help to overcome such barriers.

In regard to the first, a number of instances have already been quoted which show that they range over a wide field. Among them

10. Various authors, "Evaluation Techniques," *International Social Science Bulletin* (Paris: UNESCO).

are those deriving from linguistics, lack of information coupled with the superstitions bred from ignorance, values deriving from (or causal of?) attitudes which find their background in mysticism, animism, and religious belief, together with previous experiences resulting from intercultural contacts—i.e., with a colonial overlord.

Similarly, reference has been made to examples from the second group. Our knowledge here has in it much of the empirical for, while the first group has been the study material of anthropologists and sociologists, the second is based mostly upon the secondary experiences of field workers who are engaged in what is primarily a practical task and who now have a wide experience which needs to be formalized and orientated. So far, such attempts as have been made to capitalize on this experience have been *ad hoc* procedures by field workers themselves. A project, for example, has been associated with an appeal to the economic motive, with an existing prestige group, with the "competitive spirit," with an appeal to novelty, and even with the appeal to antiquity.

The inherent danger in such a situation is obvious, namely, the field worker will assume that what motivates him will also motivate those with whom he works. Hence, the need for orientation, and, even more, for basic research on which orientation can be based. While many field workers are alive to these dangers, they tend to see the material aspects of the situation rather than the more subtle ones. Especially is this the case in regard to the social climate of the situation. Many experts come from areas in which democracy does indeed mean "taking a man for what he is worth." Such a worker is accustomed to a considerable degree of shared responsibility, to frequent self-initiated activity, to all-embracing co-operative reviewing of situations, and to allowing his views to be altered by those with a special experience or knowledge. Much, if not all of this, is foreign to Asian societies in which authoritarianism is strongly marked, especially where caste is operative.

Only those who have lived in these societies can appreciate the pervasive effect of authoritarianism. Not only is the social group divided into the "we" and the "they" in relation to such big factors as religion, caste, or property but also into "me" and "him" in which subtle hierarchic levels appear. Age may take precedence of youth, man rank higher than woman, those with a fair complexion rate above their kind who have a dark skin, and the bus driver rank below the driver who serves a single master, so that to primary differentials there is added the halo effect of an employer. These are but a few of the subtleties which exist and which are imperatives of behavior. In a family with several children, those attending a school of higher status (because it is an "English" school or charges fees) will be better dressed than those going to the vernacular school. A bottleneck in an industrialized process may be traced to a point where skill has lifted a low-caste operative to a superior position. Signs of failure appear in what has been a successful project, because a new appointment upsets the hierarchic relationships. And as a last, almost incredible example, it may be noted that evidence was presented in an assault case to the effect that the defendant could not have been the guilty party for, as a low-caste man, he had remained at a respectful distance from the victim! In Ceylon, and doubtless elsewhere in south Asia, the concept of social distance is measurable in terms which pass beyond the psychological to the physical.

This sense of hierarchy underlying the social climate is a frequent source of difficulty to the field worker who, wishing to work in a democratic manner, tries to introduce a group technique to use in working with committees and the like. Always there are those who not only take precedence but are given it, so that official positions as chairman, convener, etc., tend always to go to the same individuals. Not only may there be too few of them, but they may be less suited to such tasks than others.

While it is common to lay the present authoritarian climate at the feet of colonial domination, which cannot be free of some part of the charge despite a democratic contribution, feudalism, sumptuary laws, caste, and other social stratifications have all played a part. Thus, today, one of the commonest comments among Western experts in south and southeast Asia is that the indigenous population is seldom ready to accept individual responsibility, or even to become involved in a situation which may in any way "single them out." Instead, they wait to be told what to do next. This, acting as both cause and consequence, results in a "top-downward" approach in which local authority gives orders and issues directives. Thus, the training and teaching situation is dominative rather than integrative, a feature which Straus,[11] in a study of agricultural extension work in Ceylon, saw as one factor militating against success.

While authoritarianism may easily suggest rigidity of social organization, it may be noted that, paradoxical though it seems, Ceylonese social organization is defined as "loose" in the sociological sense. This analysis, by Ryan and Straus,[12] may have much meaning for those concerned to introduce social change. Long ago Tennant[13] noted that the Singhalese "are by no means a plastic substance . . . capable of being moulded into any form." Embree,[14] the originator of the concept of "loose structure," noted that it permitted of social adjustment to intercultural influences without engendering drastic over-all change. Ryan[15] claimed that colonial rule had organizing rather than disintegrative effects on Singhalese social institutions, while Ryan and Straus [16] consider that loose, yet social, organization preserves basic values and normative principles, still, it does allow more readily for low-order social change. This perhaps explains why, after a new technique has apparently been accepted, the field worker is so often confused by finding that acculturation has not led to a change of values which he considers an unavoidable consequence. The villager will learn about the nitrogen cycle and use artificial fertilizers but still consult the astrologer as to the auspicious moment for planting, partly because astrology is bound up with deep-seated values and partly because the astrologist enjoys a particular social status.

To the worker in community education, all this is of relevance, indicating that he has, in some way or other, to achieve an interpersonal relationship which will have both authoritarian and democratic

11. M. Straus, "Cultural Factors in the Functioning of Agricultural Extension in Ceylon," *Rural Sociology*, 1953.

12. Bryce Ryan and M. Straus, "The Integration of Singhalese Society," *Research Studies*. Ellensberg, Washington: State College of Washington, 1954.

13. Emerson Tennant, *Ceylon: An Account of the Island*. London, 1860.

14. J. F. Embree, "Thailand: A Loosely Structured Social System," *American Anthropologist* (New York), 1950.

15. Bryce Ryan, *Caste in Modern Ceylon: The Singhalese System in Transition*. New Brunswick, New Jersey: Rutgers University Press, 1953.

16. Ryan and Straus, *op. cit.*

aspects! So seemingly impossible a task has been performed by those who have made use of the ideas of intermediate hierarchic positions. Thus, a large group may be broken into two or three tiers, with subgroups in each tier. The subgroup leaders are responsible to the next tier leaders who are fewer in number, until at the top of the pinnacle is the authoritarian figure demanded by present social structure.

Another lesson to be learned from consideration of experience in the personal-relations aspect of technical assistance is that the social situation has some degree of ambivalence. In theory, every project has a team-leader, the foreign expert from a different culture, and a "counterpart" who is functionally on the same level as the leader but who is part of the national culture pattern. The team-leader works on one side with the villagers and on the other with government officials, ranging from clerk to minister. To both groups he is "extra-cultural," a member of an out-group accepted for reasons which have no relation to local cultural values. The counterpart, however, is part of the local culture-pattern, and, while he may be looked up to by the villager, he may very well be looked down on by higher officialdom. Once the sheltering effect of the expert has gone, the project may lose prestige because the counterpart no longer commands the position he once did.

Lessons derived from consideration of social-climate and interpersonal relations appear to have a particular relevance for community-education projects. These naturally tend to have a somewhat more theoretical aspect, being often more concerned with the acquisition of new mental skills, information, and attitudes, as compared with the more practical aspects of technical programs. With a considerable verbal element, and often concerned with literacy work, extensive use is made of that convenient local figure, the teacher. While the "guru" tradition conventionally awards a high status to the teacher, his low economic position often relegates him to a comparatively low social prestige. Hence, the project itself may come to be looked upon as relatively unimportant. Thus, there is need to bolster up its prestige. One way to do this might be to associate it more directly and closely with a technical-assistance program.

## Training

A particularly important aspect of technical assistance has been the training component under which trainees have gone overseas. While there is an obvious language barrier, which has meant that trainees have inevitably been those with a relatively advanced education, there has been as little insistence as possible on this. The general value of such training schemes is unquestioned, and an urgent need is to seek means to extend them. Particularly urgent is the need to extend them to the level of operators who are the ultimate factors in a technical situation. In many countries in Asia attempts are being made to improve the fishing industry. The fishermen, on whom the industry depends, are among those nationals with least education. Thus, in this sphere, training has tended to be available to the administrator, to the research worker, and so on—not to the fisherman, except on his own coast. The same argument may be applied to the farmer, the carpenter, or the mason.

Here is a field yet to be explored in community education. "Experience," we tell each other, "is the great teacher." If we believe this, we should seek means to provide it at every level, which means we must take overseas those from the bottom of the ladder as well as those from the top. A host of problems will arise: language, food, customs, clothing—all that we mean by cultural differences. Yet, if we did not shrink from such difficulties in wartime, why should we do so in the greater service of peace? It would call for the provision of orientation courses of a particular kind. First, perhaps an intensive and rapid language course to provide limited and simple skills in communication. Next, an introduction to a new way of living, adequately supported by the vicarious experience to be obtained by the film. Next, an introduction to a new technique by practical contact with the technical-aid expert through his services (under the community-education scheme) as a teacher about his own culture. Lastly, a personal visit to that culture, by a small group, accompanied by a national with suitable language abilities, who had also been orientated for the job.

In this connection it might also be noted that foreign training tends to confer a new and enhanced status upon those who enjoy it. The "England-returned" are almost a privileged group in India and

Ceylon. Here, too, is a point to be noted, for this new status would make such individuals excellent infiltration agents for the introduction of new methods and materials, such as the spade, the shovel, the iron plowshare, or the nylon fishing line. Simple as these are, they involve changes ranging from customs to clothing, which is why they are so difficult to introduce.

Another way in which community education could be used in backing up technical-aid work is in giving to women some greater understanding of the effects of such work on the social situation. Education, in general, is less available in south and southeast Asia to girls and women than to boys and men, and the bulk of technical-assistance work is with men. While there is a growing drive for education for girls in the area, what is offered to women, under community-education schemes, tends to be concentrated upon particular segments of the domestic scene. Thus, child welfare, domestic arts and crafts, cottage crafts, and the like are offered, but little is done to offer social education in a wider sense. Yet, if technical aid affects society as a whole, it also affects families as the units of the society. It may then be suggested that we should explore what can be done to offer to women something to help them orientate family life to social change.

### Influencing Attitudes to Community Education

In order that community education may both contribute to and benefit from technical assistance it is probably necessary to bring about changes of attitude and understanding in three spheres: at top executive, administrative, and political levels; within the administrative and advisory structure or the technical agencies; and among the general public.

While it may appear that concentration upon one or another of these may be most rewarding, it is essential to realize that only a total approach, on all fronts, is likely to be effective. None of these three segments is a discrete whole; all are part of a total social situation.

The organization of the Colombo Plan, in particular, allows for an unusual degree of independence and freedom to the recipient countries in the matter of planning, and many such countries have sought foreign aid for their planning councils (and similar bodies). There is, however, a need for the development of a deeper understanding of and a more sympathetic attitude toward community education. Though the "power groups" in such countries, whether political or administrative, vary considerably in social origin, educational levels, and general experience, there is, over the area as a whole, some tendency for partisan attitudes to overrule social needs. The politician, for example, sensitive to the effect of policy on political allegiance, tends to give support to proposals which are likely to have direct and immediate results. Thus, as a platform or talking point, he would choose agriculture (which produces more food) or industrial projects (which provide work) rather than community-education projects. To him these appear to be more nebulous in character and likely to have results which are less material and more remote. In order that community education may both derive from and contribute to technical assistance to a maximum degree, it is essential to gain a greater sympathy for the former among those responsible for the latter. Here indeed is a problem in culture change, one in which the time element is of considerable significance, for those who seek such change are pressing the more remote rewards against the immediate ones. Reducing it still further to more realistic terms, they are pressing social claims against voting appeal! It is not suggested that the latter always wins. In India, for example, the long-term view has been widely accepted, so that pure research is not abandoned in favor of applied science, and community education is not neglected in favor of technical aid. There is need to seek means to develop so desirable a situation in other countries on a larger scale than that which obtains at present.

A similar need may be postulated within the technical agencies whose avowed intentions and functional structure have led to concentration on technical rather than on educative aspects. This is not to suggest entry into a new field but, rather, to suggest a greater degree of integration between the agencies. Some integration already exists; we need now to extend this and to seek new forms it might take. Ceylon, where the experts from all agencies meet monthly to discuss mutual problems, offers one avenue—and one which does not appear to be in operation elsewhere. Another possibility is to make use of orientation programs to introduce the technical expert to the concepts of community education. A third approach has been explored in the *Art of Overseasmanship*,[17] a group study sponsored by Syracuse University, U.S.A., in which it is assumed as a basic postulate that the explosive growth of America's foreign operations will need educational adaptation at home. A fourth approach might be by extension of the kind of study undertaken at the Social Science Research Center in Calcutta, which is concerned with studies of the social effects of industrialization. A fifth suggestion would be to devote more effort to evaluative research, not as adjunct to but as an integral part of every technical project, carrying it out in collaboration with either a social scientist or a local worker in community education.

At least as important as the two topics so briefly mentioned is the question of influencing the attitude of the public in regard to community education. Asian democracy is demanding education for all on an ever growing scale. Despite this, those factors which once made education the privilege of an "elite" are still to be found. There are low-caste children not in school, there are minorities suffering educational restriction,[18] and so on. The attitudes and values which conditioned these phenomena are those which are, in many cases, responsible for the low value the public often places on community education. Moreover, in countries where education is seen mostly as an agent of social mobility[19] there is lessened willingness for those forms of education which, while they necessitate public expenditure, do not appear likely to change individual status.

Changing public attitudes is not only important but also difficult! It is almost as difficult to suggest even a few lines which might be explored, largely because we are as ignorant about the motivators and determinants of public attitudes as we are about individual attitudes. Certainly the dissemination of knowledge, easily understandable and as "practical" as possible, should receive attention with the

17. Harlan Cleveland and G. J. Mangone, *The Art of Overseasmanship: Americans at Work Abroad*. Syracuse, New York: Syracuse University Press, 1957.

18. M. Straus, "Family Characteristics and Occupational Choice of University Entrants as Clues to the Social Structure of Ceylon," *University of Ceylon Review*, 1951.

19. T. L. Green, "Education and Social Mobility in Ceylon," *Ceylon Journal of Social Work* (Colombo), 1957.

aid of as many agents of communication as possible. Equally certainly we must seek to give status to community education.

The significance of education in regard to social mobility has already been noted and, on the same grounds, the apparent lack of significance in the case of community education is noted by the public. Education leads to jobs through the possession of a paper qualification. Thought should be given to this in relation to community education. Even if we do not give an award, ranging from a "chit" to a diploma to those who undergo it, we might at least invent a training course for those who provide it. It is a noticeable fact that Asian universities have given little, if any, attention to all that is comprised under such headings as extension work, extramural work, social training, or youth work. If they do so, such work would receive a wider notice and an increased approval and would provide teachers for the field of community education who would probably enjoy a greater status than many now engaged in it.

## Team Responsibilities

Not only must a regard for community education, as a potential outcome of technical assistance, be stimulated at the levels discussed above but so too must the team in the field, as a functional unit, have a similar regard. The team, too, has a dynamic structure, to which the villager reacts. This structure must be homogeneous and sincere, for team factions and lack of sincerity soon strike at the roots of trust. This is a problem far too large to enter into here, yet it is basic to success. Most field teams have an *ad hoc* structure, dependent upon the chances of selection. It might well be better to explore other methods, such as that whereby an institution in a donor or host country takes over the long-term staffing of a field project from its own staff resources, thus insuring that its members have already been able to adjust to each other before entering the field. Ensuing changes would still preserve homogeneity, because successive experts would not only have a functional tie back home but in many cases would have already worked together. Though it may never prove possible to apply sociometric techniques to the selection of teammates, it should be possible to orientate the members toward an understanding of their mutual responsibilities and interdependence. Especially is it important to insure that the designated leader is, in the sociometric sense, the functional leader. Equally important is the need to achieve an over-all acceptance of aims and methods while preserving leadership without destroying individual initiative.

While evaluation of a project will inevitably reveal something of the effectiveness of the team, it might be rewarding to insure that every team subject itself to evaluative self-analysis. "Self-Knowledge," it has been said, "is the only worth-while knowledge." If ununable fully to subscribe to this, we should at least accept for it a high degree of significance.

## Some New Basic Concepts Needed

Some of our existing shortcomings in the conceptual field have already been mentioned. A few other points deserving of attention are worthy of notice. We make a universal, for example, of the claim that culture change comes from culture contact, taking the whole history of mankind as evidence, conveniently ignoring that time is an important dimension of the process. We do not, however, appear to have considered some degree of discrepancy in our procedure for, while we assign to the expert (usually an outsider) the function of cultural change through technical process, we also accept the indigenous teacher as competent to induce change through community education. Similarly, while assuming that contact induces change, we overlook the existence of areas of minimal change but maximum intercultural contact. In other words, while we have concerned ourselves with the motivating factors in cultural change, we have neglected the conditions under which such factors operate. In brief, the conceptual bases of our beliefs and actions need critical thought.

Nowhere is this to be better seen than in regard to the value judgments inherent in the use of such descriptive labels as "progress" and "efficiency" and the application of these and other definitions outside their prescriptive culture pattern. At this point we become involved in consideration of deeper issues that cannot properly be dealt with in these pages. Here lie such issues as the value of one way of life in comparison with another, a field in which "our way of life" is accepted, by us, as inevitably better than "your way of life." It is not necessary to compare oriental and occidental patterns of living to find such differentials. Despite the common bonds of language and history, the peoples of the United States and those of the United

Kingdom jealously preserve their own ways of living. And within these national differences there are others as jealously guarded, such as those between the New England States and California, or those between Somerset and Yorkshire. To be different is to be suspect!

Seeking to change technique is the avowed purpose of technical assistance, as it is the unavoidable consequence of even the less drastic procedures of community education. Those to whom we seek to carry change react in terms which are emotional rather than rational and which are expressed as action rather than thought. Inexperienced and unsophisticated, they mirror our own procedures, judging our offerings in their terms. Too rarely, from either side of a cultural boundary do we find such studied reactions as those of Basu[20] or Leach.[21] Yet these are the types of study of which there is so great a need, for they strike deep into the philosophical roots of the value-concepts underlying cultural changes. Academic as these fields may appear to be to the technical assistance worker, they are matters of simple faith among those he works with. The expert sees the material setting of Asian life, often so reduced to the bare essentials of living that it appears to him to be totally lacking in all that he thinks makes life worth while. What he fails to see is that this is not a case of failing to achieve material rewards but a dedicated and idealistic process of voluntarily "giving up," through control, abstinence, penance, and sacrifice. Many in Asia believe, in a simple and direct way, that progress is to be measured in terms of purification of the spirit of man.

It is here that we return to points made earlier, that machines depend upon men, procedures involve personality, and values are differentiated by viewpoint. The modes in which technical assistance has made contributions to community education are many and varied, but to derive a maximal benefit from them is contingent upon wider and deeper explorations in the field of value judgment. In particular, we need to know what is meant by our use of value judgments of personality. What is meant by such words as "better" or "happier" in this connection? To such seemingly simple questions

20. A. Basu, "Moral and Ethical Implications of Technological Development: An Indian View," *Year Book of Education* (London), 1954.

21. E. R. Leach, "Educational Incentives in the Field of Technical Assistance," *Year Book of Education* (London), 1954.

any answer, despite our belief in universals, will involve culturally determined particulars, because personality is culturally determined. The individual is only able to function in a social setting. To help him function more fully or become more socially effective is our aim. Whatever the methods to be adopted, it appears clear that they must have meaning, they must integrate the social situation, they must be seen in "gestalt" terms. It is in emphasizing the need for a wider approach, set in terms of social wholes, that experience derived from the technical assistance field has made its most unique contribution to community education.

# CHAPTER X

# Community Education in Southern Illinois

RICHARD W. POSTON

## Pope County

About 1830 all of southern Illinois fell victim to a changing technology and the opening of new lands elsewhere. The completion of the Erie Canal directed pioneer traffic to the Chicago area and to northern Illinois, where land was richer and more plentiful. The important Cumberland Trail from the East to the vicinity of St. Louis skirted the northern perimeter of southern Illinois. From that time until coal-mining began in earnest, the patterns of migration bypassed the region.

Pope County, unaffected even by the coal boom, developed a cultural homogeneity of a character similar to that of the Kentucky hills where people are proud, clannish, and resistant to change.

Packet boats stopped at Golconda and other river towns several times weekly for a while, but the subsequent growth of these communities was largely intensive, with economic status dependent on local resources instead of upon thousands of transient guests. Pope County and Golconda had to face stark realities. There were no great coal and oil deposits like those in counties to the west and north. Even the rich veins of fluorspar, which support adjacent Hardin County to the north, taper off into unprofitable tricklings across the county line. The mining of lead, iron, clay, and kaolin were fruitful for only short periods of time.

Pope County's greatest asset was the beautiful Ohio. But less and less revenue came by the river route as the railroads expanded over the country. And, often, the river was more of a liability. It regularly inundated the best farm land in the county and spilled over into the principal city, Golconda, which was therefore not an ideal site for business or manufacturing industries.

Farming on the rocky, hilly soil was generally a suitable occupation only for those families easily resigned to meager subsistence
while the more adventurous were harvesting wealth in the new lands
of the West. Extensive forest areas were unmanaged and, for the
dirt farmers who had come from the South, apparently unmanage-
able. Erosion was a widespread and serious problem.

Still, the population of Pope County rose to a peak of 13,000 in
1900. It has been declining since.

More and more farmers admitted defeat and abandoned their un-
co-operative parcels of earth. Young people born in Pope County
left to search for greener pastures the day after they had ended their
schooling.

The people of Pope County, who have been concerned with the
county's problems in recent years, have naturally placed most of
their emphasis on economics. Personal and corporate bankruptcy
have been a real threat, like a black twister that can touch down
on a whim. Civic leaders held meetings. They tried to reconcile their own disagreements. They attempted to plan with the co-
operation of other groups, and, when this failed, different interest
groups went back to planning independently. Concrete results were
seldom attainable except when the federal government or state agencies intervened. Good ideas that sprang from fertile imaginations fell
unmourned upon a wasteland. Standards of living and the chances
for community rehabilitation kept going down.

### THE DEVELOPMENT PROGRAM

In their despair, the people of Pope County turned to Southern
Illinois University, sixty miles over the Shawnee Hills and through
the coal fields, for a new kind of assistance. The University had been
graduated from a teacher's college to a university primarily because
southern Illinois had a number of "Pope Counties." Farm incomes
were falling off rapidly. The coal industry no longer supported towns
to which it had given birth. Where diggings were not mined out,
a few machines had taken the place of thousands of men in the pits.
Depression-stage unemployment was rampant when other areas of
the state and nation were enjoying postwar prosperity. Towns of the
region known as "Little Egypt" had a down-at-the-heels look, and

they were intrusted in some cases to the care of the aged and others who remained only because they were too tired to leave and start life again elsewhere.

A staggering amount of tax money was going into relief for the unemployed in southern Illinois, while the state's tax income from retail sales in that area was well below the level of northern cities. Worried state officials knew, too, that the level of education, never very high in the southern section of the state, was not going to rise and generate a healthier economic climate if youngsters had to forego high school in order to help support the family.

The state chamber of commerce was deeply concerned. So were the taxing bodies, public health officials, farm groups, Chicago newspapers, and a few prominent residents of southern Illinois who were heard with respect in the state capital. University status was given to Southern Illinois Teachers College at Carbondale in the hope that it could contribute something to the rejuvenation of the thirty-one counties it served.

In addition to its teaching and research programs, the University has a number of instruments of area service designed to "help southern Illinois communities help themselves." One of these is the Department of Community Development, where the author has the privilege of directing a fifteen-man staff of city planners, industrial-development counselors, educators, farm specialists, and sociologists. Since 1953, the Department has worked closely with citizens of a dozen towns and all the communities of four counties in long-range development programs based on concerted citizen action. Scores of other towns have requested aid on special projects.

It was to this Department of Community Development that Pope County sent its request for help. Assigned to this section was Community Consultant Frank H. Sehnert, who holds a Bachelor's degree in agriculture and a Master's in rural sociology. He also has a degree in religion and experience in youth and church work.

Sehnert spent three to four days a week in Pope County for more than a year. The University paid his salary and expenses. The principal expense to Pope County was the cost of the paper used in duplicating committee reports for general distribution.

Here, briefly, is what happened:

Local citizens were directed in making a community characteristics study, sampling opinions of people throughout the county on social and economic problems and gauging their attitudes toward possible solutions.

A little later, following a series of training sessions, dozens of volunteer enumerators completed in four days a door-to-door census to collect up-to-date raw data about the county.

The Pope County Development Program was formally instituted when officers were elected and a 33-member Advisory Council named. Among its members were the chairmen of 16 study committees charged to prepare carefully and to analyze recommendations for upgrading local trades and services, government, social agencies, industrial employment, the library, health, recreation, and other aspects of community life.

Nobody expected miracles overnight. This was a completely new experience for people with a natural proclivity to move slowly and methodically.

Committee chairmen attended leadership-training sessions for a month and learned something about basic research, organizing facts, and presenting them effectively. Farmers and townspeople alike started going to community-development meetings—at first, out of curiosity or for lack of anything better to do.

It took only about a year for the program to win general approval in a region where people with much longer periods of residence are still outsiders. Acceptance came, apparently because faint signs of progress began showing up and, more important, because community development was something by and for the people, not a package gift-wrapped for Pope County by university "experts." Through their own thinking, the people were allowed to write the prescriptions for community ills and to apply the needed therapy.

To cite accomplishments of the continuing Pope County effort during its first year and a half, up to the present writing, would permit in this limited space only a laborious, albeit impressive, listing. Instead, it might be better to extract a few sketches from the county's community-development notebook.

## THE SCHOOL ISSUE

The education committee of the Pope County Development Program was one of the first to swing into action. It faced the facts and came up with a conclusion that was sound.

There were too many one-room, one-teacher schools where youngsters could hope to get no more than a second-rate education. There were, in fact, 13 one-room schools staffed by teachers without degrees who were able to spend only about 15 minutes a day with each class. This rationing of instruction, and the duplicate financial burdens in each locality for bus service and school maintenance, pointed to the need for consolidation.

It was not an idea that could be sold easily. Every tiny village zealously safeguarded its autonomy in school affairs. Each eyed with distrust a measure that would candidly hail the over-all superiority of Golconda; more rural children would have to go to Golconda where, rural residents grudgingly admitted, the school was bigger and teachers were better trained and better paid. Besides, the county superintendent of schools was already located in Golconda. The supervisor to be named for the unit schools would probably have his office there, too, and Golconda would try to run the proposed unit school board. "No, thanks," said rural residents, "we like things just the way they are."

They reverted to precedent. There was still considerable ill-feeling about the prior consolidation of the high-school district. Many still thought there should be two high schools in the county instead of one. The vote on a bond issue for a new high school several years before had clearly showed the cleavage between rural and town voters.

The need for the school was universally recognized. Golconda elementary students and all of the county's high-school students were crammed into the same building. There was no question about the voters accepting the high-school building plan; the real issue was its location. Debate on this score so obscured all other factors that none of the interested parties took care to notice an error on the election petition. A clerk in the state capitol had confused two townships and placed the new high school in the northern part of the state.

A retired attorney who saw beyond the controversy prompted a postponement of the election by kindly remarking: "I think if I were going to build a high school I'd put it in Pope County."

The second time the petition was readied for a vote it failed because none of three specified locations received a majority vote. Another long delay ensued. Finally, a compromise ballot on the high school was approved. The building was placed in a rural area near, but not too near, Golconda.

Members of the Development Program's education committee knew the unit grade school district was going to be a much harder pill for Pope County to swallow. They sugar-coated it slightly by arguing that it would mean more state education funds without higher taxes.

George McKibben, a husky southern Illinois native and an agronomist at the University of Illinois Experiment Station, found himself in an unenviable position. He was named chairman of the Development Program's education committee. He was also on the board of the small Corner School, which served the Glendale community.

McKibben was convinced the unit district was the logical choice for the whole county. In effect, he was saying to his friends and neighbors who had chosen him to govern the policies and finances of the Corner School that Glendale might be better off if the school ceased to function. That decision, if the school issue passed, would be up to a countywide board, and the residents of Glendale would have to abide by it.

Once consolidation was decided upon, there was no turning back for McKibben or the 30-odd members of his committee. Their standing in the eyes of their fellow citizens in Pope County and, indeed, the fate of the entire community-development program rested on the success of the school issue at the polls and the selection of a representative school board acceptable to all factions and geographical areas. If the measure failed—and many were certain it would—the over-all effect might not be catastrophic, for Pope County had become accustomed to the abortion of civic efforts. Yet, it would drive even deeper into the hearts and minds of people who lived there the conviction that Pope County was incapable of keeping pace with other areas. The committee members were aware of this. Like the people of other community-development committees, they had begun to know Pope County as it really was. They went to work with the fervor of men and women risking personal safety to halt an avalanche.

Their first step was to inform themselves fully of all the implications of the school merger. They sent a delegation to Springfield, the state capital, to consult the superintendent of public instruction. Twice, they invited an expert on school law from Southern Illinois University to explain to them the advantages of consolidation. They asked the county superintendent of schools to translate the measure in terms of Pope County's school system. They talked to teachers and principals and to P.T.A. leaders.

By June, three months before the election, they thought they were ready to air the question in a series of public meetings. Committee members, armed with a six-page fact sheet, went into every village and town. The early results were not very encouraging.

"Our people were still not convincing enough in that first round," said George McKibben regretfully. "Maybe we should have had a dry run with the whole committee in one town."

When a second round of meetings was held in the early fall, however, the speakers were more convincing. They could answer questions about all phases of the issue in a forthright manner.

Meanwhile, the committee enlisted the support of the *Herald-Enterprise*, the only newspaper in the county. The editor agreed to carry weekly articles written by the committee for two to three months in advance of the election. The high-school principal started authoring the series. When he went on vacation, the assignment was passed around among committee members. When the school principal returned, he told his replacements in the journalistic endeavor they were doing such a good job they might as well continue without his aid.

Just before the election, a periodical issue of the *Herald Enterprise*, which is delivered to all Farm Bureau members as well as to regular subscribers, carried a full-page advertisement about the school issue. This was written by another member of the Experiment Station staff, a forester. Bought for a cut-rate of $50.00, the advertisement carried a specimen ballot and heavy blocks of type spelling out in simple language the principal provisions of the unit law.

As the day of decision neared, the meetings of the education committee increased in intensity and drew larger crowds. To reach the people who wouldn't attend these meetings, the committee campaigned in the county's general stores where the audience sat on benches grouped around the traditional pot-bellied stove.

The unit district carried by a vote of 878 to 330. Practically everyone who was not bedridden or working away from home went to the polls.

## Brownfield

At high noon in Brownfield the only sounds came from singing birds. Periodically an automobile motor or the wailing of a child in some near-by farm house disturbed their symphony; but most of the time the birds held sway.

The post office was open for business in an unsymmetrical two-story brick structure. The front door, looking out upon a dirty street, weeded acres, and an impressive wooded bluff, opened and closed only infrequently.

Millard Farmer, supervisor of the Illinois Public Aid Commission in Golconda, scanned the vast stretch of uncultivated field that separated the silent village from its hilly perimeter. "A man couldn't sleep with so much quiet," he said.

The general store on the corner had no more traffic than the post office. The only other commercial enterprise in Brownfield, another country store, did have a few customers that day because it was going out of business and prices were cut 25 per cent.

Between the two stores was the best commercial location. It was occupied by a bank which had been closed since the depression. The boards which sealed its doorway were rotting. Bricks lay where they had fallen, on the earth beneath gaping holes in the walls.

Faintly discernible through the tall grass were railroad tracks, running east and west.

"Three passenger trains a day used to stop here," Millard Farmer said. "Over there is where the hotel stood. The stockyards were down this way. There were also three big retail stores, an implement firm, a flour and feed mill, and a railroad-tie yard."

A model-A Ford came chugging down the street, scaring the sparrows from the trees, and Farmer paused to wave to the driver.

A few seconds later the car was gone, but the sound of its motor reverberated through the village for a long time.

"When I was a boy, this place was a beehive of activity," Farmer said at length.

"How many people live here now, and what do they do?"

The young woman in the store, which was soon to be boarded up like the bank, ventured an answer: "I tried to count up as high as 75—I figured that was about right—but I guess there aren't near that many any more. Most of them are on relief, I guess. There's no place to work around here."

From there, Farmer drove his car up into the hills, which afford beautiful views of rolling hills, pasture lands, pine plantations, and little cottages tucked up against the sides of bluffs or planted at their highest peaks. From there, perspective is altered drastically. The dilapidated homes that highlight impressions in the valley appear to be part of a healthy and covetable environment when viewed from on high.

In the hills, the narrow roads were rutted and mushy after a quick thaw, and the gravel that had been dropped sparingly upon them could be seen only on the soft shoulders. The muddy miles between farm houses on such a bright, warm day would make any stranger wonder what people did when the roads became impassable.

Farmer chuckled. "The roads never become impassable. They get bad and they get worse, but, to these people, they are never impassable. If they have to go somewhere and want to go badly enough, there is no stopping them."

Earlier that day, at the crest of a steep incline, Farmer had pulled up in front of a neat frame house surrounded by several sturdy barns and rolling fields populated by large herds of sheep and cattle.

Mrs. Audrey Trovillion had been doing the farm chores during her husband's illness. Nevertheless, she came to the door in a print dress, wearing heels and makeup, and her hair was freshly done up. Her husband, a university graduate and amateur musician who had managed to hold together a community concert band in Golconda for a number of years, was out of bed but still pretty much confined to a chair.

A late-model spinet piano stood in one corner. In another was a

in this materialistic age where people want to exchange the least amount of thought and exertion for the greatest amount of personal gain. Today's Americans are reluctant to do anything unless there is a good assurance of immediate rewards.

"It takes about 10 to 15 years for the farmer to adopt ideas after they have proved sound and economical at agricultural experiment stations," Sehnert notes. "The same is probably true with new developments in the social science fields."

Trained "enablers" like Sehnert can fill the gap between ideas and people. As much educational benefit accrues to the "students" as in an organized extension course, though the teaching may not be structured according to the dictates of educational textbooks. Unlike the extension course in another way, the kind of education that Pope County is now exposed to is directed at specific problems instead of hypotheses.

To those interested in the more traditional relationships between college and community, between the man-in-the-street and the classroom professor, Pope County has one final story worth relating.

Back in the 1930's, a pair of rural sociologists conducted a thorough study of the Pope County area and made some startling recommendations. These included wholesale public purchase of land for recreation and redistribution of families in accordance with scientifically sound land-use. Fifty-six per cent of the land was suited only for forests and recreation, the researchers said, and only 17 per cent of it was good crop soil. The sociologists were in favor of consolidating schools and road districts in the county and imposing multicounty jurisdiction in government and public health. Hotels and camping sites should be constructed to promote tourist trade, the report stated, and these should be outfitted with furniture and craft items made locally with local resources.

The sociologists granted that failure to educate the people of Pope County about their problems and the methods of alleviating them would cause some of the most important directional measures to fall upon a "nonreceptive field."

The adjective *nonreceptive* was much too mild; citizens of Pope County were angry and bitter. The sociologists' report left a mark that has never been erased and probably never will. Local residents who possess a copy of the published findings would never admit to ownership. None would dare state publicly that the conclusions were valid. The general feeling was: "How can these men who never saw Pope County until a year ago tell us how they can make it better?"

Scarcely anyone mentions the 20-year-old study any more. Those who do, exaggerate its contents out of proportion. Yet, ironically, the generally accepted community-development program is pursuing independently some of the early report's boldest suggestions. The schools have been consolidated, and steps are being taken to organize a county road district. The scenic and recreational attractions of the area are now recognized and being promoted. A craft center for commercial production is in the embryonic stage. New uses are being found for the county's wood products. Businessmen interested in industrial development are concentrating on chipping mills and pulping operations.

The reasons for this apparent switch in attitudes are as basic as community education. The people refused to give blind allegiance to outside "experts." Yet, availing themselves of the opportunity to understand the issues, they reached the same conclusions and are seeking pretty much the same goals, but in their own inarticulate way.

Pope County, in a true pioneering spirit, is out to demonstrate that the people on the assembly line also have brains and resourcefulness and want only the right chance to prove that they, too, can create ideals. They can also put them to work, with boldness and confidence, as long as they live in a democracy. So can the peoples of Los Angeles, the Texas Panhandle, and the Long Island suburb.

# CHAPTER XI

# Instructional Materials in Community Education

EDGAR DALE

## Introduction

The term *materials of instruction* is broadly conceived to include all the planned experiences necessary to reach a stated educational goal. It includes the overt experiences, the demonstrations, field trips, the books, pamphlets, films, filmstrips, exhibits, tests, and evaluation devices. The materials used in instruction are influenced by three major factors: (*a*) the local, regional, or international setting or situation of the learner; (*b*) the ends or goals sought; and (*c*) the stated or assumed conceptions of learning and teaching.

The setting in which instructional materials are prepared and used for community education is not only local but is also regional, national, and international. This setting influences motivation. For example, the more than 700 million people in the newly independent nations need instructional materials which emphasize and further this independence. They need materials on life in their own country, on their history, on how to vote, on what their own government is doing nationally and internationally.

My second point is that the characteristics of materials of instruction will vary according to the general goals sought. The approach to materials of instruction will differ according to the view held as to the role of the common man in local, national, and world affairs. If governments want to help their citizens become free-ranging, mature, and independent, they will not keep these citizens on a short tether.

Training without generalization ties a person to local routines, makes his ceiling of growth a low and easily attained one, makes him eternally dependent on others for advice, guidance, or simple clear-cut instruction. He has no genuine range of informed choice.

The educated man, in contrast, becomes self-winding, self-instructing, and independent. He thinks for himself, and all the world becomes his stage. If the end in view is a thinking man, the means must match this end.

The third major factor influencing materials of instruction is our conception of learning and teaching. Teaching and learning should take place in an atmosphere aimed to develop the increasing independence of the learner. If we have a "training" concept of learning, we shall emphasize unrelated specifics, fail to develop *methods* of learning, fail to secure the possibilities of generalization and transfer. Many literates have lapsed into illiteracy because goals were too limited; the teaching of reading was *training* in "calling" words.

We could mistakenly think of community education as remedial education, aimed merely to correct some of the adult's weak points. In many situations remedial education is needed, but to assume that community education is *only* remedial would rob it of its richness and put it on a par with narrow programs of adult education with which we are familiar. It makes a difference, then, whether we conceive teaching and learning as a way of setting people free to become mature individuals or whether our plan is merely to develop routineers. The element of free, creative, disciplined choice should loom large in adult education.

Lest this approach toward the role of instructional materials seem pretentious or Utopian, we must remember the great movements of population in the Western world in the last century and realize that this movement may be even greater in Asia and Africa during the next fifty years. If we want to develop the free, flexible man in a free society, our instructional materials must reflect that point of view. We must teach so that adults *learn how to learn* and have a hunger for learning.

## *Developing the Instructional Program*

The writer has presented the background which will influence the general approach to instructional materials. Let us now move more specifically into the step-by-step procedures of such preparation.

The three steps to be followed in setting up an instructional program are these: (*a*) setting up the goals; (*b*) selecting and organizing the learning experiences, and (*c*) evaluating results.

## SETTING UP THE GOALS

Instructional materials often suffer because of blurred focus as to purposes. Here are some statements that committees in different areas have jotted down in response to questions regarding the goals of instruction: (*a*) We are trying to teach adults to read. (*b*) We are trying to get the adults in our village to hoe their corn. (*c*) We want to get our farmers to adopt more productive methods of raising rice. (*d*) We are trying to help our fishermen set up a co-operative to finance motors for their boats. (*e*) We want to teach farmers to build a brick wall around their village well. (*f*) We want farmers to improve their feeding practices for milch cows.

Some of these goals are simple and involve little more than reminding people to do acceptable things now neglected. However, some complicated abilities, such as learning to read, require not less than one hundred hours of carefully planned instruction, supplemented by much independent reading. In community education we must distinguish between these simple, easily attained skills and the complicated behaviors requiring a long time to achieve. A simple skill, "picking oranges without bruising them," adequately describes the desired response on the part of the plantation employees in Jamaica. However, the goal, "to get farm-owners to develop a land-use program," is a long-range goal and is so complex that the interacting responses between staff specialists and farmers are not easily defined.

### SELECTING AND ORGANIZING THE LEARNING EXPERIENCES

Let us suppose that we want to help adults develop their own farm-loan co-operatives. Perhaps the farmer has a horror of debt. He has seen the disastrous effects of borrowing money at high rates of interest, and he may be suspicious of government's effort to help him borrow money. He must "unlearn" before he can learn. Perhaps he needs the reassuring voice—face-to-face or by tape recording— of someone who he knows and respects. He may also need a clear explanation of the proposed measures—by film or recording. It is always easier to move along the old channels of learning than it is to cut new ones.

The farmer or landowner may be more sophisticated than a group of fishermen I met on the shore of the Caribbean Sea in Jamaica. They didn't know about possible government aid in buying a motor to reach distant fishing banks, nor had they learned to co-operate by renting a boathouse and landing facilities. The instructional experiences for them would be quite different than those of land-owners or of a sophisticated co-operative of taxi-owners in Montego Bay in Jamaica.

The American reader of this material will do well to remember that it took almost twenty years to get the farmers in Iowa to accept hybrid corn.[1] This involved no new capital; the evidence of increased yield was clear-cut. But buying and planting hybrid corn involved a change in their self-concept of the good farmer as one who selects his own seed corn.

Let us assume now that our goals are clear. We understand the motivations which can be used, the learning rewards. Our big problem is to match ends with means and means with ends. Where can one see the new method of planting rice? The plot may be distant. The weeding may be done when the farmers are doing their own work. It is hard to develop excellent demonstration plots.

We may be compelled to bring a "picture" of it to other farmers. This may be 2 × 2 color slides which show comparable land plots side by side, one using the old method, the other using the new. Or we may secure a film of the new method.

### EVALUATING THE RESULTS

Was the curriculum a satisfactory one? Did the instructional materials work? They worked if the behavioral goals set up at the outset were achieved. It is easy to evaluate the effect of the film-strip on how to pick oranges, or that of giving on-the-spot demonstrations on this simple skill. You watch to see if the quality of picked oranges improves. But the evaluation of the more complex objective, "to help farmers develop a suitable land-use program," requires a more complicated procedure. The program may extend over several years.

Many unpredicted problems arise. Perhaps the terraces get washed out; there may be unusual drouth. Or the price of sugar may decline

1. Robert A. Rohwer, "How New Practices Spread." Reprint from *Iowa Farm Science*, IV (July, 1949), 13–14.

disastrously. The instructional materials and the learning experiences cannot be neatly predicted or evaluated because the project is complex. Therefore, assistance from an agricultural specialist is needed through broadcasts, demonstrations, field trips, or reading materials where appropriate.

## Some General Principles

The writer has presented the setting in which instructional materials are prepared and has sketched the three basic steps in curriculum-making. We turn now to some of the principles or special concerns involved in the producing, using, and evaluating of such materials.

1. We are working in a voluntary, informal situation with adults, not with children. These adults read little or not at all. Their "formal" learning experiences are secured in a setting of voluntary attendance, not through compulsory and systematic experiences as in childhood education. The materials used must reflect this adult approach.

2. Widespread illiteracy will continue for a long time in most underdeveloped countries. Reading will not soon be a typical method of learning for the average adult although it may have great importance for leaders. Dramatizations, demonstrations, exhibits, and field trips are of great importance.

3. The overt, easily imitated, easily mastered experience will play a big part in the "curriculum" of community education.

4. The immediate "reward" must loom large as a factor in motivation. The rewards do not need to be material ones; the satisfaction of gradually learning to read is an important one.

5. The learning experiences must be carried out in a situation in which the adult is not embarrassed by public failure. Many adults would learn to read if they could do it secretly.

6. The beginning model must include the elements of "see and do for yourself," of personal involvement, and of direct participation. However, we must not confuse our beginning approach with what we do later. Later we shall increasingly use symbolic behavior, search for methods of transfer through principles and theory, work for adequate evaluation and a rethinking of behavior.

## The Media of Instruction

Thus far we have discussed materials of instruction chiefly as ideas, skills, or attitudes to be communicated. We have said little about the media to carry these messages, the circumstances under which each one is most effective, and the most suitable combinations.

Speaking broadly we can approach the world of reality directly and perceptually or we can approach it indirectly and conceptually. We can react by signs or by symbols to things and ideas not present. We can react to an absent person by reading a letter from him or about him. The written symbols usually use an alphabet to create the spoken symbols.

The curriculum-maker or the producer of instructional materials in community education must make a series of decisions regarding the degree of representativeness, concreteness, or abstractness of the experiences to be undergone by the student.

The specialists preparing materials of instruction must be conscious of the concrete-abstract continuum of experience and match it with the level of development of the adult learners. The curriculum-maker must know their background, how well they can react symbolically to the new experience.

We can think of teaching materials as being on varying levels of a cone of direct to indirect experience. At the bottom of the cone we have firsthand, direct, purposeful experience. The experience is unabridged, full-bodied, not compressed. We have an unedited reality. We perceptually touch, taste, smell, handle, or see. Inference is at a minimum.

A second level is the contrived experience. Reality is edited to make it easier to understand. Here we have the working model of a gasoline engine, a model hurricane-proof house, or a series of model plots on a demonstration farm. It is an "edited" farm, set up to teach. It is the real thing shifted and foreshortened to make it a teaching instrument.

A third level on the cone of experience is that of dramatization in which one is a participant. Through dramatic participation we can get closer to realities that may not be at hand in space or in time. Dramatization also edits reality—highlights here and diminishes there. It can evoke reaction through emotion. One participates empathically, gets into the other fellow's shoes.

Fourth, we have the direct and real demonstration which also edits or abridges experience to make it easier to follow, to understand, and to repeat. It is visualized explanation of an important fact or idea or process. The demonstrator may use real objects, contrived materials, recorded voices, filmstrips—indeed the whole array of audio-visual experiences. It is assumed that the persons viewing the demonstration will usually carry out the overt experience demonstrated, either then or later.

Fifth, we can use a field trip. This, too, usually means spectatorship and postponed doing. It may, however, include overt, responsible doing by the observer. There may be films and demonstrations viewed in connection with the field trip. The field trip is especially valuable in adult education since it does not smack of the classroom but has the tang and feeling of reality. The possibilities of demonstrations are illustrated by the fact that since the beginning of the Community Projects program in India, 1,129,000 demonstrations have been held by village-level workers and others in agriculture alone.[2]

The sixth level is that of exhibits. These may make use of working models, demonstrations, pictorial materials, enlarged photographs. Agricultural fairs include exhibits of fruits, crops, and manufactured products. The exhibit may occasionally permit overt participation by an observer. We may have displays of the "real thing" as well as abbreviated and edited experiences.

Here is an example of some of the problems faced in preparing exhibits for community education. From December, 1953, to May, 1955, in the rural district of Yelwal, Mysore, an experimental training scheme was held for specialists in community education. The project, carried out by UNESCO at the invitation of the governments of India and Mysore, offered training courses of nine months' duration to two groups of senior students. A team of three persons was chosen to develop a museum exhibition unit. In the manual which accompanied this unit the following statement appears:

2. Sohan Singh, "Social Education in India (Methods)," *Fundamental and Adult Education,* IX (April, 1957), 93 ff.

It is the purpose of fundamental education to help people who have not had access to formal schooling to understand and solve their immediate problems by their own efforts. It is therefore often necessary to touch, simultaneously, the understanding and the emotions of groups of people who are entirely or largely illiterate and cannot be approached through the written word.[3]

The topic chosen for the exhibit was "Trees and the Soil." The hills were bare of trees and being rapidly reduced to wasteland by overgrazing and erosion.

The material that follows describes in detail the elaborate museum project set up by this team. They made mistakes which are likely to be repeated by other museum workers in this field. Here are some comments on successes and weaknesses as noted by the authors of the pamphlet and by this writer:

1. An illuminated, three-dimensional audio-visual box which magnified the scene through lenses and provided an accompanying short lecture was very popular.
2. The three-dimensional color photographs were effective.
3. The exhibit was too complicated and too costly for the size of the audience. The unit cost per viewer was high.
4. The audio-visual materials were sometimes too complex. Some models were not recognized as such.
5. Some working models were too complicated, too fragile.
6. The human voice, whether "live" or reproduced, was needed to explain some of the exhibits and make them come alive.
7. Simple written labels proved effective. They were read to illiterates by literate viewers.
8. It is difficult to test the cumulative effect of all the exhibits.

At the seventh level up the cone we experience a further condensing or abstracting of reality by the use of television and film. Usually these media are easily interpreted by the illiterate, as parents of five-year-olds can testify. Television and film can introduce a spectator to a real event, to drama, demonstration—the whole gamut of audio-visual materials. Television can have the quality of immediacy—one may see a real event as it happens. Direct teaching may be done by television. On October 8, 1956, WKNO-TV in Memphis began a course of television lessons designed to teach

3. "Planning the Exhibition," chap. i, p. 35, in *Museum Techniques in Fundamental Education: Part II, The Mysore Experiments.* Paris: UNESCO, *Educational Studies and Documents,* No. 17.

illiterate adults how to learn to read and write. More than 1,000 students have enrolled in the courses.

With electronic media such as radio, motion pictures, and television, we introduce a new characteristic for instructional materials. They move forward mechanically at a planned speed. There is usually little or no audience interaction such as is possible with the instructional experiences previously discussed. True, the film or television program may answer the questions which the script writer may have secured from interested adults, but there is now no chance to voice new questions. Wise use of television, films, and radio must, therefore, include opportunities for some kind of planned interaction.

Electronic media introduce another important factor, namely, high initial cost and equipment needing regular repair. We must reach large audiences in order to get the unit cost per viewer down to economically manageable proportions. We must have service stations to repair equipment.

Live television can give us a picture of the unabridged real event. The motion picture, however, can both compress and expand time and space. It may reduce or increase natural size. The peasant who was not afraid of his own little mosquitoes after seeing a huge closeup of the Anopheles mosquito on the motion picture screen is now a part of the folklore of underdeveloped countries.

Early accounts of the use of film in these countries led to the suggestion that the typical films moved too quickly. Since American and British films are viewed all over the world, it is likely that most persons will learn to adjust themselves to this speed, learn how to look at motion pictures. Sometimes if the subject-matter is unfamiliar, the film story must move more slowly.

At the eighth level we have still pictures, radio, and recordings. Each uses a single sense, sight or sound. When the drawings or photographs reproduce a known reality, they can be easily interpreted. The photographs and drawings may also be projected as film strips or 2 × 2 slides, and thus we get the advantage of dramatic enlargement on a white screen. Striking use of enlarged photographs is made in traveling and stationary exhibits.

Radio can record the powerful and emotionally evocative human voice, offers drama and music. The familiar voice lends authority to what is said. Inexpensive records for 78 rpm have not been widely used but might have possibilities for instruction if such records could be developed for spring-driven phonographs.

According to the 1958 *World Almanac and Book of Facts* (p. 84), there were 300,400,000 radio sets in the world. These were distributed as follows: North America (not including the United States), 14,800,000; South America, 18,400,000; Europe, 83,000,000; Asia, 21,300,000; Australia, 9,200,000; Africa, 5,200,000; and the United States, 148,500,000. Europe (excluding USSR) and the United States have about 21 per cent of the world's population and 77 per cent of the world's radios. The United States has about half of the world's radios.

Sohan Singh reports in "Social Education in India":[4]

Programmes for women, children, farmers and villagers in general and industrial workers are broadcast from 22 centres in the country in English and in local languages.

At the receiving end there are about 900,000 domestic radio sets in the country. Education Departments, either from their own funds or from external aid, have set up community sets in many schools and social education centres.

When we are told that most radios are concentrated in the cities, we realize that India like other underdeveloped countries will have very limited numbers of farmers who listen in their homes. Such sets will usually be battery radios. Taxes and duties make the sets expensive, and service for repairs or replacements is difficult in rural areas. Widespread use of radio as a tool of community education rests upon securing durable, low-cost sets which can be bought on the installment plan.

Group listening at some central point is a possibility. In theory this planned listening is followed by discussion. Group listening to a single voice from a single station may be a temporary expedient but could lead to all the evils of a monopoly communication system.

Norman Lloyd Williams says:

4. Sohan Singh, "Social Education in India (The Radio)," *Fundamental and Adult Education*, IX (April, 1957), 93.

Recent experiments in Malaya show that it is possible to teach illiterates to read by radio—by radio alone, without the help of any teacher at the listening end.

Of 109 groups said, on the eve of the pilot experiment, to have been established, only 65 made reports at the end of the first week, and at the end of the thirteenth week only 14 groups were still functioning. It is not yet known how many survived the complete course of 25 weeks.[5]

The reader should note that "it is possible" does not mean that it worked out well in Malaya. However, the lessons could be followed easily, and Mr. Williams believed that the teaching method is sound. Still another experiment was carried on at Sutatenza, Colombia, and reported in *Fundamental and Adult Education* for April, 1955.

On the ninth level of the cone we have visual symbols—flat maps, diagrams, charts, posters, and graphs. Our adult learner may have difficulty in interpreting these symbols. The map, for example, is a highly abstracted "picture" of the area it represents. A graph symbolically compares a quantity of goods with the length of a line or the area of a circle. A diagram or chart of a land-use program may use contour lines, which may require additional instruction by the agricultural specialist.

Verbal symbols appear at the pinnacle of the cone of experience. These symbols represent the final stage in the concrete-abstract scale. Inference is now at a maximum. To get rich meaning out of printed symbols, we must put rich meaning in. If these words are spoken, they may be understood, especially if in the local dialect. But written materials may be in a literary language which the adult learner may not even know.

The foregoing description of the cone of experience is not a highly exact analysis of the levels of concreteness-abstraction. It is a metaphor with its strengths and weaknesses. We hope that it will sensitize the producer of instructional materials to the great variation in the simplicity and complexity of materials on a scale of abstraction. It may suggest, too, the importance of variety in presentation. Adults participating in community-education projects need stimulation and motivation. A variety of ways of presenting ideas is, therefore, helpful in the teaching-learning process.

5. Norman Lloyd Williams, "Teaching To Read by Radio," *Fundamental and Adult Education*, VII (October, 1955), 147, 149–50.

*Instructional Materials for Adults of Limited Reading Ability*

MATERIALS FOR USE IN UNITED STATES

In the United States the production of instructional materials for adults of limited reading abilities has been opportunistic and sporadic. Instructing prospective American citizens has been a major activity in this field. For example, a pamphlet series, *Federal Textbook Citizenship*, includes the titles "The Day Family," "On the Way to Democracy," "The Business of Our Government," "Our Constitution Lives and Grows," "The Gardners Become Citizens," "Laws for the Nation." These simply written, illustrated textbooks are available from the Superintendent of Documents, U.S. Government Printing Office, Washington, D.C. The Bureau of Indian Affairs has produced booklets at easy reading levels.

Dr. Ambrose Caliver of the U.S. Office of Education was in charge of the Literacy Education Project sponsored by the U.S. Office of Education and the Carnegie Corporation. They developed a series of readers titled, *The Brown Family Series*, later published by Washington Educators Dispatch, 100 Garfield Avenue, New London, Connecticut. Writers checked the readability of these materials with the Lorge formula. This project and related literacy activities have been described by Dr. Caliver in a series of articles appearing in *School Life*.[6]

The writer under a contract with the U.S. Armed Forces Institute prepared a series of three adult readers at the fourth-, fifth-, and sixth-grade levels which were published in 1954 and 1955. These stories deal with human relations, personal business, physical and mental health, citizenship, vocational guidance, and recreation. The titles and order numbers from the Superintendent of Documents are: "Stories for Today" (MCo02), 45 cents; "Stories Worth Knowing" (MCo03), 70 cents; "New Flights in Reading" (MCo04), 70 cents. These books were built on the "fourth-grade" literacy level gained through earlier instruction in the armed forces. All materials were field tested for interest and comprehension.

The study showed that it was possible to adapt important stories and articles or write them in such a way as to make them interesting

6. Ambrose Caliver, "Literacy Education Project Draws to a Close," *School Life*, XXXII (February, 1950), 74–75.

and comprehensible to less-able adult readers. Such readers, however, are easily "floored" by hard words, and careful grading is necessary. The materials were checked by the Dale-Chall readability formula.

The National Tuberculosis Association carried out a five-year study of their publication program and developed and readapted all of their pamphlets used for popular consumption.[7] Deficiencies of earlier publications were excessive technical vocabulary, writing pamphlets at too high a reading level, and inadequate targeting of audiences and ideas to be conveyed. A manual on simple writing was developed.[8]

### INSTRUCTIONAL MATERIALS FOR THE PHILIPPINES[9]

The National Media Production Center (NMPC) in Manila, Philippines, was established in 1953 under the American-aid program and is now a regular Philippine government agency. It produces and distributes mass media dealing with the economic-development program of the Philippines and assists all other Philippine Government agencies in producing and using the mass media.

When the information program is being formulated, the NMPC is visited by a group of officials from the Department of Agriculture and Natural Resources. This bureau has long been concerned about the relatively low yield of rice fields and the need for importing rice, thus consuming currency reserves. Yet, the Philippines could easily be self-sufficient in rice production if farmers would use improved growing techniques.

For conferences such as this one, a rough "formula" has been used to promote orderly and sound decisions. Three questions are asked and discussed with all groups seeking to develop effective communication media: (a) What, precisely, do you want to communicate? (b) To whom do you want to convey your message? (c) What media will most effectively communicate your message?

7. Edgar Dale, "How Our Health Education Materials Are Developed." New York: National Tuberculosis Association, 1947.

8. Edgar Dale and Hilda Hager, "Some Suggestions for Writing Health Materials." Available from the Bureau of Educational Research, Ohio State University, Columbus, Ohio.

9. This section was prepared by William G. Hart, Audio-Visual Advisor, International Cooperation Administration, Manila, Philippines.

*Setting Up Goals.* "What, precisely, do you want to communicate?" This question is necessary because NMPC has found that a government agency may have only a very general idea of its proposed message. The question sharpens thinking and delineates the specific problem of communication.

The agency decided that it wanted to teach farmers a series of specific techniques (seed selection, planting, cultivation, fertilizing, weed control, harvesting). No emotional impact was needed because farmers already want to have more food for their families and more cash income. But they lacked "know-how." So the communication problem was defined. We needed to teach a series of rice-growing techniques.

The next question was: "To whom do you want to convey your message?" The main target group was easily determined: the rice-growing farmers. Even in this instance, however, the usual question is asked: Can we produce "general" materials which will inform the farmer and at the same time educate the public about rice-growing? Few groups recognize the fact that really effective mass media must be specifically tailored for the target group.

*Providing Learning Experiences.* Only after several conferences are we ready to consider question 3: "Which media will most effectively communicate our message?" Here we must raise the issue of money. For example, motion pictures are relatively an expensive medium. For the cost of one motion picture, thousands of pamphlets and posters can be printed. We must decide which medium will give the best results for the money available.

How literate is the target audience? With a city audience, a carefully prepared pamphlet may be effective. A rural group, probably less literate, may require pictorial material.

Should we consider some of the less commonly used media of communication? For example, what are the possibilities of puppets, cartoons, or stage shows in communicating our message?

In all these media-planning discussions, one overriding principle is recognized. Any one medium alone is of very little value in communicating information or changing behavior. Even a good motion picture has a limited impact on the viewer. There must be follow-up, perhaps using demonstrations, posters, pamphlets. We must plan in terms of campaigns in which many media are used.

In this campaign to increase rice production, the following program was developed. A factual "how-to" motion picture, "100 Cavans per Hectare," was produced, together with a pamphlet summarizing the techniques presented in the film. The film is being shown and the pamphlets distributed by the twenty-four mobile audio-visual units of the Bureau of Agricultural Extension. Agricultural extension workers have set up demonstration plots. Pamphlets are distributed to farmers who visit these demonstration plots. Posters have been produced and are displayed in centers of population. The regular radio programs of the NMPC include spot announcements urging farmers to adopt more effective rice-growing techniques and offering the pamphlet upon request. And whenever the NMPC stage show is "on the road" similar information is included in the dialogue.

How effective are information campaigns planned in this way? How good are the pamphlets, the films, the radio programs? How much is behavior really changed by the impact of the mass media?

Obviously, an evaluation program in the field is essential. Here are some of the results of a field evaluation project recently carried out by the National Media Production Center to test the effectiveness of pamphlets already produced and distributed.

1. The distribution of printed materials has been completely reorganized. Mailing was formerly done in bulk to key government offices in each province: offices of the governor, mayor, and division school superintendent. The local school teacher was relied upon as a major community contact.

These sources have not been abandoned, but the principal emphasis is now placed on regular mailings to the 19,000 "barrio lieutenants" (elected officials of each small community). The study showed that it was the barrio lieutenant to whom rural people turn for help and advice.

2. Printed materials now carry more photographs and fewer art drawings. The research showed that rural people "believe" photographs more than drawings and believe realistic drawings more than stylized sketches.

3. More dialect translations are being made of printed materials.

4. All government agencies are being urged to plan information

campaigns which use a range of media and to follow up with their personnel. The research left little doubt that information materials distributed without supporting campaigns have little permanent effect on behavior.

## LATIN-AMERICAN FUNDAMENTAL EDUCATION PRESS[10]

*Background.* Millions of adults in Latin America are illiterate, and millions more have had only two or three years of elementary schooling. There is a dramatic scarcity of books, especially in the rural areas. Even the available reading materials present difficulties too great for this type of reader to overcome. Under these circumstances it is hard to cultivate the reading habit.

The Inter-American Seminar on Literacy and Adult Education, held in 1949 at Rio de Janeiro under the sponsorship of the Organization of American States and UNESCO, gave special consideration to this problem of reading materials. As a result, the Latin-American Fundamental Education Press was established in 1950 through an agreement between the Organization of American States and UNESCO.

*Purpose and Organization.* The main purpose of the Press is to produce and distribute educational materials. It also compiles, analyzes, and classifies materials prepared by others, organizes training courses in the production of such materials, and supplies technical information.

The main objective of the Press is to contribute to the fight against illiteracy and to the cultural and social betterment of the American peoples. Consequently, the publications of the Press cover the following categories:

1. Materials to teach adults to read
2. Basic knowledge of those subjects customarily taught in the elementary school: language and rudiments of mathematics and of the natural and social sciences
3. Civics
4. Culture and recreation
5. Health
6. Economic and social affairs
7. Agriculture

10. This section was prepared by Guillerma Nannetti, Division of Education, Organization of American States, Pan-American Union, Washington, D.C.

To date, the Press has published seventy-three titles, representing all the categories (or series), listed above, and has distributed 3,000,-000 copies in Spanish throughout Latin America. We are starting editions in Portuguese for Brazil, and in French for Haiti.

*Evaluation of the Materials.* The first edition of the booklets is considered preliminary. During this stage, the booklets are tested with individuals representative of the groups for whom they are intended. The tests determine whether the texts are easy to read and to understand, whether they awaken interest, and whether the illustrations are adequate. The first edition is revised on the basis of these tests. The final editions are then prepared, but revisions in later printings may be made as a result of the comments and the suggestions received from teachers and readers. In general, the evaluation is informal and is based mainly on the opinions of the persons for whom the booklets are intended. The readers use the simple questionnaires included in each booklet. These may be returned to the Press under the postal frank of the Pan-American Union. This directly links the Press and the users of its materials.

*Role in the Community.* The use of the booklets as a means of stimulating individual adults to learn to read by providing easy reading materials with adult content was quickly established. Collections of these booklets are now being used as the nucleus of a library or a community center where the people of the locality may come together to learn to read and also to work toward the solution of their mutual problems.

*Financing and Distribution.* The production costs are borne by the Pan-American Union. Under the Program of the Organization of the American States, hundreds of thousands of the booklets are distributed to the Latin-American governments participating in the library project. In addition, other governmental agencies, private and public organizations, and individuals buy the booklets in large quantities. A gift plan was set up to enable U.S. groups and individuals to contribute to the literacy work in Latin America by sending the booklets to groups not reached otherwise. The extent of interest in this participation is shown by the fact that during the first ten months of 1957, there were 425 instances of participation through the Gift Plan.

## THE PREPARATION OF LITERACY MATERIALS IN JAMAICA[11]

The materials produced by the Literacy Section of the Jamaica Social Welfare Commission include graded materials for direct teaching of reading. A preprimer and readers for grade levels one, two, three, and four have already been prepared. Teachers' manuals accompany these materials. The Literacy Section also prepares supplementary materials—a monthly printed newsletter for the adult reading classes, a monthly article for the *Welfare Reporter*, and a monthly contribution for *The Farmer*. Booklets are prepared at the request of other government departments and at the request of organizations such as the Jamaica Federation of Women and the Jamaica Banana Producers Federation.

The basal readers include a preprimer titled "Our Class" and the graded series of four readers titled "A Day with the Gordon's" "Introducing Willie Gordon," "Willie Saves His Land," "Willie Develops His Land," and Teacher's Manual.

The preprimer is written in the first person, uses 29 different words and has a total of 159 running words. It is completed in six to ten lessons, giving a feeling of quick mastery and helping to stimulate interest in further reading. Students are taught to write their names in the first or second lesson and learn to write the words in the book as they learn to read them.

The basal readers make literacy an integral part of a general community-education program and must help the students not only to learn the technical skills of reading and writing but also to solve basic problems.

A rural family was depicted, and the chief character named after a well-known Jamaican patriot, George William Gordon. Careful thought was given to the development of each character portrayed.

The vocabulary used in these books was carefully planned. Basic word lists were studied, and we used the Dale list of 769 words.[12] Thought was given to using the nouns most commonly spoken by Jamaicans.

11. This section was prepared by Marjorie Kirlew, Chief Literacy Officer, Jamaica Social Welfare Commission, Kingston, Jamaica.

12. Edgar Dale, "A Comparison of Two Word Lists." Columbus, Ohio: Bureau of Educational Research, Ohio State University.

Photographic illustrations were used for realistic depiction of characters and situations. These also helped build vocabulary by stimulating discussion, and students thus learned related words which do not appear in the text. For example, on page 7 in Reader I "A Day with the Gordons," a pig appears in a picture of the Gordon family. It is not referred to in the text, but the teacher is instructed to ask the students before they read the text to tell what they see in the picture. Most of them name the pig, and this word is written on the blackboard. Discussion then takes place about other farm animals, and they learn to read and write the names of these animals.

Another illustration in Reader I shows Martha washing clothes in a river. The teacher is instructed to discuss with the class how they wash their clothes and the source of available water in their area.

"A Day with the Gordons" is written in the third person and introduces a rural Jamaican family—Willie and Martha Gordon and their two children. As the title indicates, a day in the life of this family is described, Martha being highlighted as she is shown cooking and caring for her family.

There are 416 running words in Reader I with a vocabulary of 88 words, 79 being new. A limited vocabulary was used—a vocabulary of general words to which specific ones could be added as they related to the special situation in the particular community of the students.

This was a deliberate effort to combine two methods of teaching— the experience-centered method and the method in which specific teaching materials are used. In the experience-centered method, all the teaching material is developed by the teacher out of the experience of the class members.

We recommended that word analysis and word-building should be begun by the students in this first reader. Reader II has 1,104 running words with a vocabulary of 214 different words, 152 of which are new. Repetition of ideas as well as words is provided in different situations.

The student is encouraged to write down his personal problems as compared with Willie's. This tests his comprehension and his capacity to apply what he has read to his daily life. He is guided into the knowledge that he can get help from the extension officers in his area. At this stage, students are encouraged to read other simple pamphlets.

Reader III has 1,808 running words and a vocabulary of 315 different words, 128 of which are new. Here, Willie is seen considering the advice of the agricultural officer, reacting to the difficulties attached to following this advice and finally accepting it. He joins Sam's co-operative team, locally known as a "day-for-day" team and, with their help, improves his farm at comparatively little cost.

*Evaluating the Readers.* After the readers were drafted, agricultural experts were asked to check information on technical points. Persons with teaching experience were next asked for their comments.

The drafts were then amended where necessary and mimeographed copies of the readers, in book form, sent to classes, some with illustrations, some without. Teachers and students of classes were asked for comment in respect to: (*a*) the suitability of readers for enabling students to acquire the technical skill of reading and to comprehend what they read, (*b*) content, (*c*) style, (*d*) vocabulary, (*e*) usefulness, and (*f*) interest.

Visits were also made to classes by the writers and observations noted in respect to type and format. We learned that:

1. The type which we used was too small.
2. Illustrations were definitely needed.
3. Firm covers on the books were necessary.
4. There was some unnecessary detail which did not assist in creating atmosphere, developing character, or making reading easier.
5. Some of the repetition was too obvious or unnecessary.
6. In some instances, too many new words were introduced in too few running words.

After the first edition, observations were again asked for and noted, and any necessary revision made before printing the second edition.

The teachers' manual gives the broad philosophy of the Project. Teachers are told that the Literacy Project is regarded as a part of a wide fundamental-education program and that it aims at teaching adults to read with comprehension. These adults should be able to apply what they read to their daily lives and at the end of a course of reading be able to express themselves in writing so that others may understand what they have written. In other words, they should be functionally literate.

The teachers' manual also gives teachers hints on their attitudes and approach to illiterates, organization of classes, etc.

The teachers' guide for "Our Class" (preprimer) gives step-by-step directions for the use of this book and visual aids. In this guide, we suggest that the teacher try to help adult illiterates overcome their diffidence about learning to read by telling them that adults all over the world are doing the same thing. It is further suggested that teachers tell the illiterates that they and all these adults are unable to read because they were not given the opportunity to learn when they were young and that they are really people with initiative who wish to improve themselves.

## In Conclusion

This chapter has noted the procedures which might be followed in preparing material for community education. Briefly summarized, they are as follows:

1. The materials of instruction must fit into a general design of community education. An effort should be made to get intellectual and emotional re-enforcement to learning by relating these materials to the daily life of the individual learner and his family.

2. Those responsible for preparing materials of instruction should consider a total range of possible educational experiences, thus making use of the principle of variety as well as the principle of graded levels of abstraction. These experiences should be systematically related to the general educational design.

3. There should be a wise blending of locally useful materials and activities with those coming from a state or national source. The materials should be local enough to insure applicability and general enough to get the advantage of national campaigns or programs. Eventually some of the instructional materials might have international use.

4. There is a danger in having materials prepared by city-oriented authors who are physically and psychologically distant from the uses of the materials.

5. Widespread try-out in the field before final production is a safeguard against materials which do not fit local needs.

6. There must be a closer linking of the persons preparing and evaluating materials of instruction at state, national, and international levels. UNESCO fellowships have enabled specialists to visit production centers in Jamaica, the Philippines, India, Puerto Rico, the United States, Mexico, Egypt, and other countries. What is now needed is, first, a critical and detailed drawing together of the detailed and specialized experiences of these various centers; and, second, a closer, personal linking of the world-wide specialists.

# LEADERSHIP TRAINING

# CHAPTER XII

# UNESCO'S International Training Centers

## 1. Educational and Cultural Development

### WILLARD W. BEATTY

Concern for the educational and cultural development of the underdeveloped areas was expressed at the organizing sessions of UNESCO and has continued as a vital interest of the agency. Many of the men whose names have become synonymous with "mass education," "community education," "cultural missions," "mass literacy," or "each-one-teach-one" were present in person. The interests of others were presented in a report under the editorship of Henry W. Holmes, "Fundamental Education: Common Ground for All People," presented to the First Session of the UNESCO General Conference in 1946. As a result of this concern, the term "fundamental education" was adopted to designate the proposed UNESCO work for the educational and cultural development of all peoples; and in this and successive documents the term was defined to incorporate attention to the multiple physical, economic, social, and educational disadvantages under which half the world's population is suffering. James Yen, Torres Bodet, Lorenco Filho, and others who had attempted to work with adult literacy teaching as an isolated problem supplied the evidence that illiteracy seldom exists apart from other ills. In many instances the desire to alleviate illiteracy comes as a secondary result of successfully mitigating an endemic disease, improving the yield of agricultural acreage, improving the design of handicraft products, inoculating livestock against epidemics, or otherwise showing the people how to improve their physical lot.

As a result of these experiences, UNESCO proposed to carry out a program designed to help underdeveloped rural communities understand and solve the many problems that affect them in their daily lives. While the term adopted to describe this program was new, the activities included were often as old as the history of man himself. As indicated above, a variety of equivalent terms were already in use in various parts of the world to describe the activities that UNESCO included in "fundamental education."

In time, the UNESCO term "fundamental education" came into popular use throughout the world. Publications such as *Fundamental Education: Common Ground for All People* (1947) and *Fundamental Education: Description and Program* (1950), along with the founding by UNESCO of the quarterly, *Fundamental and Adult Education* (1948), helped to popularize the term.

Early seminars called by UNESCO to discuss its program revealed that there was a scarcity of trained personnel for fundamental-education work and for work in many related subject-matter fields. The UNESCO General Conference at its fourth session in Florence, Italy, in the spring of 1949, authorized the Director General to co-operate with member states as well as with the United Nations and its specialized agencies in the establishment of regional centers to train teachers and leaders to produce educational materials for rural-development activities and to carry out field research.

In response to this resolution the government of Mexico on October 3, 1949, requested that the first such regional center be established within its territory and offered to provide the land, buildings, furniture, local transportation, and domestic staff for such an international activity during the life of the center. This proposal was accepted by UNESCO, and an agreement was signed between UNESCO and the government of Mexico on September 11, 1950.

The Organization of American States (OAS) had expressed interest in collaborating in this venture and signed a co-operative agreement with UNESCO on July 7, 1950. The OAS pledged itself to contribute $100,000.00 per year for the activity, which was to be divided between the support of a Latin-American Training Center in Mexico ($40,000.00) and the establishment of a co-ordinate agency, the Latin-American Fundamental Education Press ($60,000.00), to be located at OAS headquarters in Washington, D.C., and to be devoted to the production of reading materials in Spanish for new literates. A co-ordinating committee composed of representatives of UNESCO and OAS, and a third member selected by both organizations, was established to review the proposed Center's program of studies and budget and to make recommendations to the headquarters of both UNESCO and OAS. It was stipulated that the Center should enjoy financial autonomy in the handling of the funds advanced by UNESCO, OAS, and the government of Mexico.

Believing that successful "fundamental educators" must be prepared to deal with all the concomitant problems of rural life as well as with literacy, the Center requested the co-operation of the Food and Agriculture Organization in sending experts in agriculture and animal husbandry, home economics, and the organization of co-operatives; of the World Health Organization in sending an expert in rural health; of the International Labor Organization in sending experts in handicraft improvement; and of the UN Bureau of Social Affairs in sending specialists in anthropology and community organization. During the greater part of the life of the new Latin-American Center for Fundamental Education (Centro Regional de Educación Fundamental para la America Latina—CREFAL), co-operation from these agencies has been continuous and essential.

With the election of Jaime Torres Bodet to be the Director General of UNESCO, fundamental education acquired the sponsorship of a man who, as minister of education in Mexico, had devoted a great deal of attention to the problem of literacy and had learned that successful literacy teaching could not be an isolated experience. He quickly directed the existing interest in fundamental education into a determined attack on the problem; and in 1950 and 1951, UNESCO launched a program for the development of a world-wide network of fundamental-education training centers, for which the agency had reason to believe outside funds might be supplied. This expectation was not fulfilled. However, a second international center, to be located in the Arab states, was authorized in 1951. The creation of the UN Expanded Program of Technical Assistance provided additional field operating funds to UNESCO, and the TA Board recognized fundamental education and UNESCO's support of the two centers as legitimate projects under the fund. Similarly, the other specialized agencies were permitted to spend TA funds in connection with UNESCO. UNESCO, therefore, proceeded with the establishment of a second center in Egypt under an operating agreement with the government of Egypt, similar to that with the government of Mexico. Similar co-operation from the UN Specialized Agencies was secured; and in 1952 the Arab States Fundamental Education Center (ASFEC) was established in the village of Sirs-el-Layyan, Menoufia, Egypt.

At that point it was clear that normal funds of UNESCO and its TA allotments would not be adequate to support further international centers. Furthermore, some doubt was raised as to whether it would be possible to operate other international centers successfully because of the great linguistic and cultural diversities of other areas, which appeared to present insuperable difficulties. The original program also had looked forward to the establishment of national training centers in fundamental education, as the international centers provided adequately trained leaders. Some such developments were appearing in Latin America as CREFAL trainees returned to their homes, and interest was being expressed in securing UNESCO help in the establishment of national centers elsewhere.

The first large-scale national program was launched by Thailand at Ubol in its rural uplands with assistance from UNESCO, the other Specialized Agencies, and the United States Technical Co-operation Program. A smaller scale national center was launched by Liberia at Klay, where a UNESCO pilot project had been started some years before. The result of the UNESCO pilot project in Haiti's Marbial Valley, together with Haitian CREFAL graduates, led to the initiation of a Haitian national fundamental education center. Iraq, India, and other states have taken steps of one kind or another to establish training centers for their nationals.

As the other Specialized Agencies have initiated such endeavors as the agricultural-extension programs and the community-development programs, a multiplicity of local training centers for village workers appeared. UNTA funds, UN Specialized Agency funds, USTCA funds, and the money of such private foundations as Ford and Rockefeller have supplemented national budgets for such training projects in increasing numbers.

A recent evaluation of the work of the international centers of CREFAL and ASFEC was conducted by *ad hoc* working groups of the administrative committee on co-ordination of the UN.

These working groups first pointed out that:

[Fundamental education was initially] regarded as a special contribution of UNESCO to the social and economic development of the underdeveloped areas. In this period the United Nations Expanded Program of Technical Assistance did not exist, and the various services now provided by the United Nations and Specialized Agencies had not yet developed extensive action programs among themselves and with their member states. There was, therefore, a tendency to regard fundamental education as a self-sufficient program of rural development using educational means, although requiring the support of technical services in various fields.

Since 1950, however, this situation has been rapidly changing with the development of different services by the United Nations and Specialized Agencies, notably in Social Welfare, Community Development, Rural Extension, Public Health, Rural Industries, etc.

This has called for a serious re-thinking of the philosophy and functions of fundamental education, especially in its relationship with other aspects of social and economic development.[1]

The evaluation of the Centers was undertaken in this frame of reference. The working groups found that the majority of CREFAL graduates became engaged in activities in their home states in line with the training received at CREFAL. However, a majority of these graduates came from the field of education and returned to administrative work in that field. Less use was made of ASFEC graduates in work for which they had been trained. The type of training for interdisciplinary "team work" offered by both centers has not proved entirely practical in the field.

The working group concluded "that the Centres may become interagency institutions of increasing value in the growing pattern of rural development in the two regions." Recommendations were made for modifications in student recruiting which might secure a more suitable enrolment and also for the introduction of training programs at different levels and for varying lengths of time to meet the need for specialized training of more advanced students in the different disciplines.

As will appear in the following accounts of the work of these centers, their programs are being adapted to the shifts of emphasis indicated above.

1. UNESCO Executive Board /44 Ex/7, Annex I, Paris, June 11, 1956.

## II. Training Educational Leaders for the Americas

LLOYD H. HUGHES

HISTORY OF CREFAL[2]

The Regional Fundamental Education Center for Latin America was formally inaugurated at Pátzcuaro, Michoacán, Mexico, in May, 1951. The Organization of American States, the government of Mexico, the International Labor Office, the Food and Agriculture Organization, and the World Health Organization joined with UNESCO in the support of the new institution because of a common need to develop supervisory staffs for educational and community-development programs in Latin-American countries.

Surrounded by a number of rural communities, which are representative of rural villages scattered throughout the highlands of Latin America, Pátzcuaro provided an opportunity to link observation and direct experience in villages with theoretical classroom instruction, and also to carry out experimental field studies which might lead to the discovery of new methods and materials for use in community education. The land and buildings generously donated by General Lázaro Cárdenas and the state of Michoacán were additional factors which helped to give Pátzcuaro an advantage over other sites considered.

CREFAL was directed to plan a training program for future leaders of Latin America in the philosophy, methods, and techniques of education and in methods of producing and using educational materials of various sorts. Also, emphasis was placed on the need for conducting experiments and research which would lead to the development of new methods and new materials for use in community education.

It was assumed that the students who came to the Center would already be, to some degree, specialists in education, health, agriculture, home economics, recreation, or some related field of experience. It was assumed also they would come in national teams of five, covering these fields. On graduation, it was expected the students would return to their home countries to work as national teams in educational activities.

2. The word CREFAL is derived from the initials of the Spanish name of the Center, Centro Regional de Educación Fundamental para la América Latina.

## ZONE OF INFLUENCE OF CREFAL

The work area of CREFAL consists of 21 villages and towns in the vicinity of Pátzcuaro. Colonia Ibarra, the closest, is less than two miles from Pátzcuaro; and Erongarícuaro, the farthest, is a little less than twenty miles away.

The total area of the zone is about 50 square miles, and the total population is 17,419. The villages range in population from 55 to 3,678. This tiny zone, which includes only a small portion of the area of the four municipalities closest to the Center, could easily be expanded to include many new villages. In the seven municipalities which lie within an approximate radius of 25 miles of Pátzcuaro there are approximately 150 villages, of which only 22 have been brought into the Center's zone of influence.

The inhabitants of this zone are divided roughly into two social and cultural groups: Spanish-speaking mestizos and Tarascan Indians. Language and dress are the two outward symbols of difference between these groups. An Indian who adopts Western dress and learns to speak Spanish soon ceases to be classed as an Indian and enters the mestizo or Mexican side of the population. There are three language groups in the villages of CREFAL's work area: (a) those who speak Spanish only, who represent a majority; (b) bilinguals who speak both Spanish and Tarascan; and (c) Tarascan monolinguals who form the smallest of the three groups. This situation has permitted CREFAL to use Spanish as its official language for work with the villagers and for literacy classes for children and adults.

The Center's zone of influence consists of three subareas: (a) lakeshore communities running from Tzintzuntzan to Erongarícuaro, (b) islands in the lake, and (c) a number of highland communities. It ranges in altitude from about 7,000 to 8,500 feet. The climate is cool and moist; temperatures range from about 30 degrees in the winter to a maximum of 90 degrees at the height of the dry season. Rainfall is heavy but is confined to the season from June through October.

While agriculture is the most important industry in nearly all of the villages, handicrafts are an important adjunct in many villages of CREFAL's zone of influence. Tzintzuntzan traditionally has been a village of potters, Tócuaro of wood-carving and masks, Erongarí-

cuaro of woolen and cotton textiles, Jarácuaro of hatters, Cucuchu-
cho of *petates* (woven rush mats), Ihuatzio of basket-making and
*petates*, and Janitzio of fishing nets and baskets. Handicrafts are produced primarily for the local market, but some products are also sold
to tourists. With the establishment of CREFAL, the old handicrafts
were strengthened and several new ones were introduced, but, important as handicrafts are, agriculture still forms the base of life.

PROBLEMS OF VILLAGES IN THE CREFAL ZONE

Most intravillage and intervillage conflicts stem from one or another aspect of the land problem. Lack of land and extreme fragmentation of holdings are problems in all the villages. After the Revolution, the land which had been concentrated in the hands of a
relatively few individuals was broken up into *ejidos*, and given to a
community of *ejidatarios* (members of an ejido). The members of
such a community have the right to use the land given them but not
to alienate it since ultimate ownership rests with the nation. There
are two types of *ejidos* in Mexico: individual and collective. In
CREFAL's zone almost all of the *ejidos* are individual, each member
having received a lot which he works for himself. Under a collective
*ejido* the land is worked co-operatively by all the members.

Many peasants failed to request *ejidos* of the government, feeling
that it was wrong to accept land which had been taken from its previous owners. Others, more aggressive or alert, denounced the ha-
ciendas and claimed the right to occupy them, and in the end received land from the government. As a result, they have land today,
whereas the more timid or more attached to the old way of life have
little or no land.

The result is the division of some of these villages into two mutually hostile groups: the *agraristas* who have land, influence, and control of local government, and the persons who possess what is called
*propiedad indigena* (communal Indian holdings). The dispute often
runs deep and sometimes flares into violence. It makes the job of
community education difficult, for if the field worker helps one
group he alienates the other.

The personal and social problems of the villages in CREFAL's
zone of influence are those of any underdeveloped area: poverty,
ignorance, poor health, and deficient social organization. The villages

are poor and lack many of the basic public services and utilities. Most have electric lights and all are connected to Pátzcuaro by telephone; these are services which CREFAL has helped to introduce in the communities. Only a few have public water supply systems, and none has drainage or sewage systems. Most lack markets, and none has sufficient schools to take care of all the children of school age. The average annual cash income of a villager does not exceed $150.00 per year.

Because of low income, any emergency such as sickness causes the *campesinos* to borrow from moneylenders at high rates of interest, pledging crops and future harvests as a security for such loans. As a result, many are heavily in debt and are unable to achieve a pay-as-you-go basis.

Poor health and sickness consume many working days that otherwise might be used productively. The principal diseases are of water origin, such as typhoid fever, amoebic dysentery, and gastro-enteritis. Typhus fever, malaria, and respiratory ailments such as bronchitis, pneumonia, tuberculosis, and asthma are also found in these communities. The villages are organized politically, and each has the normally established type of municipal government. However, most lack even the rudimentary type of social organization required to promote community self-help. CREFAL has tried to remedy this defect through the promotion of better types of community organization, and through the training of more effective local leaders. All of the villages have natural leaders: the teacher, the priest, the elders, a successful farmer, and the heads of important families. These people, however, require training in how to canalize the natural leadership they possess in such a way that community problems will be solved and a better life will prevail in the future.

### PROGRAM OF STUDY AND FIELD WORK

CREFAL's academic curriculum and program of field work is designed to train leaders and supervisors for fundamental education and community development activities in Latin America. As a consequence, its basic problems have been to define the attitudes, abilities, skills, and understandings that are required for success in these fields, and how best to structure an effective program for developing them. In our efforts to solve these problems, we have been guided by experience and the expressed desires of the participating governments and international agencies.

Since 1956 fundamental education has been viewed as the educational arm of a community-development program. Over-all development of the community is the goal. The fundamental educator, along with specialists in related fields such as health, agriculture, home and family life, or handicrafts, has a vitally important service to perform within this community-development process. He must possess certain special skills, plus an understanding of how all these specialized areas of competence fit together.

This kind of community educator, we are convinced, can be trained by means of a carefully balanced program of theory and practice. Academic courses are necessary, but they cannot do the whole job in an eminently practical field like fundamental education. Practice is essential, but it must be accompanied by orientation, guidance, and critical evaluation if the student is to learn effectively from his experience. These, therefore, are the principles upon which the training program is based.

CREFAL does not train multipurpose "front-line" workers but, rather, supervisory and organizational staff for education and community-development programs. The students must receive sufficient specialized training in various fields to be able to co-operate fully and competently with workers of other services of community development. The CREFAL training, therefore, aims to maintain a proper balance between specialization and generalization. It also seeks to maintain an integrated approach within each discipline and to demonstrate the relation of each discipline to the others.

The "regular" training program of CREFAL consists of an eighteen-month course for supervisors of community education. This course is divided into three periods or stages: the first, a period of orientation and theoretical-practical training which runs from April 1 to approximately December 20; the second, a period of supervised work in the communities of the Center's zone of influence, extending from mid-January to the end of July; and the third, a period of review and critical evaluation of the work previously carried out, continuing from August 1 to the end of September.

During the first period, the students attend daily classes which are designed to give them the theoretical and practical knowledge and skills required for field work in rural communities. Some of the classes are required of all students; others are open to free election in accordance with individual interest. This first period has been divided into two subperiods, one of six months and the other of two and a half months' duration. The first of these subperiods is devoted exclusively to general subjects required of all students, while the second is devoted mainly to elective subjects on a somewhat higher level.

The courses pursued during the first of these subperiods (from April to October) include:

1. *Fundamental education,* a study of the philosophy, principles, and objectives of fundamental education, their roots in social sciences, and the relation of fundamental education to community development.
2. *Problems of community development,* a survey of basic community problems in each of five subject-matter fields (health, home and family life, rural economy, recreation, and basic knowledge).
3. *Methods and media of communication,* a course which deals with modern educational methods usable in rural areas, the role of the fundamental educator in the community.
4. *Introduction to audio-visual production methods,* a course in which the students in small groups are introduced to production techniques in filmstrips, publications, graphic arts, and theater.
5. *Principles of economics,* a study of practical rural economics as related to fundamental education and community development.
6. *Library science,* a study of the organization, functioning, and services of small rural libraries.

During the second subperiod which extends from October 1 to Christmas, two required courses are given: (*a*) the problems and methods of literacy teaching, and (*b*) the methods of social research. The class in the methods of literacy teaching deals with the relationship of literacy teaching to community education and the content, methods, and materials of literacy programs. The class in the methods of social research stresses the relationship of social research to fundamental education and the methods of organizing and conducting studies and experiments.

The remainder of the time of the second subperiod is devoted to elective subjects. The electives scheduled during the morning hours deal particularly with subject-matter fields related to community education.

During the second period of the CREFAL training program, the students, organized in teams of three to five, go out to live in the communities of the CREFAL zone of influence from Monday through Thursday each week, returning to the center on Friday for an interchange of experiences.

The principal objectives of this period of field work are to give the students a chance to experience the life and work of a fundamental educator or community-development worker in a rural community, and, under guidance and orientation by the staff of the Center, to test and apply the theory and practice learned during the first period. This "front-line" experience is essential to prepare CREFAL students to train and supervise "front-line" community workers in their home countries.

During the first five years of the Center's life, student field work took the form of daily visits to the communities. This system, however, proved inadequate in several ways. In general, the students were not able to establish a close working relationship with the villages, and they did not derive the desired benefits from this artificial type of community work.

With the fifth generation of students who graduated in October, 1956, the system of establishing residence in the communities was tested. After five months of "commuting" the students spent one month living in the communities. The success of the experiment exceeded expectations. The students were virtually unanimous in declaring that their month of residence had been one of the most valuable parts of their experience at CREFAL. The villagers were equally enthusiastic, indicating that for the first time they had become well acquainted with the CREFAL students.

Encouraged by the results of this trial run, CREFAL adopted the residence system for the entire period of field work of the sixth generation. Under the new system, the students devote themselves to one community instead of two as under the former scheme. They live in the community, either with the family of a villager or in a separate house donated by the community for the use of the team.

Thus, each graduate has had direct, practical experience in community education in a rural community. If he returns to a supervisory or training position in his home country, he will be able to exercise his duties with a genuine understanding of the problems faced by the field workers.

The third period of the CREFAL course comprises two months of evaluation and criticism. The philosophy, principles, methods, and objectives of community education are reconsidered and related to field work and to the needs of the various Latin-American countries. This is done through review classes and seminars specially organized for the purpose, in which the staff and students, working together democratically, critically evaluate the work of the two previous periods of classroom instruction and field work and consider the plans, objectives, and needs of institutions of fundamental education in Latin America.

During this period the students are given free time to finish their graduation theses and to prepare for final examinations. In addition to completing satisfactorily all of the requirements already indicated, each student must present a graduation thesis written on a topic of his own choice.

The final examination is oral and consists of a defense of the graduation thesis before a specially convened committee of the faculty. Those students who satisfactorily complete all the requirements for graduation receive the degree of Specialist in Fundamental Education.

### SHORT COURSES FOR HIGHLY QUALIFIED PERSONNEL

As a new service to fundamental education and community development in Latin America, CREFAL inaugurated in June, 1957, a varied program of brief, intensive courses. These courses, of approximately three months' duration, are designed for highly trained personnel occupying responsible positions in ministries of education, health, and agriculture.

The first course began in June, 1957, and dealt with the production and use of audio-visual materials for community education. Persons experienced in photography, film-production, poster-making, publications, and the like, from various Latin-American countries worked directly with the production staff of the Center in producing and testing materials. They also received instruction which relates their production skills to the special requirements of audiences. Because of strict limitations of laboratory space and staff, enrolment in this first course was limited to twenty-five students.

## RESULTS IN THE COMMUNITIES

CREFAL's primary function, it should be noted, is to train fundamental-education organizers for all of Latin America. The field-work period is a training period; its success must ultimately be measured, not in terms of visible progress in the zone but, rather, in the future work of the students. The Center, however, has been careful not to think of the communities as laboratories and their inhabitants as guinea pigs. Within the framework of a training program, there has been an attempt to create in these communities those social and economic conditions which made genuine self-development possible.

Results in community education are necessarily slow to appear and difficult to evaluate. In reviewing the work done in the zone of influence, however, it is possible to find tangible and intangible benefits which have accrued to the people of the area. Some of these will be discussed briefly in the following paragraphs, grouped under headings which represent the primary areas of emphasis in the program.

*Improving the Economy of the Zone.* A program of supervised agricultural credit, initiated in January, 1956, has created an important new source of income for many families in the zone. Using funds loaned by a Mexican bank, FAO members of the CREFAL staff and specially trained students helped thirty families in sixteen communities to establish small poultry farms during the program's first year of operation. Each family received 125 chicks, material for building good poultry-houses and equipment, and money for purchasing carefully prepared feed, medicines, and the like. The eggs produced were collected and sold through CREFAL, and every step of the process was carefully supervised. By the end of the first year, the experiment had proved itself; the families were paying back their loans faster than anticipated and realizing monthly profits in excess of their normal earnings. In January, 1957, therefore, the bank offered a much larger sum to extend the project. Presently, 68 families of the zone of influence are participating with outstanding success, receiving profits which, in most cases, more than double their normal income.

Experiments in the establishment of village industries based on artisan activities are also proving successful. A co-operative carpentry and weaving shop established in one of our communities is now functioning smoothly and profitably under the direction of the villagers themselves; several other villages are now in process of forming similar production co-operatives modeled after this initial success. An experimental ceramics workshop has given rise, as a by-product, to a highly successful brick-making industry. Activities in these workshops have also created a demand for adult literacy classes. Carpenters, weavers, and potters, as they expand production and begin to increase their sales, must learn to read, write, and calculate. Another by-product of these workshops has, therefore, been a great increase of enrolment in adult literacy classes. Consumer co-operatives are yielding important benefits in several communities of the zone.

*Improving Health and Sanitation.* The many serious health problems existing in the zone have been attacked through the formation of health groups in each village, composed chiefly of young women who have received training in first-aid, education in the importance of hygiene and sanitation, and a knowledge of preventive measures in regard to communicable diseases. Health centers now exist in nearly all the villages, in charge of young women who have received a more intensive practical nursing course. Inoculation campaigns have been successful in most of the communities, and a regular weekly medical consultation service has been set up in all the villages. This year, with the help of the Coordinated Services of Health and Welfare of the state of Michoacan, financial aid on a matching basis is being made available to the communities for protection of public water supplies, construction of public baths and laundries, and home sanitation improvements including latrines, cement floors, etc.

*Toward a Better Home Life.* In any fundamental-education program, the most basic problems are encountered and perhaps the most important results achieved in the homes of the people. The CREFAL program in home economy seeks, through home visits and group meetings of community women, to help the people of the zone become better clothed, better fed, and better housed. As a by-product, we are beginning to see an accelerated evolution away from the position of servility which women have occupied among these people since time immemorial.

Informal classes in clothes-making are well attended in all the communities of the zone, and the sewing machines donated to the CREFAL program by CARE and other organizations are in use many hours each day. The sewing groups, many times the first out-side-the-home activity for married women, have led to demands for health and nutrition classes, literacy teaching, and recreational activities.

*Recreation in the Zone of Influence.* Misuse of leisure time for sheer lack of "something to do" is a root cause of many rural problems—alcoholism and crimes of violence among them. The CREFAL recreation program has sought to fill an almost total vacuum among the people of the region. Athletic activities, like the regional basketball and volleyball tournaments, which are held every year, are just one phase of the program. Regional folk songs and dances, which have been gradually dying out like handicraft designs, have been rediscovered and interchanged among the villages. The children of the communities are learning singing games and dances from all parts of Latin America. Puppet theaters are being organized in several communities as a result of a "portable theater" experiment conducted by students of the fifth class.

*Adult Literacy.* Adult literacy work has been greatly expanded and systematized during the past year. The students have received a new and strengthened course in literacy with particular emphasis upon teaching methods and the organizing and financing of literacy programs.

To date, the most successful literacy classes have resulted from specific needs; participants in the producers and consumers co-operatives already mentioned have been among the most eager and rapid learners because they could see the immediate usefulness of reading, writing, and arithmetic.

To encourage reading and to provide reading materials for those who have already learned to read, small community libraries have been set up in four villages, and books, periodicals, and newspapers are distributed regularly to readers in all the villages.

*Civic and Cultural Improvement.* In a variety of other ways, tangible and intangible, the communities are acquiring the skills and knowledge necessary to solve their own problems. A special two-weeks' course for carefully selected local leaders was given at the Center two years ago, and a second similar course is planned for 1958. Schoolteachers from all villages in the zone are working together with CREFAL students and staff to enrich their school program and to extend it into the community. Social centers have been established in nearly all the villages, sometimes in the school and sometimes in separate buildings supplied and prepared by the communities themselves.

Most subtle and perhaps most important of all are the changes in human relationships which are slowly becoming discernible. In the early days, the students were received with suspicion at best and a shower of stones at worst. Now, and especially since they have begun living in the communities, they are welcomed, respected, and liked. Intracommunity feuds, many of them bitter and of many years' standing, at first made community-wide activities impossible. Now, as the people begin to see how much they can accomplish by pulling together, the factions are losing their identity and meeting together for common ends.

Needless to say, all community programs have not been an unqualified success. Problems still exist, to such an extent that the casual observer notes little difference between the laboratory villages and those outside the zone. Some communities have been far more ready to accept change than others. Continuity has been difficult to achieve because of the rapid turnover of field workers; in some cases an unfortunate personality clash between a student team and a village has undone the work of several previous classes. Nevertheless, it can be said confidently that, in general, the trend in the villages is upward. They are benefiting from CREFAL's presence, and at an accelerating rate of speed.

## CREFAL GRADUATES

While there is evidence that the program of training and field work is moving along satisfactorily and that substantial though not spectacular progress is being achieved, the real test of the value of the work being done rests with the graduates. In a real sense, the "zone of influence" of CREFAL is the nineteen nations of the American continent where 284 graduates of five classes are working in commnuity education and various other activities. Only as these graduates make their influence felt throughout this enormous area, extending from the Rio Grande to Patagonia and Tierra del Fuego, can the work of CREFAL be truly evaluated and justified.

Projected against the vast backdrop of needs for community-education workers in Latin America, this number casts a small shadow; yet the facts seem to show that in the four and a half years since the first class graduated—an extremely short time in terms of progress in fundamental education—CREFAL graduates are exerting an influence out of proportion to their numbers. Several are engaged in international service in community education at CREFAL, the Rio Coco Development Project in Nicaragua, the Andean Highlands Project in Peru and Bolivia, and at the Inter-American Normal School at Rubio, Venezuela. Others occupy policy-forming positions in various ministries in posts related to community education. Many more form the basic staffs of local or national fundamental-education training centers and development projects. A considerable number are directors of normal schools or rural school districts. Some are professors in rural normal schools or supervisors of rural schools and, as such, have a direct impact on the work of rural schoolteachers who usually constitute the front-line troops for the attack on ignorance, superstition, and poverty. CREFAL graduates form the basic staff of national fundamental-education training centers of Colombia, Peru, and Venezuela, in addition to a number of pilot or demonstration projects in eleven other countries.

CREFAL is more than satisfied with the placement that has been given to its graduates by the participating countries. Most are engaged in community education or development work, many in posts of strategic importance. Through their work, the graduates are beginning to influence general educational policies in Latin America and also to demonstrate the value of community education as a means for helping to solve the problems of underdeveloped rural and urban communities.

A span of six years does not permit a thorough appraisal of the work of an educational institution. Certainly six years have not been enough to permit a scientific evaluation of the work of CREFAL. However, the staff of CREFAL is constantly engaged in informal appraisals of results, for they need to know why the different approaches they tried were successful or unsuccessful. Organized appraisals, carried out by the United Nations in 1956 and by the Inter-Agency Committee in 1957, have been even more valuable.

These internal and external appraisals all indicate that the Center has progressed and that it is meeting the needs of its patrons in a satisfactory manner. As conditions in Latin America change, so must the program of CREFAL. The program presented here is, therefore, subject to modification and adjustment. CREFAL today is in a period of transition from the original institution envisioned by UNESCO in 1949–50, to a new one which will better serve the needs of the six international agencies and twenty-one countries which are participating in the experiment.

## III. The Arab States Fundamental-Education Center

### A. HURBLI

#### THE EDUCATION OF THE MASSES

Faith in education is one of the main features of Arabic culture. Teaching as well as learning was regarded as a form of worship and was even considered more meritorious. The Arabs believed strongly in the effect of education on the prosperity of their nation. The value set upon education in early Islam is indicated by many Quoramic texts and prophetic sayings: "God will raise those of you who believe and those to whom knowledge is given to superior degrees of honor"; and the prophet Mohammed said: "It is the duty of every Moslem, man and woman, to seek learning from the cradle to the grave." Even before Mohammed, Jesus, who was another prophet to the Arabs, was often quoted as saying, "He who knows, acts, and teaches is called great in the Kindom of Heaven."

Under foreign domination, this faith faded in the Arab world. But it is now reappearing with the awakening of Arab nationalism. With this resurge of educational consciousness, it has been found that the school cannot alone cope with the educational needs of a rapidly changing Arab people. After years of stagnation resulting in an adult population which is illiterate and overwhelmed with ignorance, poverty, and disease, the Arab world cannot catch up and keep pace with the advancing civilized world if its educational program is limited to a school system which caters to children only. On the other hand, the majority of the people of the Arab states live in the rural areas which are the main source of wealth, areas which can be profitably exploited only by an educated population.

Fundamental education can help emancipate these people from ignorance by teaching them to read and write, giving them access to wider knowledge, making them better citizens, and helping them to understand the problems of their environment. It can develop their own culture and help them make creative use of their time. It can also provide support to other technical services by helping specialists in these services prepare the community for the acceptance of new ideas in such fields as agricultural techniques, conservation of natural resources, better sanitation and hygiene, improved housing conditions, and the development of rural crafts and small industries.

The growing interest in the Arab world for the education of the masses of the people and the concern for the development of rural areas has given rise to keen interest in better and more systematic literacy programs and to the establishment of "social centers," "community schools," and agricultural, health, and handicraft centers, thereby creating the need for trained personnel who can work successfully with adults—educators who can organize literacy programs with improved methods of teaching, who can communicate new ideas using educational materials suitable for an adult level of maturity and adapted to the cultures and needs of the people.

The Arab States Fundamental Education Center was established by UNESCO in Egypt to prepare those "adult educators" in the Arab world and to promote greater interest in adult education. It represents the first co-operative effort in which so many Arab states have actively participated.

The Center was established in 1952, by agreement between the Egyptian government and UNESCO at Sirs-el-Layyan, which is located in the middle of the Menouf district, about forty miles north of Cairo. The population, comprising 300,000, has a density of 2,121 people per square mile in an area of approximately 140 square miles. Situated between two branches of the Nile, the Damietta to the east and the Rosetta to the west, it is one of Egypt's more fertile regions. Within this district there are social centers, rural schools, agricultural and health units, and consolidated units.[3] Sirs-el-Layyan, with a population of 30,000, is about two and a half miles from the town of Menouf, the administrative center of the Menouf district. In 1946 it was selected as the site of a community-development project by the Egyptian government. The plan was to develop Sirs-el-Layyan

3. Institutions grouping various public services (education, health, agriculture, social affairs) in one center.

as a model experimental area in which a combined attack on ignorance, poverty, and disease was to be conducted by the ministries
of education, social affairs, health and agriculture, with the ministry
of trade and industries co-operating in the development of local
industries.

Under the agreement referred to above, the Egyptian government
provides land, premises, service staff, transport, and all other facilities.
UNESCO provides the funds required for the execution of the
program of the Center, while the United Nations, the International
Labor Office, the World Health Organization, and the Food and
Agriculture Organization provide the technical experts in the specialized subjects related to fundamental education. These subjects
include community development, rural handicrafts, health education,
agricultural co-operation, home economics, agricultural extension,
rural housing, and village planning.

The Center was housed originally in buildings which had previously been used as a rural normal school. Two years later, in
September, 1954, a new two-story dormitory building was erected
for the students and bachelor staff. It also accommodated the res-
taurant and the club. In 1957 another apartment building was erected
for the married staff, and a villa for the director. With these buildings, the Center found adequate space for the implementation of
its program.

The functions of this Center are as follows:

1. To provide regular courses in fundamental education for people who
   are mainly selected from the ministry of education in the participating
   states, namely, Egypt, Iraq, Jordan, Lebanon, Libya, Palestine, Saudi-
   Arabia, Syria, Sudan, and Yemen.
2. To provide short specialized courses in different aspects of education
   for social and economic development for the benefit of persons from
   various government departments of participating states.
3. To carry out experimental studies of educational methods and communication techniques in relation to development programs.
4. To prepare model fundamental education materials adapted to the
   needs, resources, and cultural levels of local communities in the Arab
   states and to give training in the techniques of preparing and using
   such materials.

Both experimental studies and the production of educational materials are integral parts of the programs of both the regular and
the short courses.

## THE REGULAR COURSES

The Center provides a regular eighteen-month course for students with intermediate and secondary qualifications and a twelve-month course for graduates with higher qualifications. These two courses are organized alternately.

The original aim of these courses was to train "leaders," i.e., more senior staff to train and supervise "field workers" in national services. This policy has now been modified because in many Arab states there are no organizations or training programs which could absorb such staff. Consequently, the Center now aims to produce graduates who, on return to their own countries, will be able to organize field projects, train workers for educational action in the communities, work in the field, and co-operate with representatives of technical services such as health and agriculture in concerted programs of community development. For the development of leadership, promising trainees are selected to take more responsibilities in the program.

The program of these regular courses is designed to provide an opportunity for students to develop as individuals, as well as professional workers. Moreover, the program is not limited to the acquisition of scientific and technical knowledge but also includes the cultivation of certain qualities necessary for a rural worker, such as perseverance in village work including the acceptance of manual work and respect for work with the villagers; ability to plan, record, and evaluate; initiative and leadership; participation in group action; originality and creativeness. These qualities are taken into consideration in the final evaluation of the work of the student.

The following are the various elements of the program which are carried out simultaneously, leaving place for areas of concentration such as field work:

*The general background studies* provide the trainees with the fundamental principles for the understanding of rural communities, i.e., the study of rural society, the psychology of rural groups, rural education, simple methods of social and statistical research techniques, and village planning.

*The major specialized studies* require students to select one of the following subjects for intensive study at a high level: agriculture, home economics, rural crafts, literacy, rural housing, rural recreation, co-operatives, social services, and audio-visual aids.

*Minor specialized studies* (for all students) rotate the students in groups for the study of the various fields of community development (health, agriculture, and co-operatives) so as to acquire an all-round familiarity and basic training in these fields. These studies are designed to enable the student to understand the relation of fundamental education to other aspects of community development and to work with the technical services, whether local or national, operating sometimes as educational agents to interest or promote, for example, agricultural or health services.

Early in the program the students are divided into small groups of three to five, each group being assigned to one selected village in the vicinity for part-time field experience. Team members are from different Arab states and are engaged in various facets of community development. They work on "core" projects which require the participation of all members of the team. New students are observers at first and then later share responsibility with the older students.

A period of full-time field work is provided near the end of the course, with a view to giving a complete picture of the role of the fundamental-education specialist in the village. These students live in the practice villages for four days a week for a month. In field work, problems of a fundamental nature in the villages (i.e., irrigation, roads, white-washing houses, sanitation, poultry and rabbit raising, literacy classes, etc.) are dealt with by the students.

Originally it was envisaged that graduates should work in teams in their home countries. This proved impracticable since some Arab states do not have the organization nor the finances to provide for teams such as these. Although the concept of team work in various countries has had to be adapted to reality, it has not been abandoned altogether, a provision being made for the student to work on an individual project for which he would be primarily responsible.

Recognizing the importance of the role of audio-visual aids in the communication of ideas to people, a foundation course is given to all the trainees which provides them with the general skills needed for the use and production of such educational materials and for connecting such production with field work. Students produce the media required for the implementation of their projects in the practice villages. Emphasis is laid on low-cost production, utilizing local resources. The Center also produces some prototype educational material on a professional level, which can be modified and adjusted to the needs of the participating states.

The Center trains the students in simple research techniques by carrying out basic (social and economic) surveys in the communities of the practice villages. These surveys provide data for planning and for the development of training and production. They enable the trainees to decide what should be taught in the villages and written in books, and how educational materials should be illustrated. They also help students to understand the villagers and their needs and to find efficient methods of conveying ideas to the people.

The staff responsible for the experimental and technical studies works closely with those in production and training, thus leading the way for education to be adapted to the actual situations of the villages.

A major function of this section is the literacy program. This has freed itself from the old conceptions of being exclusively for the purpose of teaching how to read and write: It has now developed into a program of general education which aims at educating the villagers as individuals and as citizens, endeavoring to change their attitudes, concepts, and superstitions whenever necessary. The program is given greater impetus by being closely related to community-development projects, in such fields as health and agriculture, carried out in the practice area. It includes general and special courses for the students, production of a series of "readers" using the global method, exercise books, follow-up materials, a series of "teach yourself" books meant especially for those (particularly women) who cannot attend classes. The Center also runs a newspaper, "Al-Saquieh," which deals with the everyday problems of rural people in the practice villages. All these publications are prototypes which can be easily adapted for use in other Arab states.

The operation of classes in the practice villages is an important part of the literacy program. They are also used for research purposes in order to test educational methods and materials and for training the students to plan and implement literacy teaching.

A course is provided for the setting up of libraries and the organization of reading rooms in the practice villages. A fundamental-education bulletin and an abstract are published in Arabic. Pertinent educational materials are collected and distributed, in particular, to Arab states. This section also prepares manuals on such topics as how to make use of the library, and it provides extension services in the practice area, relating them to the field-work program.

Courses of three months' duration are planned for about twenty supervisors and organizers of rural-development projects and technically qualified staff from various ministries who cannot be released by their governments for a longer period. These are: first, a course in the production of visual materials for community education aimed at helping Arab states train specialists in the production of simple printed materials and visual aids needed in field work to spread new techniques and convey new ideas to literate and newly literate people; second, a course on adult literacy teaching to train technically qualified persons to supervise and organize literacy teaching programs in their respective countries; third, a course dealing with the role of women in community-development projects, finding ways to obtain the participation of women in such projects and furthering knowledge and skills for working with them.

Initially, it was planned to recruit students from the ministries of education, agriculture, social affairs, and health of the participating states. Students were sought who had completed the highest level of education in a specific discipline which could be reached in their home state, who had had some experience in rural areas, were willing to return to work in a rural environment, and preferably had some working knowledge of English or French in addition to Arabic. If employed by the state, it was expected that the student would be recommended to the Center, and, if married, his salary continued to support his family. Representatives of the Center visited the participating states annually to interview candidates, final selection resting with the director of the Center. References are cleared with representatives of UN organizations operating in the home area.

In practice, the great majority of students have been recruited by the ministries of education, the other ministries being reluctant to spare their students for the length of the training period. The short courses are planned to meet the needs of representatives of ministries other than education.

The great diversity of educational progress in the participating Arab states has resulted in a hetrogeneous body of trainees, ranging from university graduates with technical training to persons with secondary-school education or less. This has created a serious problem in determining a useful level of training, either concurrently or consecutively.

Despite the enforced seclusion of rural women in many of the Arab states, one quarter of the ASFEC students during its first five years have been women, representing seven of the ten participating states.

The placement of graduates varies widely. While the majority have been placed in their respective countries in posts directly or indirectly concerned with community education, others have returned to ordinary schoolteaching. Among the former there are also several who are not concerned with actual field projects for the development of fundamental education. However, the growing awareness in the Arab states of the need to develop rural areas will undoubtedly provide more opportunities in the near future for those graduates to make full use of their education. It is also hoped that the Center's graduates will be able to stimulate the development of rural services.

Stricter recruitment procedures and a probationary period are intended to eliminate candidates who are not basically suited for rural work.

The Center has two advisory bodies: an Arab states advisory committee composed of representatives of the participating states, and an interagency advisory committee composed of representatives from the United Nations and Specialized Agencies participating in the program of the Center. Both committees meet once a year to advise the director of the Center on matters connected with the development of the program with a view to the fuller accomplishment of its objectives in relation to the needs of the participating countries and also other internationally assisted programs in those countries.

EVALUATION OF THE PROGRAM

The Arab States Fundamental Education Center is now five years old. During this period its program has been undergoing constant evaluations and changes carried out by the staff, with a view to adapting it to the needs of the countries it serves. These evaluations were not concerned merely with the technical skills, knowledge, and experience required for work in rural areas. They also included the general development of the personality of each student, with emphasis on essential attributes required for fundamental education, such as initiative, self-confidence, and courage.

A more formal evaluation was undertaken in 1955 by the United Nations.

The changes arising from these evaluations have improved the program of the Center, bringing it nearer to the needs of the participating states and giving them more confidence in the Center.

# CHAPTER XIII

# Training in Community Education and Development at the University of London

T. R. BATTEN

## Basic Problems in Community Education

Community education involves reorienting the work of the many existing extension agencies and training their field workers to use new approaches and new methods.

Specialist departments, such as health and agriculture, employ their own extension workers to "'sell" their extension policies to the people. In community education, on the other hand, the extension worker is primarily concerned with *people*, and his main interest is to help them overcome the difficulties they face in their own communities. In a very real sense this is education for community development; and since the problems people face are often many-sided, so also they often need help of many kinds to solve them. Community education rarely has its own specialist workers, but it is mainly the result of close co-operation in the field between the workers of different specialist organizations.

It is easy to say that community education is concerned with people and their problems and that it implies close co-operation between extension agencies of different kinds. But it is much harder to ensure that these ideas are adopted and implemented in the field, especially if workers have been hitherto primarily interested in im-plementing the specialist policies of their own departments and have not, in fact, been used to co-operating with one another in a holistic approach to the people's problems. Until they are convinced that community education meets a real need and that their co-operation is essential in meeting it, they are unlikely to be wholehearted in their response to it. Moreover, senior departmental officers who accept the community-education approach nearly always find that

334

they have to look critically at their existing policies. This is usually neither an easy nor a particularly pleasant task, and they are likely to tackle it with more interest and confidence if they have become aware of the methods already developed in many countries as a result of experiment during the last few years.

## Organizing the Training Program at London

Training in community education at the University of London Institute of Education has been developed to provide a solution to these basic problems. It takes experienced officers from many countries and from any kind of extension work. It helps them think out the implications of the community-education approach in relation to their own work and that of their colleagues, study human relations, and make comparative studies of community-education approaches and methods. Throughout the course there is a particular emphasis on training methods and techniques, for it is through the skill that officers develop in this field that they will most effectively be able to contribute to the success of community-education programs on their return to their own countries.

Training in community education and development at the University of London was begun in 1949, when five of the expatriate colonial-service administrative and education officers who had come to England for in-service training under the Colonial Office Second Devonshire Scheme asked for an opportunity to study community development. Started in this way, the course soon attracted other entrants, and now, in any one year, only about a fifth of the twenty officers on the course enter under the Colonial Office scheme, and of these only one or two are expatriates. The remaining four-fifths are either directly sponsored by their governments or come with UNESCO, United Nations, or British Council fellowships. Altogether, during the last eight years, the course has been attended by about one hundred and fifty officers from over thirty countries, from both inside and outside the British Commonwealth.

These officers, women as well as men, have come at all levels of seniority and from administrative, education, agricultural, health, and co-operative departments as well as from agencies engaged specifically in community-education work, and, usually in any one year, from some twelve different countries. Thus, every course is representative of a very wide range of cultures, kinds of experience, and specialist interests. It is this variety of background and experience that distinguishes the course from training courses which are oriented to one kind of extension work or to the needs of one region.

## Objectives and Methods of the Training Program

Officers pursue both group and individual studies. They meet in a group primarily to study each other's principles and methods of organizing and doing their work. These meetings are of two kinds: the *seminar*, at which they present for discussion papers outlining the objectives, organization, and methods of their own agencies, together with a brief statement of the major difficulties they encounter in their work; and the *discussion meeting*, where they discuss whatever problems they find they have in common, but always in the context of an actual situation encountered by a member of the group. The purpose of the seminar is to provide the group as quickly as possible with comparative information on agency organization and method and, incidentally, to provide each member with information about the background of the other members of the group.

The purpose of the discussion meeting is twofold: first, to give officers practice in analyzing their own problems, which many of them find it hard to do; and, secondly, to bring out into the open their very wide differences in aim, attitudes toward people and ways of dealing with them, differences which are usually also a reflection of differences in aim and method between the national agencies the officers represent. Thus, although members all agree in theory, for example, that local initiative and responsibility should be encouraged, or that officers in related departments in the same area should work as a team, they may express quite different ideas when they are discussing how to deal with problems in specific contexts and thinking mainly of getting on with the job. Then, as officers disagree and challenge each other's assumptions and opinions, real learning begins. Although each officer's first reaction is usually defensive in support of his own (or his agency's) practice, the cumulative effect of the discussions is to stimulate each member to make a critical reassessment of his values, objectives, and methods. The discussions, in fact, initiate a slow process of value and attitude change, varying with each individual according to his initial background and experience, and they provide a strong incentive for officers to investigate the widest possible variety of methods and skills. In this sense, these discussion meetings constitute the core of the course.

Ample materials for the study of a wide range of territories and of practical and theoretical topics are accumulated in the Institute library and in the files of the Community Development Clearing House. Guidance on reading is given in a series of lectures introductory to each of the major fields of study, by means of a number of select, annotated reading lists, and in tutorials. Officers are encouraged to read widely during their first term and then to select for more detailed study the one or two fields in which they are particularly interested, or which are of particular importance to them in their work. On these they write their final report.

Officers also meet weekly to discuss problems and methods of communication. At these meetings they first pool what they have learned from their own experience and then go on to study and assess the various factors affecting people's attitude to new knowledge and ideas. In specific contexts they consider how agency objectives can be reconciled with the values and customs of the people, who are the targets of communication, and how best to present ideas and information and get them discussed and incorporated into people's thinking and behavior. In the course of these meetings the group studies in some detail a variety of the actual aids used by field workers in the tropics and discusses their suitability in relation to their purpose, the kinds of audiences with which they could be used, and the techniques of using them and promoting discussion about the message they present. Individual officers are encouraged to produce sample aids for themselves, and toward the end of the year the whole group produces a sound filmstrip as a group project.

The other major field in which officers work together is in the study of community development and adult education in the United Kingdom. The group visits many of the headquarters and some of the regional offices of the national voluntary organizations to study how they are organized, how they co-ordinate (or fail to co-ordinate) their work with that of other agencies, how far local groups control or are controlled by the headquarter's organization, how the headquarters' office serves the local groups, and more particularly how it organizes and implements its leadership-training programs. Visits are also made to some of the local groups of these organizations in order to fill out the picture and enable the officers to assess the quality of the work that is being done in the field. This broad, comparative study is continued throughout the year and culminates in a two-week visit to a rural county. Here the officers study the interrelationships between the statutory and voluntary agencies operating in the area, the needs they meet, and the ways they meet them. At the same time they study the group and community organization in one sizable village, and by intensive visiting of groups and individuals try to assess the extent and nature of the influence of the agencies at work in the county.

Officers are briefed before each visit, and each visit is subsequently discussed in relation to other visits and to the group's study of developmental work in their countries. Contrary to what many of the officers initially expect, they find this broad study of community work in the United Kingdom both stimulating and relevant to the main work of the course. They find, in fact, that agencies in the United Kingdom face the same basic problems as they themselves face in finding and training leaders, stimulating initiative, and achieving specific objectives. They find that every agency has its own individual approach to these problems and that every group visited provides them with some kind of an object lesson. These visits and the ensuing discussions also have a cumulative value in training officers in the techniques of interviewing and of obtaining and assessing information which later stands them in good stead, both on visits to other countries and back on the job in their own countries.

From what has been said so far, the reader will have noticed that officers do a good deal of the work of the course in discussion groups and relatively little in formal seminars and lectures. The staff members try to serve the group, not to direct it. They provide the organization, the outline of a timetable, and facilities and guides for individual study. The staff members sometimes act purely as consultants, but they usually play a more active part, helping members analyze and discuss their problems, clarifying viewpoints, and summarizing; but at no time do they decide what shall be discussed, and they avoid making declaratory statements of their own opinions, at least until after it has become obvious that the group's members have accepted responsibility for thinking things out for themselves and that they are no longer waiting for a "lead." What this means in effect is that nothing can effectively happen in the group meetings, except at the weekly lecture and seminar, until the members of the group can agree on the content and order of their discussions. For most of them this is an unexpected and most unwelcome responsibility for they have come expecting to be taught, only to find they are expected to organize themselves for learning. Often they feel frustrated, for it may be several weeks before they are able even to agree on what they will discuss. Yet, in the end, they do not feel that this time has been wasted. As they come to accept the fact that the staff will consistently refuse to control the discussions, they realize that they must come to terms with each other, and in the process they learn a good deal about the demands a working group can make upon its members. For many individuals this is the first experience they have ever had of personal involvement in a work group which has no directive leader, and as they grapple with the many problems that arise, and sometimes derive satisfaction from solving them, they no longer want, and will no longer accept, "direction." The staff can then play a more active role, helping, advising, and suggesting, but the group's decisions do insure that the group does work which seems relevant and meaningful to its members; and the way they do it teaches them more about working with groups than any teaching situation, however "efficient," in which all real control is vested in an institutional teacher. They learn to appreciate both the difficulties and the satisfactions inherent in the democratic group process. It is this, the practical experience that the group provides, that the staff believes constitutes one of the major values, if not *the* major value, of the course.

## Attacking the Problems of the Training Course

I have now summarized the objectives and organization of the course and have briefly described the kinds of methods used. It remains to discuss some of the problems we have to face and how we try to deal with them.

One annually recurrent problem has already been referred to. Most officers arrive eager to get off to a quick start, and they quickly realize the great *potential* value of the discussion meetings. But most of them are accustomed only to situations in which they are either led or leading, and they cannot quickly adjust themselves to this new, unstructured situation. They have to try to formulate a scheme of work, and they are initially unable to agree on either the content or method of discussion.

We expect this difficulty and are not unduly worried by it because we deliberately create it, but we do take a good deal of trouble to keep the resulting frustration within manageable bounds. The course starts with a two-day orientation period which is carefully designed to give officers as much insight as possible into the character of the course and the responsibilities they will have to accept, as well as to prepare them for some frustrating experiences during the first few weeks. Moreover, although important, the discussion meetings are not the whole of the course, and, however exasperating the first experience of the group discussions may be, the weekly lecture, seminar, and visitation programs conform more closely to expectations, and we take great trouble to ensure that reading and study materials are well organized and readily accessible. Lecture references are boxed for the convenience of officers; every item on each subject reading list is classified and annotated, and so is every item in the card indexes. We have learned by experience that most of the officers who come to us have had little time for reading while they have been working in the field and that they need far more practical help and guidance in their reading than the normal student.

But the fact remains that we judge success in the course mainly by what happens at the discussion sessions, and this is true of the officers as well as of ourselves. Here we face a basic problem in every year's work. We value our method in the group as the best means of stimulating officers to define and analyze their real problems (as distinct from the general, superficial "problems" they are able to state when they come); to help them develop greater sensitivity and skill in human relations through their experiences of working with others in the group. We believe that success in reaching these objectives depends on the officers assuming full responsibility for the content and conduct of the discussions. Thus, our first task is to divest ourselves of authority as institutional teachers, and when we have succeeded we are no longer in control. I have already mentioned that once a group has tasted real freedom, it will often reject advice and waste time (as we feel) on irrelevant or unimportant topics, or by adopting ineffective methods. When this happens, we are tempted to blame ourselves for "allowing" the group to waste several precious hours. Sometimes, some members of the group are inclined to blame us too.

The fact is that in these discussions we are in much the same situation and face the same kind of problems as any field worker who is trying to help, advise, and guide groups of people over whom he has no control. Incidentally, this is one reason why we have no examinations and no award of certificates or diplomas for the work done in the course. We can try to lead the officers, but we cannot force decisions on them. We work as nondirective leaders, and, in doing so, we have to use whatever methods and techniques seem most appropriate. In effect, we are continually giving practical, "on-the-job" demonstrations of these methods and techniques in our work with the group, and officers are left to make their own assessment of their value.

No group is quite the same as any other or presents exactly the same problems, for the problems vary with the size and composition of the group. We find that the optimum size is around twelve to fifteen, and the maximum number about twenty. In a large group we invariably suggest, not always with immediate success, a partial breakdown into discussion subgroups, but most of our problems arise from the composition of the group, rather than its size. Every group contains both senior and junior officers and is an admixture of different cultural as well as personal characteristics. Officers also vary considerably in their fluency in English. All these factors affect the willingness of members to participate freely in discussion and their ability to reach agreement with one another. Participation is sometimes very uneven, especially at the early meetings, and it is easy for two or three fluent or self-confident officers to monopolize discussion. We take no direct action in the group when this kind of situation arises even if we are approached, as we sometimes are, by members who feel annoyed, but we do suggest reading[1] and also that members might like to devote a little time to discussing how they can improve the functioning of the group. We find that, in time, these two measures are enough to help most members solve their difficulties and that the difficulties themselves are welcome. They provide members with both the stimulus to learn about group skills and the need to use them. Members of the groups which get through the year without serious difficulty, as one or two have done, miss valuable experience.

The problems so far discussed are part and parcel of the course, which would be the poorer without them. But there is another problem of a different kind. The staff functions primarily to service and advise, and it is left to the members of the course to make decisions which on most training courses would be made by the staff. This approach works well with the kind of intelligent, hard-working, and experienced officers for whom the course is designed, but it is not easy to get officers exclusively of this type. However carefully applications and testimonials are scrutinized, it is impossible to insure that every officer who comes will fulfil the promise of his application, will be really keen, and contribute usefully to group discussions. Thus, on every course there is a small minority of "problem members" who are a drag on the group, at any rate for the first few months, and a trial to the officers who are really competent; and there is no certificate or diploma examination to impose an obvious penalty on slackness. And yet, after all, this type of officer has a positive function, for in his way he contributes to the problems of the group and to the learning situations it provides. There are few groups in any country which do not have their problem members. Moreover, most of our problem members improve.

### Use of Group Methods in Training

The criterion of successful training is its efficiency in meeting needs, and the experienced officers who come to London for training are well able to form their own ideas about how their needs are being met. For this reason we always invite comments on the course,

1. E.g., for initial reading, L. P. Bradford and J. R. P. French, "The Dynamics of the Discussion Group," *Journal of Social Issues*, IV (Spring, 1948), and K. D. Benne and B. Muntyan, *Human Relations in Curriculum Change* (New York: Dryden Press, 1951).

and at the end of the first term each officer is asked to submit (anonymously) his assessment in terms of his own needs and interests, together with his suggestions for course improvements, and these are subsequently discussed by the group. These evaluations, together with those held at the end of each year, have been responsible for most of the modifications and improvements to the course over the last few years.

In this chapter relatively little has been said about the content of the work done in the course, partly because the discussion and seminar content, within wide limits, varies each year and partly because officers do a great deal of specialized study in relation to their individual interests and the interests of the agencies that send them. Thus, in any one year, literacy work, project work, group and community organization, co-operation, rural industries, agricultural or health extension, and problems of working with women or with youth may all be subjects chosen by individual officers for specialist study. But in all these studies as well as in the group discussions there is a major focus on groups, on methods of working with groups, and especially on the use of group methods in training. Every officer is a potential trainer of other workers, paid or voluntary, and it is in this field of training trainers that the course makes its major contribution to community education and development.

# CHAPTER XIV

# Personnel for Overseas Service

HARLAN CLEVELAND

## Training Is Efficiency

Perhaps it goes too far to say that training and selection for overseas service are the same thing, but they should certainly be parts of a single process. The present arrangement in all government agencies is to select people first and provide the training (to the extent Congress has provided funds for the purpose) after the expert is already on the payroll. To the extent that this practice reflects the judgment that a man's *expertise* is his most important attribute, it can be readily criticized. But writing in an academic groove, I must admit that government agencies have another, even more compelling, reason for present practice: The American educational system is not providing a pool of American experts who, in addition to their professional skill, have the understanding and attitudes necessary to survival in overseas service.

The hiring agency is, therefore, on its own. Personnel men who would not dream of hiring a lawyer who hadn't been to law school, or an engineer who had had no engineering training, or an economist who had never taken a course in economics, cheerfully engage and send out into an unsuspecting world men (and their wives) who have never been abroad or given any particular attention to matters outside the United States. They will have to learn on the job, if at all, such fundamental lessons as the relativity of American values, the worth of cultural differences, the uses of humility, the essentiality of patience.

It is enough to list these few desiderata to refute the canard, so often uttered and so often uncritically believed, that a "good man at home is a good man abroad." For these are not the qualities most in demand for survival and success in most kinds of domestic em-

344

first goes abroad to work and live, to show him in easy stages how relative are the American values with which he grew up. He needs, in short, to be exposed early and often to tests of what a social psychologist might call his "cultural empathy."

Cultural empathy is the skill to understand the logic and inner coherence of other ways of thinking and the restraint not to judge them as bad just because they are different from one's own. A certain involvement in alien ways—well short of "going native"—may become the most effective device for building a bridge between cultural differences, if one uses the most universal elements in each. "You teach baseball by learning soccer" said a Brazilian to a Maxwell School interviewer. Less succinctly but more analytically, Prime Minister Nehru put it this way: "I would say of Americans that they are very friendly— and this is very good. But the fact that they are very friendly does not mean that they are *receptive*. When an American comes to India on a technical job, he is a kind of teacher. The relation between teacher and pupil is a two-way street—or it must look that way to the student. A teacher's task is not simply to tell his pupils what is in his mind but to find out what is in their minds."

About a year ago, on the island of Formosa, the United States Army was tested and found wanting on the score of cultural empathy. A soldier had killed a Chinese prowler, was court-martialed and acquitted by the American court. Local Chinese opinion was outraged, and it was not difficult for those most incensed to collect a mob on the street in front of the American Embassy and provoke it into wrecking the Embassy and the U.S. Information Building next door. What was the issue? Under Chinese law, if it is established that a person has killed, he must be adjudged guilty of the killing; only then does the question arise whether he should be punished for his guilt, or whether there are extenuating circumstances that should persuade the court to withhold punishment. Our system is the reverse: if a man kills, and there are sufficient extenuating circumstances, we judge him not to have killed. This curious twist may seem logical to us because we are used to it, but it looked upside down to the Chinese and they said so with sticks, stones, and vandalism. A more astute prediction of Chinese reaction, plus a special campaign in co-operation with the Chinese Nationalist government to explain the differences in the law just might have staved off a very ugly situation.

Sometimes the effort to see how things look on the other side of the cultural fence is not as arduous as it might seem. A charming case in point is the cartoon of the two American children squatting on the floor of their American home munching on TV dinners while viewing a favorite television program. On the screen is a picture of a Japanese family, squatting on the floor of their Japanese home, eating *their* dinner. "Well, how about that," one of the American children exclaims, "in Japan they sit on the floor to eat!"

How does the educator develop the quality of cultural empathy, assuming the expert has enough native *sympathie* to be able to put himself, for purposes of self-analysis, in the other fellow's shoes? Area studies can help, and language instruction properly handled is certainly a mighty assist to an understanding of an alien way of thought. But beyond what can be done in a training course at home, there is a strong case to be made for some form of immersion in foreign culture, a baptism which can be quite brief if it is sufficiently intensive. This implies an experience overseas *as part of the educational process*, quite apart from any in-service training (generally very meager, indeed) the expert may be exposed to, once he gets on the job abroad.

Talk to almost any administrator of an American overseas operation, governmental or private, and you will find him pleading for personnel who already have their first stint of overseas work behind them. "Nearly all of our mistakes at this post are made by people on their first tour of duty outside the United States," said an Embassy official in one Asian capital. The problem for the American educational system is to move back into the educational process the kinds of psychological experiences and adjustments which would otherwise happen to a man (and, indeed, to his wife) on his first regular job in a foreign land. It is hard to see how this can be done short of taking the student (and, if possible, his wife as well) overseas, under supervision, for a working and living experience that will both test him and mature him in the development of "cultural empathy."

#### "TO WORK WITHOUT EMBARRASSMENT . . ."

The skill to understand cultural difference may legitimately be considered an element of an expert's expertness, if he presumes to take that expertness abroad. The know-how he imparts bears the seeds of destruction of at least some of the traditional values he will find among the people who have asked him to come.

John Hersey's eloquent little book, *A Single Pebble*, describes the journey up the Yangtze River of a young American engineer filled with zeal to build a dam for the people's benefit; amid adventures on the river-boat, he comes to realize that the people closest to the river are appalled at the thought that its mysterious and turbulent flow will be changed by the action of this stranger. A similar theme runs through a play recently staged in London, the "Making of Moo" by Nigel Dennis. Here a British engineer successfully builds a dam in a "backward" country, only to see all sorts of antisocial behavior break loose when his dam is completed—for he has killed the local river god by damming the river. Since there was no longer any authority to restrain the people's baser instincts, the engineer had to set about the creation of a new religion. Most of our experts are not called upon to perform a similar feat of social invention, but they must be aware of the significance of what they are helping to destroy as well as what they are seeking to build.

Even where the host nation is politically committed to change, the sensitive expert may perceive deep-rooted resistance to it. He finds that he needs to be able to predict, recognize, and deal with the problems that arise from change in cultural norms and patterns —a kind of social-science analysis that does not occupy much space in the curriculum of the professional schools from which our experts in engineering, medicine, agriculture, and even (let's face it) education are drawn. As a result, the expert may be diffident about his role as a subversive who is undermining ancient values; in extreme cases, this diffidence actually interferes with his doing what he came to do—like the religious worker who "goes native" to such an extent that he cannot bear to upset people by teaching them about Christianity. A perceptive comment about American experts was made by an Indonesian politician I interviewed last year. "The American liberal tradition seems to make Americans uncomfortable," he said. "American liberals seem to be, if anything, too much aware of the resentment their work might create, too anxious to take into account all the cultural factors involved. Americans should recognize that they are helping to create cultural change and should be more relaxed and matter of fact about it. Too often, an American with admirably liberal inclinations is so embarrassed at his own power as to be ineffective on the job. The problem for Americans is to avoid too much rationalizing about their own role and *to work without embarrassment* at the task of changing cultures."

It is often suggested that experts should not be encouraged to run around loose without the advice and counsel of a person gifted with sensitivity and trained in the analysis of culture differences and culture change—a cultural anthropologist, let us say. Even if there were enough people trained as anthropologists, which there are not, it is not clear that their advice would always be constructively applied. Where the purpose of the exercise is change—the development of industry, for example—an expert on the existing traditions may simply serve as staff conservative, restraining change in the name of ancient values. At its worst, this may seriously harm the "backward" peoples who are thus protected; one cannot but be impressed by the fact that after more than a century of "protecting" the American Indians on their reservations from the changes represented by American growth and prosperity, we have achieved a condition in which the average American Indian has a life expectancy at birth of 39 years, while most Americans can now look forward to living almost to the scriptural three score and ten.

### EXPERTNESS AND CULTURE CHANGE

We have, indeed, been misled by "experts" on culture change almost as much as we have been assisted by their popularization of exotic cultures as a field of study. It has long been assumed, for example, that there is a very low cultural speed limit on the process of industrialization, that the whole culture pattern of primitive rural societies operated to resist rapid economic development. As a result of this assumption, which still lingers on in some quarters, we failed to see (or predict the consequences of the fact) that Japan could industrialize herself in a single generation by copying Western methods without abandoning traditional Japanese predilections for hierarchical government and rigidly defined social relations. We continued to tell ourselves that the Russians were just peasants, who couldn't be expected to show the scientific inventiveness, the technological skill, or the organizing ability to overmatch the performance of our highly industrialized society—until a fabulous rate of economic growth, topped by the drama of the first two sputniks, indicated otherwise. And we continue to this day to underinvest shamefully in world economic development, keeping the whole process on such a bush-league scale that even the Russian newcomers can compete effectively; part of the reason for our restraint on promoting economic development is certainly the persistence of the myth that the cultural resistance to industrialization is very great. Contrary to earlier impressions, much evidence these days indicates that modern industry can grow side by side with many different kinds of social and cultural institutions, and that our Western, democratic, capitalist culture is not quite as closely related to the process of modern economic development as we once supposed.

In the United States, the label "expert" refers almost exclusively to a man's competence and experience in a professional field; an expert's job assignment is usually clearly defined. Experts overseas, however, must often rely on talents that play a minor role in stateside employment. If, at home, a management expert runs across a specialized problem in budgeting, a doctor finds an eye condition he doesn't know how to treat, or an engineer is baffled by an unexpected layer of gravel on a drilling job, he will be able readily to turn to a companion expert: "Hey, Joe, what do you think we ought to do about this?" But for the overseas expert, Joe is often not around to be consulted; the expert is on his own. His *expertise* must consist not only of a sound grounding in his own specialty but must include the imagination and adaptability of the general practitioner in a much wider field of professional activity. He must constantly adapt his skill to new and challenging situations—not just situations he has never encountered before, but situations that may never have arisen before.

This difference between domestic and overseas experts may be likened to the differences between people living in the jungle as compared to those pursuing a desert existence. Domestic employment is often jungle life: An individual is part of a large bureaucratic structure which offers him cover and the protection of numbers—plus the risk and anxiety of hidden enemies. But in overseas employment, like desert life, the worker is more exposed, more vulnerable. His isolation compels him to develop a taste for independent action. Think back seventy-five years in American history, when representatives of Eastern firms would travel to the "wilds" of the western part of the nation. These men had to rely on their own initiative and ingenuity, and frequently this experience equipped them to return to the East and take high-level management positions in their firms—for training in adaptability is first-rate training for top executives. So it is with the overseasman of today. He will normally get a more varied experience than his domestic counterpart, but he must often be prepared to stand alone while his contemporary at home leads the more sheltered life of the organization man, whose duties permit a deeper specialization but are by that token more circumscribed—and who can call on the organization to extricate him if he gets in too deep.

Moreover, the "desert" existence requires a keen sense of politics and administration. Nearly every American serving abroad is more of a political man than he would need to be at home. The engineer, the public health official, and the agricultural expert who might be disinterested in "public affairs" at home must be unusually sensitive to politics, local and international, while serving abroad. Whether in their role as representatives of the United States or simply as outsiders in an area that does not clearly distinguish the national origins of its foreign visitors, the American expert is faced with the problem of getting on well with local bureaucracies and individual government officials.

Each bureaucracy is indigenous to its own locale. Given the newly developing self-assertiveness in the "underdeveloped" lands that have recently gained their independence, officials of these hotly self-conscious nations place an extraordinarily high value upon political equality in dealing with outsiders. Americans who lose sight of "face" will themselves lose effectiveness. The expert must not only learn the power structure but also the procedures and approved method of communication wherever he may be. When an American deals with a government agency that regularly loses three letters of every five it receives, it is hard for him to believe that such inefficiency is not planned in an attempt to sabotage his work. He learns that the so-called American businesslike approach to government does not apply abroad—even to the limited degree it applies at home. He learns to act on this knowledge, or else suffers the frustration that always awaits the man who declines to understand his environment.

The expert as a "political man" is inevitably an "ambassador" too. In order to interpret his own society he does not need an encyclopedic knowledge of political process, but he must have a finger-tip familiarity with the United States, its foreign policy, its culture, and the nature of its government. At his outpost the expert is the spokesman for the agency he represents; he must be able to communicate to the local population the aims and purposes of his program and to relate its aims and purposes to theirs.

Finally, the Western expert will find that while he may bear the title of "adviser," he might more accurately be called an institution-builder. An engineer accustomed to building steel structures at home will find himself building organizational structures abroad. We say of a man that he "knows how" to build a bridge—in the United States. But this merely means that he knows how to serve as the engineering member of a task force which may include such nonengineering skills as labor relations, budgeting, legal expertness, public relations, and general administration. If the engineer is sent abroad as an expert, he will be assumed by his foreign counterparts to be competent to advise on the *whole* process of building a bridge—a social process which involves not only stresses and strains on structural steel but stresses and strains on people. In one sense he will not be building a bridge at all; he will be building an organization to build bridges. This kind of "institution-building" task seems to be of the essence of overseasmanship.

## The Transferability of Institutions

Woodrow Wilson once argued that in the United States, for the first time in the modern world, man's major social relations are with institutions, not with men. The thought, debatable perhaps at the time it was expressed, is getting more nearly true all the time. Certainly the American professional man or technician overseas is nearly always an adviser on organization and procedures and on personnel and financing—which is to say, on public administration—in addition to his role as substantive specialist in his own field. The physician becomes the organizer of a mass DDT spraying program for malaria control. The artillery man, assigned to a military advisory group, finds himself training the officers who will become some of a new nation's leading politicians and administrators. The educator abandons his departmental field to energize the building of schools and the training of teachers. The agronomist forsakes his seedbed and chemical lab to advise on building an agricultural extension service. They are all, in the last analysis, in the business of "public administration" —using that much-defined term in its broadest sense. For the task of building institutions is partly a matter of helping create the elements of a well-ordered organization, which gets the "expert" into such mysteries as employment practices, budget procedures, record and accounting systems, and regular channels of communication. But the expert will often find himself going beyond administrative tools and practices to the intangibles of organizational cohesion and morale. For if the American's institution-building function is to be fulfilled, the "nationals" must ultimately cultivate some sense of identification with the new institution and take over its leadership; they must "make it theirs."

The measure of success in any technical-assistance program is this: If tomorrow you suddenly remove the foreign technical expert from the scene, what is left behind? An institutional legacy? Or just a memory?

Our confidence in our own Western institutions, plus the extravagant if uninformed admiration of Western progress on the part of the underdeveloped countries, tempts the Western technician to export to the benighted peoples outside of Europe and North America the institutions we believe to be essential to such progress. But what Paul Hoffman once said of technical assistance—that it "cannot be exported, it can only be imported"—is emphatically true of social institutions. The world is full enough of gruesome examples. In Japan, the postwar democratic constitution, which was drafted first in English and imposed by General Douglas MacArthur when he was Supreme Commander, still has not lived down its nickname, "The Translation." With good reason did an ICA office in Bagdad popularize a slogan to remind its employees of the limited transferability of institutions: "Adapt, not adopt."

It seems, therefore, that one of the key elements in successful operations by a Western expert is that he should have frankly confronted this question regarding his own specialty: "What parts of my *expertise* are transferable to underdeveloped countries, and what are merely the product of the American environment; in my specialty, what is essential and what is merely cultural?"

During a recent discussion of international technical assistance in the field of public administration, a British expert, working for the United Nations, expressed the question this way: "I always worry when I see an American personnel classification expert going out as a technical adviser," he said. "After all, the British civil service has been going on in one form or another for close to a thousand years, and it hasn't yet got around to having personnel classification experts!"

IMPLICATIONS FOR TRAINING

If the Western expert needs to be *simpatico*, if he needs to an unusual degree a sense of politics, if he needs to be an institution-builder and to have some understanding of the transferability of know-how, what do these necessities mean for education and training of experts? This is not the place to suggest a curriculum for a training course, but several observations grow naturally out of the preceding discussion.

1. At the stage when a person is subjected to formal education, he cannot normally predict where in the world he will find the right job, even if he is clear from the outset that he wants to work abroad. The American Institute for Foreign Trade at Thunderbird Field, near Phoenix, Arizona, builds its training course for businessmen around instruction in Spanish and Portuguese, together with Latin-American area studies; yet more than a quarter of their overseas alumni are in Europe or Asia or Africa.

2. "Overseasmanship" is not a new profession or a new academic discipline, but a new twist on the traditional professions and the standard academic categories of knowledge. It follows that the clientele for an overseas training program should ideally have (or be in the process of acquiring) a professional base of specialization. There is not, and probably there should not be, a substantial market outside the teaching profession for broad training in international relations not combined with a salable skill—in economics, in education, in agriculture, in public health, in public administration, in foreign trade, or whatever.

3. A training program for overseas service should be conceived in part as a recruitment and screening device.

4. Every effort should be made to immerse the student in an overseas experience, as part of his educational preparation for overseas service. Many of the psychological and intellectual adjustments required to develop and test "cultural empathy" cannot be effectively reproduced synthetically on an American campus.

5. Language instruction comes into the training picture as a subhead under "cultural empathy." The most important thing is not to try to predict the language the student will require but to develop in the student what Rowland Egger calls "a proneness to learn a foreign language"—and to enable the student to prove to himself that he can do so.

6. Similarly in the field of area studies, the inability to predict where the student will eventually land (and the probability that in some kinds of service, as with the government, he will land in a number of different countries before he completes a career in overseas service) points to the value of one exposure in one alien culture, not primarily for the purpose of getting to know that culture but to enable the student to realize the relativity of the "American way" and to develop some tools of analysis for tackling any foreign culture which he may need to absorb.

7. Realistic and practical instruction in the nature of the political process in several comparative societies, and in comparative administration, has an important place in an overseas training program for Western experts, regardless of the nature of their *expertise.*

8. In both, selection and training, stress should be placed on the process of building institutions. Those experts who have once built an organization from scratch, or have been responsible for substantial change or expansion in a going concern, may prove to be the best bets for overseas service.

9. The training program should stress those kinds of research, reading, discussion, and internship which cause the student to ask himself questions about the transferability of the technical "know-how" with which he starts. To the extent possible, such a program should confront him also with the broader form of the same question: "Which lessons and attitudes in the development of American civilization are applicable elsewhere, and which are *sui generis?"*

All of these considerations might profitably be taken into account in any training program designed to help Western experts prepare themselves for overseas service. This is not, of course, an exhaustive checklist, since it includes only those items which appear to have some general applicability and excludes special considerations that apply in a single geographical area or to a single professional category. But a training program which ignores very many of these pointers runs the risk of irrelevance to the subsequent overseas experience of the experts it trains.

# CHAPTER XV

# Educational Leadership through Workshop Procedures

THEODORE D. RICE and CHANDOS REID

In this chapter the authors will explore the workshop approach which has been used in the retraining of educational leaders in India and Pakistan and will identify features of this approach which may have value generally in the retraining of leaders in underdeveloped countries.

## Demands upon Educational Leaders

The educational leadership in these two countries is confronted with the need to develop competencies which extend beyond those previously used under more restricted settings and which will enable them to face issues of social change. Not only must attitudes and values be reformulated but, with the rise of democratic nationalism, the educator is confronted with the need to test out his competencies both by helping shape national aspirations and by helping to localize their implications for change. This requires a skill in moving from academic isolation into a working relationship with others in clarifying accepted goals and in assisting communities in making decisions. The same type of leadership which utilizes the ideas, the attitudes, and the natural urge for improvement among the people of a community must also be developed in other educators who have previously been concerned only with education focused on academic information unrelated to the culture of the community. Obviously, retraining programs should be so designed as to provide the type of leadership needed.

Training should be planned in such a way that it is related to aspirations and schemes already devised. It should exemplify the procedures and methods which are needed and should provide training in the exercise of these procedures. It should place emphasis on the analysis of local needs and the application of procedures and knowledge to local settings. Because it is designed for these purposes, the workshop seems to be a natural device for providing retraining of leaders in underdeveloped countries. It is hoped that an examination of the workshops in India and Pakistan and their results may provide suggestions concerning the value of workshops as a major way of retraining leaders in other underdeveloped countries.

## Purposes and Limitations of Workshops in India

The educational workshop is a purely Anglo-American phenomenon.[1] It is a natural outgrowth of the discussion procedures which come from an effort to put democracy to work in education as well as in government. The educational workshop, as referred to in this chapter, is designed to help people help themselves. It is seen as a problem-solving center. It begins with the premise that the program shall be developed around the problems and concerns of the participants themselves, rather than upon an organization developed by experts in the field. Its purpose is to strengthen skills in thinking and in problem-solving. The procedures used are those designed to develop leadership abilities which will be most effective in changing behavior. The role of the expert in the workshop is not one of setting direction and giving answers but that of listening to the statement of an indigenous problem and bringing pertinent information into the discussion in order to aid participation in thinking through the problems. Thus, he must not only know his field but must also be able to give help to others in using knowledge in a new setting and with new applications while teaching to the participants in the workshop the procedures he is using. The workshop, as described in this chapter, is more than a seminar procedure of sharing ideas. To the process of sharing, it adds the field of problem-solving and that of making proposals and plans for action.

It is not assumed that the workshop can do the full job. Some of its limitations, as it has been structured in India and Pakistan, include the following:

1. Mary O'Rourke and William H. Burton, *Workshops for Teachers*, pp. 4–10. New York: Appleton, Century, Crofts, 1957. See also Earl C. Kelley, *The Workshop Way of Learning*, chap. ii. New York: Harper & Bros., 1951.

1. There has not been opportunity to experience problem-solving as an interdisciplinary team of educators with specialists from agriculture, health, and social welfare.
2. The group has been an educational in-group, isolated to itself in numbers from 50 to 75 persons for six to eight weeks in training-college quarters.
3. Follow-up consultation for transfer of educational ideas developed in the workshop has been only occasional. There has been a marked gap from the workshop made up of like-minded persons to educational innovation in the isolation of a village or district little touched by social education or village improvement efforts.
4. Formal presentations from anthropology, psychology, philosophy, and specialized areas have been very limited.

### APPLICATION OF WORKSHOP TECHNIQUES TO PROBLEMS
### OF SECONDARY EDUCATION IN INDIA

Nevertheless, using the concept of "a problem-solving center" as the definition of a workshop, the United States Educational Foundation in India proposed that a team of American educators conduct workshops throughout the country to help headmasters of secondary schools think through problems of reorganization of the new secondary school in India. Work had already been done in this direction by a commission on secondary education appointed by the Indian government. The report of this commission was to be made public in the fall of 1953. However, to make the report effective, the process of thinking through the problems and proposing solutions must be carried on by the people who would have responsibility for the programs in the individual schools. The workshops were planned to provide this opportunity.

### PERSONNEL IN INDIAN WORKSHOPS

The workshops were attended by headmasters, professors from teachers' colleges, government inspectors, or other educational leaders appointed by the directors of public instruction in each of the several states in the region. Thus, the participants were recognized leaders in their states, and it was assumed that they were responsible for taking back to their states some recommendations for revising the program of secondary education. They came from villages, towns, or cities, from mission schools, government-aided schools, or government schools. They were typical of the provinces from which they were deputed and representative of the various types of schools to be found in the area. Their previous experiences away from their own homes had been in colleges. English was the only common language. While Hindi is now being taught in the schools, it is not yet a common language in many provinces. The language of the workshops, therefore, was English; and we might add, English affected by a wide variety of accents—American, Kanarese, Tamil, Telegu, Gujerati, Maharashtrian, Bengali, Assamese, and many others. Although men were in a large majority, there were at least eight or ten women enroled in each workshop. They took part in all activities and assumed their professional status in the groups.

The workshop procedures were set up so that they might be used in the home provinces. The workshops were devoted not only to the problems of secondary education but also to the procedures for meeting and developing changes in Indian education.

### WORKSHOP PROCEDURES IN INDIA

Each workshop began with an effort to define the problems with which groups were concerned and to develop a means of studying those problems and coming up with a program of action. Perhaps the best overview of workshop procedures can be gained from the participants themselves. The following description was written by students in one of the early workshops.

The course was designed to provide a study of educational trends and to give an opportunity for considering the practical application of these trends and practices in the schools from which the trainees came.

An interesting feature of the course was that the scope of work was determined in a large measure by the problems presented by the participants themselves, and the method adopted to tackle the problems was the workshop method in which the group made decisions through discussion and study, while the staff only showed the way. Lectures were few and only aimed at showing how schools in the U.S.A. faced similar problems and tried to solve them.

Each participant had his own problems which he brought from his school. All such problems were collected and grouped. So came up five broad groups: (a) curriculum, (b) teacher welfare, (c) methods of teaching, (d) guidance, (e) supervision, and (f) discipline. Each group organized its problems and sat down to work under the guidance of a staff member. So began the workshop.

The workshop generally worked in two sessions: 8:30 A.M. to 11:30

A.M. and 1:30 P.M. to 4:00 P.M., and included study groups, interviews with the staff, library study, general sessions, educational films, etc., and ended with tea at 3:30 P.M. The general session included talks by staff on general educational topics; lectures by visitors, panel discussions by staff and trainees together on problems of interest; "cracker barrel" which, like the brain trusts, invited questions on any topics to be answered on the spot and briefly; or group reports presented from time to time; discussions on follow-up work after excursions, and so on. Week-end excursions, games and tournaments, and entertainment programs too had their full share of the workshop schedule. All the work was organized in weekly schedules by the planning committee consisting of representatives of all five groups.

The workshop method was a democratic method. Each study group daily elected its chairman and had a recorder. Every participant member of the group contributed to the tackling of the issue. It was a football game where everybody gave a kick. The staff member present served as a consultant and important resource on the spot. The groups at intervals presented reports to the general assembly, thus giving an opportunity to all to share experiences and learn from everybody else.

Besides the planning committee, there were the reading-room committee, welfare committee, games committee, recreation committee, and the excursion committee. The workshop also set up an evaluation committee which reviewed from time to time activities of special interest to the trainees and so guided the planning committee in preparing the next schedule.

The evaluation committee evaluated the eight weeks' work at Baroda and showed that the workshop primarily trained the participants in the problem-solving procedure. The recommendations made by the state groups to their respective state governments showed the insight and interest the participants had developed in educational problems and procedures. There is little doubt that each individual gained a revitalized concept of his own role in the reorganization of secondary education in India. Each one has gone back to his work not only with plans as to what he can do immediately in his work but also with confidence that vision and initiative may come on the job. The workshop has done its part well; it is hoped that the participants, the managements, and the state governments will do theirs.[2]

This report, prepared by a group at the end of their eight weeks in the workshop, reflects enthusiasm in their experience. It probably fails to give the reality which many of them faced when they tried to introduce new practices at home alone. Nevertheless, the report does show awareness of the need for new directions, new pro-

2. "Report of Baroda Workshop," *Journal of Education and Psychology*, XII, No. 1 (April, 1954), 29–81 (Baroda, India).

cedures, and new leadership roles. It also shows that the workshop succeeded in extending the vision these educators have of the responsibilities for leadership. Questions submitted by participants to serve as a basis for formulation of groups also show the pressures of social change on their jobs.

## QUESTIONS OF PARTICIPANTS

A majority of the questions related to the need for change or improvement in administering the academic school in view of new demands being made upon it. Many, however, showed an awareness of the need for a closer relationship between the school and the community and the need to relate formal school programs to developments in community and basic education. They showed a searching for ways in which the school can extend its range of responsibilities and face the issues of social change. There was also recognition among participants of the need to broaden the range of responsibility and participation both within the school and within the community. The need for research was recognized. It was apparent in periods of discussion that much of the research reported in the American and English books available to the students was not very helpful. Such research indicated areas where information was needed, but the reports were so obviously Western in orientation that they could not be transferred to the Indian culture. This was one of the many ways in which procedures in the workshop study groups developed and were modified as the group worked together. In some instances plans were set up for research. In others, a school which had tried to develop some phase of democratic procedure was called upon to share its efforts and to tell how obstacles had been overcome.

## ADAPTING SCHOOL PROGRAM TO COMMUNITY SETTING

The problems pertaining to the existing school pattern were the most difficult with which to deal. There were phases of the school program, however, in which the local school did have sufficient authority to permit modification at the local level. Participants in the workshops were inclined to look for ways in which desirable activities could be made a part of the extracurriculum program. Library work might be done through a club. Activity projects in the social studies could also be used as club projects. Citizenship was already being taught through the Boy Scouts organization. In some states, schools were required to spend one day a week in social service, but the particular service to be done was left to the local community. Some schools sent students regularly to help clean up neighboring villages. Few of the schools have worked out ways to help educate the villagers so that the unsanitary conditions would not develop again. Several schools helped with teams who went out to vaccinate, but few participated in educating villagers toward understanding how disease is carried. It was in these programs of activity that the workshop participants began to find ways in which they could develop the local school program more closely in relation to its community setting. The concept of such activity as educational in purpose began to develop. Reports sent to staff members indicate some of the efforts which were made:

We have been getting the parents more interested in the work of the children at school by inviting them to observe classes and to see the work and the entertainment given separately by the classes. In this way we are able to contact different groups of parents and have discussions with them. A recreational center for children has been opened. Every day the whole school is for one period on the grounds, playing, working, digging, etc. It is very difficult to make the teachers take to physical labor, in spite of the fact that almost every day I myself work in the field. For the new admissions, we have over a hundred every year, special arrangements were made and the senior boys took charge of them and introduced them to the playfields, canteen, library, craft rooms, etc. That worked very well. The boys also took charge of parents in showing them around the school. The boys and staff have formed a school orchestra and a dramatic club. In different ways I have been trying to make the children and staff feel that everything should be a joint effort and that the school is to be considered as *our school*. Togetherness is what I am trying to achieve slowly and indirectly.[3]

SOCIAL AND COMMUNITY SERVICE IN SCHOOLS OF INDIA

In the village schools, the headmaster often worked as a team member with the village-level worker and the social director. They organized their students to assist with road-building, school- and community-building construction, house-spraying with DDT. Many

3. N. V. Tampi, Headmaster, Besant Theosophical School, Benares, October 13, 1954.

teachers taught literacy classes at night. Schools working in basic education were making real strides in relating the program of the
school to village life. This was also being accomplished in schools
which were designated as agricultural schools. Even in these schools,
however, where the headmaster was expected to develop the program in relation to the aims and interests of the citizens, there was
sometimes a concept of the school as "taking something to" the villagers rather than "working with" them. Many of the teachers who
were trained to teach in basic schools thought that they must teach
*what* they had been taught rather than *in the manner* in which they
had been taught. The result was that some classes in basic education
were learning to clean and spin and weave cotton, even though cotton had to be brought great distances to be used in the schools. In
other schools, the spirit and purpose of basic education was at work,
and the school was transforming the economy of the village through
introduction of better methods of agriculture and better methods of
marketing. An awareness of the need for close school-community
relationship was developing. After the workshop, one headmaster
wrote:

At the workshop I made a special study of community-school practices
with special reference to my country, its needs, and ideals. At the state
conference of all secondary-school headmasters, I moved a resolution that
every high school in the state should plan a program of community study
with the help of its students adopting the latest techniques of community
study, and the resolution was passed unanimously. The difficulty in all this
work is that the community around the school is not yet ready and ripe
to receive these new ideas. Hence the effort of the community school is all
mostly one-sided and progress is not rapid.[4]

Relating programs of academic schools and particularly city
schools to the life of the community was much more difficult. Because schools had taken an active part in the freedom movement,
because teachers were identified with political parties, there was
great caution about using the students in relation to political activity. This resulted in reluctance to teach even the fundamentals of the
Indian "Five-Year Plan." It militated against any kind of community
involvement in the social studies. The pressure of the examinations
also made teachers reluctant to introduce any community activities

4. M. A. Srinavasar Iyengar, Headmaster, Acharya High School, Goribidnur,
September 8, 1954.

because they would not lead to ability to answer questions on the examinations. Only in rare instances did teachers throughout a school see the additional experiences of students as actually contributing to the competence of the students. One workshopper wrote:

Of course I do not have much freedom to plan the curriculum and alter it whenever necessary. But I have freedom to develop the co-curricular activities in my own way, and it is in this sphere and in the sphere of school administration that I have sought to adopt new measures. Immediately after I returned from the workshop, I organized the teachers' council of my school on more democratic lines, and I have been consulting them on every matter of importance that concerns school life. I am happy to inform you that my teachers have responded to this change in attitude considerably, and I am receiving from them utmost co-operation and help. I have also organized pupil self-government on a similar plan with greater emphasis on pupil initiative and pupil co-operation. Now the discipline of my school is being maintained by the Students' Representative Council which has an elected president and secretary, and members drawn from the various classes.[5]

Although the focus of concern of this teacher was in the work of the school as it contributed to the curriculum and in organization which would facilitate an improved school program, yet the type of organization is also applicable to a program of community education. Organization of each group concerned in such a way that it is aware of its own responsibility for improvement and for carrying out changes which are desirable is a basic step. It is also one of the most difficult steps to achieve, since local responsibility has not previously been a part of the cultural pattern. The extracurriculum program in Indian schools seems to offer a particularly happy opportunity for this type of organization.

CARRY-OVER OF WORKSHOP PRACTICES IN INDIA

Both difficulties and achievements of the workshop are evident in these last two quotations. Certainly the direct carry-over of workshop practices was sometimes frightening and often unsuccessful. On the other hand, ideas and even overt behaviors learned there were sometimes amazingly successful. The observation of a member of the American team in 1957–58, assigned to the task of interviewing and visiting alumni of previous workshops, is interesting in this respect:

5. M. A. Srinavasar Iyengar, Headmaster, Acharya High School, Goribidnur, August, 1954.

I think you really must find a way to come back here long enough to see what has happened since 1954. They call this the age of seminars. I think it is an apt caption. Yesterday I spoke to a headmaster's seminar which is currently in progress here in Mysore. The idea of workshops and seminars has certainly caught on and, I think, is making a difference.

Everyone I have spoken to who has been in a workshop has only fond remembrances of their experiences, and, more important, most of them start to tell me of things they are doing. Off hand, it looks to me as though they are doing most in the areas outside the control of the syllabus: the library, the clubs, the committee for school improvement, etc. Some are trying things in their classrooms.[6]

This commentary bears out the observations which have been made, but it also indicates that the workshop as a device for re-education of educational leaders has been considered of value in India. We have gone into this description of the Indian workshops in some detail in order to give evidence of some of the attitudinal problems which are involved in the retraining of the technically competent as changes occur.

At the end of the first year of workshops in India, the government of Pakistan requested the same type of help in the Fulbright program there. In 1954–55, therefore, American teams worked in this manner in both India and Pakistan. The workshops have continued in both countries through the academic year of 1957–58.

## Workshops in Pakistan

### SIMILARITY OF PRACTICES IN PAKISTAN AND INDIA

The workshops in Pakistan faced problems similar to those which have been mentioned. There, as in India, little effort had been made to relate the various educational efforts of the community to each other. City schools were much less challenged by cultural changes and were less likely to be involved in community change than were schools in rural areas or in villages. To be sure, there were many schools being developed especially for the poor, but these were seen as something apart from the main streams of either education or the life of the people.[7]

6. Dr. John Robertson, Professor of Education, New York University, January, 1958.

7. The material on the Pakistan workshops was gained through interviews with two former workshop staff members: Dr. Mary O'Rourke, Massachusetts State Teachers College, Salem, Massachusetts; and Dr. Haddon James, President Emeritus, Western New Mexico College, Silver City, New Mexico.

The class structure also tended to segment the efforts which were being made to develop a universal program of education. Those who were educated were also members of the upper class. These educated adults felt little responsibility for educating adults of the poorer classes. This seemed to be almost a closed topic, as if it were assumed that they were not worthy of an education or they would have had one. Schools for the poor were almost on a basis of charity.

On the other hand, indigenous efforts to educate children to read and write were being made outside the governmental structure, but these seemed to be largely ignored by the schools and the various missions working in the field of education, either formally or in community-education projects. One of these efforts which seems to merit recognition is made by elderly mullahs who work in the post offices in Pakistan. Often these men gather children around them whenever there is time and try to teach them to read and write.

In Pakistan, as in India, the village school is much nearer the life of the people than is the city school. Here, there is the same type of emphasis on social service which is common in India. Here, also, the tendency is to do the service rather than to teach villagers to serve themselves. An exception to this is noted in a youth group which is something of a cross between the Boy Scouts movement and the National Guard. It is a group without official recognition and is often linked with mention of communistic influence. It has not been officially identified in this manner, however. The boys are taught to read and write and then go out themselves to teach adults literacy in the fundamental-education projects of the area. The teaching is necessarily on a very elementary level, for the boys are barely literate themselves. Often the methods used would be better with children than with adults. Nevertheless, this group represents a real effort to link youth with the movement in fundamental education, and the type of service which they are performing has value in relation to similar services being performed by the schools.

Pakistan workers feel that the program for women in home nursing, home education, sanitation, and disease control conducted through the American ICA efforts is an outstanding example of fundamental education at its best. There is little or no effort to link these various educational efforts to the school program or to include the same content in the syllabus of the schools. The workshops made an effort to establish a need for this relationship. School programs in Pakistan are, for the most part, looked upon as separate and different from other educational efforts. Colleges are not community oriented. They are well organized, well run, but removed from the life of the people. Through field trips, speakers, and reading materials devoted to the total scope of educational effort, the workshops called attention to the many educational ventures and to their potential relationship to desirable school practices.

In Pakistan, as in India, those in power in the various provinces are frequently unwilling to make changes in the structure of the educational pattern. In one area in Pakistan, the American staff, together with the participants who came to the workshop, went out into schools as a group to sit down with teachers and to work on problems at the local community level. This pattern had some value for relating the work of retraining teachers to the work of village reconstruction.

### NEWER PROCEDURES IN TECHNICAL SCHOOLS OF PAKISTAN

The technical schools which are being developed in Pakistan seem to hold the greatest potential for developing leaders in keeping up with the cultural changes in the country. Both at the college level, where there is training for industrial development, and in the secondary schools established to educate youth for industrial positions, the focus is on the new culture. New ways of doing things as well as new content have the effect of freeing these schools from their traditions. Perhaps the best example of this potential is taking place in East Pakistan, where the Adami Jute Mills have been constructed and a whole new city with an industrial orientation is being built. Thousands of men, women, and children are engaged in the process of building. The city is being thoroughly planned in relation to the new culture it is to represent, and the plans include a college and a library as well as sufficient schools for all the children. A visit to this developing city was a part of workshop activity in East Pakistan. From visits to such ventures where education is being seen as a part of the total community life and as oriented to the community and its improvement came a better understanding of the changes actually being effected and of the needed changes which must be made in the communities to meet the demands of the new nation.

## Lessons Learned from Workshops in India and Pakistan

### RETRAINING LEADERS

The workshops in India and Pakistan were concerned with the problem of retraining leaders in education to meet the demands of a rapidly developing new program within their countries. Each program began with problem identification and an emphasis on problem-solving and group procedures as the means of bringing about the needed changes in leadership concepts and attitudes. As Margaret Mead points out in chapter iii, change of the total stratum of the culture is much more significant than change in only one major custom while the rest of the daily living continues as before. The necessity for the schools to assume a relationship to the social changes in underdeveloped countries is intensified because these schools have already been disjointed from the existing culture. The workshops gave an opportunity to examine the needed relationships and to consider possible ways of achieving the purposes of social development.

### REALIZATION THAT IMPROVEMENTS CAN BE MADE

The workshops in both countries were also successful in achieving needed changes in concepts and attitudes. The most obvious of these is getting people to want to make improvements, to know that the improvements can be made, and to feel that they have some share in doing something about it. This is the task of the health worker who goes into a village where it is assumed that certain illnesses must be endured; but it is equally the task of the professor who works with the teachers in elementary or secondary schools. The attitude is characteristic of the culture, not of the lowest economic group alone.

Reactions of one of the American consultants in India in the fall of 1957 indicate some of the problems inherent in bringing an alien device, such as the workshop, into underdeveloped countries as a way of working on these problems:

I think the workshop was difficult but pleasant for almost everyone, including me. My most vivid impression was that the life, spirit, and creativity had been beaten out of these people by thousands of years of poverty and oppression and the development of a philosophy that encourages the individual to accept a passive role in life. The teacher in India does not see himself as an agent of change.

The workshop as a way of working was born in America. It grew on fertile soil as an institution designed specifically to solve educational problems with democratic procedures.

We transported such an institution to a land newly liberated from political servitude where freedom is desired but where the past authoritarianism grips and holds the educational institutions and stifles the spirit. Our struggle to help the Indian attain some insight into the meaning of educational democracy was begun.

The workshop participants, almost to each man, seemed to understand the significance of education for democracy. When the workshop way of working was explained to our group of participants, it was accepted intellectually but could not be implemented with actions. The difficulty was apparent. The participants could not state their own problems; could not really accept the idea that they should work out their own problems. When we did manage to get problems stated, the most frequent response was to the effect that nothing could be done about them. The teacher said the headmaster or the inspector or the director of education had to solve the problems. I can still hear them saying, "I can't," "We can't," or "It can't be done."

We struggled against passivity for weeks. In the large group meetings they listened and asked some questions and said, "But we can't." In the small groups of four or five persons they sat and looked at each other and looked to a staff member to do some talking—solve the problem. They looked at us with great respect—standing as we entered the room, calling us by our full titles—and otherwise regarding us as authorities whose main function was to solve their problems, give them the answers, with them playing the inactive role of a receptacle or a warehouse whose function was to receive, to store, certainly not to give, to plan, to think, to live, nor to practice in their workshop living.

As an old "do-it-yourselfer" and as a practical educator, I guess nothing gets me down quite so fast as seeing people so sure they can't do anything about their problems and assuming such an inactive role. I squirmed.

There is quite a happy ending to this story. The informal atmosphere of the workshop and the staff broke through the reserve of the participants and permitted and encouraged freedom of thought and action and we were on our way. About the time we pushed the small group into reporting to the large group in a form other than reading a report, the dam broke. Before we finished our reporting, all sorts of activities had been tried. We found most of our participants had a flair for the dramatic and, given a chance, could even create roles on the spot.

Many people shed a tear when we parted. I, of course, can't say for sure what we accomplished, but I think thirty participants, five staff members, three children, the sweepers, the bearers in the mess, the charvasi who carried our messages, the college president and his staff, and many Patialians who visited us sensed the power of men at work freeing themselves.

I think I saw indications of the power the workshop could release, but I also felt the tremendous strain on an institution fashioned in modern America as it was being used in modern India.

Indian educators need help of many kinds. Workshops such as ours which operate at a state and regional level are important, but if effort is not to be dissipated, in-service work at the local level should receive great support. The local state colleges of education have been entrusted with the problem of helping the local schools with the in-service training of secondary-school teachers.[8]

This letter reveals not only some of the strengths of the workshops but also some of the problems of workshops as a method of retraining educational leaders. The need for additional work at the local level is of particular importance. Only one person was deputed from a single school situation. On return, he was surrounded by the old traditions and by a faculty which had had no new experiences nor information about the purpose of the workshop to which the headmaster had been deputed. Thus, the effectiveness of the workshop efforts depended entirely upon the ability of one person to understand and then transmit his understanding to others. There has been little help for those who have difficulty, no additional interpretation if the participant had only a partial understanding. Each year there has been an effort to have workshop staff members visit local communities where participants of previous workshops are introducing new practices. It has been impossible, however, to visit all workshop alumni.

### BROADENING THE BASE OF RESPONSIBILITY

In the underdeveloped countries, the educated person is probably from the upper class, and the community-education projects within the village or city are probably being conducted with the lower class. Frequently the activities needed are those in which upper-class members of the culture have never been involved and which they consider beneath them. In many of these countries the emphasis on the respectability and desirability of manual labor has been national policy. But change in attitude toward such activity cannot be legislated. Such change in attitude is a part of the needed program of re-education. In the workshops were enrolled headmasters of

8. Dr. John Robertson, Professor of Education, New York University, December, 1957.

many different backgrounds. There was stress on the making of posters, models, and other manual activities. These contributed to needed attitudes.

If a concerted approach to the solution of the problems is to be achieved, not only must a wider group of the population assume responsibility for helping to solve problems but the communication structure and the governmental structure of the institutions involved must permit broader participation. Decisions must be made by more people, action must be initiated by a larger group. As participants took such responsibility and made decisions in the workshops, some of them came to feel that the school itself could take steps in this direction:

My staff now fully believes in the functioning of the schools and class committees. The students now realize their responsibility and engage themselves in desirable activities. Cases of delinquency are fast disappearing. Healthy contact between pupils and their teachers is enabling us to study the nature of each other closely.[9]

The purposes of these workshops were to develop better standards of health, education, and economic efficiency appropriate to the culture and potential of the countries themselves. No good is to be served by transferring a foreign system of education or economics to them. The need is for development within the countries of patterns appropriate to their tradition and their culture. In order to do this effectively in the field of education, much study, research, and experimentation is needed. Few of these countries possess the tools with which to conduct such study. The technically competent within the country must be trained in ways of conducting the needed experimentation and research for indigenous development.

DEVELOPING ATTITUDES AND SKILLS IN RELATION TO PROBLEM-SOLVING

The need for developing the attitudes and the skills essential to problem-solving is one of the greatest challenges in underdeveloped countries. In a mechanically oriented civilization, the very use of machines has made people take the attitude, "If something is wrong, how do I fix it?" When this is coupled with some form of democratic government and the kind of industrial background which

9. S. P. Nigam, Model High School, Prantiya Shiksham Mahavidyalaya, Jabalpur, December, 1954.

permits individual improvement of economic status, the attitude of the people is one of doing something about problems rather than of submitting to them. When there is a completely autocratic governmental structure, plus a centralized educational authority, plus an economic system based on self-support from handicrafts, the attitude is one of passive acceptance of the inevitable. This attitudinal problem is one of the major ones facing underdeveloped countries as they attempt to modify their cultural patterns, and especially if they try democratic procedures in doing so. Since the major focus of the workshops was on problem analysis and problem-solving, they at least afforded some practice in problem-solving procedures.

### Present Role of Workshops in India and Pakistan

The fact that the workshops and seminars have made a definite contribution to the needed re-education is evidenced by the fact that they have become a prominent part of the government program for retraining of educational leaders. The selection of people with workshop experience to take leadership in various on-going educational developments is further evidence. A headmaster of a secondary school was selected to direct the workshop follow-up conference which was held following the first year of these experiences. He was later appointed as a member of the All-India Council for Secondary Education. He writes:

> There has been a good deal of awakening, thinking anew, and planning among teachers as a result of the workshop experiences and the seminars, and I am sure the impact of all that will soon begin to be felt in better methods of teaching, in better relations between the headmaster and the staff and between the staff and students and the community. I think very much can be accomplished if only we give up the traditional method of teaching and help the children to think for themselves. Under the present system the children are not given the chance to *think*; they have only to memorize and repeat.[10]

He also indicates that the workshops since 1956 have been conducted jointly by the All-India Council and the United States Educational Foundation in India and have included an equal number of staff members from each country. He has served as a staff mem-

10. N. V. Tampi, Headmaster, Besant Theosophical School, Benares, March, 1958.

ber. This selection of a secondary-school headmaster as a staff member for advanced training is an innovation in Indian education.

This report of the workshop efforts to re-educate educational leaders in India and Pakistan has set forth the questions which were raised by participants and the problems which must be faced in retraining educational leaders, but it has indicated little of what went on in the workshop itself as these questions and problems were considered. This is as it must be, for the problems which are faced in a rapidly changing culture are too complex to lend themselves to easy answers. Furthermore, the workshops did not attempt to give answers to problems but to give consideration in such a way that the understanding of the group was broadened and deepened, that the issues became more clearly defined, that beginning steps toward emerging goals could be taken as participants returned to their own communities. Research was not conducted in the workshop, but the awareness did develop concerning the need for research and for actual research studies which could and should be done in local areas. There was no shift in the number of decisions which could be made at the local level, but participants became aware of the changes in their own attitudes toward themselves and toward decisions when they had a part in making them. The curriculum was not revised, but numerous ways of augmenting the current curriculum and of developing other facets of the learning experiences were envisioned. No single plan for working with parents was developed, but ways were shared where such efforts were already underway, and others were explored as possibilities. There were not specific decisions concerning what should be done in all schools, but ways of bringing vital experiences into the school were subjected to intense and critical examination.

In other words, the function of workshops such as those we have described is not the function of giving answers or setting up a syllabus, but rather one of clarifying and extending the scope of inquiry and understanding of the educational leaders who participate. It is a way of helping them come to a better understanding of their new role in their changing world. It was possible to examine social service activities with a critical eye and to come to the agreement that such activity should not stop with services alone but should help to educate those for whom the services were done. It was not possible to examine critically those problems which were tied too closely to the emotions of emerging nationality and political independence. All of the questions raised by participants were the subject of investigation and discussion, and always the question which permeated the discussion was, "What can I do about this when I return to my own community?"

## Values and Limitations of the Workshop Procedure

What then are the values and limitations of this method of retraining educational leaders? First, it is apparent that the participant found in the method itself and in the content of the discussions many specific things which could be used in his own school to effect immediate improvements and to solve problems which had been troubling him. Extending the responsibilities of the student council as a means of improving morale among students; developing opportunities for teachers to make decisions concerning the way things should be done; initial steps to be taken in improving the relationship of parents to the school; extending the number and variety of cocurriculum activities, such as clubs, in order to give extended learning opportunities which could utilize student drive and initiative—these were efforts which were accepted as immediately practical by a majority of participants. A few tried out new practices which had a more immediate effect on the curriculum itself. Many revised their programs of social and community services into programs for doing actual experimentation with crop improvement or programs designed to teach villagers how to improve conditions in the village.

A second value of the workshops lay in the development of leadership skills among those who attended. Workshop participants have been selected to develop the extension services of colleges because of the skills which they learned in the workshop experience. Inclusion of a headmaster with workshop experience as a member of the All-India Council on Secondary Education and on the staff of subsequent workshops has already been mentioned. Another was selected to participate in the UNESCO fundamental education project, and others were promoted to inspectorships or asked to join college staffs because of this experience. There has not been adequate follow-up of participants to indicate what percentage have been given added responsibilities as a result of this experience, but correspondence indicates that many have been called upon to share the workshop experience with others.

A third value of the workshop procedure lies in the opportunity for participants who are committed to democracy to see and experience democratic procedures and to determine through their own reactions what their value might be for application within the school and within the relationships of the school and the community.

The concentration for a six-to-eight-week period on problem-solving procedures was considered by staff members to be successful in changing the attitudes of many participants from one of apathy and resignation in the face of their problems to one of analysis, examination of assumptions, and projection of possible ways of dealing with problems.

It is the point of view of staff members who took part in this enterprise that it brought staff and students of different cultures into closer understanding than would have been possible with other procedures. There was definite improvement in willingness to discuss real problems and cultural implications of change. That this was more than friendship and familiarity is indicated in the fact that a majority of the workshop participants returned to their own schools with plans for improving their relationship with teachers in their schools. It is further indicated in continuing correspondence concerning problems as they are encountered.

Limitations of the workshop procedure have already been indicated. An additional weakness of the workshops we have described lay in the fact that they were staffed by educators only. Had they included sanitarians, agriculturists, health personnel as members of the staff, and community leaders other than schoolmen, the experience would have been more successful in effecting a new relationship between schools and the communities they serve.

In the opinion of the authors, the characteristics of the workshop procedure make it uniquely effective as a device for retraining of leaders in underdeveloped countries. The values and problems which have been described in relation to India and Pakistan, are, in our opinion, applicable to the use of workshops in other countries as well. The work of schools and other educational institutions must be related to the life of the community and to the educational programs if these programs are to become of lasting value. Similarly, the school programs must be reunited with the flow of the culture in the local communities if young people are to take effective leadership in that culture. Because of its emphasis on problems and procedures of involvement, the workshop offers promise as a means of retraining educational leaders to participate in the community improvement efforts of these countries.

# CHAPTER XVI

# The United Nations Program of Community Development

GLEN LEET

Seeking for the origins of United Nations community development, one finds that the trail leads to that first-organized intergovernmental welfare agency, the United Nations Relief and Rehabilitation Administration. UNRRA was set up, with voluntarily contributed funds from many nations, to provide relief for and to stimulate reconstruction in the devastated regions of Europe and Asia after the close of World War II.

## Community Development in the Villages of Greece

As director of welfare for UNRRA in Greece, I became convinced that giving supplies to people where there was underemployment or underdevelopment was not a real solution to their problems. If they could be persuaded to use their idle time in making environmental improvements, it would seem that a process of growth might begin. Accordingly, opportunities were sought to talk with village people about their community problems, pointing out that their unemployed days were not necessarily a burden but could be a resource of great value in the effort to realize some of their dreams for a better future. The villagers proved responsive to this approach and soon were able to define quite clearly many useful improvements, which could be accomplished by their working together.

When the collaborating nations decided to discontinue the Relief and Rehabilitation Administration in war-torn countries, the United Nations assumed some of the responsibilities which UNRRA had been carrying. Under the reorganized rehabilitation program, I became adviser to the Greek government on social policy and continued the effort to popularize the community-development movement

379

among the villages of Greece. But we did not start this campaign with a program we thought the village people ought to accept. On the contrary, we went to each village and tried to determine by popular discussion what problems the people were willing to solve co-operatively. The building of a road to a larger village, for example, was a natural project for many subsistence communities, and the farmers were quick to see that by providing access to outside markets they could ship and sell their surplus crops. This step would soon lead to the production of more crops, with a many-fold increase in their economy. Many villagers wanted to develop domestic water supplies; others were concerned with improved health and sanitation; others wanted better schools.

By this discussional approach, many thousands of village people began a wide variety of community improvements and were happy to accept a very small cash reward as a symbolic recognition of their efforts, rather than demanding full unemployment relief. The Greek government has reported[1] that, during this period, the village people built more new roads and rehabilitated or improved more subsidiary highways than had been built in the previous hundred years. At the beginning of this program, the entire national road system of Greece consisted of about 16,000 kilometers; and during the rehabilitation period the people built or rebuilt more than 5,000 kilometers of highway.

## Community Development in Greek Cities

After several years, the program was initiated in the cities. While the cities did not have the same type of underdevelopment as the rural areas they, too, needed a great deal of guidance and technical assistance on community-improvement problems. War, occupation, and civil conflict had created many urgent needs. In addition, there was the necessity for the expansion of urban facilities to meet the growth of population. Underutilized man power existed, but it was different from the seasonal unemployment of rural areas. In the cities there was both chronic unemployment and the disguised unemployment of people who continued to work at unproductive selling and

1. Glen Leet, *Greece Finds One Key to Development*, p. 2. New York: United Nations Department of Public Information, 1951.

service jobs. In the cities there was not the dramatic rise in productivity and living standards at the introduction of "Community Development Employment" (as the activity was called) which occurs when an isolated village breaks through the barrier of unemployment by building a road, which makes possible a market economy.

However, in the cities, the program had other results of an even more dramatic character. Most notable was the increased private employment, increased private investment, and increased compensation from private employment. For example, in Patras, a city of about 100,000 inhabitants, only about 10 per cent of the homes had water and sewer connections. As a part of a community-development program, an extension of the sewer and water mains was undertaken, using local rock and cement. No imported materials were used. As the mains were laid, each home-owner had to hire private labor to establish a connection; and, to save expense, 95 per cent of them did it quickly, while the excavations were still open. For these connections, the home-owners needed tile pipe. Thus, the pottery-makers developed a thriving business making the pipes. With a seven-fold increase in sewer and water connections, there was a greatly increased need for plumbing fixtures. The local factory, which manufactured plumbing fixtures, tripled its production and still could not keep up with the demand. A potter developed a crude, glazed-clay, water flush bowl that he could sell for less than three dollars and did a thriving business. Before this project began, plumbers received 17,000 drachmae per day; as a result of the project, their wages rose to 44,000 drachmae per day, and many new apprentices were trained. Even so, plumbers remained in demand.

As new streets, sidewalks, parks, and squares were built or improved through community-development projects, a high level of private investment in home construction and improvement automatically developed. Especially in the poorer sections of the city was the face of the community lifted. Through community development the pride of the inhabitants was awakened, and new and better homes were built. Even those who could not afford a new home could afford a coat of whitewash, and today the whole appearance of the city and the level of living of its people has greatly improved.

## The Egyptian Welfare Center Program

While work in Greece was proceeding, the Egyptian Ministry of Social Affairs, under Dr. Ahmed Hussein, and its Department of the Fellah and Rural Welfare, under Dr. Abbas Ammar, had been inaugurating a program of Rural Social Welfare[2] through the establishment of welfare centers in the villages of Egypt.

Egypt probably occupies the most fertile river valley in the world, but its six million feddans (a feddan approximates an acre) of agricultural land must support a farming population of over fifteen million people. Despite the fertility of the land, it cannot supply the needs of the people because of the rapidly increasing number. In contrast to many farming areas, the fellah (farmers) live in villages and go out to work on their land. Because of the population concentration, a village may embrace as many as ten to thirty thousand people. As visualized by its leaders, an Egyptian welfare center[3] is equipped to furnish resident agricultural guidance, a medical doctor, periodic visits from a veterinary-surgeon, a medical dispenser, and a plant engineer. Near by is a rural public school which enjoys the help of visiting teachers for rural industries, women's crafts, and tailoring. Appropriate simple buildings are built to provide not only classrooms for the full-time school but also places where these visiting instructors can teach and where doctors' and midwives' examinations can be given. Quarters for the resident agriculturalist, the doctor, and the teachers were also planned.

As at first outlined, such centers were to be set up in villages, and there was to be a center for each 10,000 fellah. For every thirty to forty thousand fellah, there was to be a fully equipped health unit, with a limited number of hospital beds; and for every fifty thousand feddans of land, an agricultural demonstration unit competent to service the agriculturalists at the smaller centers was to be established. A complicated interchange of services between the ministries of education, social affairs, health, agriculture, and eco-

2. "The Fellah Department," Ministry of Social Affairs, Royal Government of Egypt. Cairo, Egypt: 1950.

3. Ahmed Hussein, "Rural Social Welfare Centers in Egypt." Cairo, Egypt: Ministry of Social Affairs, 1951.

nomics was arranged, so that experts from each of these ministries could service each of the centers.

To insure that each center should reflect the support of the fellah whom it was designed to serve, the initiation of the services and the erection of the buildings was to depend on the initiative of the local people, who were supposed to be sufficiently inspired to band together and donate at least two feddans of land, together with a cash contribution of £E 1,500 (Egyptian pounds) toward the construction of the needed buildings. When the community committed itself, the government promised that it would provide £E 6,000 toward a building and about £E 1,000 annually toward its operation (to which each inhabitant was also supposed to contribute). The government also undertook to underwrite the cost of staffing the center and to buy the requisite furniture, medicines, and other supplies.

This program was widely publicized, and a few demonstration centers near Cairo drew many visitors. About 1949, the Egyptian Welfare Center program was brought to the attention of the Economic and Social Council of the United Nations by the United States delegation, with a resolution asking the Council to indorse the use of similar welfare centers throughout the world as instruments to promote social and economic progress. Other countries, whose representatives felt that Egypt was far from realizing its ambitious scheme on any large scale, preferred that a study be made of the welfare center as an instrument of social and economic progress. A resolution calling for such a study was passed and referred to the UN Bureau of Social Affairs.

At about this time, the Expanded Program of Technical Assistance was getting under way. Reports of the extraordinary successes in Greek villages and urban centers promoting self-help in community development, including the willingness of the people to invest their unemployed time for the benefit of their neighbors as well as themselves, stimulated the Technical Assistance Administration to support similar organizations in other countries. The present writer was appointed Community Development Specialist for the Technical Assistance Administration and sent on a tour of various underdeveloped areas to explain to governments what such a program of community development could mean to their people. As a result, requests for projects in community development began flowing into TAA from many parts of the world.

## The UN as an Agency of Governments

Within the United Nations itself, bureaus had been set up to care for those aspects of human well-being that had not been included in any of the specialized agencies. Out of the welfare organization which had been developed by UNRRA, a Bureau of Social Welfare had been set up in the United Nations Secretariat. A Bureau of Economic Affairs was also established. Both of these agencies became interested in the programs of community development reported by specialists of the Technical Assistance Administration. The Bureau of Social Welfare (later Social Affairs) created a new Community Development Unit in 1951. Since then, "Community Development" has been identified as a United Nations program.

The study of the Egyptian centers did not convince the UN unit that they afforded a desirable pattern for imitation in its work of community development. They believed that too much had been spent on buildings, which were often somewhat overpowering to the people they were designed to serve. The close co-ordination between the various ministries had failed to develop, and—while the ideal was admirable—the practice appeared to have by-passed the people, who were supposed to determine the program and enjoy the benefits thereof.

## Community Development Defined

The UN and the specialized agencies have defined community development, tentatively, as befits the evolution taking place:

The term *community development* has come into international usage to connote the processes by which the efforts of the people themselves are united with those of governmental authorities to improve the economic, social, and cultural conditions of communities, to integrate these communities into the life of the nation, and to enable them to contribute fully to national progress.

This complex of processes is then made up of two essential elements: the participation by the people themselves in efforts to improve their level of living with as much reliance as possible on their own initiative; and the provision of technical and other services in ways which encourage initiative, self-help, and mutual help and make these more effective. It is expressed in programs designed to achieve a wide variety of specific improvements.[4]

The concept of community development, as stated, includes: (*a*) physical improvements such as roads, housing, irrigation, drainage, and better farming practices; (*b*) functional activities such as the protection of health, education, and recreation; and (*c*) community action involving group discussion, community analyses of local needs, the setting up of committees, the seeking and use of technical assistance, and the selection and training of personnel. Thus, there should be no surprise at learning elsewhere in this book that UN community-development personnel, applying this concept, work with UNESCO fundamental-education centers around the world in training personnel for national programs.

Principles for community-development policies and practices have reached the following level of formulation:

(1) Activities undertaken must correspond to the basic needs of the community; the first projects should be initiated in response to the expressed needs of the people.

(2) Local improvements may be achieved through unrelated efforts in each substantive field; however, full and balanced community development requires concerted action and the establishment of multipurpose programmes.

(3) Changed attitudes in people are as important as the material achievements of community projects during the initial stages of development.

(4) Community development aims at increased and better participation of the people in community affairs, revitalization of existing forms of local government, and transition toward effective local administration where it is not yet functioning.

(5) The identification, encouragement, and training of local leadership should be a basic objective in any programme.

(6) Greater reliance on the participation of women and youth in community projects invigorates development programmes, establishes them on a wide basis, and secures long-range expansion.

(7) To be fully effective, communities' self-help projects require both intensive and extensive assistance by the government.

(8) Implementation of a community development programme on a national scale requires: adoption of consistent policies, specific administrative arrangements, recruitment and training of personnel, mobilization of local and national resources, and organization of research, experimentation, and evaluation.

4. "Twentieth Report of the Administrative Committee on Co-ordination to the Economic and Social Council, October 18, 1956." Annex III, E2931. New York: United Nations, 1956.

(9) The resources of voluntary nongovernmental organizations should be fully utilized in community development programmes at the local, national, and international level.

(10) Economic and social progress at the local level necessitates parallel development on a wider national scale.[5]

5. Bureau of Social Affairs, "Social Progress through Community Development." New York: United Nations, 1956.

## The UN as an Agency of Governments

In the UN galaxy, governments play the pivotal role in this process, for neither the UN itself nor any of its specialized agencies may initiate any activity within a member state. Through action of the member nations in assembly or in the general councils, a responsibility may be placed upon the Secretariats to render services to member states only when these states request the service. Thus it happened that the Social Commission, a subsidiary of the Economic and Social Council, requested the Secretary General to report on progress in the community-development field. The first inquiry to governments about ongoing programs elicited replies from more than forty countries.

This material—available from governments—plus the experiences of international organizations in serving governments on community development have led the UN and UNESCO to publish study kits on community-development techniques in English, French, and Arabic. A Spanish and Portuguese edition had an added sponsor, the Pan-American Union.

Lists of community-development projects and training facilities have also been prepared from the flow of such data coming to the UN. Seminars on a regional basis have figured prominently in UN services to interested governments. They have served as catalysts by bringing together the concerned officials with UN resource personnel. Individual fellowships have been granted under the UN Technical Assistance program to enable senior and middle-rank officials to test their insights against practices elsewhere. Study tours for groups have also been underwritten by the UN—and host governments.

Experts have been assigned to governments to serve in an advisory capacity. Up to the end of 1957, over 50 countries and territories had been served, at their request, by some four hundred consultants in community development and related fields. Eventually all governments benefit from distillations of such experience in UN reports, which collate the knowledge gained by the experts, the governments, and the UN. The UN expert is primarily an adviser to the government on national policy. But experience has shown that he is most effective when his advice is tested in demonstration projects. This is equally true whether the pilot project be in specific fields, like the use of agricultural surpluses to underwrite community development, or the training of personnel—who, in turn, need guided field experience.

Another aspect of the role of the UN is its own development of comparative data on community-development programs. A Caribbean-Mexico survey looked for the reasons for success and failure in the procedures of working with local groups. It brought out how failure frequently stems from an attempt to put into practice an externally conceived solution for a community problem. Conversely, most successes were scored when the work undertaken reflected an attempt to meet needs defined by the community.

An African survey, involving Liberia, the Gold Coast (now Ghana), the Ivory Coast, French Sudan, Uganda, Upper Volta, and Ruanda-Urundi gave indication that the contribution of community development in Africa may be even more important to mental health than to economic development. Western technology is bringing about revolutionary change, profoundly affecting tribal life. Change, due so largely to external causes, is disturbing, and, even though it results in economic advance, it sometimes contributes to a sense of inferiority and causes deep-seated resentment against those who first introduced the technology. Community development, which enables Africans to make a significant contribution themselves, involves progress on a basis which enhances dignity and self-respect in a changing society. This is increasingly important as more African states enter the world community of nations.

As the UN conveyor belt of expert services, study tours, conferences, surveys, demonstration projects, and evaluative debates by governmental spokesmen continues to deliver insights on community-development values, governments have upgraded community development as a tool for national growth. A UN World Economic

Survey notes that community development has had a measurable economic impact by bringing subsistence areas into the cash economies of a number of countries.

This is a fact of importance for the worker in the welfare, education, health, or farm-service fields. His training and experience have betrayed him if his central concern is not people. The techniques of his field are mere stepping stones in this new pattern. He has professional impact of lasting significance when he is personally integrated in his own thinking and achieves an across-the-board relationship with others.

Like all generalizations, these are susceptible to much qualification. Today, they have the greatest applicability to the underdeveloped countries. Tomorrow, the Western expert may find that he is drawing on this world experience to meet the problems of the automated industrial countries—initially in their pockets of underdevelopment, later in trying to secure human benefit from the new technologies.

### Community Development Endorsed in UN Assembly

The enthusiasm with which leaders of the underdeveloped countries are seeking the kinds of technical assistance represented by UNESCO's work in fundamental education and the UN's community-development program is evidenced by the unanimity with which the assemblies of the two organizations have indorsed these programs. At the spring (1957) meeting of the Social Commission of the Economic and Social Council (ECOSOC), a resolution requesting the Secretary General to continue to report on progress in the community-development field was passed by a vote of 17 to 0, with one member absent. This simply reflected an Assembly resolution adopted by a vote of 67 to 0 on February 21, 1957, which agreed with "the emphasis placed by the Council on community development as a part of the comprehensive measures taken by governments for raising levels of living in rural areas in particular. . . ." In November, 1957, the Twelfth Assembly noted "with satisfaction" that community-development programs "are being carried out or are being planned on a long-term basis with international co-operation."

In the debate which accompanied the consideration of these resolutions of endorsement, many national representatives took the floor to define community development as it operated within his own country and to indorse it both in actuality and in principle.

## Role of the People in Community Development

Different governments and different people may see different approaches to community development. The important fact appears to be that it is possible in almost any underdeveloped area of the world for people to raise their standards of living substantially. Three elements are involved: first, the great body of scientific knowledge now available to man—technical knowledge which, if applied to the problems of people in any environment, will enable them to raise their standards of living. Second, that ability which exists among people in their capacity to make use of their own ideas, their energy, and the resources of their locality. Third, the utilization of democratic processes which lead to a condition of growth. All the UN definitions are in consonance with this viewpoint.

People are the most significant resources in community development. For example, a better agricultural method, a better seed, a better fertilizer will usually increase the yield of cultivated land by only about 5 to 20 per cent. But, if the people of a village will apply their man power to getting control of irrigation or making a road to the market, the effective income of the community is quite commonly doubled. So, the greatest returns in improvements have been made when people and the resources which they represent are the dominant factors.

The United Nations really has not yet applied fully the principles which were set forth in the report of the Secretary General. This report said in effect that community development is a function of all appropriate agencies of government. It should not be the concern of any one department. Leadership at a high level of political insight is required. Within the functions of the United Nations, the logical inference would be that leadership for community development should be provided by the Secretary General of the United Nations; that the policy of encouraging this practice should be carried out through organs of the United Nations and various specialized agencies.

For underdeveloped countries, fundamental education and community development mean a reorienting of the relationship of government to people, so that the historically developed mechanisms of government, which were essentially to maintain order, collect taxes, and keep people down, should be shifted so that their function is to create an environment in which the qualities and capacities of people have an opportunity to grow and develop. And if the United States can more effectively relate itself to the hopes and dreams and aspirations of such emerging people, we could acquire friends and understanding instead of much of the present disillusionment.

There was reference above to the 67 to 0 vote in the Assembly favoring community development. This unanimity occurred when, in adjoining committee rooms, the cold war was frostily evident. It would be unrealistic to suggest that the unanimity on community development was made up of milk and honey, exclusively. There is a philosophic cleavage between the totalitarian regimes and others on the character of government participation in the community-development process. But it is the role of the UN to be the anvil on which these things are hammered out, where possible. And in this case, despite basic political chasms, a unanimous vote was achieved.

This raises the hope that the four hundred experts put into the field by the UN and the other specialized agencies were the forerunners of a new and different kind of international peace army. Their accomplishments are all the more remarkable when one takes into consideration some of the handicaps under which they have to operate. One of these is inadequate financing. The whole United Nations Technical Assistance program, including the expanded program carried out by specialized agencies, operates in all countries on about thirty million dollars a year. It is a highly successful pilot project, but it would require far greater financing in order to have the impact upon the problems of the underdeveloped countries that is needed.

Contrary to the popular belief, the contribution of the United States to the United Nations expanded program of technical assistance, in relation to the national income, is not the highest of any nation. The contribution of the United States for 1958 has amounted to 3.9 thousandths of 1 per cent of national income. There are eighteen nations whose contributions as a percentage of national income are greater. These nations are as follows, and the figures shown refer to thousandths of 1 per cent of national income: Netherlands, 16.3; Denmark, 15.7; Norway, 13.4; Sweden, 9.2; New Zealand, 8.5; Canada, 8.5; Colombia, 7.8; Chile, 6.9; Ghana, 6.9; Australia, 6.0; Switzerland, 5.9; Dominican Republic, 5.7; Belgium, 5.5; Argentina, 5.3; United Kingdom, 4.9; United Arab Republic, 4.6; Haiti, 4.4; and Israel, 4.3.

The principal reason for the limited financing is simply that the United States government does not choose to channel more than a very small proportion of the billions it spends for foreign aid through multilateral programs. The theory that the United States makes more friends abroad through bilateral arrangements seems not to have worked out in practice; nor is it true that the United Nations program could not utilize more funds. In almost every country and each field in which the program operates, the work could be expanded and needs to be expanded in order to reach the least-developed areas of the less-developed countries. Had funds permitted, the community development and fundamental education work would have been greatly expanded and made much more effective. It is alleged that increased United States support of a substantial character would make it so unbalanced as to lose its multilateral character. This reason is not valid. There are a number of governments that now expend on foreign technical assistance amounts many times greater than the total United Nations program. They could shift their emphasis from bilateral aid to more multilateral aid if encouraged to do so by the United States. There are also a number of countries making appropriations of small amounts to the United Nations program which have been receiving billions of dollars from United States aid. A number of these countries would gladly, if supported by the United States, substantially increase their appropriations for the multilateral program. There are literally billions of dollars in counterpart currencies from which UN programs could receive support.

United States surplus commodities, utilized with an understanding of community-development processes, could become a great resource for raising the standards of living for millions of the most underprivileged peoples of the world. In many areas these foods could nourish the physical strength and provide the psychological encouragement for community progress.

If the United Nations can become the major source of the technical personnel which is so vital to the progress of developing nations, it will truly be a greater force for peace.

## The Program Could Be Improved

One can question the wisdom of some of the relationships under which technical assistance has been provided. For example, the receiving country is expected to pay the personal living expenses and the internal transportation costs of the expert. A country receiving technical assistance should be expected to make a substantial contribution, but it is hard to find a basis that is more awkward for the receiving country and more embarrassing for the expert than the present arrangement. There would be a more gracious and tactful relationship if the United Nations paid the necessary living and travel expenses and if the government supported the work by appropriations for the program or projects for which the expert was engaged. It would help if the expert were not restricted to giving advice. As a general rule, the advice-giving relationship is sound, but, nevertheless, there are situations in which the validity of the advice can be established only through demonstrations or pilot projects carried out under expert supervision. This has especial applicability for demonstration projects such as are frequently involved in community development. A nongovernmental organization not limited by traditional restraints can often organize small demonstration projects. After seeing the results, governments often decide that they desire such projects on a national scale. The effectiveness of technical assistance, particularly in community development, would be greater if this were permitted in situations where it is desired by the government and agreed to by the UN.

Some generally accepted methods of working with village people may be based on fallacies. For example, although UNESCO has given great emphasis to the "team approach," it is doubtful that the concept involved is always valid. In a typical village, such a concentration of external ideas is apt to be confusing to the people. Better results may often be obtained from a less concentrated dose of stimulation.

There is some question as to whether the "multipurpose worker," who is considered so indispensable to the program in India, is similarly indispensable in all approaches to community development. In situations where technical services are developed, the need may be, not for a multipurpose worker, but for a *specialist in working with people*. For these community organizers, limited technical knowledge in agriculture, health, and engineering is more likely to be a liability than an asset. Their principal concern must be *with people*—their growth and development—and limited competence in functional fields is quite apt to be a distraction which interferes with their concentration upon the essence of the problem.

One of the most widely accepted principles of community development is that activities undertaken should be based upon the "felt needs" of the people concerned. The universality of agreement on this point in theory is matched only by the infrequency with which it is truly applied in practice. It is probable, however, that there is something more fundamental than the "felt needs" concept. The more fundamental concept is that of respect for people, the recognition of their dignity and their potentialities. The recognition of "felt needs" is only one of the consequences of this basic consideration of respect for people.

SECTION IV

# SUMMARY AND SELECTED READINGS

9. *Communication processes must be watched with care.* A great deal can be said on this most complex of principles. To a large extent, education depends upon communication. As Gray shows in dealing with literacy, there are channels we can now open. The techniques we employ must be chosen with skill in line with the considerations set forth by Dale.

Where individuals of different cultures come into contact, there must be conscious effort to evaluate and improve the ways in which ideas are transmitted and received. Actions, as well as words, can have symbolic meanings which carry messages of which the sender may be unaware. Facility in communicating requires thorough knowledge of languages and cultures. On the spot, it necessitates arrangements for securing "feed-back," as Doob points out. It requires a well-balanced sensitivity to the first signs that reality and daydreams are parting company so that one can discover what is going amiss. This is an area in which some few people are gloriously adept. However, if we are ever to have the numbers and kinds we need, specially organized and demanding programs of education will be required. Subtle influences of which one might not otherwise be aware are tellingly portrayed by Green in his account of problems affecting the technical-assistance programs in Asia. Some ways of preparing leaders to recognize these are the root of "overseasmanship" as discussed by Cleveland.

10. *Any culture in which one works has an integrity, a quality of wholeness, which it is important to understand and to respect.* This does not mean a sentimental refusal to aid in bringing about necessary change. It does mean that any change must be viewed in terms of what it implies for the culture as a whole. Also, the potential community educator needs to master the skills of understanding different ways of life and of guiding change processes which respect difference without negating the value of improvement. He must also be able to perceive the culture in which he is imbedded as well as the one in which he may be working. He must recognize that one change inevitably produces others.

11. *The people in every community need to be able to extend their national citizenship to include world citizenship in the larger community of nations.* This is as true for the inhabitants of now un-

derdeveloped societies as for the technologically most advanced. As Margaret Mead puts it, the goal is to help them cut into the procession near to the head. Green illustrates the same point differently when he speaks of fishermen having direct contact for learning purposes with the practitioners of their calling in advanced countries.

This means that even though in an underdeveloped area a people must first develop literacy in their own conversational tongue, in the world of today at least some will have to tap directly the sources of knowledge embodied in books written in the major languages of science. To open channels for both individual and social growth, many people must become world-mobile, able to work in, gain from, and contribute to the larger world in which they live.

## Problems for American Education

For the educational institutions of the free world, the potential significance of community education raises problems in two somewhat different dimensions. On the one hand, there is need for a citizenry sensitive to the problem and able to support, if not demand, that both national and international agencies work effectively in this area. On the other hand, our colleges and universities must develop programs for producing the experts and leaders who can do the job well.

For the first problem, in this period of concern with education, school people must enlist all possible aid in preserving those aspects of social studies which make for sensitive citizenship. In particular, schools should devote energy to helping young people both to understand the nation in which they live, and be able to see how other peoples look upon the Western countries.

Just as educators are now learning to live with themselves without complacency, we must help the children of the free world to recognize that admiration of them is far from universal and that critical viewpoints have some basis in fact.

More important, this is a time for all people, youth included, to give thought to our fundamental values and to see what programs of action give expression to those values. Inevitably, in considering the very fact that our globe houses underdeveloped countries, that free nations contain within their borders underprivileged regions, that cities contain slums, young people will want to consider also what can be done. If this much necessary education is achieved, clearly the pupils and students will have to learn about community education.

Among those who see this as a need, many may come to see it as a duty, as a vocation which will give more meaning to their lives than some other possibilities. For those who reach this decision now or in the future, our educational institutions must be ready.

This suggests the second question, how our institutions of higher learning may give the necessary training not only to our own citizens but also to the thousands of students from underdeveloped countries who come seeking technological expertness without realizing fully that they need to learn how to educate people to put technology helpfully to work.

For the job to be done right involves not only the construction of curriculums but the collecting of necessary information. Obviously, there are languages of great importance in many countries for which instruction is not readily available in the Western world. Even for languages known and taught, we need to consider seriously whether there should not be more emphasis upon developing competence in the communication of technical information rather than an appreciation of literary masterpieces. Be that as it may, we clearly need to tackle the entire problem of linguistic competency, particularly in reference to Asia and Africa.

Along with this must go an equal emphasis upon anthropology and those sciences which further an understanding of cultures. This would be sterile if we did not also tackle the problem of how men and women can learn to communicate well and live fruitfully in cultures other than their own.

There is a question, too, of values of living. The young American whose highest values are derived from luxury living, as symbolized by the Cadillac, Lincoln, or Chrysler, is bound to feel ill at ease, if not resentful, when asked to live in the style which would be "one of us" to an Afghan, Burman, or Ghanian. Perhaps if he had decided for himself what makes a life worth living, if he felt he was making the world better for freedom by toiling in self-imposed discomfort, he would be a better ambassador and a happier man. We wonder, perhaps hesitatingly, how many of his professors today would look on him with pride. So, possibly, there is a rather sticky task of self-re-education on the faculty level.

## Conclusion

As we review the road traveled in this study of community education, we recognize how much educational thought is all of one piece. Just as Donne, in his "for whom the bell tolls" couplet, declares that the loss of one life detracts from all, so we may find that the betterment of any is a gain for all.

As we concentrate thought on finding ways of helping other people improve their living, we are making discoveries we can apply at home. The ultimate goal is to aid them to achieve human dignity. Could we want more than this for ourselves?

HAYDEN, HOWARD. *Moturiki: A Pilot Project in Community Development.* London: Oxford University Press, 1954. Pp. 180.

A complete description of an experiment in community development on a small South Pacific island. The project was developed by a trained native team and lasted for a limited period. The author, who directed the project, draws conclusions from the experiments in the final chapter.

HUGHES, LLOYD H. *The Mexican Cultural Mission Programme.* Monographs in Fundamental Education, No. III. Paris: UNESCO, 1950. Pp. 77.

Reviews the historical background of the cultural missions; describes the organization and program; gives examples of typical missions at work and an assessment of achievements and problems.

INDIA PLANNING COMMISSION, COMMUNITY PROJECTS ADMINISTRATION. *Manual on Social Education.* Delhi: The Commission, 1955. Pp. 104.

A handbook of suggestions for social education workers; deals with aims and nature of social education, describes functions of the social education officers, and reproduces useful resource materials for carrying out the practical task.

LAIDLAW, ALEX. *A Factual Outline of the Antigonish Movement.* Antigonish, Nova Scotia: St. Francis Xavier University, Extension Department, 1952. Pp. 27.

Among the problems which faced Nova Scotia, New Brunswick, and Prince Edward Island, the most serious were the emigration of the youth and the uneconomical methods of marketing local produce. In 1929 the Extension Department was founded and launched its program to overcome these difficulties through co-operative action and adult education. The various aspects of this program are briefly described, and examples of successful achievement are cited.

MARIER, ROGER. *Social Welfare Work in Jamaica.* Monographs in Fundamental Education, No. VII. Paris: UNESCO, 1954. Pp. 165.

A detailed study of the work of the Jamaica Social Welfare Commission from its inception up to the date of publication. The commission carried out a diversified program of social, cultural, and economic development; its approach is based on self-help, group work, community organization, and community education.

MILBURN, S. *Methods and Techniques of Community Development in the United Kingdom Dependent and Trust Territories: A Study Prepared for the United Nations.* (Series on Community Organization and Development, ST/SOA/Ser.O/21; ST/TAA/Ser.D/21.) New York: United Nations, 1954. Pp. 111.

A comprehensive analytical study of the subject. Describes the evolution of the concept and formulation of government policy; the various methods and techniques adopted for community development according to local needs and conditions.

ORATA, PEDRO T. *Fundamental Education in an Amerindian Community.* Washington: Bureau of Indian Affairs, U.S. Department of the Interior, 1953. Pp. 220.

Describes the work undertaken in an Indian reservation to establish a community school through the joint effort of the staff, the school children, and the adults to implement a program aiming at self-support, self-government, better housing, better health, and improvement of native culture.

RUOPP, PHILIPPS. *Approaches to Community Development.* A symposium introductory to problems and methods in village welfare in underdeveloped areas. The Hague: W. van Hove, Ltd., 1953. Pp. 352.

Aspects considered are the sociology and economics of community development and education for community development. The contribution by non-governmental organizations to community development is discussed.

"The Scope and Nature of Fundamental Education," *Fundamental and Adult Education,* IX (April, 1957), 51–59.

Gives the new definition of fundamental education adopted by UNESCO and its relationships wtih community development.

*Social Progress through Community Development.* New York: United Nations Bureau of Social Affairs, 1955. Pp. 120.

Five main sections deal respectively with: definition and content of community development, community development and international assistance, and community development as a world-wide trend; types of community welfare centers, institutions, and programs; national programs; methods used in community development; and training local leaders.

*Study Kit on Training for Community Development.* New York: United Nations Department of Economic and Social Affairs, 1957. Pp. 69.

Sets out some of the general principles for the training of personnel for community development, methods of selection, and technique of training. The annexes contain descriptions of practical experiences in different parts of the world.

THOMSON, R. *Educational Aspects of Community Development.* Technical Paper No. 74. Noumea, New Caledonia: South Pacific Commission, 1955. Pp. 89.

A compilation from existing sources. Its aim is to give departmental officers of the South Pacific Commission some account of what is going on in this field in other parts of the world.

U.S. OFFICE OF EDUCATION. *Education for Better Living: The Role of the School in Community Betterment.* Yearbook on Education around the World, 1957. Washington: Government Printing Office, 1957. Pp. 339.

Group accounts by different authors of a wide range of programs—the school, adult-education projects, leadership training, etc.—showing a world-wide trend toward relating education to community needs and educating communities for improving their own conditions.

*World Illiteracy at Mid-Century: A Statistical Study.* Monographs on Fundamental Education, No. XI. Paris: UNESCO, 1957. Pp. 200.

A world-wide survey of illiteracy based on official statistics. After reviewing the situation by groups of countries and territories, the study turns to examine the relationship between illiteracy and school enrolment, national income, and urban industrialization.

PERIODICALS

*Community Development Bulletin.* Quarterly. (London: Community Development Clearing House, University of London, Institute of Education.)

*Fundamental and Adult Education.* Quarterly. (Paris: UNESCO.)

# INDEX

# Index

Adapting school program to community setting, 363–64

Adult reading, measurement of, 143–45

Agricultural assistance, frequent failures in, 22–23

Agricultural extension education, assistance of land-grant colleges in development of, 48

Agricultural improvement measures in underdeveloped countries, difficulties encountered in, 22–23

American Technical Co-operation Administration, bilateral-assistance programs of, 170

Anchau development scheme in Nigeria, failure of well-planned project in, 39

Ancient wells and cisterns, use of, in modern technical-assistance program, 41

Application of workshop techniques to problems of secondary education in India, 360

Arab States Fundamental Education Center: education of the masses through, 325–27; origin of, 310; recruitment of students for, 331–32; regular courses in, 327–30

Asian-African Solidarity Conference in Cairo, 65

Asian villager, problems of, 191–94

Basic education: definition of, 38; and social education in India, proposals made by Ghandi for, 58–60

Bilateral assistance programs in aid of underdeveloped countries, 170–71

Bilateral programs in education, advantages and disadvantages of, 187–90

Bilateral programs, relation of, to multilateral procedures, 190–91

Bodet, Torres, 175, 307

Brook Farm Colony, 46

Buddhist and Islamic missionaries, stimulation of advances in literacy by, 45–46

Carry-over of workshop practices in India, 366

Case studies of cultural adaptation to the more sophisticated mores of newly contacted populations, 79–90

*Centres of Attraction*, multipurpose program aiming at community development in French Africa through, 38

Changes involved in introducing literacy to an uneducated population, 70–73

Channels of communication to adults in underdeveloped areas: relation of, to community education, 103–4; significance of feedback in connection with, 105

Chiang, Kai-shek, promotion of popular interest in education, sanitation, and community development by, 52

Colombo Plan of the British Commonwealth, 170; of technical assistance for under developed areas initiated by representatives of British Commonwealth of Nations, report of case studies of contributions of various voluntary organizations to, 237–46

Committee on Co-ordination of the Economic and Social Council of the United Nations, redefinition of fundamental education by, 175

Community-center concept, use of, by California Catholic Missions in cultural transformation by persuasion, 43–44

Community centers for Indians in Mexico, 43

Community development: defined, 384–86; movement in villages and cities of Greece, 379–81; program of the United Nations, origin of, 379; relation of literacy programs to, 23–24; use of, by Incas to impose their culture upon conquered peoples, 39–40

Community education: development of, 3–4; and development among displaced people of Marshall Islands, 220–30; emphasis of, in the United States, on agricultural improvement and rural standards of living, 47–48; reorientation of work of extension agencies involved in using new methods and new approaches to existing problems, 334; social significance of, 11–13; variety of motivational bases for, in different countries, 62–63; viewed as aid to and beneficiary of technical-assistance program, 261–63

Community-improvement projects of elementary- and high-school pupils successfully co-ordinated with science and other school subjects, 166–69

Community schools in the Philippines, development of health and sanitation in, 152–56

Compost fertilizer, increased productivity of gardening activities of school children through experimentation with, 158–62

County agent programs, use of demonstration techniques in, 49

Cultural anthropology, contributions of, to community education, 73–76

Cultural change: by Mitamae system of Incas, 39–40; social and economic causes of, 13–18

Cultural transformation: by cultural missions in Mexico, 55–58; by force, under dictator regimes, 39

Democratic community organization, as ultimate object of community education, 20

Developing attitudes and skills, 373

Drives representing evaluative reaction of learner to acceptance or rejection of newer or older form of behavior, factors determining degree of satisfaction or dissatisfaction with, 109–12

Economic development of Yap District in Pacific Islands territory, enlistment of services of school children in, 234–36

Evaluation: of programs for community education, 36–37; of results of teaching, 286–87

Externalization-internalization, significance of, in comparative reactions of native and alien observers to new forms of behavior, 108

Factors affecting learning among people of underdeveloped areas, 99–100

Factors limiting progress of technical-assistance projects, methods of overcoming obstacles to normal progress in such situations, 249–59

Filho, Lorenco, 307

Firka movement in South India, 195

Folkhouse, use of, in cultural transformation movement in Turkey, 53–55

Food and Agriculture Organization, 64, 309

Fourier, Charles, organization of co-operative villages by, 46

Functional literacy, definition of, 118

Fundamental education: definition of, 307–8; redefined in recognition of services of UN Specialized Agencies, 311; similarity of, to other movements envisioning community development, 38; UNESCO support for, in various parts of the world, 124–26; unique significance of, as envisaged by UNESCO, 39; value of services of women in programs of, 35–36

Ghandi, M. K., proposals for basic and social education in India initiated by, 58–60, 196

Good-neighbor policy of Franklin Roosevelt, 173

Gray, William S., 23

Group-training scheme for fundamental education in India, 130–31

Handwriting, the teaching of, 142–43

Holmes, Henry W., 307

Hughes, Richard, 64

Industrial revolution: impact of, on community education, 46–47; influence of, on community-education programs in the United States, 46

Institute for Inter-American Affairs, 173

Instructional materials: for the Philippines, 295–97; for use in United States, 294–95

Inter-American Educational Foundation: relationship of, to community education, 178; contributions of, to community education in America, 177-79

International Labor Organization, 64

International technical-assistance programs in behalf of underdeveloped countries, 170-71

Kemal, Mustafa, cultural transformations in Turkey under leadership of, 53-55

Knapp, Seaman A., promotion of agricultural extension work by, 49

Land-grant colleges in the United States, 48

Language problems in underdeveloped countries, 23-25

Latin-American Fundamental Education Press, purpose and organization of, 298-99, 308-9

Laubach, Frank: literacy campaign of, in the Philippines, 52-53; reading materials for adults, prepared by, 136

Leaders, role of, in the introduction of new forms of behavior in relatively backward societies, 99-103

Learning to read, benefits derived from, 23-24

Levels of literacy, 128-29

Literacy: importance of, in community development, 23-24; role of, in community education, 126-27

Literacy campaigns: relation of, to public education in the Philippines, 131-32; in the Soviet Union, 60-62

Literacy instruction, organization of, 136-37

Literacy statistics on population of the Philippines following Spanish-American War, 149

Local responsibility for community participation in development of educational programs in Trust Territory of Pacific Islands, 231-33

London School of Oriental Languages, 31

Lorge, Irving, 144

Manus of the Admiralty Islands, 84-86

Mass education: definition of, as defined by the British, 38; movement in China, 51-52

Materials of instruction, factors influencing decisions of school officials with respect to, 283-84

Mead, Margaret, 14, 37

Media of instruction, importance of, in relation to community education, 288-91

Medieval monasteries, stimulation of community development by exchange of ideas through, 42-43

Mexican Cultural Missions, 33

Motivational basis for community education in different countries, 62-63

Multipurpose village workers in Asia, 201-3

National Advisory Committee on Illiteracy appointed by President Hoover, 123

National development program of Greece, 38

National literacy campaigns in various areas after World War I, 122-24

Neijs, Karel, 130, 135

New health practices, influence of, on community development in underdeveloped areas, 20-22

Newer procedures in technical schools of Pakistan, 369

Nongovernmental agencies, offers of technical assistance to underprivileged populations by, 170-71

Orata, Pedro, 33

Organization of American States, collaboration of, with UNESCO in developing training centers for promotion of fundamental-education programs under UNESCO, 308

Overseas employment, training programs for, 30-32, 335-39, 344-46

Payne, E. George, 210

Penn School at St. Helena (South Carolina), 49-51

People of underdeveloped countries, influence of fundamental education and community development programs of United Nations upon, 389-92

Pope County (Illinois) development program, a case study of community participation in proposed up-grading of various public and private agencies in period of economic depression, 268–71

Poverty and chronic illnesses, effects of, on progressive economic deterioration of underdeveloped countries, 4–6

Preparation of literacy materials in Jamaica, 300

Principles of acculturation deduced from anthropological approaches to change, 73–79, 91–93

Principles governing procedures to be adopted in planning for the development of effective community education in underdeveloped areas, 397–401

Principles of selection and organization of instructional materials, 287

Problems of American education, 402–3

Program providing technical assistance for less-developed societies, proposed by Harry S. Truman, 64–65

Protestant missionary movements in England and America, stimulation of improvements in health, education, and agriculture by, 45

Psychological factors related to community education, summarization of, 117–18

Psychological principles involved in the acculturation of relatively unsophisticated populations, 97–100

Puerto Rico Reconstruction Administration, accomplishments of, 15–17

Racial theories of inferiority, effects of, on cultural change, 67–68

Regional Fundamental Education Center for Latin America (CREFAL): academic curriculum and program of field work in, 315–19; graduates of, 323–25; history of, 312–14; primary function of, 320–22; problems of villages in area of, 314–15

Revolutionary trends of early twentieth century, 7–9

Road-building by medieval monks, as a type of community education, 42

Rochdale Pioneer movement, as an example of co-operative enterprise among workers in food distribution, 46

Rockefeller, Nelson, 173

Roman Empire, expansion of, as illustration of modern technical-assistance program, 40–41

Save the Children Federation of New York, self-help program of, on behalf of underprivileged children in the United States and overseas, 207–16

Selection of trainees for participation in overseasmanship service under auspices of UNESCO and UN, prevailing need for more consideration of training provided for, 344–46

Self-government, importance of local initiative in, 34–35

Self-help practices in community-development movements, 11–13

Self-help programs, emphasis upon, in technical-assistance projects for community development, 176

Servicio system of bilateral programs in the field of education, 183–84

Settlement houses, movement promoting self-improvement practices through, 47

Significance of cultural change as a factor in community education, 39

Social and community service in schools of India, 364–65

Social education, purposes of, in India, 38

Southern Illinois University Department of Community Development, effective planning for desirable reorganization of rural school system of Pope County (Illinois) with technical assistance of, 272–75

Soviet countries, recent offers of technical assistance to underdeveloped countries by, 170–71

Teacher education in bilateral programs, 184–85

Teaching adults to read, recognized aims of, 135–36

Technical assistance, relationship of community education to values of, 261–64

Technical co-operation in Latin America established by United States government in 1939, 172–73

Ten-fold self-help plan established by the Save the Children Federation operating on principle of minimum external aid, 207–16
Trainees for technical-assistance projects, problems of recruitment of, for overseas service, 260–61
Training program at University of London, objectives of, 335–36
Truman's Point IV proposal, 173
Trusteeship for administration of Micronesia: agreement for, 217; objectives of, 217–20

Underdeveloped countries, effects of widespread chronic illnesses and poverty on further deterioration of, 4–6
UNESCO: General Conference, development of centers for training teachers approved by, 308; group-training scheme for fundamental education, 130; programs of fundamental education, 179; reports providing basis for estimating extent of illiteracy, 124–25; world-wide study of teaching of reading and writing by, 133–34
United Nations: as an agency of government, 386–88; Expanded Program of Technical Assistance, relation of, to UNESCO programs of fundamental education, 309, 311; Relief and Rehabilitation Administration, objectives of, 379–81
United States: Department of Agriculture, influence of, on community-school programs in farming areas, 48; Technical Co-operation Program, 310
University of London Institute of Education, emphasis on comparative studies of community-education approaches and methods in, 334–39
Urban rehabilitation: inadequate promotion of, 18–19; types of, in underdeveloped countries, 18–19

Variability in responsiveness of different racial groups to opportunities for learning, 97–99
Vasco de Quirigo, 43
Vasconselos, José, movement for the education of the masses and the redemption of the Indians started by, 55–58
Village people of India, government co-operation with, 199
"Villages of Co-operation and Union" established by Robert Owen in response to impact of industrial revolution on educational and social improvement, 46
Villages of India, government leadership in improvement of, 195–97

Watson, Elkanah W., and the Berkshire Agricultural Society, 48
Winslow, C. E. A., 4
Workshop procedures in India, 361–62, 367–68
World Health Organization, participation of, in programs of fundamental education, 64, 309

Yen, James C., 51, 52, 309

# INFORMATION CONCERNING THE NATIONAL SOCIETY FOR THE STUDY OF EDUCATION

1. PURPOSE. The purpose of the National Society is to promote the investigation and discussion of educational questions. To this end it holds an annual meeting and publishes a series of yearbooks.

2. ELIGIBILITY TO MEMBERSHIP. Any person who is interested in receiving its publications may become a member by sending to the Secretary-Treasurer information concerning name, title, and address, and a check for $6.00 (see Item 5).

Membership is not transferable; it is limited to individuals, and may not be held by libraries, schools, or other institutions, either directly or indirectly.

3. PERIOD OF MEMBERSHIP. Applicants for membership may not date their entrance back of the current calendar year, and all memberships terminate automatically on December 31, unless the dues for the ensuing year are paid as indicated in Item 6.

4. DUTIES AND PRIVILEGES OF MEMBERS. Members pay dues of $5.00 annually, receive a cloth-bound copy of each publication, are entitled to vote, to participate in discussion, and (under certain conditions) to hold office. The names of members are printed in the yearbooks.

Persons who are sixty years of age or above may become life members on payment of fee based on average life-expectancy of their age group. For information, apply to Secretary-Treasurer.

5. ENTRANCE FEE. New members are required the first year to pay, in addition to the dues, an entrance fee of one dollar.

6. PAYMENT OF DUES. Statements of dues are rendered in October for the following calendar year. Any member so notified whose dues remain unpaid on January 1, thereby loses his membership and can be reinstated only by paying a reinstatement fee of fifty cents.

School warrants and vouchers from institutions must be accompanied by definite information concerning the name and address of the person for whom membership fee is being paid. Statements of dues are rendered on our own form only. The Secretary's office cannot undertake to fill out special invoice forms of any sort or to affix notary's affidavit to statements or receipts.

Cancelled checks serve as receipts. Members desiring an additional receipt must enclose a stamped and addressed envelope therefor.

7. DISTRIBUTION OF YEARBOOKS TO MEMBERS. The yearbooks, ready prior to each February meeting, will be mailed from the office of the distributors, only to members whose dues for that year have been paid. Members who desire yearbooks prior to the current year must purchase them directly from the distributors (see Item 8).

8. COMMERCIAL SALES. The distribution of all yearbooks prior to the current year, and also of those of the current year not regularly mailed to members in exchange for their dues, is in the hands of the distributor, not of the Secretary. For such commercial sales, communicate directly with the University of Chicago Press, Chicago 37, Illinois, which will gladly send a price list covering all the publications of this Society. This list is also printed in the yearbook.

9. YEARBOOKS. The yearbooks are issued about one month before the February meeting. They comprise from 600 to 800 pages annually. Unusual effort has been made to make them, on the one hand, of immediate practical value, and, on the other hand, representative of sound scholarship and scientific investigation.

10. MEETINGS. The annual meeting, at which the yearbooks are discussed, is held in February at the same time and place as the meeting of the American Association of School Administrators.

Applications for membership will be handled promptly at any time on receipt of name and address, together with check for $6.00 (or $5.50 for reinstatement). Applications entitle the new members to the yearbook slated for discussion during the calendar year the application is made.

5835 Kimbark Ave.     NELSON B. HENRY, *Secretary-Treasurer*
Chicago 37, Illinois

i

# PUBLICATIONS OF THE NATIONAL SOCIETY FOR THE STUDY OF EDUCATION

NOTICE: Many of the early yearbooks of this series are now out of print. In the following list, those titles to which an asterisk is prefixed are not available for purchase.

POSTPAID
PRICE

*First Yearbook, 1902, Part I—*Some Principles in the Teaching of History.* Lucy M. Salmon....
*First Yearbook, 1902, Part II—*The Progress of Geography in the Schools.* W. M. Davis and H. M. Wilson................
*Second Yearbook, 1903, Part I—*The Course of Study in History in the Common School.* Isabel Lawrence, C. A. McMurry, Frank McMurry, E. C. Page, and E. J. Rice................
*Second Yearbook, 1903, Part II—*The Relation of Theory to Practice in Education.* M. J. Holmes, J. A. Keith, and Levi Seeley................
Third Yearbook, 1904, Part I—*The Relation of Theory to Practice in the Education of Teachers.* John Dewey, Sarah C. Brooks, F. M. McMurry, et al................ $0.53
Third Yearbook, 1904, Part II—*Nature Study.* W. S. Jackman................ .85
Fourth Yearbook, 1905, Part I—*The Education and Training of Secondary Teachers.* E. C. Elliott, E. G. Dexter, M. J. Holmes, et al................ .85
*Fourth Yearbook, 1905, Part II—*The Place of Vocational Subjects in the High-School Curriculum.* J. S. Brown, G. B. Morrison, and Ellen Richards................
*Fifth Yearbook, 1906, Part I—*On the Teaching of English in Elementary and High Schools.* G. P. Brown and Emerson Davis................
*Fifth Yearbook, 1906, Part II—*The Certification of Teachers.* E. P. Cubberley................
*Sixth Yearbook, 1907, Part I—*Vocational Studies for College Entrance.* C. A. Herrick, H. W. Holmes, T. deLaguna, V. Prettyman, and W. J. S. Bryan................
*Sixth Yearbook, 1907, Part II—*The Kindergarten and Its Relation to Elementary Education.* Ada Van Stone Harris, E. A. Kirkpatrick, Marie Kraus-Boelté, Patty S. Hill, Harriette M. Mills, and Nina Vandewalker................
Seventh Yearbook, 1908, Part I—*The Relation of Superintendents and Principals to the Training and Professional Improvement of Their Teachers.* Charles D. Lowry................ .78
Seventh Yearbook, 1908, Part II—*The Co-ordination of the Kindergarten and the Elementary School.* B. J. Gregory, Jennie B. Merrill, Bertha Payne, and Margaret Giddings............ .78
Eighth Yearbook, 1909, Parts I and II—*Education with Reference to Sex.* C. R. Henderson and Helen C. Putnam. Both parts................ 1.60
*Ninth Yearbook, 1910, Part I—*Health and Education.* T. D. Wood................
*Ninth Yearbook, 1910, Part II—*The Nurse in Education.* T. D. Wood, et al................
*Tenth Yearbook, 1911, Part I—*The City School as a Community Center.* H. C. Leipziger, Sarah E. Hyre, R. D. Warden, C. Ward Crampton, E. W. Stitt, E. J. Ward, Mrs. E. C. Grice, and C. A. Perry................
*Tenth Yearbook, 1911, Part II—*The Rural School as a Community Center.* B. H. Crocheron, Jessie Field, F. W. Howe, E. C. Bishop, A. B. Graham, O. J. Kern, M. T. Scudder, and B. M. Davis................
*Eleventh Yearbook, 1912, Part I—*Industrial Education: Typical Experiments Described and Interpreted.* J. F. Barker, M. Bloomfield, B. W. Johnson, P. Johnson, L. M. Leavitt, G. A. Mirick, M. W. Murray, C. F. Perry, A. L. Safford, and H. B. Wilson................
*Eleventh Yearbook, 1912, Part II—*Agricultural Education in Secondary Schools.* A. C. Monahan, R. W. Stimson, D. J. Crosby, W. H. French, H. F. Button, F. R. Crane, W. R. Hart, and G. F. Warren................
*Twelfth Yearbook, 1913, Part I—*The Supervision of City Schools.* Franklin Bobbitt, J. W. Hall, and J. D. Wolcott................
*Twelfth Yearbook, 1913, Part II—*The Supervision of Rural Schools.* A. C. Monahan, L. J. Hanifan, J. E. Warren, Wallace Lund, U. J. Hoffman, A. S. Cook, E. M. Rapp, Jackson Davis, and J. D. Wolcott................
Thirteenth Yearbook, 1914, Part I—*Some Aspects of High-School Instruction and Administration.* H. C. Morrison, E. R. Breslich, W. A. Jessup, and L. D. Coffman................ .85
Thirteenth Yearbook, 1914, Part II—*Plans for Organizing School Surveys, with a Summary of Typical School Surveys.* Charles H. Judd and Henry L. Smith................ .79
Fourteenth Yearbook, 1915, Part I—*Minimum Essentials in Elementary School Subjects—Standards and Current Practices.* H. B. Wilson, H. W. Holmes, F. E. Thompson, R. G. Jones, S. A. Courtis, W. S. Gray, F. N. Freeman, H. C. Pryor, J. F. Hosic, W. A. Jessup, and W. C. Bagley .85
Fourteenth Yearbook, 1915, Part II—*Methods for Measuring Teachers' Efficiency.* Arthur C. Boyce................ .79
*Fifteenth Yearbook, 1916, Part I—*Standards and Tests for the Measurement of the Efficiency of Schools and School Systems.* G. D. Strayer, Bird T. Baldwin, B. R. Buckingham, F. W. Ballou, D. C. Bliss, H. G. Childs, S. A. Courtis, E. P. Cubberley, C. H. Judd, George Melcher, E. E. Oberholtzer, J. B. Sears, Daniel Starch, M. R. Trabue, and G. M. Whipple................
*Fifteenth Yearbook, 1916, Part II—*The Relationship between Persistence in School and Home Conditions.* Charles E. Holley................
*Fifteenth Yearbook, 1916, Part III—*The Junior High School.* Aubrey A. Douglass................

POSTPAID
PRICE

*Sixteenth Yearbook, 1917, Part I—*Second Report of the Committee on Minimum Essentials in Elementary-School Subjects.* W. C. Bagley, W. W. Charters, F. N. Freeman, W. S. Gray, Ernest Horn, J. H. Hoskinson, W. S. Monroe, C. F. Munson, H. C. Pryor, L. W. Rapeer, G. M. Wilson, and H. B. Wilson...............................................................

*Sixteenth Yearbook, 1917, Part II—*The Efficiency of College Students as Conditioned by Age at Entrance and Size of High School.* B. F. Pittenger........................................................

Seventeenth Yearbook, 1918, Part I—*Third Report of the Committee on Economy of Time in Education.* W. C. Bagley, B. B. Bassett, M. E. Branom, Alice Camerer, J. E. Dealey, C. A. Ellwood, E. B. Greene, A. B. Hart, J. F. Hosic, E. T. Housh, W. H. Mace, L. R. Marston, H. C. McKown, H. E. Mitchell, W. C. Reavis, D. Snedden, and H. B. Wilson............ $0.85

*Seventeenth Yearbook, 1918, Part II—*The Measurement of Educational Products.* E. J. Ashbaugh, W. A. Averill, L. P. Ayers, F. W. Ballou, Edna Bryner, B. R. Buckingham, S. A. Courtis, M. E. Haggerty, C. H. Judd, George Melcher, W. S. Monroe, E. A. Nifenecker, and E. L. Thorndike.....................................................................

*Eighteenth Yearbook, 1919, Part I—*The Professional Preparation of High-School Teachers.* G. N. Cade, S. S. Colvin, Charles Fordyce, H. H. Foster, T. S. Gosling, W. S. Gray, L. V. Koos, A. R. Mead, H. L. Miller, F. C. Whitcomb, and Clifford Woody.................

Eighteenth Yearbook, 1919, Part II—*Fourth Report of Committee on Economy of Time in Education.* F. C. Ayer, F. N. Freeman, W. S. Gray, Ernest Horn, W. S. Monroe, and C. E. Seashore   1.10

*Nineteenth Yearbook, 1920, Part I—*New Materials of Instruction.* Prepared by the Society's Committee on Materials of Instruction.............................................

*Nineteenth Yearbook, 1920, Part II—*Classroom Problems in the Education of Gifted Children.* T. S. Henry.....................................................................................

*Twentieth Yearbook, 1921, Part I—*New Materials of Instruction.* Second Report by the Society's Committee.........................................................................

*Twentieth Yearbook, 1921, Part II—*Report of the Society's Committee on Silent Reading.* M. A. Burgess, S. A. Courtis, C. E. Germane, W. S. Gray, H. A. Greene, Regina R. Heller, J. H. Hoover, J. A. O'Brien, J. L. Packer, Daniel Starch, W. W. Theisen, G. A. Yoakam, and representatives of other school systems............................................................

*Twenty-first Yearbook, 1922, Parts I and II—*Intelligence Tests and Their Use.* Part I—*The Nature, History, and General Principles of Intelligence Testing.* E. L. Thorndike, S. S. Colvin, Harold Rugg, G. M. Whipple, Part II—*The Administrative Use of Intelligence Tests,* H. W. Holmes, W. K. Layton, Helen Davis, Agnes L. Rogers, Rudolf Pintner, M. R. Trabue, W. S. Miller, Bessie L. Gambrill, and others. The two parts are bound together.................

*Twenty-second Yearbook, 1923, Part I—*English Composition: Its Aims, Methods, and Measurements.* Earl Hudelson.....................................................................

*Twenty-second Yearbook, 1923, Part II—*The Social Studies in the Elementary and Secondary School.* A. S. Barr, J. J. Coss, Henry Harap, R. W. Hatch, H. C. Hill, Ernest Horn, C. H. Judd, L. C. Marshall, F. M. McMurry, Earle Rugg, H. O. Rugg, Emma Schweppe, Mabel Snedaker, and C. W. Washburne........................................................

*Twenty-third Yearbook, 1924, Part I—*The Education of Gifted Children.* Report of the Society's Committee. Guy M. Whipple, Chairman...................................................

*Twenty-third Yearbook, 1924, Part II—*Vocational Guidance and Vocational Education for Industries.* A. H. Edgerton and Others...............................................................

Twenty-fourth Yearbook, 1925, Part I—*Report of the National Committee on Reading.* W. S. Gray, Chairman, F. W. Ballou, Rose L. Hardy, Ernest Horn, Francis Jenkins, S. A. Leonard, Estaline Wilson, and Laura Zirbes.......................................................   1.50

*Twenty-fourth Yearbook, 1925, Part II—*Adapting the Schools to Individual Differences.* Report of the Society's Committee. Carleton W. Washburne, Chairman...........................

*Twenty-fifth Yearbook, 1926, Part I—*The Present Status of Safety Education.* Report of the Society's Committee. Guy M. Whipple, Chairman..........................................

*Twenty-fifth Yearbook, 1926, Part II—*Extra-curricular Activities.* Report of the Society's Committee. Leonard V. Koos, Chairman.........................................................

*Twenty-sixth Yearbook, 1927, Part I—*Curriculum-making: Past and Present.* Report of the Society's Committee. Harold O. Rugg, Chairman...............................................

*Twenty-sixth Yearbook, 1927, Part II—*The Foundations of Curriculum-making.* Prepared by individual members of the Society's Committee. Harold O. Rugg, Chairman.............

Twenty-seventh Yearbook, 1928, Part I—*Nature and Nurture: Their Influence upon Intelligence.* Prepared by the Society's Committee. Lewis M. Terman, Chairman...............   1.75

Twenty-seventh Yearbook, 1928, Part II—*Nature and Nurture: Their Influence upon Achievement.* Prepared by the Society's Committee. Lewis M. Terman, Chairman...............   1.75

Twenty-eighth Yearbook, 1929. Parts I and II—*Preschool and Parental Education.* Part I—*Organization and Development.* Part II—*Research and Method.* Prepared by the Society's Committee. Lois H. Meek, Chairman. Bound in one volume. Cloth...................   5.00
   Paper..........................................................................................   3.25

Twenty-ninth Yearbook, 1930, Parts I and II—*Report of the Society's Committee on Arithmetic.* Part I—*Some Aspects of Modern Thought on Arithmetic.* Part II—*Research in Arithmetic.* Prepared by the Society's Committee. F. B. Knight, Chairman. Bound in one volume. Cloth   5.00
   Paper..........................................................................................   3.25

Thirtieth Yearbook, 1931, Part I—*The Status of Rural Education.* First Report of the Society's Committee on Rural Education. Orville G. Brim, Chairman. Cloth.....................   2.50
   Paper..........................................................................................   1.75

Thirtieth Yearbook, 1931, Part II—*The Textbook in American Education.* Report of the Society's Committee on the Textbook. J. B. Edmonson, Chairman. Cloth.........................   2.50
   Paper..........................................................................................   1.75

Thirty-first Yearbook, 1932, Part I—*A Program for Teaching Science.* Prepared by the Society's Committee on the Teaching of Science. S. Ralph Powers, Chairman. Cloth..............   2.50
   Paper..........................................................................................   1.75

Thirty-first Yearbook, 1932, Part II—*Changes and Experiments in Liberal-Arts Education.* Prepared by Kathryn McHale, with numerous collaborators. Cloth...................   2.50
   Paper..........................................................................................   1.75

POSTPAID
PRICE

Thirty-second Yearbook, 1933—*The Teaching of Geography*. Prepared by the Society's Committee on the Teaching of Geography. A. E. Parkins, Chairman. Cloth.................. $4.50
Paper........................................................................ 3.00
Thirty-third Yearbook, 1934, Part I—*The Planning and Construction of School Buildings*. Prepared by the Society's Committee on School Buildings. N. L. Engelhardt, Chairman. Cloth 2.50
Paper........................................................................ 1.75
Thirty-third Yearbook, 1934, Part II—*The Activity Movement*. Prepared by the Society's Committee on the Activity Movement. Lois Coffey Mossman, Chairman. Cloth.............. 2.50
Paper........................................................................ 1.75
Thirty-fourth Yearbook, 1935—*Educational Diagnosis*. Prepared by the Society's Committee on Educational Diagnosis. L. J. Brueckner, Chairman. Cloth........................... 4.25
Paper........................................................................ 3.00
Thirty-fifth Yearbook, 1936, Part I—*The Grouping of Pupils*. Prepared by the Society's Committee. W. W. Coxe, Chairman. Cloth............................................ 2.50
*Thirty-fifth Yearbook, 1936, Part II—*Music Education*. Prepared by the Society's Committee. W. L. Uhl, Chairman. Cloth.............................................
Paper........................................................................
Thirty-sixth Yearbook, 1937, Part I—*The Teaching of Reading*. Prepared by the Society's Committee. W. S. Gray, Chairman. Cloth........................................... 2.50
Paper........................................................................ 1.75
Thirty-sixth Yearbook, 1937, Part II—*International Understanding through the Public-School Curriculum*. Prepared by the Society's Committee. I. L. Kandel, Chairman. Cloth........ 2.50
Paper........................................................................ 1.75
Thirty-seventh Yearbook, 1938, Part I—*Guidance in Educational Institutions*. Prepared by the Society's Committee. G. N. Kefauver, Chairman. Cloth............................. 2.50
Paper........................................................................ 1.75
Thirty-seventh Yearbook, 1938, Part II—*The Scientific Movement in Education*. Prepared by the Society's Committee. F. N. Freeman, Chairman. Cloth............................. 4.00
Paper........................................................................ 3.00
Thirty-eighth Yearbook, 1939, Part I—*Child Development and the Curriculum*. Prepared by the Society's Committee. Carleton Washburne, Chairman. Cloth......................... 3.25
Paper........................................................................ 2.50
Thirty-eighth Yearbook, 1939, Part II—*General Education in the American College*. Prepared by the Society's Committee. Alvin Eurich, Chairman. Cloth............................. 2.75
Paper........................................................................ 2.00
Thirty-ninth Yearbook, 1940, Part I—*Intelligence: Its Nature and Nurture. Comparative and Critical Exposition*. Prepared by the Society's Committee. G. D. Stoddard, Chairman. Cloth 3.00
Paper........................................................................ 2.25
Thirty-ninth Yearbook, 1940, Part II—*Intelligence: Its Nature and Nurture. Original Studies and Experiments*. Prepared by the Society's Committee. G. D. Stoddard, Chairman. Cloth 3.00
Paper........................................................................ 2.25
Fortieth Yearbook, 1941—*Art in American Life and Education*. Prepared by the Society's Committee. Thomas Munro, Chairman. Cloth....................................... 4.00
Paper........................................................................ 3.00
Forty-first Yearbook, 1942, Part I—*Philosophies of Education*. Prepared by the Society's Committee. John S. Brubacher, Chairman. Cloth.................................. 3.00
Paper........................................................................ 2.25
Forty-first Yearbook, 1942, Part II—*The Psychology of Learning*. Prepared by the Society's Committee. T. R. McConnell, Chairman. Cloth.................................. 3.25
Paper........................................................................ 2.50
Forty-second Yearbook, 1943, Part I—*Vocational Education*. Prepared by the Society's Committee. F. J. Keller, Chairman. Cloth....................................... 3.25
Paper........................................................................ 2.50
Forty-second Yearbook, 1943, Part II—*The Library in General Education*. Prepared by the Society's Committee. L. R. Wilson, Chairman. Cloth.............................. 3.00
Paper........................................................................ 2.25
Forty-third Yearbook, 1944, Part I—*Adolescence*. Prepared by the Society's Committee. Harold E. Jones, Chairman. Cloth..................................................... 3.00
Paper........................................................................ 2.25
Forty-third Yearbook, 1944, Part II—*Teaching Language in the Elementary School*. Prepared by the Society's Committee. M. R. Trabue, Chairman. Cloth........................... 2.75
Paper........................................................................ 2.00
Forty-fourth Yearbook, 1945, Part I—*American Education in the Postwar Period: Curriculum Reconstruction*. Prepared by the Society's Committee. Ralph W. Tyler, Chairman. Cloth ...... 3.00
Paper........................................................................ 2.25
Forty-fourth Yearbook, 1945, Part II—*American Education in the Postwar Period: Structural Reorganization*. Prepared by the Society's Committee. Bess Goodykoontz, Chairman. Cloth.. 3.00
Paper........................................................................ 2.25
Forty-fifth Yearbook, 1946, Part I—*The Measurement of Understanding*. Prepared by the Society's Committee. William A. Brownell, Chairman. Cloth........................... 3.00
Paper........................................................................ 2.25
Forty-fifth Yearbook, 1946, Part II—*Changing Conceptions in Educational Administration*. Prepared by the Society's Committee. Alonzo G. Grace, Chairman. Cloth.................. 2.50
Paper........................................................................ 1.75
Forty-sixth Yearbook, 1947, Part I—*Science Education in American Schools*. Prepared by the Society's Committee. Victor H. Noll, Chairman. Cloth............................. 3.25
Paper........................................................................ 2.50
Forty-sixth Yearbook, 1947, Part II—*Early Childhood Education*. Prepared by the Society's Committee. N. Searle Light, Chairman. Cloth...................................... 3.50
Paper........................................................................ 2.75

POSTPAID
PRICE

Forty-seventh Yearbook, 1948, Part I—*Juvenile Delinquency and the Schools.* Prepared by the
Society's Committee. Ruth Strang, Chairman. Cloth................................. $3.50
Paper...................................................................................... 2.75
Forty-seventh Yearbook, 1948, Part II—*Reading in the High School and College.* Prepared by the
Society's Committee. William S. Gray, Chairman. Cloth............................. 3.50
Paper...................................................................................... 2.75
Forty-eighth Yearbook, 1949, Part I—*Audio-visual Materials of Instruction.* Prepared by the
Society's Committee. Stephen M. Corey, Chairman. Cloth............................ 3.50
Paper...................................................................................... 2.75
Forty-eighth Yearbook, 1949, Part II—*Reading in the Elementary School.* Prepared by the So-
ciety's Committee. Arthur I. Gates, Chairman. Cloth............................... 3.50
Paper...................................................................................... 2.75
Forty-ninth Yearbook, 1950, Part I—*Learning and Instruction.* Prepared by the Society's Com-
mittee. G. Lester Anderson, Chairman. Cloth...................................... 3.50
Paper...................................................................................... 2.75
Forty-ninth Yearbook, 1950, Part II—*The Education of Exceptional Children.* Prepared by the
Society's Committee. Samuel A. Kirk, Chairman. Cloth............................. 3.50
Paper...................................................................................... 2.75
Fiftieth Yearbook, 1951, Part I—*Graduate Study in Education.* Prepared by the Society's Board
of Directors. Ralph W. Tyler, Chairman. Cloth................................... 3.50
Paper...................................................................................... 2.75
Fiftieth Yearbook, 1951, Part II—*The Teaching of Arithmetic.* Prepared by the Society's Com-
mittee. G. T. Buswell, Chairman. Cloth.......................................... 3.50
Paper...................................................................................... 2.75
Fifty-first Yearbook, 1952, Part I—*General Education.* Prepared by the Society's Committee.
T. R. McConnell, Chairman. Cloth............................................... 3.50
Paper...................................................................................... 2.75
Fifty-first Yearbook, 1952, Part II—*Education in Rural Communities.* Prepared by the Society's
Committee. Ruth Strang, Chairman. Cloth......................................... 3.50
Paper...................................................................................... 2.75
Fifty-second Yearbook, 1953, Part I—*Adapting the Secondary-School Program to the Needs of
Youth.* Prepared by the Society's Committee. William G. Brink, Chairman. Cloth....... 3.50
Paper...................................................................................... 2.75
Fifty-second Yearbook, 1953, Part II—*The Community School.* Prepared by the Society's Com-
mittee. Maurice F. Seay, Chairman. Cloth........................................ 3.50
Paper...................................................................................... 2.75
Fifty-third Yearbook, 1954, Part I—*Citizen Co-operation for Better Public Schools.* Prepared by
the Society's Committee. Edgar L. Morphet, Chairman. Cloth....................... 4.00
Paper...................................................................................... 3.25
Fifty-third Yearbook, 1954, Part II—*Mass Media and Education.* Prepared by the Society's
Committee. Edgar Dale, Chairman. Cloth.......................................... 4.00
Paper...................................................................................... 3.25
Fifty-fourth Yearbook, 1955, Part I—*Modern Philosophies and Education.* Prepared by the
Society's Committee. John S. Brubacher, Chairman. Cloth.......................... 4.00
Paper...................................................................................... 3.25
Fifty-fourth Yearbook, 1955, Part II—*Mental Health in Modern Education.* Prepared by the
Society's Committee. Paul A. Witty, Chairman. Cloth.............................. 4.00
Paper...................................................................................... 3.25
Fifty-fifth Yearbook, 1956. Part I—*The Public Junior College.* Prepared by the Society's
Committee. B. Lamar Johnson, Chairman. Cloth.................................... 4.00
Paper...................................................................................... 3.25
Fifty-fifth Yearbook, 1956, Part II—*Adult Reading.* Prepared by the Society's Committee.
David H. Clift, Chairman. Cloth................................................. 4.00
Paper...................................................................................... 3.25
Fifty-sixth Yearbook, 1957, Part I—*In-service Education of Teachers, Supervisors, and Adminis-
trators.* Prepared by the Society's Committee. Stephen M. Corey, Chairman. Cloth....... 4.00
Paper...................................................................................... 3.25
Fifty-sixth Yearbook, 1957, Part II—*Social Studies in the Elementary School.* Prepared by the
Society's Committee. Ralph C. Preston, Chairman. Cloth........................... 4.00
Paper...................................................................................... 3.25
Fifty-seventh Yearbook, 1958, Part I—*Basic Concepts in Music Education.* Prepared by the So-
ciety's Committee. Thurber H. Madison, Chairman. Cloth.......................... 4.00
Paper...................................................................................... 3.25
Fifty-seventh Yearbook, 1958, Part II—*Education for the Gifted.* Prepared by the Society's
Committee. Robert J. Havighurst, Chairman. Cloth................................ 4.00
Paper...................................................................................... 3.25
Fifty-seventh Yearbook, 1958, Part III—*The Integration of Educational Experiences.* Prepared
by the Society's Committee. Paul L. Dressel, Chairman. Cloth...................... 4.00
Paper...................................................................................... 3.25
Fifty-eighth Yearbook, 1959, Part I—*Community Education: Principles and Practices from World-
wide Experience.* Prepared by the Society's Committee. C. O. Arndt, Chairman. Cloth..... 4.00
Paper...................................................................................... 3.25
Fifty-eighth Yearbook, 1959, Part II—*Personnel Services in Education.* Prepared by the Soci-
ety's Committee. Melvene D. Hardee, Chairman. Cloth............................. 4.00
Paper...................................................................................... 3.25

*Distributed by*
THE UNIVERSITY OF CHICAGO PRESS, CHICAGO 37, ILLINOIS
1959

## DATE DUE

| MAY 21 65 | | | |
|---|---|---|---|
| DEC 22 78 | | | |
| | | | |
| | | | |
| | | | |
| | | | |
| | | | |
| | | | |
| | | | |
| | | | |
| | | | |
| | | | |
| | | | |
| | | | |
| | | | |
| | | | |
| | | | |
| | | | |
| | | | |
| GAYLORD | | | PRINTED IN U S A. |